T0185198

Objective-C Programmer's Reference

Carlos Oliveira

Apress·

Objective-C Programmer's Reference

Copyright © 2013 by Carlos Oliveira

This work is subject to copyright. All rights are reserved by the Publisher, whether the whole or part of the material is concerned, specifically the rights of translation, reprinting, reuse of illustrations, recitation, broadcasting, reproduction on microfilms or in any other physical way, and transmission or information storage and retrieval, electronic adaptation, computer software, or by similar or dissimilar methodology now known or hereafter developed. Exempted from this legal reservation are brief excerpts in connection with reviews or scholarly analysis or material supplied specifically for the purpose of being entered and executed on a computer system, for exclusive use by the purchaser of the work. Duplication of this publication or parts thereof is permitted only under the provisions of the Copyright Law of the Publisher's location, in its current version, and permission for use must always be obtained from Springer. Permissions for use may be obtained through RightsLink at the Copyright Clearance Center. Violations are liable to prosecution under the respective Copyright Law.

ISBN-13 (pbk): 978-1-4302-5905-3

ISBN-13 (electronic): 978-1-4302-5906-0

Trademarked names, logos, and images may appear in this book. Rather than use a trademark symbol with every occurrence of a trademarked name, logo, or image we use the names, logos, and images only in an editorial fashion and to the benefit of the trademark owner, with no intention of infringement of the trademark.

The use in this publication of trade names, trademarks, service marks, and similar terms, even if they are not identified as such, is not to be taken as an expression of opinion as to whether or not they are subject to proprietary rights.

While the advice and information in this book are believed to be true and accurate at the date of publication, neither the authors nor the editors nor the publisher can accept any legal responsibility for any errors or omissions that may be made. The publisher makes no warranty, express or implied, with respect to the material contained herein.

President and Publisher: Paul Manning
Lead Editor: Jonathan Gennick
Developmental Editor: Douglas Pundick
Technical Reviewer: Ron Natalie
Editorial Board: Steve Anglin, Mark Beckner, Ewan Buckingham, Gary Cornell, Louise Corrigan,
    Morgan Ertel, Jonathan Gennick, Jonathan Hassell, Robert Hutchinson, Michelle Lowman, James Markham,
    Matthew Moodie, Jeff Olson, Jeffrey Pepper, Douglas Pundick, Ben Renow-Clarke, Dominic Shakeshaft,
    Gwenan Spearing, Matt Wade, Tom Welsh
Coordinating Editor: Jill Balzano
Copy Editor: Mary Behr
Compositor: SPi Global
Indexer: SPi Global
Artist: SPi Global
Cover Designer: Anna Ishchenko

Distributed to the book trade worldwide by Springer Science+Business Media New York, 233 Spring Street, 6th Floor, New York, NY 10013. Phone 1-800-SPRINGER, fax (201) 348-4505, e-mail orders-ny@springer-sbm.com, or visit www.springeronline.com. Apress Media, LLC is a California LLC and the sole member (owner) is Springer Science + Business Media Finance Inc (SSBM Finance Inc). SSBM Finance Inc is a Delaware corporation.

For information on translations, please e-mail rights@apress.com, or visit www.apress.com.

Apress and friends of ED books may be purchased in bulk for academic, corporate, or promotional use. eBook versions and licenses are also available for most titles. For more information, reference our Special Bulk Sales–eBook Licensing web page at www.apress.com/bulk-sales.

Any source code or other supplementary materials referenced by the author in this text is available to readers at www.apress.com. For detailed information about how to locate your book's source code, go to www.apress.com/source-code/.

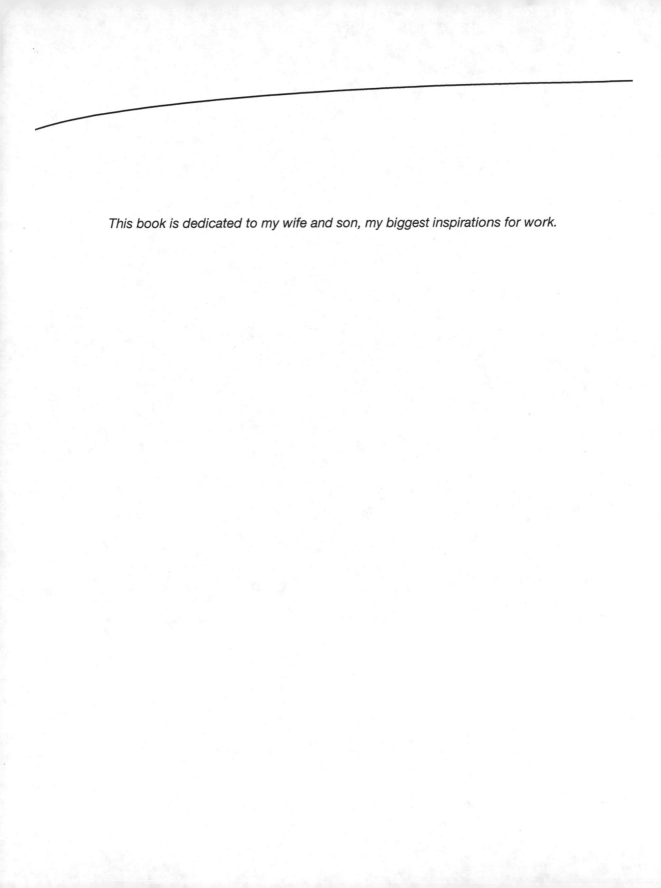

This book is dedicated to my wife and son, my biggest inspirations for work.

Contents at a Glance

Contents

About the Author

Carlos Oliveira is a software engineer working for the financial industry, with more than 10 years of experience in Objective-C and C++ programming. During his career, Carlos has developed several large-scale applications for companies big and small. Carlos Oliveira obtained a PhD in Systems Engineering and Operations Research from the University of Florida, an MSc in Computer Science from UFC (Brazil), and a BSc in Computer Science from UECE (Brazil). Carlos has also performed academic research in the field of combinatorial optimization, with applications in diverse areas such as finance, telecommunications, computational biology, and logistics. He has written more than 20 papers on optimization aspects of these topics, and co-authored *Mathematical Aspects of Network Routing Optimization* (Springer, 2010).

Carlos Oliveira currently works in New York City and lives in New Jersey with his wife, Janaina, and his son, Lucas. You can contact Carlos Oliveira at his web site, `http://coliveira.net`.

About the Technical Reviewer

Ron Natalie has 35 years of experience developing large scale applications in C, Objective-C, and C++ on Unix, OS X, and Windows. He has a degree in electrical engineering from the Johns Hopkins University and has taught professional courses in programming, network design, and computer security.

He splits his time between Virginia and North Carolina with his wife, Margy.

Acknowledgments

It would be very hard to write a book like this without the help of a competent and dedicated group. I would like to acknowledge the help of the editorial team at Apress for their great support.

First, thanks to Editor Jonathan Gennick for giving me the opportunity to write this text; his help has been appreciated. The Technical Reviewer, Ron Natalie, has done a great job of pointing out any issues found in the programming topics. Editors Jill Balzano and Douglas Pundick have been incredibly helpful in all practical aspects of the project.

Last but not least, thanks to my family for their loving support during my whole career and especially during the time spent writing this book.

Introduction

Welcome to *Objective-C Programmer's Reference*. This is a book targeted at developers who have prior experience with other languages such as Java, Python, Ruby, or C++ and would like to leverage that knowledge into the Objective-C world.

Maybe you have played with the iPhone and would like to know how to develop that app that you wish were available on the AppStore. Or maybe you want to create a new desktop application in Mac OS X. Still, you may want to program in Objective-C just because you need to support iOS devices at your company. Whatever the reason, this book will help you to move from knowing concepts of programming in other languages to learning how to and (I hope) enjoying programing in Objective-C.

This book is also written with the goal of reaching readers who already know Objective-C but would like a concise reference to the most commonly used techniques in the language. You will be able to understand topics that are of real importance when working with Cocoa and Cocoa Touch, the two largest and most important frameworks in Objective-C. You will also learn fundamental topics that can be leveraged into any programming situation where Objective-C is needed.

You may not have the time to invest in more traditional books, which usually spend hundreds of pages to explain simple concepts that are already part of the standard vocabulary of working developers and advanced programming students. That's why this book tries to convey only the most important topics with concise examples. We also include a quick reference to the most commonly used classes, so you don't need to spend too much time looking at these documents online.

Objective-C Programer's Reference is an excellent choice for developers that want to use their knowledge effectively, while learning one of the most sought after and marketable skill sets for modern application and mobile development.

Topics Discussed

Objective-C Programmer's Reference provides all the tools necessary to build working solutions in Objective-C. Starting from the basic building blocks of the C language, I discuss how to create correct and efficient applications, leveraging knowledge of object-oriented programming as well as structured programming.

I make extensive use of concepts mastered by developers who are fluent in other languages such as C++, Java, Perl, and Python. In writing this book, my goal is to provide such readers a fast-paced path to achieve proficiency in Objective-C.

On the other hand, this book introduces Objective-C in a logical and structured way, so that even novice programmers will have an easy time absorbing the most important topics and competencies necessary to develop applications that use the language.

We work in an industry where typical books are thousands of pages long and where most of that length is filled up by introductory topics that are not of great concern for professional developers. In this book, I strive to provide a more concise and focused reference to the language, offering readers much more value for their reading efforts. This book does the following:

- Takes you quickly through fundamental concepts such as interfaces and class implementations in Objective-C.

- Provides a concise and handy reference to the Foundation framework that is all-important when programming in Objective-C.

- Highlights key differences between Objective-C and other popular languages such as Java or Python.

- Shows how to create full applications using advanced concepts such as container classes, selectors, and key-value interfaces.

- Provides the fundamentals of writing Cocoa and Cocoa Touch applications, which are the standard for Mac OS X and iOS development.

What You Will Learn

Here are some of the topics that you will learn in this book:

- The basic syntax of the Objective-C language.

- How to create classes in Objective-C.

- How methods and the message passing mechanism work to simplify your code and avoid deep class hierarchies.

- The key-value system for storing and accessing dynamic data, and how it ties with Objective-C interfaces to simplify application programming.

- The effective use of container classes in Objective-C, such as arrays and dictionaries, with their immutable and mutable versions.

- Basic topics in Cocoa programming, which can be used to create simple applications in the Mac OS X and iOS environments.

Here is a quick summary of the topics you will learn in each chapter.

Chapter 1: The C in Objective-C

The Objective-C language was created as an extension of C, which means that any program written in C is also a valid Objective-C program. As a result, many of the basic expressions in Objective-C are identical to their equivalents in C. To become a good Objective-C programmer, you need to have a basic understanding of the C language. In this chapter, I provide a quick introduction to the most important concepts from the C language as used in Objective-C.

Chapter 2: Classes

In Objective-C, classes are the building blocks of applications. They are the syntactic construct used to define the methods and variables that become the components of an object. This chapter gives an introduction to the concept of Objective-C classes, and how to define them. One of the main features of classes is how they can be described in separate files, one for the interface and another for the implementation. This clear separation makes it possible to share only the important aspects of a class, while hiding any implementation information that is not needed by clients.

Chapter 3: Strings and Container Classes

One of the main characteristics of Objective-C programs is the constant use of dynamic objects to simplify the management of memory and other resources. Among the most fundamental classes in the Objective-C runtime are the classes used to handle strings, numbers, and collections of objects. In this chapter, I show how to use these basic classes and their methods.

Chapter 4: Protocols and Categories

Objective-C promotes a clear separation between implementation and interfaces. One of the techniques used to encourage this separation is the concept of protocols. A protocol allows classes to communicate by just describing a subset of the methods they respond to. Another way to promote this separation of concerns is to extend classes through categories: instead of making everyone aware of the methods available at a particular class, a programmer can add categories as they are needed. This results in a much cleaner implementation, which reduces dependencies on other parts of the application.

Chapter 5: Inheritance

Object-oriented programming is the main idea that motivated the creation of Objective-C. An important aspect of OOP is the ability to create new classes that inherit the methods, variables, and properties of existing classes. The proper use of inheritance, however, requires a certain care in both the design phase and the proper implementation of derived classes. In this chapter, I cover the main ideas that you need to be familiar with when creating class hierarchies.

Chapter 6: Block Syntax

Objective-C provides another technique to reduce programming effort through its block syntax. A block is a piece of code that can be passed around to other parts of the application. A block not only retains information about the code but also about variables that were in scope at the time the block was created. In this way, blocks are similar to the concept of closures available in other languages. By defining blocks, you can make the implementation of certain algorithms more extensible. You can also use blocks to implement code that will run in other threads, as accomplished by some Objective-C libraries.

Chapter 7: Dynamic Binding

One of the biggest advantages of Objective-C is that it allows programmers to choose the right combination of speed and flexibility, depending on their needs. The runtime system of Objective-C is the main mechanism that can be used by programmers to switch between dynamic and static programming. In this chapter, you learn how to explore the runtime system to achieve the best combination of static checking and dynamic flexibility in your software.

Chapter 8: Memory Management

One of the advantages of working with an object-oriented language with dynamic features is that memory management can be simplified, with system libraries doing most of the hard work. Objective-C uses a reference-based model for memory management, with rules that make it almost straightforward to allocate and release memory in any application. In this chapter, I review the simple rules that you need to master in order to write correct objective-C code. I also cover the latest techniques provided by Apple compilers, which practically remove the need for manual intervention in their memory management mechanisms.

Chapter 9: Key-Value Programming

A very common way to interact with objects in Objective-C is to set values for particular property names, also referred to as keys. Key-value programming is very important because it is used in so many libraries in Objective-C. It allows an object to be used through a simple interface, avoiding the need to create multiple subclasses when the only difference between objects is the set of values they contain.

Chapter 10: The Filesystem

Objective-C libraries provide a simplified mechanism for accessing system resources. One example is how the Foundation framework can be used to access files and directories. In this chapter, I show how the classes in this standard Objective-C framework can be used to create files, read and write data to existing files, and manipulate the content of directories.

Chapter 11: The Foundation Framework

Classes in Objective-C are organized into frameworks for ease of distribution and use. The Foundation framework provides classes needed to write programs interacting with the environment. The basic utility classes, such as strings, dictionaries, and arrays, are also contained in the Foundation framework. In this chapter, I provide a reference to the Foundation framework classes, with examples when necessary.

Chapter 12: The Compiler

To use Objective-C effectively, it is important to understand the basic infrastructure of the language. The compiler plays a special role in the software development cycle, since it determines how source code is translated into executable programs. In the Apple environment, two main compilers are used: gcc, the traditional compiler used by Mac OS X, and the new compiler based on the LLVM (Lower Level Virtual Machine), which has been developed by Apple in the last few years. In this chapter, I take a look at several options provided by the Objective-C compilers and how to use them to write fast and reliable code.

Chapter 13: The Preprocessor

Objective-C comes with a powerful preprocessor that can simplify the input of repetitive code into a program. The preprocessor, however, may be the source of numerous programming pitfalls if you are not careful with its usage. In this chapter, I present the main features of the preprocessor and how to avoid some of its rough edges.

Chapter 14: Unit Tests

Test-driven development is a software methodology that requires that every feature of a program be thoroughly tested with unit testing code. Test-driven development is a great way to employ the modularity of object-oriented languages such as Objective-C. In this chapter, you learn how to create unit tests in the Objective-C language. You also learn how to manage and run unit tests using the Xcode IDE.

Chapter 15: Debugging

Any programmer knows how difficult it is to write defect-free software. That is why every platform has a number of integrated debugging aids. Xcode provides a complete solution for writing and debugging programs, which makes it much easier to find bugs in a new or existing application. In this chapter, I explain how to use these debugging features. Using a tutorial style, I describe how to use breakpoints, watch windows, conditional expressions, and the logging terminal.

Chapter 16: Building a OS X Application in Cocoa

The most important use of Objective-C is in the implementation of applications that employ the Cocoa frameworks. As an Objective-C programmer, your may become involved in the creation of iOS apps or full Mac OS X applications. In this chapter, I introduce Cocoa, the framework used to develop desktop applications in the Mac OS X.

Chapter 17: Building an iOS App on Cocoa Touch

Cocoa Touch is the framework used to create rich applications for iOS, the operating system that powers the iPhone, iPad, and iPod touch. While using technologies similar to Cocoa, iOS provides a simplified architecture in comparison to the full-featured Cocoa framework. Cocoa Touch also provides access to mobile resources such as cameras, the accelerometer, and other hardware managed by iOS.

Compiling the Code Samples

The examples given in this book have all been compiled on OS X using the freely available Xcode IDE. To use Xcode you need to have a Mac OS X machine. If you don't have Xcode installed in your computer, you can download it from Apple's developer web site at

`http://developer.apple.com`

Another way to install Xcode is to use the App Store application on your Mac. Search for Xcode and click to install the app.

The next time you start Xcode, create a new project by clicking File ➤ New ➤ Project. This will bring up a wizard window where you can give some basic options for the new project, such as its location, name, and target operating system (use Mac OS X as the target).

With the new project, you can create files and enter the examples as displayed in the book. To download the complete set of examples included here, visit the web page for this book at `http://coliveira.net` or `www.apress.com`.

Part 1

The Language

The C in Objective-C

In this chapter, we will introduce the main concepts common to the Objective-C and C languages. Objective-C is based on the original C language. As a result of this special relationship, any program that is valid C code is also valid from Objective-C's perspective. This is why it is so important to be familiar with the basics of C, as well as how they relate to areas of object oriented programming, such as classes, messages, and interfaces.

Topics such as arrays, structures, pointers, variable declarations, variable types, and functions are part of the common vocabulary shared by these languages. Programmers who are fluent in such basic Objective-C techniques have a much better time at understanding and using object-oriented concepts.

To get you up to speed with the advanced abilities of Objective-C, we start the book with an overview of the most frequently used features inherited from the C language. In the next sections, you will see how to use such fundamental techniques to create simple programs that will be the building blocks of your future Objective-C applications.

> **Note** As you read the next few sections, please keep in mind the implicit assumption that every feature discussed here as being part of Objective-C is also available in plain C. This will be true throughout this chapter, unless explicitly stated.

Simple Statements

Programs in Objective-C are composed of syntactical elements that may be further categorized into functions, classes, and variable declarations. Functions contain statements, or variable declarations. Each statement in the language is ended by a semicolon or is enclosed in brackets (in the case of compound statements), which makes them easy to recognize by both human beings and compilers.

Unlike languages that use indentation to define the possible end of declarations, Objective-C has an unambiguous way to mark their end using semicolons. For example, here are a few valid statements and variable declarations (their meaning will be explained in later sections):

```
int numberOfEmployees;
```

```
double totalPayment;
```

```
totalPayment = numberOfEmployees * 1000;
```

```
NSLog(@"test log");
```

```
if (1 > 2) totalPayment = totalPayment + 10;
```

Each of these lines is either defining an executable instruction or declaring an entity that will be later used by the program. We will examine in detail the syntax used in each of these cases, but for now it is important to recognize the nature of Objective-C statements and how they combine to create valid programs.

Variables

A variable is a location in memory where values can be saved and modified. Variables in Objective-C have to be of a particular type, which is explicitly defined when the variable is declared. Here are a few examples:

```
int anIntegerVariable;
```

```
float aFloatingNumber;
```

Note that the variable type is the first element in the declaration. The name of the variable follows, ended by semicolon, which marks the end-of-statement character. These two variable declarations create an integer and a floating number variable. Integer variables are required to contain only whole numbers, and the compiler will check that this is always the case. Even when a programmer forces a value of a different type into an integer variable, the content will still be converted to an integer number in all expressions where they appear.

More than one variable can be declared in a single statement. This is done by having additional variable names in the same statement, separated by commas. Here is another example showing multiple variables declared in the same expression:

```
int anIntegerVariable, aSecondIntegerVariable;
```

```
bool booleanVariable1, booleanVariable2;
```

There are a few rules that need to be observed when naming variables. The first rule is that variables can start only with alphabetic characters or the underscore character. The same is valid for additional characters in a variable name; however, numeric characters are also allowed, starting from the second position. Here are a few valid variable declarations:

```
int var1;

int _single_2_Position;

int long_variable_name;
```

In Objective-C, the underscore character is frequently used as a separator for long variable names. The goal is to increase readability for these long names without resorting to a mix of uppercase and lowercase letters. Some programmers, however, see no problem in mixing cases in the same variable. The following example, thus, is also very common:

```
int longVariableName.
```

> **Note**   Variable naming is a style issue. Different programmers have different opinions on what looks better. However, we recommend that you be consistent in the use of variable naming styles. Don't use variables with mixed case in one place and variables separated by underscores in another. The basic idea is to avoid confusion and reduce the number of decisions you need to take each time you introduce a new name in a program.

Variable names, as well as all other identifiers in Objective-C, are case sensitive. This means that the following are two valid declarations for different variables:

```
int myVariable1;

int myvariable1;
```

The fact that case is significant in variable names makes the use of a unified naming style even more important. It would be very unfortunate to have a program failing because of the indiscriminate use of two variables that differ just by a single misspelled character.

> **Note**   In the C language, names starting with single or double underscores followed by a capital letter are reserved. Only the compiler can use them, for the purposes of language implementation. Avoid the use of such names, since they may conflict with internal names used in future versions of the language—even if they seem to work in your current compiler implementation.

Variable Initialization

A variable declaration can also be used to define the initial value of a variable. This is done using the assignment operator. Here is a simple example:

```
int daysInTheWeek = 7;
```

```
int monthsInTheYear = 12;

float PI = 3.14;
```

An initialization can also make use of arithmetic expressions or even function calls. Thus, it is possible to write code like this:

```
int secondsPerHour = 60 * 60;
```

> **Note**   Variables should always be initialized to suitable values, since lack of proper initialization is one of the most common sources of programming errors. Variable initialization is combined with definition in Objective-C exactly to reduce the occurrence of such mistakes.

Variable Types

A variable needs to be declared of a particular type before it is used. There are several types that can be used in Objective-C. They can be generally classified as native or user-defined types.

A native type is predefined by the language and compiler implementation. These types are available without the use of any libraries or header files, so they can be used in any function or class defined in Objective-C. User defined types, on the other hand, are specified by programmers. They can either be part of libraries or of user code. I will first consider the available native types; structures and classes will be discussed later.

There are a small number of native types. Most of them are numeric, but they can also be used to store alphanumeric data as well as logical values. Finally, native types can also be used to store memory addresses, which are called pointers.

Among the numeric types, the most common are integers and floating point numbers. For example, an integer value is denoted by the type int. Floating point numbers, a computational approximation for the real numbers used in mathematics, can be represented by native types such as float or double.

Integer Types

Integer types are used to store whole numbers and comprise the types char, int, short, long, and long long. The need for different numeric types arise from the different storage capacities that each one has, along with the memory necessary to represent such a number in memory. For example, integer numbers defined as int are commonly represented using 4 bytes in a 32-bit machine. This means that it is possible to store numbers up to about four billion. On the other hand, values of type short may be as small as 2 bytes, which would be enough to store numbers up to about two million. Here are some examples:

```
char val0 = 12;

int val1 = 123400;
```

```
short val2 = 123;
```

```
long val3 = 12345;
```

```
long long val4 = 12345678;
```

The size of long and long long variables depends on the compiler and machine used, but the values they can store are usually larger than what is allowed for an int.

Types for integer values can also be declared as signed or unsigned. A signed number can be either positive or negative, since the sign is stored along with the number representation. Unsigned numbers cannot be negative, ranging from zero to the maximum allowed by the variable size.

Unsigned numbers are useful when representing quantities that are known to be non-negative. For example, memory sizes are frequently represented by unsigned numbers. The common approach, however, is to use the more generic signed type—unless it is know with certainty that a number cannot be negative. By default, integer numbers declared as int, short, long, or long long are signed.

Floating Point Numbers

A floating number is a computer representation of a real number. Since computers have limitations on the amount of stored data, real numbers cannot be stored exactly. For some numbers, such as 0.3 for example, only an approximation can be stored in a computer due to errors introduced by the use of a binary representation. For other real numbers, such as Pi, it is well known that there is no finite representation.

Objective-C programs use a floating-point representation where the real number is stored in two parts: the mantissa and the exponent. You don't need to know the intricacies of such a representation, but it is important to be aware of the difference between these numbers and integer numbers. It is also important to know that operations in floating point numbers may result in rounding errors that are difficult to understand and track down.

Floating point numbers can be declared in two forms: they can be either float or double values (although a double can receive the long modifier). The difference between float and double is due to the amount of data used to store each type. The exact number of bytes is dependent on the machine used, but double numbers have double the precision and exponent as a float number. Here are some examples:

```
int degrees = 360;
```

```
float e = 2.7182;
```

```
double elarge = 2.718281828459;
```

Characters

A common native type that is supported by Objective-C is the character (char). Characters can store any of the standard ASCII values, which commonly range from 0 to 255. Although used to store elements of character strings, the character type is just one of the integer number types mentioned previously, and as such it behaves similarly to types such as int or short. A type char can also be declared as signed (when negative numbers are allowed) or unsigned (in case it is known that no negative number will be stored).

Logical Values

A variable can also store a single logical value, true or false. Although the C language doesn't have a specialized Boolean value, in Objective-C you use the BOOL type to represent this kind of variable. A variable of type BOOL can store the values YES or NO, which can also be spelled as TRUE or FALSE. The language, however, allows the conversion of any integer type into a Boolean. In that case, the value zero is converted to FALSE, while anything different from zero is considered to be TRUE. This may be a source of mistakes for programmers that are not careful with the conversion rules between these types.

Pointers

Objective-C supports variables that store memory addresses, and this is one of the most flexible methods to refer to data stored by a program (the use of such variables will be covered later in this chapter). Pointers are declared using the star notation, and here is an example of declaring pointers to common types:

```
int *pointer_to_int;

double *double_pointer;
```

The first example is a variable that can store the address of an integer. The second is a pointer that can be used to store the address where a value of type double is contained. The pointer notation is frequently used when creating objects in Objective-C, as you will see in the next chapter.

The void Type

The keyword void is a special type name used in Objective-C. Unlike the other type names, void doesn't represent a real data type, but instead signifies the absence of data, or the fact that the type is unknown. The type void can appear only in a few situations. One case happens when a function has no return value. This is indicated by the use of the void keyword in place of the return type.

Another situation in which void is employed is to mark pointers to unknown data types. When a type is unknown and void is used instead, the resulting pointer will have no information about the actual data type stored in that memory location. Such a variable can be used in Objective-C as a generic pointer, which can be applied to any data type. You will see examples of this use when learning about pointers in a later section.

> **Note** Since void is just a special keyword, it is not possible to declare a variable of void type. For example, trying to declare a variable like void var; will result in a compilation error, since the compiler won't be able to deduce the real type of the variable.

Comments

Software used in a large-scale project is not always easy to understand. Although every effort should be made to make code easier to comprehend, complicated algorithms and other assumptions may hinder the understanding of a particular area of the program. That is why there is always the need for adding documentation to the program itself.

Objective-C uses two different styles of code comments. The first style, and the simplest one to use, employs the sequence // as the beginning of a new comment. Any comment started this way will be in force until the end of the line.

```
int integerVariable; // this variable holds an integer

float floatVariable; // a floating number variable
```

A second comment style is used for comments that span multiple lines. In that case, the comment is started with the characters /*. All text from that position on is considered to be part of the comment, until the pair of characters */ are reached.

```
/* this is an example of multiple line comments. The
following expressions are used to define variables of
the type integer and floating point, respectively */

int integerVariable;

float floatVariable;
```

Multi-line comments cannot be embedded. That is, if you already have a comment, you can't just use a second pair of comment characters around them. That will not work because the first time the characters */ are seen, they will close any multi-line comment started previously, not just the latest.

```
/* a new comment
  /* original comment, not embedded */
this is not a comment, since the first multi line comment
was already closed. */
```

> **Note**   One of the reasons why some programmers avoid the use of multi-line comments is that they can lead to confusion, as noted above. To avoid this, use only single-line comments, and reserve multi-line comments for specific situations, such as the general comment at the top of an Objective-C file.

Arithmetic Expressions

One of the simplest ways to use variables is as part of arithmetic expressions. These are used to calculate numeric quantities, using one of the common operators such as addition, subtraction, multiplication, and division.

Objective-C has a rich set of operators that can be used in numeric expressions. The most evident way to use such operators is to express the four common arithmetic operations. A not-so-obvious operator, however, is the remainder operator. It returns the integer remainder of the division of the first number by the second.

```
int remainder = 10 % 4;
```

The result of this operation should be equal to two. A common use for this kind of expression is to decide if a number is even.

```
if (number % 2 == 0)
{
        /* this is an even number */
}
```

Expressions can be combined using parenthesis, so that programmers can control the order in which the operations will be grouped by the compiler.

```
int value = 25;

int result = (10 + value) * (2 / value);
```

Function Fundamentals

Objective-C programs are composed of a mix of functions, declarations, and classes. Functions are the basic concept used by C programs, while classes are the basic extension mechanism provided by Objective-C. Accordingly, in this section we will only discuss functions; we'll introduce classes in the next chapter.

Every program starts in a function called main. The main function is not called from any part of the program, but instead it is called by the programming environment whenever the application is started. The program ends exactly when the main function returns. Here is a simple example of a main function:

```
int main()
{
   NSLog(@"hello to objective-C");
   return 0;
}
```

The purpose of this program is to write a single logging string. The program achieves this using the NSLog function, which is part of the Foundation framework provided by Objective-C, and therefore is not available in standard C programs. The argument to NSLog is a string literal that starts with the @ character; such string literals are also exclusive to Objective-C. Everything else in the program is there just to comply with the requirements of the language.

The name of the function is main, and the pair of parenthesis after the name of the function is used to determine any parameters that are required as arguments. In this particular case, the main function has been defined with an empty set of parameters, meaning that there are no arguments. Some applications, however, expect to receive arguments, which can be provided from the command line. If that is the case, the main function can also be declared in a slightly different way.

```
int main(int argc, char *argv[])
{
    NSLog(@"hello from objective-C");
    return 0;
}
```

In this example, the program is receiving two parameters: the first is an integer value `argc`, also known as the argument counter, which specifies the number of arguments passed to the program. The second parameter, `argv`, is an array of pointers to characters, which can be used to store each of the arguments passed to the application. In future examples, you will learn how to use these arguments in your programs.

Defining New Functions

A function is a simple way to package a set of instructions so that programmers don't need to repeat themselves. For example, here is a simple function to calculate the average of two numbers:

```
float avg(float a, float b)
{
    return (a+b)/2;
}
```

There are several advantages in using functions whenever possible.

- *Simplifying a program:* Whenever a common operation needs to be performed repeatedly, you can instead create a function that encapsulates the operation. In the example above, by calling the function avg you don't need to repeat in other parts of your code the addition and division operations used to calculate the average. This may seem unnecessary here because the function is so simple. However, when an algorithm is more complex, it becomes even more important to streamline its use. For example, you could have a routine for mathematical integration as part of a large-scale engineering package. Or you could have a window-drawing routine in a graphical application. In each case, using functions will result in a simplification of the resulting program.

- *Improving maintenance:* Things change, and programmers have to adapt to change on a daily basis. If the client decides to modify the way a calculation is made and you are not using a function, then the required changes have to be propagated to all places where the calculation is currently done. On the other hand, if you were clever enough to use a function instead, there's only one place where the change needs to be applied. Every place in the code where the function is called will use the updated version automatically. Such use of functions can reduce the maintenance burden. In some cases, modifications can be avoided in hundreds or thousands of lines of code—and remain contained to just a single place.

- *Improving documentation:* Creating a function is also a way to document a procedure. Whenever you create a function, you need to give it a name that describes what it does. If this is done well, callers will have at least a high-level idea of what the function does. This technique can be seen as a simple but effective form of self-documentation. Such a practice, when use regularly by everyone in a programming project, can result in code that is much more maintainable and future-proof.

Because of all these advantages, functions are widely used in Objective-C, and are in fact the basic principle of code organization in the C language as well. You will see in the next chapter that classes can be seen as a generalization of functions, so that you can achieve even more by using these principles.

Function Syntax

The syntax of a function is determined by its input arguments and result type, along with the braces and the set of statements contained within them. The argument list is the set of parameters displayed inside parenthesis, after the name of the function. Even if no argument is needed by a function, it will have a pair of empty parenthesis after its name. The name of the function is preceded by the type of values that are returned as result. For example,

```
int add_values(int a, int b)
{
    return a + b;
}
```

will always return an integer value that depends on the two arguments a and b.

The following examples in this chapter will use the syntax for functions, so that you can have an idea of how functions may be used in programming projects.

Conditional Operations

A conditional operation is used to codify logical statements. In a programming language like Objective-C, any expression that produces a non-zero value is considered to be true, while zero (or NULL) values are considered to be false. Logical operations are used to manipulate such true or false expressions, and form the basis for conditional execution using the if statement, for example. Consider the following code fragment:

```
void test_function(int x)
{
    if (x > 10)
        NSLog(@"Number is greater than 10");
}
```

This function illustrates the use of the expression (x > 10) as part of an if statement. Logical expressions can use one of the operators: >, <, >=, <=, ==, &&, ||, or !. The first five operators provide a way to express the logical relations of greater, less, greater than, less than, or equal to. They can be applied to numbers or characters, as well as to Boolean values.

These five operators can be used in expressions that compare integers, characters, Booleans, or floating-point numbers. The result of such expressions will be a logical value such as YES or NO.

You can also combine such Boolean values using the logical operators &&, ||, and !. The first combines two logical values, resulting in YES if both are true. The second operates on two logical values, resulting in YES if at least one of them is true. Finally, the third operator performs logical negation. It results in YES when the value is false and NO when the value is true. These operators can also be applied to numeric or pointer values. When this happens, a number or pointer is considered to be false if it corresponds to zero or NULL. The value is otherwise considered to be true.

Complex logical expressions can also be grouped using parenthesis so that they are easier to understand. Here is an example of using these logical operators:

```
void logical_func(int x, int y)
{
    if ((x > 2  && x <= 10) ||
        (y > 15 && y <= 20)
        )
        NSLog(@"the numbers are acceptable");
}
```

In this code, the variable x is compared to 2 and 10, so that the value of x is in the interval between 3 and 10. The variable y is also compared to 15 and 20, so that the only acceptable numbers are between 16 and 20. If x or y satisfy these requirements, the function will print a message saying so.

The if statement

An if statement, as seen in the example above, can be used to perform an action based on a logical expression. The simplest case of the if statement is similar to the following:

```
if (<logical expression>)
  <statement>;
```

This variety of the if statement is useful but cannot be used when there is more than one statement that needs to be executed. If that is the case, you should instead group the expressions into a single block (also known as a compound statement). A block is a common way to group expressions in Objective-C, and is similar to the grouping defined by a function. Here is an example:

```
void logical_func2(int x, int y)
{
    if ((x > 2  && x <= 10) ||
        (y > 15 && y <= 20)
        )
    {
        NSLog(@"the numbers are acceptable");
        NSLog(@"the total value is %d", x + y);
    }
}
```

This code performs two actions whenever the logical expression is true: you print a log string and display the value of x + y. For this to work, you need a block of expressions, defined between curly braces, as seen above.

There is a third version of the if statement that is even more useful. Suppose that you have some action that needs to be done when the logical expression is true, and another when the expression is false. This can be done by adding an else case to the if statement. The else case can be either a single statement as well as a block. Here is another example:

```
void logical_func3(int x, int y)
{
    if ((x > 2  && x <= 10) ||
        (y > 15 && y <= 20))
    {
        NSLog(@"the numbers are acceptable");
        NSLog(@"the total value is %d", x + y);
    }

    else
    {
        NSLog(@"the numbers are not acceptable");
    }
}
```

Loops

Programming may be described as the art of defining repetitive tasks. But without a method for controlled repetition, it is very difficult to perform a programming task. That's why every language provides a set of statements that allow for the repetition of expressions. A loop is the common name given to statements that are used primarily to repeat a set of instructions, and where the repetition depends on the result of a logical condition.

The loop expressions available in Objective-C are the for, while, and do while loops. Each of these loop forms provide the syntax needed to performed controlled repetitions. You will see how each of them works in the next sections.

The while Loop

The while loop is the simplest of the three loop forms. The basic format of the while loop is

```
while (<logical expression>)
    <statement>
```

where <statement> can either be a single or a compound statement. For example,

```
void printNums(int min, int max)
{
    while (min < max)
    {
        NSLog(@"Value %d", min);
        min = min + 1;
    }
}
```

The while loop is executed by evaluating the given logical expression and entering the loop only if the result is true. All the expressions in the block defined inside curly braces are executed. Then the logical expression is evaluated again, and the process repeats. When the logical expression is false, the whole block is skipped and the program continues execution in the first line after the block.

Just like the if statement, the while statement also allows a single expression instead of a block. Thus, one can write the following code:

```
bool isOdd(int num)
{
    while (num > 0)
        num = num - 2;

    return num == -1;
}
```

The do { } while( ) Loop

Another variation of iteration statements is the do/while loop. The difference between this and the previous while form is that the test for its execution is performed at the end of the body (where the while keyword is located). This makes the do/while loop effective in situations where the block needs to be repeated at least once.

A do/while loop can be thought of as a way to avoid the initial test, as opposed to the standard way in which a while loop works. With this extra repetition, it is possible to encode a large set of algorithms that may require an initial execution before the logical test is evaluated.

For example, consider an algorithm to process input read, say, from a file. Suppose that the file contains a set of numbers, and the last one is -1. The algorithm, in that case, consists of reading the numbers in a file, doing some processing possibly using the number, and stopping when the number is -1. If you suppose that there exists a function called nextNumber(), which returns the next number in the file, then the algorithm could be represented as

```
void process_numbers()
{
    int number;

    do
    {
        number = nextNumber();
        // perform other tasks
    }
    while (number != -1);
}
```

Notice that this function will always read the next number and perform associated tasks at least once. This is the situation where a do/while loop may be the best tool for the job. The test will at the end evaluate to true whenever you have a number that is not equal to -1. When that expression is false, the repetition stops and the function ends its current execution.

The for Loop

Among the three loop statements in Objective-C, the for loop is the most versatile. The reason is that it can be used to perform different actions at the beginning (or end) of each iteration. Combining the power of the other, more focused iteration statements, the for loop is probably the most used of the control structures that you have seen so far.

The syntax of the for loop is composed of a preamble, enclosed by parenthesis, and the body—just like the while loop. Unlike a while loop, however, the pair of parenthesis contains three expressions separated by semicolons. The first section is an initialization expression. The second is a logical expression, similar to what you would write in a while loop. This logical test determines if the body of the for loop will be executed, and it is repeated every time a new iteration is about to start.

Finally, the third section is executed every time the end of the body is reached. Therefore, just like the middle section of the loop, this last part is executed once per run of the body of the loop. Here is a simple example:

```
int for_test(int max)
{
    int i;

    for (i=0; i<max; i=i+1)
    {
        NSLog(@"value is %d", i);
    }
}
```

This is a minimal case of how such a loop works in practice. In the first part of the expression at the top of the for loop, you see the initialization. In this case, the objective is to assign the initial value of zero to the counter variable i. The middle section will check if the number is less than the maximum value. If that test is true, then the body is executed, where the number is printed to the application log.

The last section of the for multi-part expression is executed only at the end of each iteration. In this case, the value of i is incremented by one. This will make the counter increase its value at the end of each iteration until it reaches the maximum value provided. When that happens, the logical test fails and the loop ends.

The switch Statement

Objective-C provides another way to select two or more options for execution. Other than the if statement, you can use the switch/case composite statement when there are two or more options that can be chosen based on a single value.

For example, suppose that you are given a character that can contain only three values: 'B' for blue, 'R' for red, and 'G' for green. In this case, you can use a switch/case to execute three different options depending of the content of this variable. Here is the example code:

```
void switch_test(char value)
{
    switch (value)
```

```
  {
  case 'R':
     NSLog(@"red");
     break;

  case 'G':
     NSLog(@"green");
     break;

  case 'B':
     NSLog(@"blue");
     break;
  }
}
```

Notice that the switch control structure receives as a parameter the variable that controls the switch. Then, for each valid case you have a case label. The case defines the point where the execution begins. In this example, it prints the color associated with the character.

After each valid code path is a break statement. The reason this is necessary is that the switch control structure will not stop execution when a new case is introduced. In fact, in the absence of a break instruction, the remaining code would continue to be executed until the switch block has been completed. To prevent this from happening, the break statement will move the program to the next instruction after the end of the body of the switch.

Another element that can be used in a switch/case statement is a default label. Such a label can be used to check for invalid input. Here is an improved version of the function shown above:

```
void switch_test(char value)
{
   switch (value)
   {
   case 'R':
      NSLog(@"red");
      break;
   case 'G':
      NSLog(@"green");
      break;
   case 'B':
      NSLog(@"blue");
      break;

   default:
      NSLog(@"error: invalid color code");
   }
}
```

It is also possible to have multiple cases targeting the same code. This is done by not adding a break to cases that will fall through to the next. Consider the following example:

```
void vowel_test(char x)
{
    switch(x) {
        case 'A':
        case 'E':
        case 'I':
        case 'O':
        case 'U':
            NSLog(@"vowel\n");
            break;
        default:
            NSLog(@"consonant\n");
    }
}
```

Assignment Operators

Objective-C provides a general kind of expression employed to update the value of variables, which uses the assignment operator. Such assignment expressions are frequently used due to the fact that they may accomplish more succinctly certain tasks that would require two or more steps in other languages.

The basic assignment operator uses the = symbol and modifies the variable in the left side to contain the result of the expression in the right. This is the common way to update variables, and you have encountered it in examples seen so far. Beyond this basic use, however, the assignment operator can also be used as a subexpression occurring in other contexts. The result is that you can embed an assignment so that it becomes part of other expressions as well.

```
bool check_total(int a, int b)
{
    int total;
    if ((total = a + b) > 10)
    {
        NSLog(@"total value of %d is too high", total);
        return false;
    }
    return true;
}
```

In this example, the variable total is used to store the sum of a and b. The if statement checks if the sum of the two parameters is greater than 10. However, the test also assigns the result of a + b to variable total, so that it can be later used in the call to NSLog. The expression (total = a + b) not only performs the assignment, but also results in the value assigned, so that other expressions can have access to that value.

> **Note**   In this example, it is clear that total could have been updated elsewhere, but in more complex code there are situations where the assignment as a subexpression is the more natural thing to do. When creating this kind of code, try to see if alternative ways of solving the problem would result in a better and more maintainable solution.

Another use for this property of the assignment operator is in chained assignments. The basic idea is that the same value can be assigned to more than one variable; this can be done by just having two or more variables share the same assignment expression.

```c
int height, width;
void make_square(int dimension)
{
    height = width = dimension;
}
```

Function make_square is used to update the height and width variables to the same quantity. This is accomplished by chaining the assignment between these two variables. In fact, the proper way to read this assignment would be from right to left.

```c
void make_square(int dimension)
{
    height = (width = dimension);
}
```

Clearly the same idea can be extended to as many variables as necessary.

Increment and Decrement Operators

A simple form of assignment is the increment operator. This operator was created to perform a unit increment to variables containing integer values. Similarly, a decrement operator also exists, and its application decreases by a single unit the value assigned to a variable. The increment operators are frequently used in loops, for example, to update the value of temporary counters.

```c
int print_forwards_and_backwards(int n)
{
    int i;

    for (i=0; i<n; i++)
    {
        NSLog(@"value is %d", i+1);
    }

    for (i=n; i>0; i--)
    {
        NSLog(@"value is %d", i);
    }
}
```

In this example you have the opportunity to use both increment and decrement operators to move the counter variable i. The increment and decrement operators also have a version that can be used inside of another expression, in a similar way to how an assignment an assignment operator can be used. The pre-increment operator increments a variable by one unit, but it also makes sure that the increment happens before other parts of the containing expression are executed. Similarly, there is a pre-decrement operator with a similar property.

```
int print_forwards_and_backwards(int n)
{
    int i;

    for (i=0; i<n; )
    {
        NSLog(@"value is %d", ++i);
    }

    for (i=n; i>0; )
    {
        NSLog(@"value is %d", i--);
    }
}
```

This example shows the difference between using the pre-increment and post-increment operators. In both loops we removed the increment and decrement operators from the loop expression. They have been moved and became sub-expressions of the NSLog call. In the first, case, however, we want to increment the variable before it is printed, so we use the pre-increment operator. In the second case, the goal is to print the variable as it is and then perform the increment, which is accomplished by the post-increment operator.

> **Note**   Increment and decrement operators cannot be used more than once for the same variable in the same expression. When that happens, the compiler will not know the expected value of the variable, and the result will most probably be incorrect. As a matter of programming discipline, avoid using increment operators in large expression where this may happen by accident.

Compound Assignment

A class of assignment operators exists that generalize the increment and decrement operators. For example, to add integer values to a variable, you can use the += operator. Thus,

```
width = widht + 10;
```

is equivalent to

```
width += 10;
```

As an example, the following code increases the dimensions of a rectangle:

```
int width, height;

void increase_rectangle_dimensions(int increase)
{
    width += increase;
    height += increase;
}
```

And similarly for subtraction:

```
void reduce_rectangle_dimensions(int reduction)
{
    width -= reduction;
    height -= reduction;
}
```

There is a version of the compound assignment operators for each of the arithmetic operators: *=, /=, %=, <<=, >>=. They are easy to understand, and you will see examples of their use in other sections of this book.

Structures

A structure is a user-defined type containing other data elements that can be accessed using tags. A structure is declared with the keyword struct.

```
struct address
{
    int number;
    NSString *street;
    NSString *city;
    NSString *state;
    int postal_code;
};
```

This struct defines a new data type that contains five pieces of data that can be accessed as part of the address structure. To use such a structure, you just need to create a variable of the newly defined type.

```
void create_address()
{
    struct address famous_address;
    famous_address.number = 1600;
    famous_address.street = "Pennsylvania Av";
    famous_address.city = "Washington";
    famous_address.state = "DC";
}
```

The great advantage of structures is that they allow information to be packed into logical units, so that you don't need to deal with several unrelated variables. Instead, you just need to work with a single data representation. So, for example, using the address structure described above you can create functions that receive addresses as parameters, instead of dealing with a set of unrelated items.

```
void print_address(struct address an_address)
{
    NSLog(@"street: %@", an_address.street);
    // ... print other fields in address
}
```

You can also think of structures as a primitive version of an object that contains only data. In the next chapter you will see how Objective-C provides user-defined data types that have not only associated data, but that can also respond to messages.

Pointers

A pointer is an address to a location in memory. Objective-C provides convenient access to memory addresses through the use of pointers to particular types. The main advantage of pointer types is that they allow you to interpret any memory address as the potential location of a variable. Therefore, you are not limited to use variables that have been previously declared: you can convert any memory location into data types that can be manipulated by algorithms.

To declare a pointer, you start with an existing data type and apply the star character to the right of the desired data type. For example, you can define pointers for integers and doubles in the following way:

```
int *pointer_to_int;
double *my_double_pointer;
```

> **Note**   A pointer declaration will merely define an address to a data type, but will not create any memory associated with that data type. For example, the variable pointer_to_int shown above has no integer variable associated to it. To be able to use a pointer you need first to have it pointing to valid memory.

Once you have a pointer, you can use it to manipulate existing variables. You can do this by using two operators: the star operator is used to retrieve the data stored in the memory at which it is pointed. For example,

```
void print_value(int *pint)
{
    NSLog(@"the value is %d", *pint);
}
```

The expression *pint means that you are dereferencing the value stored in the memory pointed by pint. In summary, the star operator allows you to use a pointer in place of a variable of the given type.

The second operator used with pointers is the address-of (ampersand) operator &. This operator is required to retrieve the memory address of an existing variable. When combined, the star operator and the address-of operator allow you to retrieve addresses from variables, and to access and modify data stored at these memory addresses. They provide the programmer with the basic tools necessary to manage memory in an application. Here is a simple example:

```
void modify_value(int *pint, int new_value)
{
    *pint = new_value;
}

int width, height;

void init_rectangle_dimensions()
{
    modify_value(&width, 100);
    modify_value(&height, 50);
    NSLog(@"Now width = %d and height = %d", width, height);
}
```

This code is using a pointer to modify the content of an integer variable. This indirect operation is useful because now the same code can be use to modify any integer variable, regardless of its actual name in the program.

Parameter Passing

This is a good moment to explain the idea of parameter passing conventions. Each function is defined by its name, parameters, and return type. Parameters passed to functions in Objective-C are always copied. This means, for example, that when passing an integer number to a function, the value used inside the function is just a copy of the original integer. In particular, if you modify the value of a parameter, you are not changing the value of the original variable that was passed. For example,

```
void try_to_change(int value)
{
    value = 10; // a new value
    NSLog(@"value is now %d", value);
}
void use_change()
{
    int orig_value = 20;
    try_to_change(orig_value);
    NSLog(@"after change %d", orig_value);
}
```

If you run this function, you'll see that the stored value didn't change after the function try_to_change was executed. We say that the variable orig_value was passed by value to try_to_change. If you really want to change the value of a variable, you need to have not just a copy of it, but its memory address. This can be done using a pointer, as shown in the previous section. So, the correct thing to do in this example is

```
void really_change(int *value)
{
    *value = 10; // a new value
    NSLog(@"value is now %d", *value);
}
void use_change()
{
    int orig_value = 20;
    really_change(&orig_value);
    NSLog(@"after change %d", orig_value);
}
```

Notice that now, instead of passing a value around, you are passing a memory address, so that you will be able to access that memory using the star operator. After the function try_to_change is called, the value of orig_value has changed from 20 to 10, unlike the previous time. This means that the function really_change is performing the modification on the contents of the original variable, not just on a copy.

> **Note**   Understanding how the language uses pointer parameters is important because this is also how objects are manipulated. All objects in Objective-C are created and used as pointers.

Arrays

An array is a way to store multiple values of the same type in a sequential manner. For example, suppose you wanted to store the ages for all students in a school. One way of doing this is to create a large number of variables to store that data, such as

```
int age1, age2, age3; // ... more here
```

This arrangement can be easily seen as too inflexible to maintain. Clearly this will require code that stores data in different variables.

```
age1 = 11;
```

```
age2 = 9;
```

```
// ... more here
```

This is not only inconvenient but also error prone. Arrays provide a way to solve this problem. If all you need is to store students' ages, you can create an array of 1,000 integers that can be indexed by values from 0 to 999.

```
int ages[1000];
```

Now you can write code that accesses and modifies the array as needed. For example, to store all ages, suppose you have a function returning the number of students, and another function returning the age of student number i. Then, you can write the following code to calculate the average age:

```
void average_student_age()
{
    int total_age = 0;
    int max = number_of_students();
    int i;
    double denominator = max;

    for (i=0; i<max; ++i)
    {
        ages[i] = age_of_student(i);
    }

    for (i=0; i<max; ++i)
    {
        total += age[i];
    }

    return total / denominator;
}
```

This function first reads the data into the ages array, and then calculates the average (the total age divided by the number of students).

The array declaration syntax is similar to the way single variables are declared. However, to create an array of a particular size, you type the number of elements between square brackets. In the example above, you have an array with 1,000 integers. In order to declare an array, you need a fixed size, such as 1,000. For variable sized arrays, you will later use Objective-C container classes such as NSArray, which provides a more flexible mechanism for array creation and resizing.

To access the elements of an array, you just need to address the required element using brackets. For example, to assign a value to the third element of the array, you need to use the following code:

```
ages[2] = value;
```

This code fragment will store the contents of value to the third position of the array ages.

> **Note**   Objective-C arrays are zero-based, so the first element is located at position zero. This may be confusing for people learning the language, but you just need to remember that the index represents how far from the beginning of the array you want to reach. The first element is at distance zero from the beginning of the array, so the index is zero. Similarly, the second element is at distance one.

Arrays and Pointers

One of the most important properties of arrays in Objective-C is that they are closely related to pointers. The relationship between these two concepts comes from the way the memory for arrays is created in an Objective-C application. Arrays are just stored as memory blocks, with elements that are accessed based on the distance to the beginning of the array.

For example, consider the array ages described in the previous example. When reading the array declaration, the compiler will reserve a memory area large enough to contain as many elements as requested.

To access a particular element, the compiler will take the address of the beginning of the array and add a particular displacement. Therefore, the following code is possible:

```
int ages[1000];

// some code to initialize the array ...

void print_item(int pos)
{
    int *pointer = ages;

    NSLog(@"item value: %d is the same as %d", *(pointer + pos), ages[pos]);
}
```

What this code illustrates is the fact that an array can be converted to a pointer of a similar type. Also, adding a value to a pointer is similar to accessing a particular element of an array. So, the code above is equivalent to the following, in which the array is accessed differently:

```
int ages[1000];

void print_item(int pos)
{
    int *pointer = ages;

    NSLog(@"item value: %d is the same as %d", pointer[pos], (ages+pos));
}
```

Given the way that arrays are stored in memory by Objective-C compilers, using pointers to access array elements is not only possible, but also frequently done by professional programmers.

Summary

In this chapter we provided a quick overview of the main concepts common to both the C and Objective-C languages. While we don't have space to describe every detail of the syntax and semantics of the C language, the basic elements discussed here can be used to create complex and useful applications.

The programming methodology of the C language, structured programming, calls for the division of programs into related functions. In Objective-C, on the other hand, the main concept is the decomposition of programs into classes, which encapsulate both the code as well as the data used by their methods. Moreover, Objective-C provides a flexible mechanism for runtime code execution through the concept of message passing. This is the main topic of the next chapter, in which you will begin the exploration of the concepts of object-oriented programming.

Chapter 2

Classes

In an object-oriented programming language such as Objective-C, classes are the building blocks of applications. They are the syntactic construct used to define objects, which are composed of methods and variables. For programmers new to the language, it is important to understand that object-oriented programming (OOP) features are the keystone of all techniques used in Objective-C.

Without a proper understanding of object-oriented design concepts, it is difficult to become proficient in the libraries used on Mac OS X or iOS, since they make heavy use of OOP. For this reason, I start this chapter with a concise overview of OOP. One of my first objectives is to explain how OOP differs from other popular programming paradigms. While structured programming tries to decompose programs by means of simple functions, OOP considers the combination of functions and data as the real defining concept of programming abstraction. Therefore, OOP languages avoid the separation of data from the methods operating on that data. Another great advantage of programming in terms of objects is the idea of sending a message to other objects and letting these objects decide on the best way to respond to the message.

After an initial introduction to OOP, this chapter gives a detailed description of the concept of classes in Objective-C. Special attention is given to the syntactical aspects—especially how to create new objects from existing classes. I explain how to associate data to these classes, and then proceed to add methods to the objects. Methods in Objective-C can also be associated to the class itself, as you will see in the examples.

One of the main features of classes in Objective-C is how they can be neatly decomposed into two separate files: one containing the interface and one containing the implementation details. This clear separation makes it possible to share only the important aspects of a class, while hiding any implementation information that is not needed by clients. In this chapter, you will see all the details of the syntax used to create classes that provide this simple interface to other parts of the application.

Finally, I provide examples of how to define instance properties, a simple mechanism that exposes data to other objects while retaining control over how that data is interpreted and saved. These are the main building blocks of UI objects, and learning how to define them will enable you to create flexible classes that can respond immediately to changes in other parts of the application. For example, properties are used to maintain separate views of the same object, while making sure that updates are immediately reflected in each view of the data.

Object-Oriented Programming

The primary goal of this chapter is to discuss the main features of Objective-C targeted at object-oriented programming. OOP is a style of programming in which we are encouraged to organize code into classes defined according to the desired functionality. The word "class" is a good metaphor since we are trying to classify code and data into suitable abstractions.

Unlike standard implementation technologies such as structured programing, OOP provides a flexible mechanism for sending messages to other objects in order to execute code. Instead of directly calling a function, as we have been doing up to this point, OOP applications just tell other objects what they would like to be executed. By sending messages instead of using functions defined at compilation time, objects are free to dynamically modify the way they respond to messages.

The messaging mechanism provided by OOP also facilitates the separation of concerns between areas of an application. Using this strategy, an object can concentrate only on the basic functionality it provides. At the same time, objects can request any additional functionality from other existing objects in the system.

A class can be interpreted as a prototype for an object. In Objective-C, a class is defined in two parts, which are introduced by the keywords @interface and @implementation. These definitions encompass all the information needed by the language in order to create runtime objects.

An object is the runtime instantiation of a particular class. In most of the contexts discussed in this book, an instance is equivalent to a runtime object. Therefore, you see that objects are created through the explicit instantiation of existing classes.

Why Are Objects Important?

In the last 30 years, OOP languages came to the forefront of programming research and practice due to their advanced mechanisms for program decomposition and extensibility. While it is true that older languages such as C can simulate all features in an OOP language, achieving the same results requires a high level of complexity that is unnecessary when using OOP.

As a result, most application software is currently designed for OOP languages such as Objective-C. Due to the practical importance of objects, it is necessary to be aware of the main differences between OOP and other programming paradigms.

The classical definition of OOP identifies a number of functionalities that need to be present in an OOP language. Since OOP languages are so numerous these days, it becomes hard to present features that are common to all of them, other than the concept of objects and methods associated to them. Nonetheless, a classical definition of OOP includes a number of important elements, which are available in Objective-C as well as in many other OOP languages.

1. *Encapsulation*: This means that objects are supposed to contain data and code in the same unit. For example, an object that defines a financial statement will contain the data used by a financial statement, plus code that can be used to manipulate financial statements.

2. *Inheritance*: Classes can inherit variables and code from other classes. This relationship is called inheritance. The inherited class is referred to as the super class, parent class, or base class. The inheritance relationship is

recursive, therefore forming a class hierarchy. In Objective-C, only single inheritance is possible; that is, classes can inherit data and code from a single class only (but this can be made more flexible by the use of the protocol mechanism, as you will see in a future chapter).

3. *Polymorphism*: This is a central concept in OOP, since it allows the same message to be responded to in different ways depending on the object that receives the message. The syntax of Objective-C allows a pointer to a base class to be used to refer to an object or a derived class. This flexible mechanism allows programmers to send messages to objects without having to define exactly how the receiver will react, and what is going to happen as a result. Objects receiving the message can choose to interpret it according to their own needs. This provides for extensibility that would be very difficult to achieve without the use of objects.

Object-oriented programming has been used in the last few decades to define the building blocks of many important technologies. For example, Apple has used the strengths of OOP through Objective-C to design the Mac OS X operating system interface. More recently, all the UI and system code for the iOS has been created using Objective-C.

Now that you understand the advantages of using OOP, let's take a look at how Objective-C provides support for the main concepts of object orientation, including how to define new classes with variables, and their methods.

Using Objects

A program in Objective-C makes extensive use of objects. Although it is always possible to create structures and functions, as you saw in the previous chapter, applications are supposed to use objects in order to comply with the Objective-C framework and to have access to the extensibility options available in the language.

The first thing you need to understand is how to properly use existing objects. An object in Objective-C is created when you send a create message to its class. Then, the object will become active and you can start sending messages to it.

In practice, you work with pointers to objects, since it is not possible to directly create a variable of a particular class. Consider for example the Objective-C class for strings, `NSString`.

> **Note**   All classes in the Objective-C framework provided by Apple start with two letters that are used as a common prefix. The NS prefix is used by all classes in the Foundation framework. These two letters have been used since Objective-C was still a product developed by NextSTEP. Other frameworks use different combinations of letters. In particular, code developed by application writers should avoid this prefix.

```
void printMessage(NSString *text)
{

    NSLog(@"Message is %@", text);

}
```

In this example, there is an object of class NSString, which implements the string type. Objects are always manipulated through a pointer, since you cannot know exactly the type of the object passed to the function, other than the fact that it derives from NSString. This is the basic principle of polymorphism and is used whenever you manipulate an object.

The most important thing you can do with an object is sending messages to it. The syntax for message sending is the following:

```
[<object pointer> <message>];
```

For example, consider the following function:

```
void printMessage(NSString *text)
{
    int len = [text length];

    NSLog(@"Message length is %d", len);
}
```

In this example, you use text, a pointer to a string object, and send to it the message length, which returns an integer value. The length message is part of the interface of NSString objects, so it can be called anytime you have an available NSString.

Method Parameters

The length message discussed above is a very simple one, without any arguments. If a message has a single argument, it is passed after the name of the message and a colon, like so:

```
void printsubstr()
{

        NSString *text = @"My Example String";
        NSString *substr = [text substringToIndex:5];
        NSLog(@"substring is %@", substr); // prints "My Ex"
}
```

In this example, the substringToIndex message is sent the text object. This message is defined as returning a new string containing all the characters in the original string, up to the character number provided. In the last line of this function, you use the NSLog function to print the resulting substring to the console.

If a message needs two arguments, it has a specific format that describes the use of each argument. Here is an example using the message stringByReplacingOccurrencesOfString:withString:

```
NSString *replaceOne(NSString *myString)
{

        return [myString
                stringByReplacingOccurrencesOfString:@"1"
                withString:@"one"];
}
```

As the name of the message clearly states, its goal is to return a new string by replacing occurrences of the first argument with the second argument. The arguments are always supplied after the colon separator. This is true for as many arguments as required by the message.

> **Note**   Many programmers, used to the way methods and functions work in languages such as C++ or Java, feel that Objective-C is very verbose when it requires an additional keyword for each argument. There are some advantages, however, in choosing the long-style syntax for messages. First, it promotes the creation of methods with a small number of arguments. This is a good side effect, since a large number of arguments can make functions harder to understand, no matter what syntax is used. Second, Objective-C messages are self-documenting, since they are required to use words to describe each of the parameters.

The id Type

One of the singularities of the OO features in Objective-C is the use of a generic object type called id. A variable of type id can be used to hold a pointer to any object, independent of its original type. The objective-C compiler will also allow you to send any message to that variable, since the process of message dispatching will be performed at runtime, rather than at compile time.

The id type is used in some important messages, such as alloc, which allocates memory for a new object. The return type for that message is id, so that it can be used to create any type of object.

Since id can be used as a generic type for objects, it is important to understand when to use id or a specific pointer type, such as NSString *. The advantage of using a well-defined type is that the compiler can tell exactly which messages are available for that type. If an incorrect message is sent to an instance of NSString, the compiler will present the user with an error message. Therefore, it is easier to work with objects of particular types if the code assumes that this is the only possible target of the desired messages.

On the other hand, there are many situations in which you might want to write code valid for a generic type. Also, a few library objects return id as a type. In these cases, it is necessary to work with an id instead of a well-defined type.

Creating New Objects

Creating new objects is a two-step process. The first step is to send a message to the desired class requesting a new object. This is done with the `alloc` message, which allocates enough space for the object and returns a pointer to it.

The second step consists of initializing the newly created object. This is a task performed by an instance method. A standard method called `init` exists and is inherited by any class deriving from NSObject. It is also possible for an object to define its own `init` method. More complex objects can also be initialized through a special purpose method, for example when additional parameters are needed.

> **Note**   Remember that classes in Objective-C are also objects. Once a new class is defined (as you will see in the next section), the compiler will automatically create a runtime object representing the class. Just like any other object, classes can have their own methods. Moreover, such methods can run independently of any instance of the class.

To illustrate this, consider the process of creating an array of numbers using the NSArray and NSNumber classes:

```
NSArray *createArray()
{

        NSMutableArray *array = [[NSMutableArray alloc] init];
        for (int i=0; i<3; ++i)
        {
                NSNumber *number = [[NSNumber alloc] initWithInt: i+1];
                [array addObject:number];
        }
        return array;
}
```

In this example, first you create a mutable array by sending an `alloc` message to the NSMutableArray class. Then, you ask the object to initialize itself by sending the `init` message. Although you want to return an NSArray object, you create an NSMutableArray because it allows you to add elements as needed. Polymorphism allows you to use an NSMutableArray as if it were an NSArray. Inside the loop, you create an NSNumber object for each value between 1 and 3. You first send an `alloc` message to the class, but then use the `initWithInt`, which is a special purpose initializer method for the NSNumber class. It receives an integer, which then becomes the value stored by the NSNumber.

Defining New Classes

A class is defined by creating a pair of elements: the interface and the implementation. An interface is usually entered in a separate header file and is used to define the content of a class to their users. The interface is then made available to other modules of the application.

From that interface definition, other classes will receive a detailed description of which messages can be sent to a particular object. For example:

```
@interface Employee : NSObject
{
    // list of variables here, if any
}

// a list of messages

@end

@implementation Employee

// list of message implementations

@end
```

> **Note**   When programming on Apple-related platforms, you should always use NSObject as a superclass. This is not a requirement when defining a new class, since it is possible to create classes that are independent of NSObject. For example, you may want to define you own hierarchy of objects with different semantics. However, in practice you always want to use the common methods provided by NSObject, which was designed to be a common denominator for all objects across the system.

The @interface keyword is used to introduce an interface. The keyword is followed by the name of the class, and optionally a colon and the name of the superclass used by the object, if there is one.

The @implementation keyword is used to start the class definition. It is used as part of the .m (messages) file, and contains the definition of every message that the object responds to.

> **Note**   Reserved words used by Objective-C are prefixed by the @ character, which is not used in the syntax of C. This practice avoids possible clashes with existing C code. This is a convenience for programmers integrating existing C code into Objective-C. For example, @class is a keyword so it is still possible to use the name "class," which is a legal name in a C application. By doing this, Objective-C avoids a common problem that exists when porting code from C to C++. Whenever Objective-C uses keywords without a @ character, these are restricted to just a small number of contexts, so there is no possible clash with application-defined names.

In the next sections, you will see how to add instance variables and instance methods to a class definition.

Instance Variables

An instance variable is used to store data for a particular object. The defining characteristic of member variables is that they are defined for each object of a particular class. In this sense, they are similar to the data stored in a plain C structure. On the other hand, instance variables are accessible inside the implementation of a class.

For example, an Employee class would have data stored for each object of that class. An Employee would typically have instance variables such as age, salary, and address. These instance variables would be represented in the following way:

```
@interface Employee : NSObject
{
    int salary;
    NSString *address;
    int age;
}
@end
```

Once an instance variable is declared in the class' interface, it can be used in the implementation. For example, suppose that you declare a new method called incomeTax.

```
@implementation Employee

-(double) incomeTax:(double)taxBracket
{
    return salary * taxBracket;
}

@end
```

Instance variables can be designated as public or private, thus limiting the access provided to other classes. A private variable can only be used by methods of the same class, unlike public variables, which are available to any code that uses objects of that class. This mechanism makes it possible for application writers to change the internal implementation of a class, while at the same time reducing concerns about the consequences on other code that uses it.

To define an instance variable as private, just use the keyword @private before the definition of the variable. Similarly, one can make a variable public by using the @public keyword. If you want an instance variable to become accessible by a class and its subclasses, use the @protected keyword. By default, private instance variables are private; that is, they are available only to the class itself, and not to its descendants. Once an accessibility keyword is used, it affects all variables declared after it, until the accessibility level is changed by the appearance of another keyword.

An instance variable can also be made available only in the package in which it is defined. For this purpose, the keyword @protected exists. Its use is similar to the way private and protected variables are marked.

> **Note**   In general, Objective-C programmers don't make extensive use of public or protected instance variables. Due to its dynamic nature, classes in Objective-C are used through their methods, using the message passing mechanism. This means that direct access to variables is of little use and should be avoided in practice.

Adding and Defining Instance Methods

Methods are the main mechanism used to define behavior in a class. It is the set of methods in a class that define the messages that an object can answer directly (for derived classes, this also includes the methods in the super classes). Therefore, one of the main goals in OOP is to include only methods that are directly related to the functionality that you want to expose to users.

An instance method defines the behavior of an object instance whenever the object receives a particular message. For example, suppose that you want to respond to the sayHello message. This can be done as follows:

```
@interface SimpleObject  : NSObject

-(void) sayHello;

@end

@implementation SimpleObject

-(void) sayHello
{
    NSLog(@"hello");
}

@end
```

This example shows a class that provides limited functionality through its single method. To access the method, you can create an object of the SimpleObject class, and send the sayHello message.

```
SimpleObject *object = [[SimpleObject alloc] init];
[object sayHello];
```

As previously discussed, methods are declared with a segmented syntax, where each parameter is introduced by a word describing its meaning. The method sayHello doesn't have any argument, therefore there is no colon following its name. On the other hand, consider the method printText shown bellow:

```
@interface SimpleObject2  : NSObject

-(void) printText:(NSString *)message;

-(void) printText:(NSString *)message withSuffix:(NSString *)suffix;

@end
```

```
@implementation SimpleObject2

-(void) printText:(NSString *)message
{
        NSLog(@"message is: %@", message);
}

-(void) printText:(NSString *)message withSuffix:(NSString *)suffix
{
        NSLog(@"message is: %@%@", message, suffix);
}

@end
```

Here, the new class defines an object that responds to the printText message. When sending a message to this object, you need to provide a parameter after the colon separator, like so:

```
void printTextExample()
{
        SimpleObject2 *obj = [[SimpleObject2 alloc] init];
        [obj printText:@"My message"];
}
```

Similarly, when two or more parameters are needed, they are given after the corresponding colon that separates argument keywords from actual arguments. Here is an example using the message printText:withSuffix:.

```
void printTextAndSuffixExample()
{
        SimpleObject2 *obj = [[SimpleObject2 alloc] init];
        [obj printText:@"My message" withSuffix:@"here"];
}
```

The Difference Between Messages and Functions

There is a subtle difference between sending messages to an object and calling a function in Objective-C. When executing a function, both the programmer and the compiler know exactly what is going to be executed as a result. For example, when a function like printf is called, you know that some well-defined code to print the arguments to the log will be executed. Similarly, when calling the exp function, you can be certain that the function in the mathematical library that calculates the exponential will be called.

However, when it comes to working with objects, a message sent to an object doesn't guarantee that a particular piece of code will be executed in each case. This is especially true when you send messages to objects that you didn't create. The difference has to do with the concept of polymorphism. Polymorphism means that any object can respond to messages in a different way—in a way that is most appropriate to its objectives. For example, an InkJetPrinter object may respond to the print message differently from a LaserPrinter object. However, only these objects need to understand how the implementation of these methods is different. OO languages provide this level of separation between the object sending a message and the object receiving the message.

Consider the following example, in which you create an Employee class:

```
@interface Employee : NSObject
{
        // add any necessary variables here
}

-(double) calculatePay;

@end

@implementation Employee

-(double) calculatePay
{
    return 0;
}

@end
```

You also have an hourly employee class, which represents employees that are paid by the number of hours worked.

```
@interface HourlyEmployee : Employee
{
    int numWorkedHours;
    double hourlySalary;
}

@end

@implementation HourlyEmployee

-(double) calculatePay
{
    return numWorkedHours * hourlySalary;
}

@end
```

Finally, you have full-time employees, whose payment is established in a yearly basis.

```
@interface FullTimeEmployee : Employee
{
    double yearlySalary;
}

@end

@implementation FullTimeEmployee
```

```
-(double) calculatePay
{
    return yearlySalary / 12;
}
```

```
@end
```

From a design point of view, there are three classes: Employee, the base class, and two derived classes, HourlyEmployee and FullTimeEmployee. These classes have implementations for the method calculatePay. But the implementation used in each of these classes is different. In the first class, you have just a basic implementation, where the value zero is returned, since there is no information about the type of Employee being described.

The second class has an implementation that depends on the variables numWorkedHours and hourlySalary. This information is used to calculate the salary that needs to be paid to an hourly-based employee. The third class is also derived from Employee, but in that case the salary calculation is much easier, since a full time employee receives the yearly salary in monthly installments.

Suppose you use these classes as follows:

```
void send_payment_message(Employee *employee)
{
    double total = [employee calculatePay];
    NSLog(@"salary total is %d", total);
}
```

In that case, although the value passed to the function is of type Employee, you don't know for sure which kind of Employee is being used: it can either be an object of the original Employee class or one of the derived classes. In each case, the value stored in total will be different, leading to a calculation that depends on different information. This is possible because messages in Objective-C are resolved only at runtime.

Polymorphic Messages

When the message is sent to an object, the runtime system determines which method can be used to respond to that particular message. If a suitable method is found, it will be used to handle the message. If no method is found matching the message, then the runtime system will search for that method in the superclass (the parent class). If the method is not found there, this process will continue until either a method is found that matches the message in one of its super classes, or an error is generated.

In the case presented above, objects are related by inheritance to the class Employee. For this reason, the compiler can be sure that there is a valid implementation for that particular message. However, this is not always the case, since validation by the compiler is not strictly necessary. To make it possible to send messages that are now known at compile time, Objective-C allows any message to be sent to an object of the generic type id. For example, you could have the following function:

```
void send_pay_message(id object)
{
    double total = [object calculatePay];
    NSLog(@"salary total is %lf, total);
}
```

The code is very similar to the example above, but now the object is declared as just an id, the generic type that can be used for any object, instead of the fixed type Employee. In that case, no compile-time check is performed, but the runtime system will still perform the same work it did before. The only difference is that the compiler cannot guarantee that the message will be correctly sent during runtime. In that case, the programmer needs to be careful enough to send certain messages only to objects that can possibly respond to them (in that case, only objects that respond to the calculatePay message should be used).

The Special Variable self

When implementing instance methods, it becomes necessary to access the data stored in instance variables. This is possible through the use of the self variable. In the interior of a method, self is a special variable that is set to a pointer to the object itself. Thus, it can be used as the target of messages as well as to access instance variables. For example, consider the following definitions:

```
@interface Person : NSObject
{
        NSString *firstName;
        NSString *lastName;
}

- (void)setFirstName:(NSString *)firstName;

- (void)setLastName:(NSString *)lastName;

- (void)printFullName;

- (void)setFirstName:(NSString *)first lastName:(NSString*)last;

@end

@implementation Person

- (void)setFirstName:(NSString *)aFirstName
{
        self->firstName = aFirstName;
}

- (void)setLastName:(NSString *)aLastName
{
        self->lastName = aLastName;
}

- (void)printFullName
{
        NSLog(@"Full name is %@ %@", self->firstName, self->lastName);
}
```

```
- (void)setFirstName:(NSString *)first lastName:(NSString*)last
{
    [self setFirstName:first];
    [self setLastName:last];
}
@end
```

Notice here that you can access the value of `firstName` and `lastName` through the variable `self`, which is just a pointer to the current object. While this is useful, it needs to be noted that an instance variable can be freely accessed from inside a method, even without the use of `self`. For example, the `setLastName` method could also be written as

```
- (void)setLastName:(NSString *)aLastName
{
        lastName = aLastName;
}
```

The second use of the variable `self` in the class implementation shown here is as a target for other messages in the same object. Since it is frequently necessary to invoke methods in the same object, the special variable `self` is essential. Without a reference to the current object, there would be no way to send a message that could be responded by other methods in your own class.

Defining Class Methods

A class method is different from an instance method in that it is triggered by a message sent to the name of a class, not to a particular object. Therefore, it is possible to send messages to a class even before a single object of that class has been created. This is a simple but effective way to perform creation and initialization of objects. For example, consider the following code that uses the `NSString` class:

```
NSString *copyString(NSString *string)
{
        NSString *copy = [NSString stringWithString:string];
        return copy;
}
```

The objective of this function is to copy the original string, returning a pointer to the new object of the `NSString` type with the same text content. To do this, you send a message to the `NSString` class, asking it to create a new string object and to initialize it using the single string passed as argument. Notice that, as a consequence, the class is asked to perform all of these tasks: the `NSString` instance is not responsible for the result.

Let's see an example of how to add a new class method, called `performClassTask`, to a class interface and implementation. To define a class method, the syntax used is almost identical to an instance method definition. The only difference is that such methods start with a plus symbol (+) instead of a minus (-).

```
@interface MyClass : NSObject

+ (void) performClassTask;

@end
```

```
@implementation MyClass

+ (void) performClassTask
{
    // implementation goes here
}

@end
```

Another difference when implementing a class method is that it doesn't have access to instance variables of the object through the self keyword. This makes logical sense because such a method is not running as part of the object. A class method is attached instead to the class object, of which only one exists for each class in the application. The variable self, in this case, refers to that class object.

As you saw in the first example, class methods are a convenient way to create and initialize new instances of a particular class. Since they operate at the class level, they can be invoked before the object exists. Thus, it is possible to use a class method to perform any number of prior steps necessary for the creation of a complex object.

To see several examples of the concept of class methods, just look at some of the most common classes in the Foundation framework. For example, the NSString class has a number of class methods that create and initialize a new string based on input provided by the client. Here is a sample code that creates a new string based on an existing pointer to characters:

```
NSString *stringFromCArray(const char *text)
{
        return [NSString stringWithUTF8String:text];
}
```

As you see, the message is sent to the NSString class directly. The class method is then responsible for allocating a new object and properly initializing it with the provided pointer. This example also shows how to convert text stored as in legacy code written in C. Since the C language doesn't have objects, strings are represented as simple arrays of characters terminated by a null (zero value) character. While this is a fast way to represent strings, it is also hard to manipulate and it requires manual maintenance of the memory used by the string. The NSString object is, in contrast, much easier to use and it can be updated in a way that is similar to other objects in the system.

The init Method

The init method performs an important function among other methods in a class. It is the method called right after an object has been created, in the two-step alloc/init pair. The init method is declared in the NSObject class, but it is frequently necessary to override its definition in new classes.

One of the reasons you may want to redefine the init method is to provide a customized initialization for one or more of the instance variables in the object. By default, instance variables are initialized to zero, if they are numbers, or nil (the null value for pointers) if they are objects. On the other hand, it may be necessary or desirable to initialize instance variables to something else that is more sensible for the class.

For example, suppose you have a class representing Cash. The only two instance variables for this class are quantity and currency. For quantity, it is OK to have the default value of zero. However, for currency you want the default to be USD. Here is how you can do that:

```
@interface Cash : NSObject {
        double quantity;
        NSString *currency;
}

@end

@implementation Cash

- (id)init {
    self = [super init];
    if (self) {
        currency = @"USD";
    }
    return self;
}

@end
```

First, you define the interface for the class, where the two instance variables are declared. Notice that it is not necessary to add init as a method in the class interface: init is already part of the interface by inheritance, since NSObject is its superclass.

Next, you provide an implementation for the init method in the @implementation section. The implementation has to follow a structure similar to what is displayed here to conform to the expectations of users of the class. Therefore, the first action needs to be calling the init function in the parent class, through the special variable super. Second, you check that self points to a valid object and, in the positive case, initialize its variable currency to the value @"USD".

The same process needs to be followed for any class that needs to define an initializer method. You can also declare initializers that accept parameters. For example, an init method that receives the currency name as a parameter could be coded as follows:

```
- (id)initWithCurrency:(NSString*)aCurrency {
    self = [super init];
    if (self) {
        currency = [NSString stringWithString:aCurrency];
    }
    return self;
}
```

In this case, you still call the init class in the parent class, but the argument aCurrency is now used to initialize the currency instance variable.

Defining Properties

Instance variables are used to store data associated with an object. Instance methods are used to implement the functionality provided by objects of a particular class. Together, these two elements are enough to deliver all of the main advantages of OOP. However, there are cases in which it is helpful to work with a combination of methods and variables. This is the reason why properties were introduced to the language.

A property is a syntax used to simplify the creation of methods for setting and getting a particular value associated to an object. Although a property is similar in use to an instance variable, it doesn't need to be associated to any variable in particular. A property is a practical way of providing access to data that needs to be properly handled by the application.

Consider, for example, the case in which some data is used in two or more areas of an application. Consequently, it is desirable to trigger an update mechanism every time the data is changed. This is a case in which a property could be used to provide a simple interface for data access.

```
@interface Person : NSObject
{
        NSString *name_;
}

@property(readwrite,retain,nonatomic) NSString *name;

@end

@implementation Person

-(void) setName:(NSString*)aName
{
        name_ = aName;
        // notify UI of name change
}

-(NSString *)name
{
        return name_;
}

@end
```

In this example, you have a Person object that contains a name property (I will explain the attributes between parentheses later). Associated with that property are two methods: the first is used to set the property, and the second returns the value currently stored. To store the content of the property, class Person uses an instance variable called name_.

Using Properties

Once these definitions are available, you can use the property in some code, like so:

```
-(void)useProperty:(NSString*) newName
{
    Person *myPerson = [[Person alloc] init];
    myPerson.name = @"new property value";
}
```

Notice how this code uses the property as if it were a field in a structure. This is a special syntax that works only on properties, since myPerson is a pointer, and pointers don't have data members (since they are not structures). What this syntax is doing, instead, is calling the setter method in the Person class. Whenever this happens, the code in the setName: method will perform any action necessary to update the UI, as required.

Of course, you could achieve the same result calling the method directly, like so:

```
-(void)usePropertyAgain:(NSString*) newName
{
    Person *myPerson = [[Person alloc] init];
    [myPerson setName: @"new property value"];
}
```

Similarly, a read access will call the getter method.

```
-(void)readProperty:(NSString*) newName
{
    Person *myPerson = [[Person alloc] init];
    myPerson.name = @"new property value";
    NSLog(@"The name is now: %@", myPerson.name);
}
```

Synthesized Properties

In general, properties are a great way to simplify the interface to functionality exposed in a class. This is particularly true when changes in a property result in changes to other parts of the application. The property mechanism can also be used when a particular data is calculated in terms of variables stored in the object. For example, you could create a property called temperatureInCelsius that could share the same data as temperatureInFahrenheit. The only difference is that the getter and setter methods would be responsible for the conversion between these two representations.

The implementation of properties can be simplified if all you are doing is storing and retrieving data from an instance variable. In that case, Objective-C provides a default mechanism that can be used to automatically create the getter and setter methods. Therefore, the implementation of the above property could be simplified to the following:

```
@implementation Person

@synthesize name = name_;

@end
```

Here, you don't need to directly implement any getter or setter. The compiler will do that automatically, while you are just responsible for providing the variable name (in this case, the variable is called name_).

```
@interface Person : NSObject {
        NSString *name_;
}

@property(readwrite,retain,nonatomic) NSString *name;

@end

@implementation Person

@synthesize name = name_;

@end
```

Finally, Objective-C provides an even simpler way to implement properties. This is possible by leaving the instance variable to be defined solely by the compiler. In that case, the previous example can be changed to

```
@interface Person : NSObject

@property(readwrite,retain,nonatomic) NSString *name;

@end

@implementation Person

- (void) useName
{
        NSLog(@"name is %@", self.name);
}

@end
```

Then, the method useName is able to access the property and print its value, even though no instance variable has been assigned using @synthesize. In that case, the corresponding instance variable is automatic generated, which by default uses the same name as the property with a leading underscore added to the name.

Property Attributes

As shown above, properties have a number of attributes that describe how it will be synthesized or defined in the @implementation section. Here is a list of some of the most common attributes associated with properties:

- *readwrite*: This attribute is used for properties can be read and modified by client code. That is, other objects can use the notation object.property to read as well as to set the corresponding property (this is the default).

- *readonly*: This attribute may be used to mark a property that cannot be modified. This is useful when you just want to provide access to a particular data contained in the object, but at the same time you don't want to allow modifications to its value. For example, a property may have its value synthesized from other instance variables—which means that you don't want to allow for independent modifications.

- *atomic*: This attribute is useful when working with multithreaded code. It means that the operations defined by this property cannot be interrupted once they start. For example, multiple threads will be required to read and write values in a single transaction. Notice that this option may result in unnecessary overhead if the atomic operation is not necessary, but is also the default assignment method.

- *nonatomic*: The opposite of the above attribute, this indicates that the operation can be interrupted. Useful when writing single-threaded applications that don't have a need for atomic operations.

- *getter*: This attribute can be used to define a custom name for the getter method. For example, you may want to use a method that has already been defined. The compiler will route all read accesses using the notation `object. property` to this method. The proper syntax is `getter=methodName`.

- *setter*: This can be used to define a custom name for the setter method. The use of this attribute is similar to getter, as described above. The proper syntax is `setter=methodName`.

- *copy*: The setter method will store a copy of the object passed as an argument, instead of the object itself. This may be used to avoid additional references to an existing object, and to isolate changes to the copied object from the original one.

- *retain*: When using this option, the data will be retained for memory management purposes. Any other object currently stored in that property will be released.

- *assign*: This attribute indicates that the data passed as argument to the setter method will be directly assigned to the variable used by the property.

> **Note**   Some of the options above deal with the way memory is managed by objects. Don't worry if you don't understand the difference between these memory management strategies: I will discuss these implementation techniques in Chapter 8. For now, just remember that different attributes can be used to determine how data is stored and released by a property setter.

Classes and File Structure

Objective-C uses two main kinds of source code files: header files and module implementation files. A header file is used to contain the interface section of a class. Other elements, such as constants and auxiliary type definitions, can also be included in the header file.

The second type of file, a module definition, is saved with the `.m` extension. The module definition is where the bulk of the implementation of a class is contained. It will have not only the implementation section, but also any other functions and type definitions necessary for the module.

The header file is necessary to provide a public interface for the class. Other modules in the project will access the class through its public interface. Therefore they need access to the header file where this interface is defined.

There are two ways to have access to definitions in a header file. First, there is the traditional C style include. For example, to include a standard I/O library in C-style, you can use

```
#include <stdio.h>
```

This is necessary to include definitions for traditional and legacy code available to the application. Objective-C, however, provides a second method for header file inclusion. This second style is used to simplify the creation of interfaces. You can include such interfaces using the import directive, like so:

```
#import <Foundation/NSObject.h>
```

This will import the NSObject.h header contained in the Foundation framework. It is common to organize classes into frameworks, and the notation FrameworkName/ObjectName.h is an easy way to remember where an object may be located.

Here is a complete example of what the header and implementation files may look like for a simple class. First, the header file for a Loan class, where you represent common properties of loans such as principal and interest.

```
// file Loan.h

@interface Loan : NSObject
{
    double principal;

    double interest;
}

- (double)getMonthlyPayment;

@end
```

And this is the corresponding method implementation file:

```
// file Loan.m

#import "Loan.h"

@implementation Loan

- (double)getMonthlyPayment
{
    return principal * (interest/12);
}

@end
```

Once you have the code for a class split into these two files, the header Loan.h is the only part that needs to be available to other objects. This means that modifications in the implementation file Loan.m have no influence in how the other classes in the system are compiled unless the interface is changed in some way.

One of the great things that you can do using this method of separating interface and implementation is to update the implementation in a way that is independent of the interface. For example, you can decide to change the way getMonthlyPayment is implemented. Suppose, for example, that you want to have the interest calculated in a separate method, instead of using an inline expression as you are doing right now. This would result in the following implementation file:

```
// Loan.m

#import "Loan.h"

@implementation Loan

- (double) interestPerMonth
{
        return interest/12;
}

// updated calculation of month payments
// using the new interestPerMonth method.
- (double) getMonthlyPayment
{
        double monthlyInterest = [self interestPerMonth];
        return principal * monthlyInterest;
}
@end
```

Notice how the new calculation uses another method called interestPerMonth. While the result is still the same, the new organization resulting from this change allows for other changes in the future. For example, you may have to use a more complicated technique for calculating monthly interest, depending on the financial score of the borrower. This is now possible since the calculation of interest has been separated from the calculation of the monthly payment.

Another aspect of this example should be noticed: if a method is used only inside the implementation, then it is not necessary to add it to the interface. This is an important fact because it helps to reduce the amount of entries in the @interface section. Only methods accessible to other classes need to be included in the interface section, while methods that are used locally need to appear only in the implementation section. As long as you add a method before its first use, this is all you need to do. In a later chapter you will see a more general way to add internal methods to an existing implementation.

Summary

Classes provide the building blocks of object-oriented programming. As OOP is the main focus of Objective-C, it is very important to understand the concepts of classes. In this chapter I presented everything you need to create and manipulate classes in Objective-C.

Initially, you saw how OOP may be an important tool for software development. The concepts of OOP—such as encapsulation, polymorphism, and inheritance—provide the basis for the design of modern software by allowing an adequate level of abstraction during the design and development phases of the project. OOP has been used for the last 30 years, and Objective-C is a language that fully embraces the concepts proposed by the OOP community.

You learned how to define new classes in Objective-C using the `@interface` and `@implementation` sections. The syntax for classes allows such definitions to be split into public header files and private implementation files.

You have also seen how to define the interface variables and methods necessary to provide the full functionality of any object. Instance methods have access to the instance variables declared in the class. They also have access to other methods in the same class through the use of the `self` variable.

Finally, you learned about properties, an effective way to simplify the process of setting and reading data from and to an object. Properties are very flexible, and provide several ways for class writers to interact with instance variables as well as intercept changes and accesses to these properties. For example, you can provide this functionality by the use of the `@synthesize` keyword.

With the essential understanding about classes and objects acquired in this chapter, you are ready to delve into the objects provided by the Objective-C frameworks. You start this exploration in the next chapter, which will discuss strings and containers.

Chapter 3

Strings and Container Classes

In this chapter I discuss some of the most common classes available in the Foundation framework. In particular, I discuss the NSString class, used to manipulate all character sequences in Objective-C. NSString offers a convenient interface to create strings, retrieve part of a string, compare string values, and convert them into other formats.

Another important class in the Foundation framework is NSNumber. Numbers are one of the most basic concepts in computer programming, and they are usually handled by the C language as native data types. However, there are times when a number needs to be passed to or stored by other objects. When that is necessary, a wrapper class such as NSNumber is the best way to simplify the conversion between the C and Objective-C worlds.

I also discuss the two main collection types provided by Objective-C. NSArray is a simple class interface for a sequence of objects. With the help of NSArray objects, you can efficiently store and retrieve elements in a simple sequence.

NSDictionary is a class that provides the general service of storing key/value pairs. Each key has a unique value stored in the dictionary, so that it can be efficiently retrieved. NSDictionary gives programmers a rich set of messages that can be used to query, retrieve, and process objects stored in such a dictionary container.

Strings

A string is a sequence of characters. The NSString class provides all the functionality necessary for creating and modifying strings, and it is used throughout Cocoa and related frameworks. Strings are used not only for messages, but also when you need a textual representation of a component that is represented internally in binary, such as an integer number, a floating pointer number, or an object.

Creating Strings

To create strings, you use the NSString class, which is part of the Foundation framework. To create an empty string, you just send an alloc message to the NSString class, followed by an init message that will properly initialize the members of the class.

```
- (void)createString
{
        NSString *myStr = [[NSString alloc] initWithCString:"my original string"
                                            encoding:NSASCIIStringEncoding];
        NSLog(@"the string is %@", myStr);
}
```

The first thing you do in this function is send the alloc message to NSString, like you may do with any Objective-C class. Then, you send the initWithCString:encoding: message to the allocated object. The first parameter to that method is a C string, enclosed in single quotes. The second parameter is the encoding type for the characters. The most common option is the one shown, the ASCII encoding, but several other options are available.

Of course, it would be boring to go through all of these steps just to create a string. That's why there's another, simpler option, which you have been using since the first chapter: by adding the character @ to the beginning of a double quoted string, you tell the compiler to create a new NSString object with the standard encoding. The compiler is responsible for calling alloc and the right version of init for the resulting object. This is a great effort reduction, and it also shows the great amount of work that the compiler performs on your behalf when processing Objective-C code.

NSString Methods

NSString provides a rich interface for text manipulation. There are methods that can be used to access single characters or a range of characters. Some methods can be used to compare different strings, while others can be used to return information about prefixes and suffixes.

The length method is used to return the number of characters in a string. For example, you could rewrite the above function in the following manner to display the size of the string passed to the constructor:

```
- (void)createString
{
        NSString *myStr = [[NSString alloc] initWithCString:"my original string"
                                            encoding:NSASCIIStringEncoding];

        NSLog(@"the length of the string is %d", [myStr length]);
        // prints the length of the string is 18
}
```

The method `characterAtIndex:` returns a single character that is located at the given index position. Remember that, as with plain C arrays, `NSString` objects use a zero-based index. That is, the index 1 is used for the second element, and so forth. The following function will always return YES:

```
- (BOOL) compareString
{
        NSString *myStr = [[NSString alloc] initWithCString:"my original string"
                                         encoding:NSASCIIStringEncoding];

        return [myStr characterAtIndex:4] == 'r';
}
```

The following function will return YES if both strings have the same characters:

```
- (BOOL) stringsEqual:(NSString *) :(NSString *)b
{
        NSUInteger n1 = [a length];
        NSUInteger n2 = [b length];

        if (n1 != n2)
        {
                return NO;
        }

        for (int i=0; i<n1; ++i)
        {
                if ([a characterAtIndex:i] != [b characterAtIndex:i])
                {
                        return NO;
                }
        }
        return YES;
}
```

> **Note** `NSUInteger` is a type defined by the Objective-C library to refer to an unsigned integer. It is typically the same as `unsigned int`, but it is left as a separate type to facilitate porting of Objective-C code to other platforms. Since there is no guarantee that an `unsigned int` will have the same size on all platforms, it is a good idea to use `NSUInteger` to achieve uniformity, especially when you are writing code that is related to memory sizes, such as string lengths.

While it is possible to use `characterAtIndex:` to compare two strings, as you did in the previous example, it is much more convenient to use the `compare:` instance method for this job. When using `compare:`, the return value is of type `NSComparisonResult`, and there are three possible values. `NSOrderedAscending` means that the original string comes before the argument string in lexicographical order. A result of NSOrderedSame means that the two strings are identical. The remaining option is denoted by NSOrderedDescending. Here is an example:

```
- (void) compareString:(NSString *)a with:(NSString *)b
{

        NSComparisonResult res = [a compare:b];
        if (res == NSOrderedAscending)
        {
                NSLog(@"String %@ comes before %@", a, b);
        }

        else if (res == NSOrderedDescending)
        {
                NSLog(@"String %@ comes before %@", b, a);
        }
        else
        {
                NSLog(@"The strings are identical");
        }
}
```

Finally, if you are interested just in simple equality testing (that is, if you don't care if the two strings are lexicographically in ascending or descending order), there is an even faster way to achieve it. The method isEqualToString: will take as a parameter another string and return YES or NO, depending on the equality of all corresponding characters on both strings.

The same kind of tests discussed above can be performed using case-insensitive comparison. For example, NSString has a method called caseInsensitiveCompare: that behaves similarly to compare: with the exception that characters such as "a" and "A" are considered to be identical.

Substrings

Another kind of operation that can be performed on NSStrings is retrieving subsets of the sequence of characters. The methods extract parts of the current string based on the position where they appear and return a new NSString containing only the desired characters. For example, to find a substring that contains all the characters from the beginning of a string up to a given index, you can use the substringToIndex: method. Here is some sample code:

```
- (void) initialSubstring
{
        NSString *original = @"Original string";
        NSString *partial = [original substringToIndex:4];
        NSLog(@"The partial string is %@", partial);
}
```

This code would print "Orig", the first four letters in the original string, into the log screen. Another method that has a similar use is the substringFromIndex: method. It can be applied to a string in such a way that the return value is composed of the last characters if the sequence, starting at a particular position. For example, suppose that a function is designed to detect plural words. A simple way to do this is to look at the suffix of the given string and check if it is equal to "s".

```
- (BOOL) isPluralWord:(NSString *)word
{
        int length = (int)[word length];
        int initialPosition = length - 1;
        if (initialPosition < 0)
        {
                return NO;
        }
        NSString *suffix = [word substringFromIndex:initialPosition];
        return [suffix isEqualToString:@"s"];
}
```

This code determines the length of the received string, and then calculates the position, starting from the beginning, for the last character. This is at position `length - 1` because indices always start from zero. If the resulting position is less than zero, then it must be an empty string and you return NO. Otherwise, you determine the suffix of the word and compare it to "s" to determine if this is a plural word.

With these two methods you could select any internal substring of a given string by using a combination of substringToIndex: and substringFromIndex:. However, there's also a method called substringWithRange:, which takes a range composed of two positions and returns a substring containing all the characters between the given range. For example, suppose you received a quoted string (that is, a string where the initial and final characters are a quote). You can design a function to remove the quotes from such a string using the substringWithRange: to return the internal part of the NSString object.

```
-(NSString *) removeQuotes:(NSString *)str
{
        int len = (int)[str length];
        if (len < 2)
        {
                return @"";
        }
        NSRange range = NSMakeRange(1, len-2);
        return [str substringWithRange:range];
}
```

In this example, you first calculate the length of the string passed as a parameter, and then check if the string has at least two characters (otherwise you return just the empty string). Then, you create a range starting from position 1 and with length equal to the original length minus two positions. As a result, you then return the substring calculated by substringWithRange:.

The NSNumber Class

When working with objects, it is frequently necessary to store or retrieve numbers using an OO interface. After all, the main strength of Objective-C is to be able to write flexible code, passing messages between objects rather than using fixed interfaces defined by functions and C operators.

Also, while numbers such as integers and doubles are easy to manipulate using C functions, objects need to support an additional range of operations derived from the basic NSObject class. For this reason, Objective-C provides a special purpose class, NSNumber, which can be used to store a number from any of the standard C numeric types.

NSNumber is a generic interface. It can be used to wrap any of the native numeric types provided in the C language. The types of numbers that can be represented by an NSNumber include integers (int), long integers (long int), short integers (short), as well as unsigned integers (unsigned int). Very small numbers can be represented in C as characters, so NSNumber also provides support for the char type. Floating-point numbers (float) as well as double floating numbers (double) are also represented. Finally, NSNumber can wrap values of Boolean type (BOOL).

To create an NSNumber, you just need to call the alloc/init combination, where the init function will depend on the type of number you want to wrap. Here are some examples:

```
- (void) createNumbers
{
        int aInt = 1;
        long aLong = 23456;
        double aDouble = 3.14;
        BOOL aBool = YES;
        char aChar = 'A';

        // here are the corresponding NSNumber objects
        NSNumber *objInt = [[NSNumber alloc] initWithInt:aInt];
        NSNumber *objLong = [[NSNumber alloc] initWithLong:aLong];
        NSNumber *objDouble = [[NSNumber alloc] initWithDouble:aDouble];
        NSNumber *objBool = [[NSNumber alloc] initWithBool:aBool];
        NSNumber *objChar = [[NSNumber alloc] initWithChar:aChar];
        NSLog(@"Here are the values: %@, %@, %@, %@, %@ ",
                objInt, objLong, objDouble, objBool, objChar);
}
```

While this is the standard way to create such number objects, there are other avenues for object construction. For example, it is possible to simplify this by using a class method to perform the allocation and initialization in the same step. That would become

```
- (void) createNumbers2
{
        int aInt = 1;
        long aLong = 23456;
        double aDouble = 3.14;
        BOOL aBool = YES;
        char aChar = 'A';

        // here are the corresponding NSNumber objects
        NSNumber *objInt = [NSNumber numberWithInt:aInt];
        NSNumber *objLong = [NSNumber numberWithLong:aLong];
        NSNumber *objDouble = [NSNumber numberWithDouble:aDouble];
```

```
        NSNumber *objBool = [NSNumber numberWithBool:aBool];
        NSNumber *objChar = [NSNumber numberWithChar:aChar];
        NSLog(@"Here are the values: %@, %@, %@, %@, %@ ",
                objInt, objLong, objDouble, objBool, objChar);
}
```

Hopefully, if you have access to some modern version of Xcode, you will be able to use the latest syntax for number literals. The new syntax works by using the @ character as an indicator that the following literal value needs to be converted to an NSNumber. This trick works for literal numbers (or for variables as in the above), and therefore you can apply it to the preceeding example for further simplification, like so:

```
- (void) createNumbers3
{
        NSNumber *objInt =  @1;
        NSNumber *objLong = @23456;
        NSNumber *objDouble = @3.14;
        NSNumber *objBool = @YES;
        NSNumber *objChar = @'A';

        // print the values as objects
        NSLog(@"Here are the values: %@, %@, %@, %@, %@ ",
                objInt, objLong, objDouble, objBool, objChar);
}
```

Accessing an NSNumber

The other side of the coin for NSNumbers is to be able to access their values. This can be done with a set of methods that provide access to each of the values that may be stored in an NSNumber. For example, for integer values, there's the integerValue method. For characters, there's the charValue. Similarly, access methods exist for each of the types directly supported by NSNumber. The following example shows how to access the data stored in NSNumbers:

```
- (void) accessNumberValue
{
        NSNumber *objInt =  @1;
        NSNumber *objLong = @23456;
        NSNumber *objDouble = @3.14;
        NSNumber *objBool = @YES;
        NSNumber *objChar = @'A';

        // print the values as native data types
        NSLog(@"Here are the values: %d, %ld, %lf, %d, %c ",
                (int)[objInt integerValue],
                [objLong longValue],
                [objDouble doubleValue],
                [objBool boolValue],
                [objChar charValue]);
}
```

> **Note**   Retrieving data from NSNumber does not guarantee that the right format will be used. Since the internal data stored in NSNumber is just a number in binary format, the accessors will try to convert the internal data so that it fits the requested format. This may result in the loss of data. For example, storing a long and trying to access it with a request for a char will result in truncation. Before accessing the data stored in a NSNumber, however, you can use the objCType method to determine the exact type contained in it.

When to Use an NSNumber?

The next question to address is when to use NSNumber. Although it is nice to be able to send messages to an object instead of calling functions, this is not always necessary. Moreover, there is a performance penalty paid every time an object is used instead of native types. Objects require allocation and message passing, which are expensive when compared to the efficient way native types, such as integers and Booleans, are handled by the compiler.

Therefore, there is little reason to use objects instead of native types if the situation requires high performance. For example, numerical algorithms that make frequent calculations are much better handled by native types, which can benefit from all optimizations enabled by the C language.

On the other hand, there are situations in which you would like to treat numbers as if they were objects. This happens whenever you want them to be part of some kind of collection that responds to well-known messages. For example, suppose that you want to create an array of objects. These objects will all receive a certain set of messages, such as deallocate, when the array is destroyed. To make it possible to add numbers to such an array, it must be possible to represent the number as an object. Thus, instead of adding numbers directly to an array of objects, you create object wrappers to the numbers.

Collections of objects are a main reason for using the NSNumber class. In the next few sections, you will see how container classes do their job of maintaining arrays and dictionaries.

> **Note**   Consider performance reasons before using NSNumber objects. If you need to perform fast calculations, prefer the native types. NSNumber objects are necessary, however, whenever you need to treat the number as an object, such as when interfacing with methods that receive objects only, or when adding numbers to a container.

Containers

When data is stored in the form of objects, it is useful to be able to manipulate a collection of elements as just another object. The Foundation framework provides a set of container classes that make it easier to achieve this goal. The containers supplied by the Foundation framework include arrays and dictionaries, both in mutable and immutable forms. In the next few sections I explain how to create, update, add, and remove elements from such containers.

Arrays

An array is a set of objects stored in contiguous memory. As you saw in the first chapter, C provides a flexible and efficient implementation for native arrays. However, arrays may be difficult to work with, especially for dynamic arrays that require explicit memory management. The NSArray class was introduced with the goal of providing a simple yet powerful interface for array objects. With the help of NSArray you can execute a number of operations on arrays using the message passing mechanism.

First, consider how to create and add elements to an array. The simplest way to create an array is to call a pair of alloc/init methods. Once the array object has been properly initialized, it is possible to create a new array by adding new elements to the original NSArray.

```
- (void) createSimpleArray
{
        NSArray *a0 = [[NSArray alloc] init];

        NSArray *a1 = [a0 arrayByAddingObject:@"My First Object"];
        NSArray *a2 = [a1 arrayByAddingObject:@"My Second Object"];

        NSLog(@"The size of the array is %d", (int)[a2 count]);
}
```

The function createSimpleArray creates an array with two string elements, and prints to the system log the size of the resulting array, called a2. To achieve this, you send the arrayByAddingObject to an instance of NSArray. Additionally, to find the number of elements in an array, you send the count message to the resulting array.

While the technique above can be employed so that you may add elements to any array, it would be much easier to add both elements in a single step. This can be done using a special version of the init method for the NSArray class, like so:

```
- (void) createSimpleArray2
{
        NSArray *array = [[NSArray alloc] initWithObjects:
                                        @"My First Object",
                                        @"My Second Object", nil];
        NSLog(@"The size of the array is %d", (int)[array count]);
}
```

While the results are identical for the two examples, the function createSimpleArray2 uses a special version of the init method. The method initWithObjects: is able to receive a sequence of objects as arguments. The only detail you need to be careful about is that the last element needs to be nil, since that is the sentinel value that indicates the end of the sequence. The nil value, however, will not be stored as part of the array.

The description of the initWithObjects: instance method shows you a very important aspect of the NSArray class. The class accepts only non-nil values as members of the array. This means that a nil element must be translated into some other representation before being stored in a NSArray (or any other container). For this particular purpose, there is a class called NSNull, which represents a nil (or NULL) as a single object.

Adding elements to an array via the `initWithObjects:` message is a simple way to perform this vital task. However, it is still cumbersome to have to use two messages in the same line. To simplify this common workflow, NSArray also has a class method with a similar functionality, the `arrayWithObjects:` method. The advantage of this method is that you can pass the sequence of elements directly to the NSArray class, instead of having to call `alloc` first. This simplifies the code by removing the need for an extra method call. The above example could be more concisely presented as

```
- (void) createSimpleArray3
{
        NSArray *array = [NSArray arrayWithObjects:
                                        @"My First Object",
                                        @"My Second Object", nil];
        NSLog(@"The size of the array is %d", (int)[array count]);
}
```

The methods `arrayWithObjects:` or `initWithObjects:` can be used to create arrays with any number of elements. As long as you end the list of elements with nil, there is no limit in the number of entries. However, there are situations in which you may create an array with just one element. That is possible with the methods `arrayWithObject:` or `initWithObject:`. They are similar to the ones that you have seen, with the exception that they accept a single element only.

```
- (void) createSimpleArray4
{
        NSArray *array = [NSArray arrayWithObject:
                                        @"My Single Object"];
        NSLog(@"The size of the array is %d", (int)[array count]);
}
```

While we are in the topic of array creation, note that there are other versions of `init` and `arrayWith` that can be used with NSArray. For example, you can initialize an NSArray with another, previously created array. For example, suppose that you would like to have a copy of the array constructed above. This could be done in the following way:

```
- (void) createArrayAndCopy
{
        NSArray *array = [NSArray arrayWithObjects:
                                        @"My First Object",
                                        @"My Second Object", nil];
        NSLog(@"The size of the array is %d", (int)[array count]);
        NSArray *copy = [NSArray arrayWithArray:array];
        NSLog(@"The size of the copy array is also %d", (int)[copy count]);
}
```

Finally, you might be interested in creating an array from an existing C array. That is also possible with NSArray, but you are required to also submit the number of elements in the array. This is needed because, by their nature, C arrays are equivalent to a pointer, and as such they don't store the number of elements.

```
- (void) createArrayWithCArray
{
        NSString *orig_array[] = { @"Obj1", @"Obj2" };
        NSArray *array = [NSArray arrayWithObjects:orig_array count:2];
        NSLog(@"The size of the array is %d", (int)[array count]);
}
```

In the first line of this example you are creating a C array with two objects. The declaration in the first line means that you are creating an array (indicated by []) of NSString *, which is the type used by string objects. The notation inside curly brackets is used by C functions to initialize an array of identical elements. Next, you pass the name of the array that, as you have seen in the first chapter, is equivalent to a pointer, to the arrayWithObjects:count: method.

Knowing all of these ways to create an NSArray object is useful because data may be available in many formats. It would be hard to convert these different data formats into a single format just to use it with NSArray. And you have not even exhausted the possibilities for conversion. For example, other ways of creating an NSArray are by reading data directly from a file (see arrayWithContentsOFFile:) or from an URL (see arrayWithContentsOfURL:).

Adding Other Object Types to an NSArray

In the examples you have seen so far, all the objects added to an NSArray are of type NSString. I have done this for simplicity only. In fact, NSArray is a dynamic container, which means that you can add objects of any type to an array. Here is an example of how this can be done:

```
- (void) createArrayWithDiffferentObjects
{
        NSNumber *num1 = [NSNumber numberWithInt:42];
        NSArray *array = [NSArray arrayWithObjects:num1, @"str2", nil];
        NSLog(@"The size of the array is %d", (int)[array count]);
}
```

The first object is an NSNumber, while the second is an NSString. They are now part of the same array. The only problem raised by such an array is how to distinguish elements based on their type. The answer to this question depends on what you want to do with the members of this array. If you are going to use only generic messages such as description, then there is no problem with mixing objects of different types.

The safest way to work with NSArray collections, however, is to create collections based on their types. For example, if you are creating an application that deals with geometric shapes, some of your arrays should contain shapes only. This is where inheritance gives you an advantage in handling dynamic objects: a set of geometric shapes can have a common class, used to classify different shapes.

For example, shapes such as Oval or Rectangle should be subclasses of a generic Shape class. Using this superclass, it is possible to restrict the elements in an NSArray to objects deriving of Shape. Thus, it would be possible to send messages that are specific to a Shape, and understood by them all.

If you are mixing objects of different types that are not related by a superclass, then you need some other way to determine which object is from a particular class. Although this is not recommended, there are ways to determine if an object is of a particular class. First of all, every object has an instance method called class, which returns a representation of the class. You could, in principle, compare the class returned by an object to a particular class representation, like so:

```
- (void) checkPersonClass:(Person *)person
{
        if ([person class] == [Employee class])
        {
                NSLog(@"This is an Employee");
        }
        else
        {
                NSLog(@"This is not an Employee");
        }
}
```

While this may work in some situations, it is also a dangerous way of solving the problem. The main issue is that checking for a particular class will also exclude objects that are in a subclass. For example, if you are looking for objects of class Shape, you will miss objects of type Rectangle. However, Rectangles are also a kind of Shape, and the resulting code will stop working on that situation.

To avoid this problem, you can use a method from NSObject called isSubclassOfClass:. This method is able to test if a given class is identical or a subclass of a given class. The following example shows how to test if an object is an NSNumber or an instance of a subclass of NSNumber:

```
- (void) checkClass2
{
        NSNumber *num1 = [NSNumber numberWithInt:42];

        // check if the object is a number of one of its subclasses
        if ([[num1 class] isSubclassOfClass: [NSNumber class]])
        {
                NSLog(@"This is a NSNumber");
        }
        else
        {
                NSLog(@"This is not a NSNumber");
        }
}
```

The call to class is necessary to return the class of the object. On the other hand, class is also sent to NSNumber to request the class object for that class. Another way of getting the same information is using the isKindOfClass method, which is derived from NSObject.

Using the Literal Notation

If you have access to Xcode 4.5 or later, you should be able to use the new literal notation introduced by Apple compilers. The traditional way to create arrays involves the use of alloc/init, or one of the helper class methods discussed above. While such initialization techniques work well, they are still cumbersome when compared to the initialization of native types, such as integers or native arrays.

The new literal notation makes it as easy to initialize an NSArray as a native type. Instead of sending messages to the NSArray class, the new notation uses a simple syntax to handle the process of creating an array. Here is an example:

```
- (void) createArrayWithNewSyntax
{
        NSArray *array = @[@"obj1", @"obj2" ];
        NSLog(@"The size of the array is %d", (int)[array count]);
}
```

Notice that the result this function produces is similar to what you have seen in previous examples. However, by means of the @[notation, an NSArray is created automatically by the compiler. There is no need to send messages to allocate or initialize the resulting object, since these operations will be performed automatically by the generated code.

One additional advantage of the new notation for array initialization is the reduction in potential errors. By using a simpler syntax, it is easier to spot simple mistakes, such as duplicate objects or nil elements, which could be otherwise introduced in the original notation.

On the other hand, the fact is that the new syntax doesn't totally remove the need for NSArray initializers. One example is using an existing C array as the initial contents of an NSArray. In that case, it is still necessary to use the form arrayWithArray:, which allows a C-based array to be passed, along with the array size.

Accessing an Array

In most programs, creating an array is just the beginning of the process. The other side of the coin is to access data stored in the resulting container. NSArray provides a simple way to access data through the objectAtIndex: method. With that method, you can pass the zero-based index of the stored object. Consider the following example:

```
- (void) accessArrayData
{
        NSArray *array = @[@"obj1", @"obj2" ];
        NSLog(@"The second element of the array is %@", [array objectAtIndex:1]);
}
```

The result of calling objectAtIndex: is the object that was stored at the requested position. Since the index is zero-based, requesting the index 1 will return the second element, the same convention used for native arrays in C.

While `objectAtIndex:` is powerful enough to provide access to any element, there are other ways to achieve this objective. For example, if you are using the array as a simple queue (last-in/first-out), you may be interested in the last element only.

```
- (void) accessLastElement
{
        NSArray *array = @[@"obj1", @"obj2" ];
        NSLog(@"The second element of the array is %@", [array lastObject]);
}
```

So the example above is equivalent to the previous one. Another way to access the elements of an array is by first comparing them to other existing objects. In that case, you may want to find the index of the object that has been previously stored in the array. This can be easily done with the `indexOfObject:` method, like so:

```
- (void) getIndexOfElement
{
        NSString *secondObj = @"obj2";
        NSArray *array = @[@"obj1", secondObj, @"obj3" ];
        int position = (int)[array indexOfObject:secondObj];
        NSLog(@"The index of the second element is %d", position);
}
```

In the first line of the function, you are creating a new object of type `NSString`. The second line creates an array that contains that object. The third line sends a message to the array, asking for the position of the known object, which is then printed to the log.

Finally, the new syntax introduced for `NSArray` and other containers has also a simplified way of accessing elements. If you have an `NSArray`, now it is possible to directly access elements with the same syntax of native arrays.

```
- (void) accessWithNewSyntax
{
        NSArray *array = @[@"obj1", @"obj2" ];
        NSLog(@"The second element of the array is %@", array[1]);
}
```

Behind the scenes, the compiler is generating code similar to what you saw before, with calls to `objectAtIndex:`. However, the syntax makes it much easier to visualize the way you are accessing elements, which is a big advantage for code maintenance.

Mutable Arrays

One issue that surprises programmers new to Objective-C is that a standard `NSArray` object cannot be modified. Once an object is created with one of the `init` functions described in the previous section, the only thing you can do is to access data, or request a new array based on the original content. In other words, an `NSArray` is an immutable data structure.

The reason for the immutability of NSArray is that such objects are optimized for fast access. Updates to an array, such as adding and removing elements, have the potential to generate new allocations and/or memory moves. Given the simple implementation of NSArray, this is considered to be undesirable. To allow for modifications, however, NSArray was subclassed into a modifiable form, the NSMutableArray class.

Everything that I said about the functionality of NSArray is still true for an NSMutableArray. However, the later is also able to add and remove elements, among the other important tricks it has learned. Creating an NSMutableArray is very much like what you did for an NSArray.

```
- (void) createMutableArray
{
        NSMutableArray *array = [NSMutableArray arrayWithObjects:
                                                @"My First Object",
                                                @"My Second Object", nil];
        NSLog(@"The second element of the array is %@", [array objectAtIndex:1]);
}
```

An NSMutableArray, however, is able to add elements at any time, not only during creation. So, the same mutable array could be created using the following code:

```
- (void) addElementsToArray
{
        NSMutableArray *array = [[NSMutableArray alloc] init];
        [array addObject: @"My First Object"];
        [array addObject: @"My Second Object"];
        NSLog(@"The second element of the array is %@", [array objectAtIndex:1]);
}
```

Another operation you can perform in such a mutable array is element removal. For example, you can remove any element by providing the index for the desired object.

```
- (void) addAndRemoveArrayElements
{
        NSMutableArray *array = [[NSMutableArray alloc] init];
        [array addObject: @"My First Object"];
        [array addObject: @"My Second Object"];
        NSLog(@"The second element of the array is %@", [array objectAtIndex:1]);
        [array removeObjectAtIndex:1];
        NSLog(@"The array now has %d elements", (int)[array count]);
}
```

Another use of a mutable array is as a simple queue data structure. A queue is a useful data storage mechanism that uses the first-in/first-out (FIFO) strategy. There are a large number of algorithms that benefit from the use of FIFO data structures, including language parsers and simulation systems, among others. To implement a queue using an NSMutableArray, you can use the methods addObject: and removeLastObject. Here is how you can enqueue and dequeue elements into this kind of data structure:

```
- (void) enqueue:(NSMutableArray *)array forId:(id) object
{
        [array addObject: object];
}

- (id) dequeue:(NSMutableArray *)array
{
        id element = [array lastObject];
        [array removeLastObject];
        return element;
}
```

Dictionaries

A dictionary is a data structure used to maintain a relationship between a set of keys and their corresponding values. You can think of a dictionary as a generalized array, where the keys may be not just integer numbers, but also any type of object. Therefore it is possible to use a dictionary to maintain a set of related objects, such as the list of countries and their capital cities: ("Canada","Ottawa"), ("France", "Paris"), ("USA", "Washington D.C."), etc.

The interface to a dictionary object, called NSDictionary, is familiar if you know how NSArray works. NSDictionary is an immutable class; therefore it allows only creation and data retrieval operations. The reasons for immutability are also very similar to the NSArray case: it is desirable to avoid changes in the underlying data structure for performance and maintenance reasons.

There are several initialization methods that can be called to create a new dictionary. For example, you can use initWithObjectsAndKeys:, where the values and keys are entered in a list that is ended by nil. Notice that supplying an incorrect number or entries or forgetting to enter a nil element will result in an error.

```
- (void) createDictionary
{
        NSDictionary *dict = [[NSDictionary alloc] initWithObjectsAndKeys:
                                        @"first", @"one", @"second",
                                        @"two", @"third", @"three", nil];

        NSLog(@"The number of elements in the dictionary is %d", (int)[dict count]);

}
```

Another way to achieve the same thing is to use arrays for values and keys. In that case, you need to make sure that both arrays have the same number of elements, or a runtime error will be raised during program execution.

```
- (void) createDictionaryFromArrays
{
        NSArray *values = [NSArray arrayWithObjects:@"first", @"second", @"third", nil];
        NSArray *keys = [NSArray arrayWithObjects:@"one", @"two", @"three", nil];

        NSDictionary *dict = [[NSDictionary alloc] initWithObjects:values forKeys:keys];
        NSLog(@"The number of elements in the dictionary is %d", (int)[dict count]);
}
```

While this is an easier to way to achieve the same result, there are other creation methods that might be more convenient, depending on how the data is available. For example, it is possible to create a new NSDictionary from data stored in a file using dictionaryWithContentsOfFile:, and even from an URL, using the method dictionaryWithContentsOfURL:.

Finally, for anyone using one the latest versions of the Apple compiler, it is possible to initialize an NSDictionary with a simple and intuitive notation, which is very similar to the one available for arrays. Here is an example:

```
- (void) createDictionaryWithNewSyntax
{
        NSDictionary *dict = @{ @"one": @"first", @"two" : @"second", @"three" : @"third" };
        NSLog(@"The number of elements in the dictionary is %d", (int)[dict count]);
}
```

The syntax uses the @{ sequence to introduce key/value pairs. The result is similar to using the method initWithObjectsAndKeys:, but keys are introduced in the first position. Also, keys and values are separated by a colon character. Finally, there is no need for a nil object at the end of the sequence, as is the case when a creation method is used.

Accessing Dictionary Elements

Once a dictionary is created, it is possible to access its elements using a few specialized methods in the NSDictionaryClass. The simplest way to retrieve an element is using the objectForKey: method. By sending this message to a dictionary, the value associated to the given key is returned. If no value is stored for the requested key, the return value is nil.

```
- (void) retriveDictionaryElement
{
        NSDictionary *dict = @{ @"one": @"first", @"two" : @"second", @"three" : @"third" };
        NSLog(@"The number of elements in the dictionary is %d", (int)[dict count]);

        NSLog(@"The element associated to two is %@", [dict objectForKey:@"two"]);
}
```

Another way to retrieve elements is to use the objectsForKeys: instance method. This method has the advantage of returning several items at the same time, which can speed up operations that depend on dictionary look-ups.

```
- (void) retrieveSetElementSet
{
        NSDictionary *dict = @{ @"one": @"first", @"two" : @"second", @"three" : @"third" };

        NSArray *objects = [dict objectsForKeys:@[@"two", @"three"]
                              notFoundMarker:[NSNull null]];
        NSLog(@"The number of object found is %d", (int)[objects count]);
}
```

In the call to objectsForKeys:, a second argument is the notFoundMarker:. The objective is to have some way to identify elements in the array of keys that don't correspond to any of the elements in the dictionary. Therefore, the value passed should be unique and not used in the dictionary. A possible solution is to use the null object of the NSNull class.

Retrieving Keys

Another way of accessing the data in an NSDictionary is by retrieving all the keys stored in the container. This might be useful when you want to check the keys in use. The NSDictionary makes this operation possible through the allKeys: method. The result of that method is an array containing all keys currently in use.

```
- (void) retrieveKeys
{
        NSDictionary *dict = @{ @"one": @"first", @"two" : @"second", @"three" : @"third" };

        NSArray *keys = [dict allKeys];
        NSLog(@"The number of keys in the dictionary is %d", (int)[keys count]);
}
```

The allKeys method is the simplest way to retrieve keys, but not the only one. The NSDictionary class provides a rich set of methods giving access to the list of keys. For example, a closely related method is allKeysForObject:, which returns an array with all keys that are associated with the object passed as a parameter. This message is useful when dealing with dictionaries where the same object may be stored for several keys.

An example would be an application where food ingredients (keys) may be associated to recipes (values). Since a recipe has several ingredients, it is common to have an object associated with several keys in such an application. Therefore, to find all the ingredients used to prepare a cake, you might want to use the allKeysForObject: method.

```
- (void) findIngredientsForCake:(NSDictionary *)ingredientDictionary
{

        NSArray *ingredients = [ingredientDictionary allKeysForObject:@"cake"];
        NSUInteger size - [ingredients count];
```

```
NSLog(@"The number of ingredients for cake is %d", (int)size);
for (int i=0; i<size; ++i)
{
        NSLog(@"cake ingredient: %@", [ingredients objectAtIndex:i]);
}
```

}

Similarly, you may want to access all values in a dictionary using an array. This is possible through the allValues method, which is similar in usage to allKeys. Clearly, there is no need for an allValuesForObject, since there is just one value per key. In its place, you will find the objectsForKeys:notFoundMarker:, which I have already discussed.

Using Dictionary Enumerators

Another way of accessing objects and keys is using NSEnumerator. With an object of type NSEnumerator, it is possible to retrieve a sequence using a simple for loop, which requests one element per iteration. The NSEnumerator class provides the method nextObject, which returns the next object in the enumerator. For example, to receive an enumerator for all the objects in a dictionary, you can send the message objectEnumerator to NSDictionary and iterate over the resulting elements. Here is some sample code:

```
- (void) enumerateDictionaryObjects
{
        NSDictionary *dict = @{ @"one": @"first", @"two" : @"second", @"three" : @"third" };

        NSEnumerator *objects = [dict objectEnumerator];
        id obj;
        while ((obj = [objects nextObject]))
        {
                NSLog(@"The dictionary contains object %@", obj);
        }
}
```

This example shows how to acquire an NSEnumerator that can be used to visit every object contained in the NSDictionary. The test in the while loop has two functions. First, it sends the nextObject message. Second, it checks if the returned value is not nil, in which case the body of the while loop is executed for the retrieved object.

In a similar fashion, you can use an enumerator to access the keys in a dictionary. The method responsible for this is called keyEnumerator, and it works as shown in the following example:

```
- (void) enumerateDictionaryKeys
{
        NSDictionary *dict = @{ @"one": @"first", @"two" : @"second", @"three" : @"third" };

        NSEnumerator *keys = [dict keyEnumerator];
        id key;
```

```
        while ((key = [keys nextObject]))
        {
                NSLog(@"The dictionary contains key %@", key);
                NSLog(@"The corresponding object is %@", [dict objectForKey:key]);
        }
}
```

Notice that enumerating an object by its keys is even more useful, since it allows one to traverse the dictionary in such a way that will reveal both keys and associated values.

Still another way to enumerate elements in a dictionary is using the fast enumeration protocol. Fast enumeration simplifies the process of visiting each element of a collection, although it works only on the latest versions of Apple's operating systems.

```
- (void) enumerateDictionaryObjects
{
        NSDictionary *dict = @{ @"one": @"first", @"two" : @"second", @"three" : @"third" };

        for (NSString *key in dict)
        {
                NSLog(@"The dictionary contains key %@ and value %@",
                        key, [dict objectForKey:key]);
        }
}
```

Mutable Dictionaries

Just as NSArray is an immutable sequence of objects, NSDictionary is also immutable. This means that, once created, it is not possible to insert new keys in it. Moreover, for a given set of keys, it is not possible to change the key/value associations included in the dictionary. The reason for this is similar to the reason NSArray is immutable: unchangeable data is more efficient and easy to handle by algorithms. So, this allows NSDictionary to have a small overhead, which is important when considering a data structure that is so frequently used.

On the other hand, it is very frequently necessary to consider mutable dictionaries, in which it is possible to add keys and change associations as needed. To satisfy this requirement, the Foundation framework provides a mutable version of NSDictionary, called NSMutableDictionary.

The NSMutableDictionary class inherits from NSDictionary, so that any NSMutableDictionary object is also an NSDictionary object. This means that everything I said about NSDictionary is also true in this case. Moreover, a few new methods have been added to modify the contents of the dictionary.

The first method is setObject:forKey:. The first parameter to this method is the value you want to set, while the second parameter is the associated key. Using setObject:forKey: it is possible to add new elements to a NSMutableDictionary, as in the following example:

```
- (void) changeDictionary
{
        NSDictionary *immutable_dict =
    @{ @"one": @"first", @"two" : @"second", @"three" : @"third" };
```

```
NSMutableDictionary *dict = [NSMutableDictionary
                                    dictionaryWithDictionary:immutable_dict];

[dict setObject:@"fourth" forKey:@"four"];
[dict setObject:@"fifth" forKey:@"five"];

for (NSString *key in dict)
{
        NSLog(@"The dictionary contains key %@ and value %@",
                key, [dict objectForKey:key]);
}
}
```

This code creates an initial dictionary, called immutable_dict, and then uses that dictionary to initialize an instance of NSMutableDictionary. This is possible with the use of method dictionaryWithDictionary:. Then, you add two key/value pairs using the setObject:forKey: method. The resulting dictionary is then printed using a for loop that iterates over the keys and retrieves the object for a given key using objectForKey:.

Another method you may call on NSMutableDictionary is removeObjectForKey:, which can be used to delete entries from the dictionary. The use of this method is straightforward: objects associated with the given key are removed from the dictionary after the message is processed. If you want to delete more than one key, this is possible using the removeObjectsForKeys: method. The argument for removeObjectsForKeys: has to be an NSArray, with all the keys for objects you want to remove. For instance, you could amend the example above to delete two entries in the dictionary using an array of keys, like so:

```
- (void) deleteFromDictionary
{
        NSDictionary *immutable_dict =
        @{ @"one": @"first", @"two" : @"second", @"three" : @"third" };

        NSMutableDictionary *dict = [NSMutableDictionary
                                    dictionaryWithDictionary:immutable_dict];

        [dict setObject:@"fourth" forKey:@"four"];
        [dict setObject:@"fifth" forKey:@"five"];

        for (NSString *key in dict)
        {
                NSLog(@"The dictionary contains key %@ and value %@",
                        key, [dict objectForKey:key]);
        }

        NSArray *keys_to_delete = @[ @"two", @"three" ];
        [dict removeObjectsForKeys:keys_to_delete];
```

```
for (NSString *key in dict)
{
        NSLog(@"The dictionary still contains key %@ and value %@",
                key, [dict objectForKey:key]);
}
}
```

Summary

In this chapter I discussed some of the most important classes in the Objective-C Foundation framework. First was the NSString class, used to store and manipulate character strings. Then I talked about the NSNumber class, which serves as a wrapper for common values such as integers, floating-point numbers, characters, and Booleans. Finally, I discussed in detail the container classes, which include NSArray and NSDictionary.

Strings are important because they are the most common way to encode input and output data. The NSString class provides several initialization methods that can be used in various situations, depending on how the string data is supplied to the application. Common facilities include substring matching and comparison methods.

Numbers can be handled in Objective-C in two ways. The native types are the same as the ones used in the C language. They are the most indicated for high performance algorithms. However, many Objective-C classes require a reference to an object. In these situations, it is possible to wrap the number in an instance of NSNumber. That class provides methods to access the data in the desired format, including int, long, float, double, char, and BOOL.

Collections are objects used to maintain sets of other objects. The NSArray class defines the interface for objects that are stored in a sequence. Objects of the class NSArray can store and retrieve elements by index, starting from zero. The NSMutableArray is a subclass of NSArray that maintains arrays with a mutable interface, which allows elements to be added and/or removed.

The NSDictionary class provides a collection of elements associated to keys. You need to supply a valid key to retrieve elements. The NSMutableDictionary gives users the ability to add and remove entries from the dictionary.

Together, these classes provide most of the infrastructure necessary to write more complicated algorithms, ranging from graphical interfaces to game programming logic. In the next chapter, you will see how to make classes even more flexible for applications that need to extend them. With protocols and categories, you will learn about two mechanisms that can be used to add advanced capabilities to existing classes.

Chapter 4

Categories and Protocols

A category can be used in Objective-C to add methods to classes, even when you don't have complete access to the original source file for the class.

For example, using categories it is possible to add new methods to common classes in the system, such as `NSString`, `NSNumber`, or even `NSObject`. Doing this will make the added methods available to any user of the original class, as long as the category is loaded into the application.

If you need to add a complex responsibility to a new class in the context of a new library, or if you're just trying to add a single convenience method, categories may save the day, and are another reason why programming in Objective-C is so productive.

The design of adaptable interfaces is another area of strength for Objective-C, when compared to other object-oriented languages that enforce a strong type mechanism. By declaring a protocol, it is possible to create interfaces that are independent of a particular class and that can, therefore, be used by any client who wants to conform to a particular set of messages, as previously stated in the protocol declaration.

In this chapter, I consider these two mechanisms, categories and protocols, and how they can be used to create better applications. You will first investigate how to create new classes that benefit from the use of categories. In the second part of the chapter, you will see how protocols are employed in Apple's libraries, and how client code can profit from their use.

Categories

Due to its object-oriented philosophy, Objective-C promotes a clear separation between interface and implementation. One facet of this separation of concerns is the ability to extend classes through the addition of methods. This is made possible through the use of categories, a flexible mechanism that can be used by class designers, as well as clients of a particular class interface. Using a category, for example, it is possible to add new methods without requiring a recompilation of the original class file. This is of great help when working with existing libraries provided by third parties. The same principle can be used to manipulate the classes of frameworks provided by Apple, such as Cocoa and Cocoa Touch.

For instance, suppose that you need to add a method that could be applied to any string. A simple way of doing this would be to create a subclass of NSString and have the method attached to that subclass. You could then create strings by instantiating the new class, and such strings would be able to access the new method you declared. Since you can rely on polymorphism to be handled by Objective-C runtime, every method that accepts a string would also accept your new class.

However, this solution is not entirely satisfactory because in many cases you cannot control how an instance of NSString is created: such strings are frequently returned by other methods. Another problem is that by using a custom class you give away some benefits, such as the possibility of using string literals, for example.

Another way of proceeding would be to create a new category of NSString instead. In that case, you could add this method as an integral part of the NSString class interface. By importing the new category, any other class in your project that uses NSString will be able to access the added method, as if it was part of the original string class.

> **Note**   Extending existing classes through a category is a technique commonly used in the Cocoa frameworks. In this way, Cocoa allows classes such as NSString to incorporate features that make sense only in the context of a particular library. For a well-known example, the text-drawing framework adds a category to NSString that provides the ability to draw strings directly on the screen.

Creating a New Category

To declare a new category, you can use a syntax that is very similar to the implementation section of a normal class. However, in a category you will add the category name between parentheses after the class name, so that the compiler will recognize that the subsequent declarations are defining an extension to the original class, not the class itself.

After a method is added through a category, it behaves in all ways as if it was declared directly in the original class. For example, you can call these methods using the same syntax used to call one of the original methods of the target class. Classes derived from the original class that is being extended by the category will also inherit the methods defined in this way.

Here is an example of a category that implements an extension to the NSString class. The category consists of just one utility method: reverse, returning a new string that is the reverse of the original one.

```
@interface  NSString  (utility)

- (NSString *) reverse;

@end
```

Notice the name of the category following the class name, which distinguishes this declaration from a standard interface. The implementation is straightforward.

```
@implementation NSString (utility)

- (NSString *) reverse
{
        NSMutableString *resultString = [[[NSMutableString alloc] init] autorelease];

        int n = (int)[self length];
        for (int i=n-1; i>=0; --i)
        {
                [resultString appendFormat:@"%c", [self characterAtIndex:i]];
        }
        return resultString;
}

@end
```

This code uses the NSMutableString class, which allows data to be added to a string using methods such as appendFormat:. In contrast, an NSString is an immutable object, as it is common for many of the collection classes discussed in the last chapter.

Categories are used not only to extend existing classes in the standard frameworks. In general, imagine that you have just created a class with a handful of methods that implement a very specific responsibility. After using the class for some time, however, you figure out that a second type of responsibility could be added to the class, making it even more useful to its clients. The problem, however, is that you would like to keep the original interface as simple as possible.

When that is the case, Objective-C provides the concept of categories as a possible way to encapsulate additional functionality in a class, without compromising the original code and interface. The same technique can be applied to a class that you created as well as to an existing class.

Using a Category Header File

Categories can be used to extend the behavior of any class in the system. However, in order to enjoy the advantages of a new category, the client code needs to have access to its declaration.

This can be done using the standard mechanism of header file inclusion. As is common practice, the original class has its interface stored in a header file in the project. For example, the header file for class Employee would be named Employee.h. Now, suppose you want to extend the Employee class by declaring a new category called ExecutiveOptions. In that case, you would create a corresponding header file, Employee+ExecutiveOptions.h, containing the definition of the new category. The name of the header file, then, is a concatenation of the name of the class with the category name.

> **Note**   The logic behind this header file naming convention is to avoid a conflict with other classes. For example, it is conceivable that another class in the system could be named ExecutiveOption. In that case, you would have two header files with the same name, making it hard for users to simultaneously employ both the class and the category. Similarly, using just the name of the class without a suffix could result in nomenclature clashes.

The naming convention for category header files also helps with the maintenance of the system. Using the convention, it is very clear that any category file will have the added plus sign as part of the file name, which makes it easy to find a list of all categories in a project.

It is import to note, however, that not all categories are stored in a separate header file. For the same reason that sometimes it is better to store related classes in the same header, it may also be easier to add categories in a file that holds some other class declarations. This is frequently the case in the Foundation and Cocoa frameworks. The objective there is to minimize the number of header files that programmers need to import in order to employ a set of related classes and categories.

Categories and Private Methods

In an Objective-C class it is possible to declare instance variables with varying degrees of visibility. For public variables, any class or function that has a pointer to the object can access their content. Private ivars (instance variables), on the other hand, are available only to the class itself. Finally, Objective-C also provides protected ivars, which can be read or written by the class where they are defined, as well as any class that inherits from it. These accessibility levels provide some assurance that the compiler will enforce the visibility of a particular variable. This, in turns, contributes to a better code organization since an instance variable will only be visible or modified by a small part of the code base.

It would be great to have the same levels of accessibility for methods as well as for ivars. However, the design of Objective-C does not allow messages to be restricted in this way. Messages are resolved only at runtime, which means that the compiler has no way to enforce such access rules during compilation, as it can do for instance variables.

While there is no way to enforce access rules on methods, you can use categories as a simple way to reduce the visibility of methods that you would like to use in private. This is possible because a category can be created as an effective way to encompass one or more methods that are known only in the local context of a file.

To achieve this, you need to define a new category at the beginning of an implementation file. You can use any name for that category. Traditionally, people have used the name Private for this purpose, but Objective-C also allows the name of the category to be empty, resulting in anonymous categories. In that case, you don't need to worry about the right name for the category. But the greatest advantage of using anonymous categories is that there is no need to create a separate implementation section in your file, thus reducing the amount code to maintain.

The content of the anonymous category will be composed of all the methods you would like to make private. These methods can be accessed only by code pertaining to the original class and contained in the same implementation file. Here is an example where you implement a Library class with an anonymous category. The only method in this category is getPrivateBookTitles.

```
// file: Library.h
@interface Library : NSObject
{
        // instance variables here
}
// standard methods here
@end

// file: Library.m
@interface Library ()

- (NSArray *) getPrivateBookTitles;

@end

@implementation Library

- (NSArray *) getPrivateBookTitles
{
        NSArray *books = @[];
        // code to find private books
        return books;
}

@end
```

Even when using anonymous categories, it is necessary to keep in mind that the mechanism doesn't offer runtime protection for methods declared in this way. After all, it is still possible for the user of a class to send a message that will be resolved to a method in such a category. Remember that the mechanism of message dispatching works in such a way that doesn't care about the target of the message, as long as the message can be dispatched successfully. If you really don't want some code to be executed by external classes, the best way to achieve this is to use a static C function, since C functions aren't subjected to the message dispatching rules of Objective-C.

Adding Properties to Categories

As you have seen, categories can make our lives easier by allowing the extension of existing classes with new methods, using a simple syntax. However, when we're talking about enhancing the feature set of a class, it is frequently necessary to have some additional memory to store data associated with the new feature. For example, an Employee class may want to store health information for each person. The method addHeathRecords: would need to use one or more instance variables to keep track of the information as needed.

It is not possible, however, to add new instance variables directly to a category. After all, the objective of a category is to provide new methods, and not to change fundamentally the contents of an object. However, Objective-C provides an exception to this rule when adding an anonymous category.

Remember that anonymous categories are basically a way to add methods that are not named in the public interface of a class. As a result, an anonymous class is viewed by the compiler as part of the original class itself and uses the definitions of properties contained there as a basis for synthesized ivars. This combination of properties and their synthesized variables gives us a way to indirectly add data, which can be used throughout the methods declared in the main implementation section.

Here is an example of how this works. Consider again a class used to model a physical library, with information about books contained in it.

```
// file: Library.h

@interface Library : NSObject
{
        // instance variables here
}
// methods here
@end

// file: Library.m

@interface Library ()

@property(retain) NSString * privateCollectionName;

@property(retain) NSNumber * numericProperty;

- (void) setValues;

@end

@implementation Library

@synthesize numericProperty = _numberOfBooks;        // give a different name

- (void) setValues
{
        self->_privateCollectionName = @"MyLibrary"; // generated by the compiler
        self.numberOfBooks = @1000;                  // declared with @syntesize
     NSLog(@"setting collection name to %@", self. privateCollectionName);

}

@end
```

In this code is a header file with the main interface to the Library class (the methods and instance variables in the class are not displayed for brevity). The Library.m implementation file contains an anonymous category where two properties are declared: privateCollectionName and numericProperty. Finally, the methods in the Library class are defined inside an @implementation section.

Since you are using an anonymous category, it is also appropriate to add the definition for the method setValues in the class @implementation section. Similarly, the @synthesize declarations that are used by the compiler generate an instance variable with a name that is different from the name specified by the property.

The first property (privateCollectionName) uses the standard variable name synthesized by the compiler. Therefore, no @synthesize declaration is needed. The instance variable is created automatically by the compiler and named _privateCollectionName. Notice that you refer directly to this ivar inside the method setValues.

The second property, however, has an internal name that is different from the name declared by the @property. This might happen, for example, because you want an internal name that is easier to type, while its property name would remain more descriptive. In this example, the property is called numericProperty, while the synthesized ivar is called _numberOfBooks.

The setValues method shows how you can use both types of instance variables. Each property can be accessed either as an instance variable or directly as a property. The syntax for instance variables works by using self as a valid pointer to the object. Therefore, it uses the -> notation. The property syntax, on the other hand, employs a dot to indicate where the compiler should generate special code to get or set the property contents.

Protocols

A *protocol* allows classes to interact using a well-known interface. Many classes have the need to interact with other services (or a set of services) by just calling a few methods that implement the desired functionality. One solution for this problem is to have a base class that implements the needed features, and then having lots of subclasses inheriting the same interface.

However, this solution doesn't scale well with the number of classes and services available in a large system. The need to implement services may inflate the number of classes in the application, for the simple reason that you need to customize how a class interacts with other parts of the system. This proliferation of types in languages like C++ with fewer options to extend classes is unnecessary in Objective-C.

A solution provided by Objective-C is to declare a protocol and require that certain classes implement that protocol to interact with a particular service. In this way a client can extend existing class by just implementing the new protocol, instead of having to create an entirely new class for that purpose.

There are two ways in which a protocol can be declared. The first method defines an informal protocol, which is just a communication mechanism between objects, documented through the use of categories.

The second way to implement a protocol is by using a specific syntax. That technique supports not only the definition of new protocols but also the implementation of one or more protocols by a class.

Informal Protocols

An *informal protocol* is just a way to define a set of methods that should be present in a class in order to provide a service. It is called informal because it is not defined by a particular syntax, but simply by the expectation that a client class will define the appropriate methods. For example, suppose that you are writing an application to interact with moneylenders. There are several classes of moneylenders, such as banks, credit unions, and private investors. However, any such lender would provide to their clients a set of methods such as

```
- (BOOL) canLend:(float)amount;
```

```
- (BOOL) lendRequest:(float)value toLoaner:(NSString*)loanerId;
```

The first method is used to determine if the lender is able to loan the required amount of money. The second method will try to satisfy the lending request for the requested amount and for the provided loaner identification. The return value of lendRequest:toLoaner: is YES when the lending process finishes successfully.

Any class that wants to act as a lender needs to provide these two methods. However, how they are going to provide these methods is not precisely defined by your interface. In fact, there are a few options for how to detect and use the right implementation for the methods listed above. The first technique you are going to see is based on categories defined in NSObject.

As you know, NSObject is the base class for most objects in Objective-C. By defining a category of NSObject, you are able to provide a particular behavior to all objects in the system. Thus, you may just want to add an empty implementation for the methods above. Here is how this would look like as a category:

```
@interface NSObject (MoneyLender)

- (BOOL) canLend:(float)amount;

- (BOOL) lendRequest:(float)value toLoaner:(NSString*)loanerId;

@end
```

This is the interface for the new category, declaring the two new methods that you want to be added to all objects of the system. The implementation will be empty, so that you can call these methods on any object:

```
@implementation NSObject (MoneyLender)

- (BOOL) canLend:(float)amount
{
        return NO;
}

- (BOOL) lendRequest:(float)value toLoaner:(NSString*)loanerId
{
        return NO;
}

@end
```

The methods simply return NO to the requests. This means that it is safe to call these methods, knowing that they will only return YES when there is a real implementation, not the empty one you just created.

What is missing now is a way to call these methods. The traditional way of doing that includes receiving a pointer to the target object. This will show up in the class calling the interface. Let's say that the class is called InvestmentAdvisor, with a method findLoan. The class also has a property called loanSource.

```
@interface InvestmentAdvisor : NSObject
{
        // other ivars here
}

@property (nonatomic, retain) NSObject *loanSource;

- (void) findLoan:(float)amount;

@end
```

The implementation for this class will use the value stored in the property loanSource and try to find a loan for a particular client.

```
@implementation InvestmentAdvisor

- (void) findLoan:(float)amount
{
        if ([self.loanSource canLend:amount])
        {
                BOOL result = [self.loanSource lendRequest:amount
                                                toLoaner:@"InvestmentClient"];
                if (result)
                {
                        NSLog(@"The loan application was accepted");
                }
        }
}

@end
```

You first use the value stored in self.loanSource to determine if the given source can lend the requested amount of money. If that is possible, then you send the lendRequest: message to the lender in order to complete the loan process. If everything goes well, you then print a message to the system log.

Note   In the code above you are using loanSource property without knowing if its value has been set. Despite this, the code still works because of the way Objective-C handles message passing to nil pointers. If the target of a message is nil, then the code generated by the compiler will automatically return NO for messages returning BOOL. Similarly, messages returning numbers will default to zero. The advantage of these special processing rules for null pointers is that you can avoid checking for nil each time you use a variable or property. This also reduces the number of null pointer exceptions that are so common in C and C++ code.

Suppose now that you want to create a class implementing the interface for MoneyLender. For that to happen, you just need to define your own class, containing the two methods included in the MoneyLender category. Here is an example:

```
// MyLoanSource.h
@interface MyLoanSource : NSObject

- (BOOL) canLend:(float)amount;

- (BOOL) lendRequest:(float)value toLoaner:(NSString*)loanerId;

// other methods here

@end
```

I show only the methods that are part of the protocol, but a real implementation would have several other methods. Here is the corresponding implementation:

```
// MyLoanSource.m
#import "MyLoanSource.h"

@implementation MyLoanSource

#define MAX_LOAN 1000 * 1000

- (BOOL) canLend:(float)amount
{
        return amount < MAX_LOAN;
}

- (BOOL) lendRequest:(float)value toLoaner:(NSString*)loanerId
{
        if ([@"" isEqualToString:loanerId])
        {
                return NO;
        }


    if (value > MAX_LOAN)
        {
                return NO;
        }

        return YES;

}

@end
```

You still need to create the code that will use the object defined above as an input to the LoanAdviser class.

```
- (void) useLoanSource {
        MyLoanSource *loanSource = [[MyLoanSource alloc] init];
        InvestmentAdvisor *advisor = [[InvestmentAdvisor alloc] init];
        advisor.loanSource = loanSource;
        [advisor  findLoan:10000];
}
```

This code will first create an object of type MyLoanSource, which implements the protocol defined by LoanSource. Then, the next line creates an advisor object, which is responsible for using the loan source. The property loanSource is set up with this newly created object. Finally, you send the findLoan: message, with a loan value of $10,000. As a result of this message, the loan source will be used, and the requested loan satisfied.

Checking for Protocol Compliance

While the technique presented above works well as a way of implementing a protocol, it suffers from a small drawback. By creating new categories on the NSObject class, you are making general message dispatching a little more inefficient for everyone else. The reason is that such an informal protocol requires that all classes derived from NSObject contain the two methods specified. That can become a problem when the number of protocols increases. It is not difficult to visualize a situation where most of the methods in the dispatch table for NSObject would be composed of empty protocol methods.

To avoid this, you can check at runtime if the required methods exist, instead of making these methods become part of every object in the system. This requires a little more work on the part of the code that sends the messages, but it can definitely make things easier for everyone else using that class. Here's a modified version of the InvestmentAdvisor class that checks if the loan source supports the required methods:

```
- (void) findLoan:(float)amount
{
        SEL canLendSel = @selector(canLend:);
        SEL lendReqSel = @selector(lendRequest:toLoaner:);
        if([self.loanSource respondsToSelector:canLendSel] &&
           [self.loanSource respondsToSelector:lendReqSel])
        {
                if ([self.loanSource canLend:amount])
                {
                        BOOL result = [self.loanSource lendRequest:amount
                                                    toLoaner:@"InvestmentClient"];
                        if (result)
                        {
                                NSLog(@"The loan application was accepted");
                        }
                }
        }
}
```

The new version of `findLoan:` differs from the previous one in the test at the beginning of the method. First, you create two selectors for the methods you are trying to invoke.

> **Note**   A selector is the name given to the internal representation of a method. With selectors it is possible to manipulate and get information about a method. For example, it is possible to answer the question "Is this method implemented by a given class?" The type of a selector variable is always SEL.

Once the selectors have been retrieved, you use the `respondsToSelector:` message to determine if the object that was passed as a `loanSource` can respond to the requests you want to make. If that is true, you can execute the same code contained in the original version of `findLoan:`.

Using this new definition for `findLoan:`, you can now remove the category MoneyLender from the definitions. Since you will only call any of the methods in that category when they are defined as part of the given object, there is no need to add an empty version of such methods to each object of type `NSObject`.

A final glitch with this new version of `findLoan:` will be noticed after you completely remove the MoneyLender category; the compiler will display a warning about not knowing if `loanSource` can respond to the messages sent. This happens because there is no way to know at compilation time if the methods can be successfully dispatched. You shouldn't worry about this, though, because the `if` statement guarantees that this will be true at runtime. It is possible to avoid these warnings, however, by using runtime functions to call the selectors directly. Don't worry about this for now, however.

Formal Protocols

Calling methods that have been defined in an informal protocol, as you did above, provides a clear solution for the problem of defining an interface. However, by using `NSObject` categories or checking if the object can respond to a particular message, you are just being creative about the runtime flexibility of Objective-C. The truth is that such mechanisms don't explicitly show the intention of the code, which is defining a well-established protocol between objects.

To improve the readability and simplify coding, Apple introduced a formal syntax for protocols, using the keyword @protocol. Employing this syntax, the previous example could be written with the following protocol declaration:

```
@protocol MoneyLender

- (BOOL) canLend:(float)amount;

- (BOOL) lendRequest:(float)value toLoaner:(NSString*)loanerId;

@end
```

At a first impression, there is not much difference here between the previous declaration, based on a category, and the formal protocol declaration, other than the obvious fact that the keyword @protocol is used. However, once MoneyLender is declared in that way, it can be used by client classes that want to implement the methods contained in the protocol.

Thus, a major difference in such a declaration is that you want it to become known by client classes, by placing the protocol declaration in a header file. In contrast, an informal protocol defined as a category of NSObject can be kept as private to the class using it.

Another difference is in how classes implement the protocol. With informal protocols, the only thing you need to do is to add a valid implementation of the required methods. With formal protocols, you need to explicitly indicate that the class implements the protocol. This is done using angle brackets to enclose the list of protocols, right after the name of the base class. Here is an example:

```
@interface AccreditedLoanSource  : NSObject <MoneyLender>
{
    // ivars go here
}

// other methods here

@end
```

The class AccreditedLoanSource has an interface definition similar to other classes, with the difference that it implements the MoneyLender protocol. When such a protocol is identified as part of the interface, the Objective-C compiler checks if the required methods in the protocol are part of the implementation. Here is an example of the implementation section, with just two implementation stubs:

```
// file AccreditedLoanSource.m

@implementation AccreditedLoanSource

- (BOOL) canLend:(float)amount
{
        return YES;
}

- (BOOL) lendRequest:(float)value toLoaner:(NSString*)loanerId
{
        return YES;
}

@end
```

> **Note** From the point of view of code packaging, formal protocols have another difference with regard to informal protocols. In the later, it was not necessary to provide a public interface through a header file. But with formal protocols, this is not only desirable, but also necessary. The compiler needs to see a declaration of the protocol when the interface for the new class is defined.

The next step in the use of formal protocols is defining variables and properties that guarantee that the protocol is implemented. This is done by declaring a variable and using angle brackets after the type of the variable. If all you want is an object implementing the methods in the protocol, then it is customary to define the type of the object as NSObject <ProtocolName>.

The modified version of InvestmentAdvisor using protocols can be written as

```
@interface InvestmentAdvisor : NSObject
{
        // other ivars here
}

@property (nonatomic, retain) NSObject <MoneyLender> *loanSource;

- (BOOL) findLoan:(float)amount;

@end

@implementation InvestmentAdvisor

- (BOOL) findLoan:(float)amount
{
        BOOL canLend = [self.loanSource canLend:amount];
        if (canLend)
        {
                BOOL result = [self.loanSource lendRequest:amount
                                                 toLoaner:@"InvestmentClient"];
                if (result)
                {
                        NSLog(@"The loan application was accepted");
                        return YES;
                }
        }
        return NO;
}
```

Notice that in this version of findLoan: you don't need to worry if the methods canLend: and lendRequest:toLoaner: are defined or not. Once the compiler knows that the property loanSource points to an object implementing the protocol, these two methods can be validated at compilation time. The last step, then, is to create the right object and use it to initialize the property loanSource.

```
- (void) useLoanSource
{
        AccreditedLoanSource *loanSource = [[AccreditedLoanSource alloc] init];
        InvestmentAdvisor *advisor = [[InvestmentAdvisor alloc] init];
        advisor.loanSource = loanSource;
        BOOL res = [advisor  findLoan:10000];
        NSLog(@"result is %d", res);
        [advisor release];
        [loanSource release];
}
```

Notice that the only real difference here is how you created the loanSource object, which now provides a complete implementation of the MoneyLender protocol.

> **Note** An instance variable or property that implements some functionality required by current class and is supplied by an outside user is known as a *delegate*. For example, the loanSource property is a delegate for the InvestmentAdvisor class. Requiring a delegate to implement a specific protocol is an often-used idiom in Objective-C libraries. For example, the Cocoa framework requires users to define delegates to supply most of the functionality associated with GUI objects.

Optional Methods

In a formal protocol, it is possible to define if a method is required or optional. A required method will be checked by the compiler, which will emit a warning if the method is not present. An optional method can be left out of a class that implements a protocol.

It is possible to declare two different levels of requirement for the members of a protocol.

- **Required methods:** These are the ones that need to be present in every object that implements the protocol. You may think of such methods as providing essential functionality that define the protocol. A method included in a protocol without qualification is considered a required method. Additionally, any method following the @required keyword is considered to be required.

- **Optional methods:** These are methods that may provide additional features that are not essential to the definition of the protocol. A class implementing the protocol is free to include or exclude such methods. An optional method is defined with the help of the @optional keyword. All methods following this keyword are considered optional.

When using optional methods, you need to determine if they have been defined or not in the target object. The method to do this is similar to what you would do when using an informal protocol: just send a respondsToSelector: message to the target in order to check if the method is available. For example, suppose that you want to add an optional method to the protocol MoneyLender.

```
@protocol MoneyLender

@optional

- (BOOL) canExtendLoan;

@required

- (BOOL) canLend:(float)amount;

- (BOOL) lendRequest:(float)value toLoaner:(NSString*)loanerId;

@end
```

Now, you can write code that uses the `canExtendLoan:` method, but only after testing for its existence.

```objc
- (BOOL) checkLoan
{
        if ([self.loanSource respondsToSelector:@selector(canExtendLoan)])
        {
                if ([self.loanSource canExtendLoan])
                {
                        NSLog(@"The loan can be extended");
                        return YES;
                }
        }
        return NO;
}
```

Summary

In this chapter, I covered two of the most important topics in the design of effective classes in Objective-C. Using categories and protocols, it is possible to extend the capabilities of classes created by yourself, as well as other classes that already exist in libraries shipped with the system or from third-party vendors.

Categories support the addition of methods to the interface of an existing class. As long as you provide the code for the extension methods—along with a header file with the category definition—other classes can use the category methods as if they were part of the original class. This provides a great way to customize common classes, such as `NSArray` or `NSString`, with code that is useful in the context of your applications.

Protocols provide a way for classes to define a limited interface that will be used only by a particular service. A protocol may be defined in an informal way, by just listing one or more methods that need to be part of the interface. To implement such an informal protocol, classes can provide a set of empty implementations through a category, usually attached to `NSObject`. A second technique is to check if the required methods exist on the target object, using the runtime API provided by Objective-C.

A formal protocol is defined with a syntax that is similar to a class declaration. However, its main goal is to define a simple interface that can be independently implemented by other classes. Much of the Objective-C libraries rely upon protocols to provide services without the necessity of adding new classes for each new feature. For example, Cocoa uses protocols as the main tool to define delegates for UI components.

Categories and protocols show some of the dynamic aspects of objective-C, but they only scratch the surface of the possibilities. In the next chapter, you will investigate more deeply the concept of dynamic binding and see what it can help you accomplish.

Chapter 5

Inheritance

In the previous chapters you explored some of the basic ideas of object-oriented programming in Objective-C. As you have seen, OOP is the main software development concept that motivated the creation of the language. A chief feature of OOP is the ability to create new classes that inherit methods, variables, and properties from other existing classes. You see, then, that to master the language you need to attain a good working knowledge of the concept of class-based inheritance.

The proper use of inheritance, however, requires a certain amount of attention both during the design phase as well as with the implementation of base and derived classes. In this chapter you will explore topics related to inheritance in Objective-C, covering some of the necessary background required to design effective class hierarchies.

You will take a more in-depth look at how inheritance works, along with the mechanism of method overriding among classes in the same hierarchy. Furthermore, you will see how to address some issues raised by the way inheritance is implemented in Objective-C. For example, you will learn how to simulate the use of multiple-inheritance, or how to avoid deep class hierarchies.

The Concept of Inheritance

Classes describe the general behavior of objects. In an OO language, a class works as a blueprint for objects that will be created and maintained by the system. By defining a new class, you outline a list of behaviors that objects of that type respond to, as well as the data storage available to each object. As such, a class introduces an independent unit of code that the rest of the application can use and interact with.

Just being able to create objects of a given type would be enough to deliver great functionality, and it would offer overall impressive software quality in itself. However, creating and using new objects is not sufficient to simplify the process of producing classes with more complex behavior. Let's look at a characteristic example, where you want to define a class for the concept of Employee.

```
// file Employee.h

@interface Employee : NSObject
{
        NSString *name;
}

- (void) setName:(NSString*) aName;

- (double) calculateSalary;

@end
```

Here is the corresponding implementation file:

```
// file Employee.m

@implementation Employee

- (void) setName:(NSString*) aName
{
        self->name = aName;
}

- (double) calculateSalary
{
        double salary = 0;
        // perform salary calculation
        return salary;
}

@end
```

With these definitions, it becomes very easy to create and use objects with the behavior specified by the Employee class. As you have seen in the previous chapters, you can just send a pair of alloc/init messages to the Employee class to create a new object of that particular type.

However, suppose that you are interested instead in using a slightly modified version of Employee, one that was not envisioned by the creators of the original class. For example, you may want to represent an hourly employee, one that receives a salary that depends on the number of hours worked, instead of a fixed value determined every year. Without inheritance, you would be forced to create a new, separate class for that concept.

```
// HourlyEmployee.h
@interface HourlyEmployee: NSObject
{
        NSString *name;
        int hoursPerWeek;
}

- (void) setName:(NSString*) aName;
```

```
- (double) calculateSalary;

- (int) getHoursPerWeek;

@end

// HourlyEmployee.m
@implementation HourlyEmployee

- (void) setName:(NSString*) aName
{
        self->name = aName;
}

- (double) calculateSalary
{
        double salary = 0;
        // perform salary calculation for hourly employee
        return salary;
}

- (int) getHoursPerWeek
{
        // return number of hours
}

@end
```

This definition and the contents of the class would be very similar to those used in the Employee class, with just a small number of modifications to account for the variances between the two concepts. In an application that depends on the definition of objects that are, in some ways, variations on a basic concept, this would amount to a huge code duplication—leading to programs that are both hard to create and maintain. The reuse of existing code in such a situation would be hard to accomplish because most of the interface for these classes would need to be replicated across the system.

Now, consider the same class using the concept of inheritance:

```
// file HourlyEmployee.h

@interface HourlyEmployee : Employee

- (int) getHoursPerWeek;

@end

// file HourlyEmployee.m

@implementation HourlyEmployee
```

```
- (double) calculateSalary
{
        double salary = 0;
        // perform salary calculation, as discussed later
        return salary;
}

- (int) getHoursPerWeek
{
        // return number of hours
}

@end
```

Now HourlyEmployee is not a free class in the system; instead it depends directly on the definitions provided by Employee. The main benefit of this organization is that you won't need to repeat every method and instance variable contained in the original class. Not only the interface, but also the implementation of the methods in the base class are also inherited, so that a programmer can concentrate on the aspects of HourlyEmployee that are unlike what is found in the original class— instead of having to codify again any existing functionality.

Notice also that, as a result of Objective-C type system, HourlyEmployee can be used whenever an Employee object is required. This means that you can also take advantage of any available method that in some way provides a service for Employee objects. On the other hand, as you will see in a later section, this type of substitution is not free: it requires that classes derived from a given subclass also subscribe to the same contract that is defined in the original class.

Inheritance and Overriding

Overriding is the action of replacing a method from a superclass with a more specific version of itself. Overriding methods is the primary way by which you can customize the behavior of the classes participating in a hierarchy.

In Objective-C, any method can be overridden. It doesn't make any difference if the method is part of class in your application or in a third party framework. The only requirement is that the overriding method needs to use the same keyword names and arguments as the original one.

A peculiarity about overridden methods in Objective-C is that you don't need to mention them in the interface of a subclass. Consider again an Employee. Suppose that you want to introduce another subclass called Contractor. In that case, you would like to adjust the implementation so that it reflects the different responsibilities of a contractor. For illustration purposes, let's assume that the original class will be augmented with the provideJobEvaluation method, like so:

```
// file Employee.h

@interface Employee : NSObject
{
        NSString *name;
}
```

```
- (void) setName:(NSString*) aName;

- (double) calculateSalary;

- (void) provideJobEvaluation;

@end
```

This method is used to create a routine, internal evaluation for each completed job. Now let's see how you could declare an interface for the Contractor class:

```
// file Contractor.h

@interface Contractor : Employee
{
        NSString *thirdPartyCompany;
}

@end
```

It is clear from here that the Contractor has additional storage needs. However, there is no indication here that the Contractor class is implementing a new version of any of the methods in Employee. This doesn't make any difference for users of this class, however. In the implementation section, you are free to override any of the methods in the parent class.

```
// file Employee.m

@implementation Contractor

- (void) provideJobEvaluation
{
        // steps for contract job evaluation here
}

@end
```

With this definition, whenever a new object of class Contractor is created, the provideJobEvaluation method will perform the correct calculation for a contract, even though the override was not explicit in the class interface. The same can also be said for categories. For example, you could create a new category for Contractor that would declare yet another adjustment for the class behavior, like so:

```
// Contractor+NameHanding.h
@interface Contractor (NameHanding)
  // no new methods declared here
@end
```

It would have the following implementation:

```
// file Contractor+NameHanding.m

@implementation Contractor (NameHanding)
```

```
- (void) setName:(NSString*) aName
{
        self->name = [NSString stringWithFormat:@"contractor %@", aName];
}

@end
```

This would change how names are displayed for any contractor created in the application, as a result of overriding the setName: method.

Invoking Methods in Superclasses

As part of a hierarchy, subclasses have access to data and methods inherited from superclasses. This allows objects of the subclass, for example, to call any method defined in the classes above it in the hierarchy.

When the method in the superclass has a different name, calling that method is just a matter of sending a message to self, using the traditional message-sending notation. The message dispatch mechanism will automatically find the correct implementation. For example, consider a class that represents the type of an entry in the file system.

```
// file FileType.h

@interface FileType : NSObject
{
        // ivars listed here
}

- (NSString*) getExtension;

@end

// file FileType.m

@implementation FileType

- (NSString*) getExtension
{
        NSString *ext = @"";
        // retrieve extension
        return ext;
}

@end
```

Suppose now that you are interested in implementing a new subclass for documents, which you will call DocumentType.

```
// file DocumentType.h

@interface DocumentType  : FileType
```

```
{
        // ivars here
}

- (BOOL) isValid;

@end

// file DocumentType.m

@implementation DocumentType

-(BOOL)isValid
{
        if ([@"" isEqualToString:[self getExtension]])
        {
                return false;
        }
        return true;
}

@end
```

In this example, the DocumentType class needs to use the method getExtension from the superclass. To do this, it just needs to send a message to self, using the following notation:

```
[self getExtension]
```

Now, suppose that instead you are implementing a new version of the getExtension method. In this case, you may want to be able to call the original version of the method. For example, you may want to take the original extension calculated with the getExtension method in FileType, and perform some post-processing to return a modified extension. However, if you send the message getExtension to self, you will end up receiving a recursive call, instead of a call to the implementation in the superclass.

To solve this issue, Objective-C introduces the special variable super. The goal of super is to redirect the message-sending mechanism so that a suitable method is searched starting from the superclass, instead of the current class. When sending a message to super, the compiler can detect that the message resolution mechanism needs to be slightly changed, in such a way that the message will reach the correct method.

Note that when a subclass overrides a method that was declared in the superclass, it may be for two reasons:

- *Replacing the original behavior with a completely new implementation*: In this case, the new behavior is coded totally on the subclass, without any need to refer to the original implementation. This is the easiest case to handle, since there is no need to interact with the base class to implement the modified method.

- *Extending the original behavior with additional code*: In this case, it is necessary to refer to the original implementation of the method you're trying to override.

In the second case, a programmer can refer to the implementation of a method in the superclass using the special variable super. With the help of this variable, it is possible to skip the current class level when using the message dispatch mechanism. Therefore, the compiler will generate code that searches for a match for the required message starting from the parent class, instead of the current class. Using super, therefore, is a common way to reuse code that was written for the base class, while at the same time providing an enhanced implementation of the same method. For example, when overriding a method from a base class, it is very common to use the following idiom:

```
- (void) overridenMethodName
{
    [super overridenMethodName];
    // additional code goes here
}
```

That is, you first call the original method in the base class, followed by any additional code necessary to customize the behavior of the method.

Template Methods

Method overriding is one way of introducing polymorphic behavior. However, overriding a single method may not be enough to achieve the customization you need. In some cases, the behavior of a class is determined by an algorithm with several steps, and each of these steps can be customized in an independent way. When that happens, the best strategy is to use a template method that embeds the knowledge about the exact sequence of steps used by the class.

For example, consider a class that represents a cook. The class has a method called prepareRecipe, which performs the main steps of food preparation.

```
// file Cook.h

@interface Cook : NSObject

- (void)prepareRecipe;

- (void)acquireIngredients;

- (void)mixIngredients;

- (void)cookDish;

@end
```

The implementation has the basic outline of prepareRecipe, along with empty implementations for each of the remaining three methods.

```
// file Cook.m

@implementation Cook

-(void) prepareRecipe
{
        [self acquireIngredients];
        [self mixIngredients];
        [self cookDish];
}

- (void)acquireIngredients
{
}

- (void)mixIngredients
{
}

- (void)cookDish
{
}

@end
```

Here you have a method, prepareRecipe, which is called by clients of the class. The method, however, is just a shell (or template) that calls three other methods where the real work takes place. To implement an instance of Cook that really does something useful, you need to create a derived class first and then implement the three methods (acquireIngredients, mixIngredients, and cookDish) in a sensible way.

What you have in Cook is a class that provides a generic interface with three operations, and a method that determines the sequence in which these operations will be called. Subclasses are required to provide the details for this type of template method to work.

> **Note**   You can classify the class displayed above as an abstract class. An abstract class is one in which an implementation is not provided for one or more of the methods of its interface. This might happen for a few reasons: an implementation for a feature does not exist at a particular level or you want to force a subclass to provide its own implementation. This is the case when a base class needs some information that can be supplied only by subclasses.

Object Initialization

Proper object initialization is one of the main concerns when creating a new class, and it is also directly affected by inheritance. After all, a class is a template for runtime object instances, but they need to be a valid representation of the intended concept in the first place.

The most common way to initialize a class in Objective-C is to send `init` or one of the `initWith` messages. The `init` method is defined originally in the `NSObject` class, and it has to be overridden in any class that wishes to provide custom initialization.

But when more than one initialization method is available, it becomes essential to coordinate the way they interact with each other. This is necessary to maintain consistency across different ways of initializing the state of the object.

You have seen already some examples of classes that offer alternate initialization methods. A typical example is `NSString`, which has the following initializers, among others:

```
- (id)init;

- (id)initWithCharactersNoCopy:(unichar *)characters length:(NSUInteger)length
freeWhenDone:(BOOL)freeBuffer;

- (id)initWithCharacters:(const unichar *)characters length:(NSUInteger)length;

- (id)initWithUTF8String:(const char *)nullTerminatedCString;

- (id)initWithString:(NSString *)aString;

- (id)initWithData:(NSData *)data encoding:(NSStringEncoding)encoding;

- (id)initWithBytes:(const void *)bytes length:(NSUInteger)len encoding:(NSStringEncoding)encoding;

- (id)initWithBytesNoCopy:(void *)bytes length:(NSUInteger)len encoding:(NSStringEncoding)encoding
freeWhenDone:(BOOL)freeBuffer;
```

Even though a class may have a considerable number of initializers, there is always a particular version that is marked as the designated initializer. This is a version of the `init` or `initWith` method that is responsible for performing a complete initialization for objects of the class and calling the parent initializer. Clients may call other `init` methods in the class, but these methods will ultimately call the designated initializer to complete the process.

Whenever you create a new subclass, it is necessary to determine the designated initializer and use it to perform the proper configuration of the parent class. In this way, you can make sure that the base class is in a valid state before the subclass is able to jump into action. Therefore, new subclasses should be designed in a way that makes it clear which version of the `init` method is the default initializer.

For example, consider the class LibraryHolding, which is part of an application used to manage libraries. This class has three initialization methods, as shown:

```
// file LibraryHolding.h

@interface LibraryHolding : NSObject
{
     NSString *patron;
     NSString *title;
}

- (id)init;

- (id)initWithPatron:(NSString*)patron;

- (id)initWithPatron:(NSString*)patron title:(NSString*)aTitle;

@end
```

The designated initializer here is the third one, because it is the only one that needs to call the init method of the parent class directly. You can see this clearly in the following implementation:

```
// file LibraryHolding.m

@implementation LibraryHolding

- (id)init
{
     return [self initWithPatron:@""];
}

- (id) initWithPatron:(NSString *)aPatron
{
     return [self initWithPatron:aPatron title:@""];
}

- (id) initWithPatron:(NSString *)aPatron title:(NSString *)aTitle
{
    self = [super init];
    if (self)
    {
        self->patron = aPatron;
        self->title = aTitle;
    }
    return self;
}

@end
```

As a helpful rule, if an initialization method has more arguments that all others, then it usually is the one chosen as the designated initializer, since it can be used to simulate the others. Now, suppose that you want to create a derived class, called `PeriodicalHolding`, used to represent periodicals such as magazines and newspapers. Here is a possible interface:

```
// file PeriodicalHolding.h

@interface PeriodicalHolding : LibraryHolding
{
        int issue_number;
}

- (id)initWithTitle:(NSString*)aTitle number:(int)aNumber;

- (id)initWithPatron:(NSString*)patron title:(NSString*)aTitle number:(int)aNumber;

@end
```

Here is the corresponding implementation:

```
// file PeriodicalHolding.m

@implementation PeriodicalHolding

- (id)initWithTitle:(NSString*)aTitle number:(int)aNumber
{
        return [self initWithPatron:@"" title:aTitle number:aNumber];
}

- (id)initWithPatron:(NSString*)aPatron title:(NSString*)aTitle number:(int)aNumber
{
    self = [super initWithPatron:aPatron title:aTitle];
    if (self)
    {
        self-> issue_number = aNumber;
    }
    return self;
}

@end
```

Notice again that the designated initializer is the one with more arguments. The second initializer just calls the designated one with the desired parameters.

The Substitution Principle

When a class inherits from another class in the system, it not only shares a privilege, but also an obligation. The main privilege is to inherit the non-private interface and implementation provided by the base class. As such, a derived class can be used in any context where a base class could be used. For example, a `HourlyEmployee` is effectively a type of `Employee` object. Therefore, it can be used whenever an Employee is required: if an object expects to receive an Employee, and sends a message to it, then it should be able to do so with a HourlyEmployee as well.

On the other hand, inheritance requires a responsibility from subclasses: they need to be able to satisfy the expectations set by the base class. For example, if the base class says that it can calculate employee salaries, then the subclass also needs to be able to do so.

```
// file Employee.h

@interface Employee : NSObject
{
        NSString *name;
}

- (void) setName:(NSString*) aName;

- (double) calculateSalary;

- (void) provideJobEvaluation;

@end
```

But what happens if the new subclass HourlyEmployee has a different way to calculate salaries? The simple solution is just to override the calculateSalary method and provide a new implementation.

```
// file Employee.m

@implementation Employee

- (void) setName:(NSString*) aName
{
        self->name = aName;
}

- (double) calculateSalary
{
        double salary = 0;
        // perform salary calculation
        return salary;
}

- (void) provideJobEvaluation
{
}

@end
```

Doing this is a valid use of inheritance. But suppose, on the other hand, that the class HourlyEmployee has no way to calculate the salary. Assume, for example, that the salary is based on commissions that are not available to the class until the beginning of next year. When that happens, the contract defined by the base class breaks, and the subclass will have difficulties in posing as similar to the superclass. For example, here are two options for the implementation of calculateSalary:

```
- (double)calculateSalary
{
    return 0;
}
```

```
- (double)calculateSalary
{
        @throw [NSException exceptionWithName:@"salaryException"
                                    reason:@"no salary available"
                                    userInfo:NULL];
}
```

In the first case, the application will receive an incorrect value, since an hourly employee clearly doesn't receive a salary of zero. In the second option, the application cannot continue after the method generates an exception. In both cases, the result is not what the clients expected of an Employee object. This means that SalaryEmployee is not a good fit for a subclass of Employee.

The substitution principle states that, when a class is derived from a base class, objects of the subclass should be able to substitute for objects of the subclass in any situation where this is required. The class HourlyEmployee doesn't comply with this general principle, as you have seen. It cannot respond to calculateSalary messages in the same way that the original class responds. Therefore, in this case it would be preferable to avoid the direct use of inheritance. One possible solution would be to split the responsibility for salary calculation into a separate class, so that the original class would respond to a message such as canCalculateSalary. In any case, it is necessary to consider if a subclass can be really used in any context where the base class is used, and make any design changes necessary in case this is not possible.

Class Clusters

A class cluster is a set of classes related by inheritance, which offer a complete implementation for a feature that can have variations depending on the concrete types used. The main distinction of a class cluster is that only one class at the top of the hierarchy is visible to clients. All other classes of the cluster are hidden, so that it is not possible to instantiate them directly. Instead, concrete classes of the cluster have to be created through the main interface, which usually contains init methods, as well as class methods, that can return the right object for each situation.

Class clusters offer a powerful way to control the complexity of maintaining and exposing a large number of related classes in a hierarchy. When using a class cluster, you don't need to know the name of the exact class that implements the right version of the functionality you need. The base class of the cluster will cooperate with derived classes to create the exact object that will satisfy your needs. On the other hand, the classes that derive from the main class of the cluster have the responsibility to implement a concrete version of the methods that interact with local storage. The methods that need to be overridden in a concrete implementation of the cluster are called primitive methods, since they provide the primitive functionality that is used by the class cluster to implement other high level features.

The definition can be more easily understood through a use case. Suppose that a class can assume two or more functional configurations, with independent data storage that determines how these classes will act. Moreover, the class has a common interface for each of these configurations, so that it is possible to access them in a unified way. When that is the case, it is possible to organize the classes in a way that only a base class can be made visible, while the concrete functionality is implemented by its subclasses.

Class clusters are considered to be a basic design pattern in Objective-C. A typical example of class cluster in the Foundation framework is NSNumber. While it appears to clients as being a single class, the real implementation of NSNumber happens to contain a class cluster, where the main abstract class acts as a wrapper around concrete classes, which handle the state of the object. Among the concrete classes in the NSNumber cluster, you will find implementation models for integers, floats, and Booleans, for example.

Using a class cluster is straightforward, in the sense that the programmer doesn't need to know which class is created by the class initializers. In the NSNumber example, you have a number of initialization methods, named for instance initWithInteger:, initWithFloat:, and initWithChar:. These methods return an object that correctly represents the data stored on it. However, the exact subclass of the returned object is hidden from users.

From the point of view of the creator of a new class cluster, there are some practical issues that must be considered. First, it is necessary that the public interface of the abstract base class be the only point of contact between clients and the other classes in the cluster. Therefore, the interface of the base class in the cluster must contain all methods that will be used to interact with any member of the cluster. Among the methods of the abstract class you will find primitive methods, the ones that need to be implemented in each derived class. The second class of methods, derived methods, contains those that are implemented in the base class and use the primitive methods in their definition. Therefore, such methods don't need to be overridden in the concrete classes.

A class that derives from the abstract root of the cluster needs to provide its own instance variables for data storage. The abstract class in a cluster doesn't have local storage by design, since each concrete class may have a different way to store data.

Another example of a class cluster can be seen in the collection classes, such as NSArray. The object returned when you call init implements the interface of NSArray, but may be from different subclass in the cluster, including NSMutableArray; it all depends on how the NSArray constructor performs the object initialization tasks. As you will see later, class clusters are one example of a general strategy to hide implementation specific information from other clients occurring in a library or in a big application.

Preventing Subclassing

Finally, despite the many advantages of subclassing that have been discussed in this chapter, there are also legitimate problems that can result from its incorrect use. Therefore, in some cases it may be necessary to avoid inheritance from occurring for a few specific classes; in other words, you may want to prevent a class from becoming the basis for another class.

> **Note**   One of the major drawbacks of inheritance is what is known now as **fragile base classes**. When creating a class hierarchy, classes will frequently use implementation information provided by parent classes. However, there is no such a thing as perfect design, and changes to a base class may eventually be necessary. Such changes may cause subclasses that rely on those internal details to stop working. A good hierarchy design should try to minimize this possibility.

Some languages provide direct support for this feature, by marking a specific class as immutable from the point of view of inheritance. For example, in Java it is possible to identify a class with the `final` keyword, so that developers are not allowed to inherit from it after this syntactic annotation has been applied. Among newer languages, C# also allows this type of distinction between classes.

Objective-C designers decided not to add a mechanism to avoid inheritance. This choice was probably made to maintain the simplicity of the language, and perhaps because this is a feature that is not very frequently used. However, even though there is no direct support in the form of a `final` keyword as in Java, it is still possible to take a few measures to prevent a class from being subclassed.

The general strategy you can use involves reducing the visibility of a class. The principle here is that you cannot subclass a class that exists somewhere in the application but that cannot be seen at compile time by clients. So, for example, you can create a class but never provide a header file for it. In that case, the class would be accessible only through an external interface (such as a protocol or an abstract class), but the internal details of the class would never be accessible.

Let's see how you could implement such a non-inheritable class. First, consider the class `ConcreteMatrix`. It has a lot of data used to store a matrix, as well as special details such as dimensions, the largest entry, and other utility methods.

```
@interface ConcreteMatrix2 : NSObject
{
        double *contents;
        int size;
         // other ivars here
}

- (void) initializeMatrix:(double *)vector size:(int)size;

- (void) performMatrixOperation;

// other methods here

@end
```

Although this is a general-purpose class that should be available for the whole application, the internals of the class are so tightly coupled that it would be really hard to crate a correct subclass. To do this, a programmer would need detailed information about the internals of the class, such as the instance variables used and when they should be updated, for example. So, while you want to make the class available as widely as possible, you don't intend to allow subclasses of it.

The solution is to avoid providing any direct access to the class. However, you still want the functionality to become accessible to clients. So, you create a class that provides a suitable interface to the object you want to hide. This external object is visible to others, but it has nothing other than a reference to the object that really implements the functionality.

```
// file AbstractMatrix.h

@interface AbstractMatrix : NSObject

- (void) initializeMatrix:(double *)vector size:(int)size;

- (void) performMatrixOperation;

+ (AbstractMatrix*) getMatrix;

@end
```

This version can now be used without any information about the internals of the class. Notice that you removed all internal data storage, and added a class method that returns a new object of type AbstractMatrix. As a side effect of making an abstract class, you now need a method such as getMatrix to return a new matrix object. This is necessary because AbstractMatrix can't be instantiated itself, since it is missing the implementation of some of its methods.

On the other hand, the original concrete class can remain hidden in an implementation file. However, it still needs to inherit from the abstract class so that it can provide the same interface.

```
@interface ConcreteMatrix : AbstractMatrix
{
        double *contents;
        int size;
         // other ivars
}

- (void) initializeMatrix:(double *)vector size:(int)size;

- (void) performMatrixOperation;

// other methods here

@end
```

The method getMatrix will be responsible for creating a ConcreteMatrix and returning it to users.

```
@implementation AbstractMatrix

+ (AbstractMatrix*) getMatrix
{
        return [[ConcreteMatrix alloc] init];
}

// other implementation methods here

@end
```

A class can now create a `ConcreteMatrix` using code such as [`AbstractMatrix getMatrix`]. All the functionality listed on the `AbstractMatrix` interface will be available to them, even though they have no way to access the internals of `ConcreteMatrix`.

> **Note** This example uses a mechanism similar to the one employed by a class cluster, although here the goal is just to protect the single class that provides the concrete implementation, instead of offering an array of classes conforming to the same abstract interface.

Multiple Inheritance

What you have seen in the previous sections covers what is called single inheritance, a type of subclassing where the new class can have only one parent. Objective-C, as well as other OO languages such as Java and Smalltalk, provides support for single inheritance only. Other languages, such as C++, are able to derive new classes from multiple parent classes. Multiple inheritance is the name given to this style of subclassing.

Since only one superclass is allowed when a new class is created under single inheritance, the resulting hierarchy looks like a tree-shaped structure where the initial base class is at the root of the tree. With multiple inheritance languages, however, the hierarchy looks much more like a network of connections with classes that can get data and method implementations from two or more sources.

In Objective-C, it is not possible to create such a network of inheritance connections. One of the reasons is to avoid the overhead that might affect dynamic message dispatching. Just consider that, instead of looking for method implementations in a single class tree, it would be necessary to look for methods in several unrelated ancestor classes.

There are, however, ways of simulating some of the conveniences of multiple inheritance. The most common method is to use formal protocols to define extra functionality that should be provided by a class. For example, suppose that you want to create a class that has two kinds of responsibilities: being a vehicle and a place for living. Here is a list of such responsibilities:

```
// file Vehicle.h

@interface Vehicle
- (void) drive;
@end

// file LivingPlace.h

@interface LivingPlace
- (void) setAddress:(NSString *)address;
@end
```

Now, suppose that you want to define a class representing a boat, which happens to be a Vehicle as well as a LivingPlace. The problem you have now is that Objective-C classes can have only one superclass. The first thing you need to do is to decide on making either Vehicle or LivingPlace the base class for Boat. The other problem is how to add the functionality for the second class to your new subclass. I discuss in the next section a potential solution for this problem.

Simulating Multiple Inheritance

One possible solution is to make LivingPlace a protocol, instead of a class. In this way, LivingPlace can have a fixed interface that can be implemented by any number of classes, even when they are not related by a single hierarchy. The following is a definition for this protocol:

```
// file LivingPlace.h

@protocol LivingPlace
- (void) setAddress:(NSString *)address;
@end
```

Then Boat could be defined as a class deriving from vehicle, but also implementing the LivingPlace protocol.

```
@interface Boat : Vehicle <LivingPlace>
{
        NSString *_address;
}
@end

@implementation Boat

- (void) setAddress:(NSString *)address
{
        self->_address = address;
}

@end
```

This solution will answer the issue of using single inheritance, but still doesn't provide the whole functionality of multiple inheritance. After all, the LivingPlace protocol is just a well-defined interface, without any associated implementation. When a class implements that protocol, it has to provide code for the desired functionality.

If you want to offer not only an interface but also a default implementation, a possible solution is to create a concrete implementation class for the protocol, which will be used by other classes. A client class can use such a default implementation by creating a new instance of the default class and saving it as an instance variable for later use.

```
// DefaultLivingPlace.h
@interface DefaultLivingPlace : NSObject <LivingPlace>
{
      NSString *_address;
}
@end

// DefaultLivingPlace.m
@implementation DefaultLivingPlace

- (void) setAddress:(NSString *)address
{
      self->_address = address;
}

@end
```

Now, whenever a class needs to implement the LivingPlace protocol, it can count on the default implementation to provide standard methods.

```
@interface Boat : Vehicle <LivingPlace>
{
      NSString *_address;
       DefaultLivingPlace *livingPlaceImp;
}
@end
```

The methods of the interface still need to be defined in the class. However, the implementation can now become just a message call that forwards the message to the default implementation.

```
@implementation Boat

- (void) setAddress:(NSString *)address
{
      [self->livingPlaceImp setAddress:address];
}

@end
```

Inheritance versus Delegation

In this example, you used an implementation member variable instead of inheritance to provide new coding features. This is an illustration of the more general opposition between inheritance and composition. In the first case, some functionality is made available to an object because it was inherited from a base class. In the second case, functionality is provided by an external object and made available through an instance variable. While inheritance is a richer way of providing functionality, it turns out that composition through delegation is more flexible for a few reasons.

- *There is no need for a deep connection between the two classes*: With inheritance, it is possible for the subclass to access a lot of details from the superclass, such as protected variables and methods that are not made accessible to external clients. This generates some problems when things change in the base class. With delegation, you don't need to worry about the connection between the implementation and its client, since you can rely on the mechanisms provided by the language to avoid undesirable access.

- *A class is free to use containment with as many objects as necessary*: Thus, a class can receive messages and forward them to any appropriate object as needed. With inheritance, however, only one superclass can be used.

What this means is that you don't need direct inheritance to enjoy some of the benefits of code reuse. On the other hand, delegation provides a few extra benefits that may increase the flexibility of your code and even make it easier to handle problems that would be typically solved through multiple inheritance.

Summary

In this chapter you explored class inheritance, one of the most important concepts in object-oriented programming. Objective-C offers great support for inheritance, and learning to use the possibilities will help you design better classes, as well as use the Foundation and other frameworks more effectively. You have seen how inheritance helps in avoiding code duplication, by assembling useful methods in base classes and reusing them later through the subclassing mechanism.

Inheritance also gives rise to some patterns that are frequently used in Objective-C. For example, you have seen how clusters allow programmers to hide concrete classes under a single façade, defined by an abstract class. This technique is frequently used in classes from the Foundation framework, including NSNumber and NSArray.

There are also moments when you would like to disallow the creation of new classes from one of your base classes. This can be done to avoid unnecessary coupling between your methods and third party code. Preventing the creation of subclasses can be done by the application of some strategies reviewed in this chapter, such as using delegates that comply with a well-defined protocol.

In the next chapter, you will explore the block syntax, a unique feature in Objective-C that allows your code to refer directly to arbitrary blocks of code. With blocks, you can simplify some operations that would otherwise require lots of boilerplate code, while using an elegant method for transferring code.

Chapter 6

Blocks

One of the overall goals of Objective-C is to reduce the effort necessary to program complex applications through the use of object-oriented concepts, which can help to simplify and clarify the relationship between programming entities. In this chapter, you will learn how to create and use blocks, a syntactical feature that makes the language much easier and more expressive.

A block is a piece of code that can be passed around to other parts of the application, without the need to create a separate function, method, or class. Moreover, a block not only retains information about the code contained in it, but also about the variables that were in scope right at the time that the block was created. In this way, blocks are similar to the concept of closures, which are available in other programming languages such as Python and Ruby. In Java, the similar functionality would be provided by anonymous classes, and in C++ by lambda functions.

By defining blocks, you can make the operation of certain algorithms more extensible, as clients are now able to provide key parts of the implementation in the form of block parameters. Because of these features, blocks have wide applicability in Objective-C programs. For example, you can also use blocks to implement multi-processing code that will seamlessly run in parallel threads, as currently accomplished by some Objective-C libraries.

In this chapter, you will first learn about the basic concepts of blocks. Then, you will get more information about accessing variables from inside blocks, including local and instance variables. I will then discuss the issues influencing the memory allocation of blocks as well as accessing them outside the context in which they were created. Finally, you will see a few examples of using blocks both in your own applications and in classes of the Foundation framework.

Introducing Blocks

A block is a set of instructions that can be manipulated by the program. For example, a block can be saved in a variable and executed when needed. A block can superficially be compared to a pointer to a function, in that both provide a mechanism to store and execute code. However, there are some important differences between these two concepts.

The first difference between blocks and function pointers is that a block literal can be declared in any place that an executable statement may be present. So, for example, a block can be declared right in the middle of a function, or as part of a method call. This is not possible with functions, because they cannot be nested: according to the rules of the C language, functions can only be declared at the top level of an implementation file.

The second difference between blocks and function pointers is also one of the biggest advantages of using blocks. A block can capture the values and addresses of any variable that is active in the context where it is defined. For example, a block may use a local variable declared in a method, even after the execution of original method itself has finished. This property is also one of the defining properties of a closure, a programming construct used with great effect in functional languages.

These features of blocks allow for the creation of some interesting algorithms that otherwise would be hard to replicate with the same conciseness. For example, blocks can be used to simulate the use of control structures, such as a for loop, over complex data types. They can also be used to provide alternate code for sorting procedures, as you will see later in this chapter.

Declaring Blocks

Blocks can be stored in variables. To declare a block variable you use a notation similar the one employed to declare function pointers. Instead of using a star, however, you use the ^ character to mark its definition. Here is a simple example that will be explained in the next paragraphs:

```
- (void) simpleBlock
{
        int (^b)(int);      // declare a block variable

        b = ^ int (int a)  // create a block and store it in b
        {
                return a + 1;
        };
}
```

To use a block as part of a variable or method declaration, it is first necessary to declare the type of block you are interested in using. As hinted previously, blocks are related to pointers to functions, since they both provide a means of referencing executable sections of code. Therefore, it is natural that they use similar declaration styles. Blocks, however, have a few syntactical subtleties, as you will see next.

To declare a variable as holding a block, you need to use the caret notation. In this notation, the name of the variable appears after a ^ character and inside parenthesis, in the same position that the name of a function would normally appear. For example, to declare a block that receives two integers and returns a double, you would use the following declaration:

```
- (void) divisionBlock
{
        double (^division)(int, int); // declare a block
        // use block here...
}
```

After a block variable has been defined, the next logical step is to set its value to hold a new block. You can do that using block literals, with the following syntax illustrated:

```
- (void) divisionBlock
{
        double (^division)(int, double);        // declare a block

        division = ^ double (int a, double b)  // save block on variable
        {
                return a / b;
        };
}
```

Here, you set the value of the `division` variable to hold the block that comes after the caret. Notice that the way the block is defined is also very similar to how a function is implemented, with the difference that its definition can appear directly on the location where it will be used, just as with other literal values.

While the above notation differs little from a function definition, the block syntax offers a number of simplifications, which can substantially reduce the amount of code you need to write in these situations. For example, it is possible to omit some elements of the definition if they become clear from the context. The first thing that can be omitted is the return type, since the compiler can get that information from the return value itself.

```
- (void) divisionBlock
{
        double (^division)(int, double);

        division = ^ (int a, double b)
        {
                return a / b;
        };
}
```

Second, it is possible to omit the list of parameters in the case that the list is empty. That is, there is no need for the extra parenthesis if no argument is being passed to the block. Here is an example:

```
- (void) getPI
{
        double (^f)(); // declare a new block
        f = ^ {
                return 3.14;
        };
}
```

This code defines a new block variable f, and then assigns to it a block that returns a literal number representing the mathematical constant Pi.

To call the code defined by a block, it is possible to employ the name of the block variable in the same way that a function is used.

```
- (void) divisionBlock
{
        double (^division)(int, double);    // declare a block
        division = ^ (int a, double b)      // save block on variable
        {
                return a / b;
        };

        double result = division(1, 2);
        NSLog(@"the result is %lf", result); // will print 0.5
}
```

Reading Complex Block Declarations

A block may not only be stored in a local variable, but also used as a parameter to a function or method, or even as a return value. When that happens, the declaration aspect of blocks keeps getting more complicated. For instance, here is how a block, similar to what you have seen before, can be used as a parameter:

```
- (void) useBlock:(double (^)(int, int))aBlock
{
        aBlock(1, 2);
}
```

You can read this declaration by looking at the characters (^) as defining a block, while the types around them are the return value and argument types. As any other parameter to an Objective-C method, they are wrapped inside a pair of parenthesis, followed by the formal name of the argument, which in this case is called aBlock.

Finally, here is an example of how to declare a method that returns a block:

```
- (double (^)(int, int)) returnABlock
{
        // return block here
}
```

The process of reading such declarations is similar to what I explained in the previous example. However, you will notice how complicated this can become with an increasing number of parameters and return values. One way to simplify this process is to use the typedef mechanism offered by the C language.

A typedef is just a shortcut for a longer type declaration. However, despite the introduction of a new name, types declared with a typedef are exactly the same as the original name for all practical purposes. A simple use of a typedef would be

typedef int MyNewIntType;

In this case, MyNewIntType can now be employed as a type name anywhere you expect to use the int type. A better use of typedefs, however, is in the simplification of complex block (as well as function pointer) variable declarations. Here is how you can improve the previous example:

```
typedef double (^MathBlock)(int, double);

- (void) divisionBlock
{
        MathBlock division; // declare a block
        division = ^ (int a, double b)
        {
                return a / b;
        };

        double result = division(1, 2);
        NSLog(@"the result is %lf", result);
        // this will print result as 0.500
}
```

First, there is the typedef statement, which declares MathBlock as the new name for the block type. As a general rule, the new name for the type in a typedef expression appears in the same location that the variable name would normally appear. After MathBlock is declared, you can use it everywhere the type name would be needed. The main advantage of using a typedef is that you don't need to retype a complex block definition like this one. It also makes it much easier to initialize the block in the same line as the declaration. For example, the above example could also be written as

```
- (void) divisionBlock
{
        MathBlock division = ^ (int a, double b)
        {
                return a / b;
        };

        double result = division(1, 2);
        NSLog(@"the result is %lf", result);
        // this will print result as 0.500
}
```

This allows you to initialize the block in the same line as the declaration. The same typedef can also be used in the declaration of method arguments. Therefore, one of the previous examples can be rewritten in the following way:

```
typedef double (^DoubleIntIntBlock)(int, int);

- (void) useBlock:(DoubleIntIntBlock)aBlock
{
        aBlock(1, 2);
}
```

and similarly for return values:

```
- (DoubleIntIntBlock) returnABlock
{
  // return block here
}
```

Passing Blocks as Parameters

As you have seen, it is easy to create function methods that receive blocks as parameters. Similarly, it is relatively straightforward to pass blocks as parameters to functions or methods. For example, consider the previously defined method,

```
- (void) useBlock:(DoubleIntIntBlock)aBlock;
```

To use such a method, you can first define a variable an pass it as a parameter, like so:

```
- (void) callBlockMethod
{
        DoubleIntIntBlock myBlock;
        myBlock = ^ double (int a,int b)
        {
                NSLog(@"the values passed are %d and %d", a, b);
                return 1.0 + a + b;
        };

        [self useBlock:myBlock];
}
```

Another way of doing this is to use the block directly as part of a message call.

```
- (void) callBlockMethod
{
        [self useBlock:^ double (int a,int b)
        {
                NSLog(@"the values passed are %d and %d", a, b);
                return 1.0 + a + b;
        }];
}
```

Here, you are defining an unnamed block and immediately using it as the sole argument to a method call. The block is passed as a parameter to the useBlock: method, which can call it directly or save it for later use.

Accessing External Variables

One of the features of blocks, which separates that concept from standard function pointers, is that a block can have access to variables that are in the enclosing sections of code. This makes the work with blocks much easier, because there is less need to copy the value of variables using either function parameters or additional classes. Blocks have by default read-only access to local variables or instance variables accessible from the location they are defined. It is also possible to modify such variables through the use of the special keyword __block. The simplest case of data access is read-only access of local variables. When creating a block, this is allowed without any additional effort on the part of programmers.

```
- (void) showReadAcccess
{
        int myVariable = 2;
        int (^getMultiple)();

        getMultiple = ^ {
            return 5 * myVariable ;
        };

        NSLog(@"Here is a the result: %d", getMultiple());
        // this should print the value 10
}
```

In this example, you declare a variable called myVariable, which contains an integer value. Then, you define a block, named getMultiple, which returns a multiple of the value stored in myVariable. The log window should then display the result of the computation as the block is called.

A similar kind of data access is possible for instance variables of the class where the function is defined. For example, consider the following class declaration, where there's a single integer instance variable,

```
// file Blocks.h
@interface Blocks : NSObject
{
        int _myIntValue;
}

- (void) callBlockMethod;

@end
```

followed by an implementation,

```
- (void) showInstVarReadAcccess
{
        _myIntValue = 3;
        int (^getMultiple)();
```

```
        getMultiple = ^ {
            return 6 * _myIntValue ;
        };

        NSLog(@"Here is a the result: %d", getMultiple());
        // this should print the value 18
}
```

The method implementation is similar to the previous example, but this time it shows how the block has easy access to the instance variable _myIntVariable, which is part of the class. Of course, it is not impressive that you may do so when the block is called from inside the class itself, but consider the following scenario:

```
// file UseBlock.h
@interface UseBlock : NSObject
{
        int _myIntValue;
}

- (void) receiveBlock:(int (^)())aBlock;

@end

// file UseBlock.m
@implementation UseBlock

- (void) receiveBlock:(int (^)())aBlock
{
        NSLog(@"the result is now: %d", aBlock());
}

@end
```

This class is supposed to receive a block and call it, without any knowledge about the location where the block originated. Let's now see how this class can be used.

```
- (void) showVariableReadAcccess
{
        _myIntValue = 3;
        int myVariable = 2;

        UseBlock *useBlock = [[UseBlock alloc] init];

        [useBlock receiveBlock:^
        {
                return 5 * myVariable + 2 * _myIntValue;
        }];
}
```

When this method is run, it results in the execution of a block that references a local variable as well as an instance variable. Even though the UseBlock class doesn't have any knowledge about the location and contents of these variables, it is still able to run the requested instructions.

The reason why a block can have access to local data, no matter which context it is called from, is due to the way Objective-C handles them through the runtime system. During runtime, a block is an object like any other, and the compiler implicitly sets data access to refer to object instance variables that are known only by the block object. The block syntax provides a simple way to declare a complex object that has access to data stored in other objects.

Read-Write Access to Local Variables

The standard data access provided to local variables located outside a block is read-only, as you saw in the previous examples. The variables accessed by the block are just copies of the values stored in the current method or function, when the block was created. However, Objective-C also provides a mechanism for modification of such values, though the __block keyword.

The use of the __block keyword forces the compiler to create not just a copy of the data, but also a reference that can be used to modify the same object or value as stored in local variables.

It's easy to modify one of the previous examples to show this distinction.

```
- (void) showWriteAcccess
{
        __block int myVariable = 2;
        int (^getMultiple)(int);

        getMultiple = ^ (int base)
        {
                myVariable = base;
                return 5 * myVariable ;
        };

        NSLog(@"Here is a the result: %d", getMultiple(3));
        // this should print the value 15
}
```

This is a similar example where the local variable is referenced inside the block. However, now the block also has the responsibility of changing the value stored in the local variable. Unlike in the previous example, the code stored in the block now needs to have writing access to the local variable. This intention is made explicit by the Objective-C keyword __block, which is added before the declaration of myVariable.

What happens under the cover, as this code is processed by the compiler, is that the a shared copy of this variable becomes accessible to the block, as well as to any other statement that need read-write access permissions. The shared reference to the local variable can be used by the block in whatever context it is called, including with methods that are part of other classes.

When modifications are made to instance variables, however, there is no need to add __block directly to the variable definition. The compiler will automatically store a reference to the object whenever the block needs to update one of its instance variables.

> **Note**   The mechanism for sharing local and instance variables described above is called, in other languages, a closure. For example, in Python, Ruby, or Lisp, it is possible to create closures, that is, sections of code that refer to variables that are active at their point of declaration. Objective-C blocks achieve essentially the same goals, while maintaining the type checking inherent to the C language.

Blocks and Memory Management

Blocks offer a lot of flexibility for programmers, who need additional tools to structure their code implementation. With blocks, for example, it is easier to share behavior between classes without the need to create separate objects. This flexibility, when not used properly, however, can cause subtle issues that are difficult to debug.

One issue that can confuse new programmers is the scope of blocks. While a block can be used in other locations of a program, this doesn't mean that all the memory in a block is managed automatically. The main issue is that the creation and use of a block also involve managing the memory associated with it. While Objective-C can automatically set up the necessary references for the data accessed from inside a block, it doesn't manage memory directly.

The issue of block memory management may sometimes be confusing. The main problem occurs when someone tries to access a block outside of the execution scope in which it was created. For example, consider a block created inside an if statement (the same also applies for blocks declared in a for, while, do/while).

```
- (double) invalidBlock:(BOOL)initBlock :(BOOL)callBlock :(int)x1 :(int)x2
{
        double (^division)(int, double) = nil;

        if (initBlock)
        {
                division = ^ double (int a, double b)
                {
                        return a / b;
                };
        }

        if (initBlock && callBlock)
        {
                return division(x1, x2); // This doesn't work.
        }

        return 0;
}
```

The intended meaning of this method is clear: it initializes and creates a block according to the parameters passed. If both are true, then the block is invoked and the file returned.

The problem, however, is that the block variable (division) is initialized within a group of statements (defined by the if statement) that has finished by the time the block is called. Since the default storage for a block is held on the program stack, its associated memory is released at the end of the if statement. This means that the block variable division is invalid when it is called.

Memory for a block is stack allocated for performance reasons. However, it is possible to create a dynamically allocated copy of a block. This can be done in the same way you copy any other object in the system, that is, by calling the copy method.

```
- (double) callValidBlock:(BOOL)initBlock :(BOOL)callBlock :(int)x1 :(int)x2
{
        double (^division)(int, double) = nil;

        if (initBlock)
        {
                division = [^ double (int a, double b)
                {
                        return a / b;
                }
                copy];
        }

        if (initBlock && callBlock)
        {
                return division(x1, x2);
        }

        [division release];
        return 0;
}
```

With this version, it is now correct to execute the block from the location where the call currently is. This is possible because the copy method will store a properly allocated version of the block, which will persist after the if statement is completed. Since you made a copy, however, you need to call release at the end of the method, to guarantee that its memory is properly released (I will discuss this and other rules for memory management in a later chapter).

A similar approach is necessary when a method returns a block. Since such a block needs to be accessed outside the stack environment in which it was created, you need to return a valid copy.

```
- (double (^)(int, double)) returnBlock
{
        return [[^ double (int a, double b)
                        {
                                return a / b;
                        }
                copy] autorelease];
}
```

This example is similar, but since you are returning the block to a client, you also call the autorelease method, which takes care of automatically disposing the memory associated to an object whenever it is not in use.

Using Blocks with the Foundation Framework

Using blocks in your own applications gives you lots of opportunities to simplify your code and reduce the number of classes needed to achieve a specific goal. However, blocks are also useful when dealing with the Cocoa libraries. In this section, I will show you a few examples where blocks can be used to interact with the Foundation framework.

A good application of blocks is to execute similar code on a set of elements. This is explored in the collection of classes of the Foundation framework. For an example, look at the NSArray class. If you want to determine the number of elements in an array that satisfy a particular condition, it is possible to check each element of the array using a for loop, for example. Alternatively, the NSArray class allows you to pass a block to test for the condition, using the method indexesOfObjectsPassingTest.

```
- (void) countPositivesInArray
{
        NSArray *array = @[ @-1, @-2, @1, @2, @3];

        NSIndexSet *indices =
        [array indexesOfObjectsPassingTest:
         ^ BOOL (id obj, NSUInteger idx, BOOL *stop)
         {
                NSNumber *num = (NSNumber*)obj;
                return [num integerValue] > 0;
         }
         ];

        NSLog(@"There are %d positive elements", (int)[indices count]);
        // this will show a result of 3
}
```

Notice that, using indexesOfObjectsPassingTest, you don't need to manually set up a for loop and keep a count of the number of elements satisfying the test for positives, since this this is automatically done by the NSArray class. In general, it is a good idea to delegate repetitive tasks to specialized methods, and that is the biggest advantage of using blocks: you can let other methods take care of the details, while defining only the important aspects of a computational task.

A similar approach is demonstrated by the sortedArrayUsingComparator method. Here, the goal is to perform the comparison of two elements in an array as part of a sorting procedure. Based on the result of the comparison, the sortedArrayUsingComparator can decide if the position of the two elements should be swapped or not. In a normal sorting procedure, this is done by passing a function pointer, or by subclassing an existing base class. Using a block, however, you can more easily decide how the elements should be compared without having to create additional boilerplate code. Let's see an example.

```
- (void) sortArray
{
        NSArray *array = @[ @-1, @2, @100, @4, @-3];

        NSArray *sorted = [array sortedArrayUsingComparator:^  (id a, id b)
        {
                if ([a integerValue] > [b integerValue])
                {
                        return (NSComparisonResult)NSOrderedDescending;
                }
                else if ([a integerValue] < [b integerValue])
                {
                        return (NSComparisonResult)NSOrderedAscending;
                }
                else
                {
                        return (NSComparisonResult)NSOrderedSame;
                }
        }];

        for (id item in sorted)
        {
                NSLog(@"value is %@", item);
        }

        // this will print the items in sorted order
}
```

In this method, you sort the NSArray defined in the first executable line. Then, you call the method sortedArrayUsingComparator on the original array, and pass a comparison block to it. The comparison block receives two objects as parameters and returns an NSComparisonResult, which is defined as an enumeration with only three values. Depending on how the first object compares to the second, you return NSOrderedDescending, NSOrderedDescending, or NSOrderedSame. The sorting method of NSArray uses this information to decide if the two objects are in order or not. Finally, the sortArray method prints all elements of the sorted array, which should be now in sorted order.

These two examples taken from NSArray show how blocks are used in the Cocoa frameworks. Many other classes of these frameworks use blocks where they offer the best benefit: simplifying the execution of small sections of code that can be supplied in place. As you explore the functionality provided by the Cocoa and Cocoa Touch libraries, you will see other examples where blocks are also used.

Summary

In this chapter, you have seen an overview, along with examples, of how to use blocks in Objective-C. With the help of blocks, you are able to create code fragments that can be sent to other methods or saved for later use in a context different from that where they were created. While blocks look similar to functions, and have the ability to simulate other functions or instance methods, they are a much more succinct way to implement small sections of code.

Even more importantly, blocks enable a simple and efficient mechanism to implicitly share data (both local and instance variables) with other parts of the program. This allows applications to reduce the amount of support code necessary to coordinate the access to variables in the system. Instead of creating explicit methods to get and set data in a separate class, you can use blocks to simplify data access when that seems to be a natural solution to a programming problem.

As you have seen, blocks are important not only as a way to organize your own code, but also to interact with other classes in Cocoa. The Foundation framework, for example, presents several methods where programmers are required to use blocks to accomplish a particular task. You have seen a few examples of this approach being used by the NSArray class.

New frameworks in the Cocoa and Cocoa Touch frameworks are introducing even more opportunities to use blocks. Some application areas for this technique are parallel programming, where blocks can be set up in such a way that they can be executed in different threads, or graphical programming, where blocks can be used, for example, to draw scenes in a 3D animation sequence.

In the next chapter, you will get an in-depth view of the dynamic binding mechanisms provided by Objective-C. In particular, I will discuss how to interact with the runtime system to improve the flexibility of your applications.

7

Dynamic Binding

One of the biggest advantages of Objective-C is that it allows programmers to choose the right combination of speed and flexibility, depending on their real needs. Code written in this language can enjoy the safety of compiler-checked expressions and method calls, where the compiler verifies every statement during the process of creating an executable. A lot of features, however, are runtime-driven, and this allows programmers to delay some decisions until a piece of code is executed.

The runtime system of Objective-C is the main tool used by programmers to switch between dynamic and static programming behaviors. In this chapter, you will explore some of the features provided by the runtime system. You will see that programmers have a lot of room for defining how to answer the messages sent to an object. For example, manipulating methods through the use of selectors is one of the most powerful features used by advanced programmers.

You will also see how you are allowed to forward messages to other objects at runtime. With this ability, it is possible to design software that seamlessly combines two or more existing interfaces. Finally, you will see how to use these same features to improve the performance of code that uses the message sending mechanism in Objective-C.

Method Selectors

When creating new methods in Objective-C, keep in mind that a method is defined by a message name, a return type, and a set of formal parameters. These elements of a method are used later on during a message call. When you send a message to an object, you are implicitly telling the compiler what kind of method name, return type, and parameters you are looking for.

The identity of the method targeted by a particular message call is of great importance in an object-oriented application. To find the right implementation, the compiler first looks up the list of known messages and finds the one that exactly corresponds to the request.

Because Objective-C is a dynamic language, decisions about how to respond to a message are taken at runtime, rather than at compilation time. Therefore, unlike in static compilation based languages such as C++, the compiler needs some way to internally represent the message during program execution. This ability is provided by the use of selectors, which are a runtime representation of a message. Selectors can also be stored as variables of type SEL, and therefore can be easily created and manipulated by programmers.

From the programmer's point of view, a selector is an identifier that can be used at runtime to determine which message you are looking for. Every message has an associated selector: you can retrieve and store the selector, and you can use it to perform message calls. Here are a few reasons why you may want to access a method selector in your program:

- *Calling a generic method*: One possible use of this functionality is to make a generic method call that can vary depending on the method selector that is passed as a parameter. Similarly to function pointers, selectors allow one to make method calls without knowing exactly the name of the method that will respond.

- *Storing a selector for later use*: Your goal may be to have a list of selectors that will be used later, in response to an event, for example. Methods employed in this way are referred to as callbacks. This is a common way to interact with events that are triggered by an UI application, as you will see in a later section.

- *Introspection*: Some applications need to determine the methods associated with a particular class. If you have this need, selectors may be the right way to define how a class responds to incoming messages.

A Simple Example

To better understand how selectors work, let's start with a sample class that employs selectors in its implementation.

```
// file Selectors.h

@interface Selectors : NSObject

- (void) printValue:(id)obj;

- (void) createSelector;

@end

// file Selectors.m

@implementation Selectors

- (void) printValue:(id)obj
{
        NSLog(@"printing the value of object: %@", obj);
}

- (void) createSelector
```

```
{
        SEL sel = @selector(printValue:);
        // use selector here
}

@end
```

The Selectors class gives you an example of how to retrieve the selector for a generic method. The method in question is printValue:, which simply prints its parameter obj to the logging window (when a colon is appended to the name of a method, as in printValue:, it means that it requires an argument). The method createSelector, however, is responsible for getting the selector of the first method and storing it in the local variable sel. To do this, you employ a special operator made available by Objective-C that returns the selector for a message passed as argument.

The @selector operator can be used anytime you need to convert existing methods into selector values. In a sense, @selector returns an object that is similar to a pointer or reference, since it can be later used to identify the message and to pass it as a parameter to other parts of the code.

Once you have a selector, you can use it on methods that accept this type of parameter. The simplest way to use a selector is to call it on a particular object. This can be done, for example, with the performSelector: method, like so:

```
// file Selectors.m

@implementation Selectors

- (void) displayData
{
        NSLog(@"The value is 1");
}

- (void) createSelector
{
        SEL sel = @selector(displayData);
        // use selector here
        [self performSelector:sel];
        // this should print "The value is 1"
}

@end
```

The performSelector: method has the ability to trigger a message call using the provided selector on the targeted object. Thus, in the example above, the line

```
[self performSelector:sel];
```

is identical to calling the method directly, like

```
[self displayData];
```

Clearly, in this example you are not gaining anything by adding the extra indirection, but in a real application the selector would be retrieved by another part of the code, passed as a parameter, for example. In that case, the current class would have no information about the targeted message. This is a common situation that is explored in several areas of the Cocoa frameworks, as you will see in the next sections.

Additional Parameters

If you want to execute a message that has a parameter, then you need to use a slightly modified version of the `performSelector:` message so that it can become possible to pass the required parameter as an argument to the destination method. To do this, you use the `performSelector:withObject:` version, like so:

```
// file Selectors.m

@implementation Selectors

- (void) printValue:(id)obj
{
        NSLog(@"printing the value of object: %@", obj);
}

- (void) createSelector
{
        SEL sel = @selector(printValue:);
        // use selector here
        [self performSelector:sel withObject:@"parameter"];
        // this should print "the value of object is parameter"
}

@end
```

This kind of mechanism is very useful when you want to allow a class to determine which message to call when a particular event happens. For example, suppose that class `MailService` is able to deliver mail to other classes. One possibility is to have the destination saved in an instance variable that matches a particular protocol (say `MailReceiver`). When the message is available, then a particular message is sent, in this case the `onMailIsAvailable:` message. Let's first see what the class interface would look like.

```
// file MailService.h

@protocol MailReceiver <NSObject>

- (void) onMailIsAvailable:(id)mail;

@end

@interface MailService : NSObject
{
        id <MailReceiver> _receiver;
}
```

```
@property(retain) id <MailReceiver> receiver;

- (void) processMail;

@end
```

Here the `MailReceiver` protocol is defined, containing a single method called `onMailIsAvailable:` that will be called by `MailService` when the mail is available for processing.

Then you need an interface for the `MailService`. That class will contain a property that stores a pointer to an object called `_receiver`. The notation `id <MailReceiver>` means that this object satisfies the `MailReceiver` protocol. It also contains a method `processMail`, which performs the main tasks of mail processing.

When the `processMail` method is called, it retrieves the mail data and calls the `onMailIsAvailable:` message on the receiver object.

```
// file MailService.m

@implementation MailService

- (void) processMail
{
        id myMail = nil;
        // do something else to initialize myMail...
        [_receiver onMailIsAvailable:myMail];
}

@end
```

Here, you use the message defined by the `MailReceiver` protocol to transfer the `myMail` data to the interested object.

Using Selectors

The design you have seen up to now for the mail processing system is consistent with the techniques discussed in the previous chapters. However, it also has a few problems.

- It requires that a protocol be used during the class interface definition. This is possible in many cases, but not always. For example, suppose that you are writing a category extension to an existing class. In this case, you cannot change the protocols implemented by the class in its original interface definition.

- The method used always has the same name: this limits the way you can respond to `MailService` messages. For example, suppose that you want to subscribe to two `MailService` objects for different types of messages. In this case, both `MailService` objects will call the same method, and you will have a difficult time making a distinction between the calls.

- It needs the extra complexity of a protocol definition. Sometimes you may want to use a simpler solution that could be used in several similar places. Removing the need for an additional protocol is a better way to handle such situations. Even if an informal protocol is used, the two problems mentioned above are still present.

Using selectors provides an alternative way to solve these problems while avoiding many of the issues created by the introduction of a new protocol. In a nutshell, the idea is to allow the client to pass a selector that identifies the target method. That method will then be called when the expected event or condition is raised. In that way, it is possible to have several target methods responding to as many MailService objects as necessary.

Each instance of MailService may have a distinct selector, so it will respond in a different way. When receiving the message call destined to a specific selector, the MailReceiver can be sure of what particular version of MailService generated the call. Let's see how such an approach could be implemented.

```
// file MailService.h

@interface MailService : NSObject

@property(retain) id receiver;

@property SEL selector;
- (void) processMail;

@end
```

The MailService interface is updated to contain an additional property: the selector property, which holds a selector for the message you want to send when mail is available. Also notice that the receiver doesn't need to be restricted to a particular protocol. Since you will not be calling any method directly, there is no need to request a particular interface for this object.

```
// file MailService.m

@implementation MailService

- (void) processMail
{
        id myMail = nil;
        // do something else to initialize myMail...
        if (_selector && _receiver)
        {
                [_receiver performSelector:_selector withObject:myMail];
        }
}

@end
```

Some changes in the implementation section are necessary to make use of the new property. Once mail data is available for processing, you check if the receiver and selector properties have been set. Then, you call performSelector:withObject: on the receiver object, passing the selector as parameter, along with the data stored in myMail.

You can also slightly increase the safety of the processMail method by checking if the selector is really implemented by the receiver. Such a test can avoid programming errors where the receiver object doesn't implement the method specified by the selector. This can be achieved with the use of the method respondsToSelector:, which checks if an object can process a message call to the given selector.

```
- (void) processMail
{
        id myMail = nil;
        // do something else to initialize myMail...
        if (_selector && _receiver)
        {
                if ([_receiver respondsToSelector:_selector])
                {
                        [_receiver performSelector:_selector withObject:myMail];
                }
                else
                {
                        NSLog(@"error: the receiver doesn't respond to the given selector");
                }
        }
}
```

RHere, you check if the selector can be called as a message sent to _receiver. If that is not possible, then you log an error message that can later be traced by developers.

Finally, the following code shows how you can use this selector-based implementation:

```
// file MailReceiverImp.h

@interface MailReceiverImp : NSObject
{
        MailService *_service1;
        MailService *_service2;
}

- (void) receiveMail1:(id)data;

- (void) receiveMail2:(id)data;

- (void) setupServices;

@end
```

First, you define an example class that will have two mail services. This will show how such services can be handled independently using the selector-based approach. The MailReceiverImp class has two instance variables used to store the MailService objects in use. The class also has two methods that can receive mail data. Finally, you declare a setupServices method, which will be responsible for the initial setup of the mail processing subsystem.

```
// file MailReceiverImp.m

@implementation MailReceiverImp

- (void) receiveMail1:(id)data
{
        NSLog(@"receiving email data from source 1");
}
```

```
- (void) receiveMail2:(id)data
{
        NSLog(@"receiving email data from source 2");
}

- (void) setupServices
{
        _service1 = [[MailService alloc] init];
        _service1.selector = @selector(receiveMail1:);
        _service1.receiver = self;

        _service2 = [[MailService alloc] init];
        _service2.selector = @selector(receiveMail2:);
        _service2.receiver = self;
}

@end
```

The implementation section of the class provides the details for using the two MailService objects. The two receiveMail methods are similar and are displayed here just for completeness. A real implementation would do different things with the data received. The setupServices method, however, performs a useful role. Its goal is to allocate and initialize both services. Then, you set the two properties expected by each service: a selector and a receiver. The receiver is always self, since you are interested in processing the mail data directly. This could be different if you wanted to send the results to another object, however.

You also set the selector property to different methods, one for each MailService object. The selectors are retrieved using the @selector keyword, applied to each of the target methods.

The biggest advantage of this type of code is that it can handle as many MailService objects as necessary. There is no limitation imposed by a particular protocol, for example. All a class needs to do is add a new method and use the @selector keyword to retrieve its associate selector and pass it to the service object.

As you will see in the next section, this type of strategy is useful not only on your own user-defined classes, but also when interacting with the Cocoa frameworks. In fact, event processing using selectors is one of the basic design patterns used in GUI programming for the Cocoa and Cocoa Touch libraries.

Target-Action on Cocoa

A common use of selectors is in defining the target for a particular message, which is typically generated in response to an event. As such, there is a great potential for using these selector-based strategies in UI code. This design pattern is called target-action and is frequently employed in the Cocoa frameworks to handle events that need to be processed by application classes.

The Cocoa UI library uses the target-action design pattern to achieve a greater level of abstraction and independence between the target of an event and the UI control that generates the event. Similar to the application we discussed in the previous section, the goal of the UI toolkit is to allow each class to be the target of multiple GUI controls. At the same time, the GUI control shouldn't be required to know about any particular protocol implemented by the target.

The result of these requirements is a design pattern where the GUI control object has two properties: a target and an action. The target property designates the object that will receive the message when the desired event occurs.

Consider, for example, an application with a single window and a button that can be used to trigger a user-defined action. Although I haven't described how to create such applications in Cocoa (see the last chapter for a complete example), here is the basic code necessary only to set up and process the event:

```
// file ButtonTest.h

@interface ButtonTest : NSObject

- (void) doWhenButtonPressed:(id)button;

- (void) setupButton:(NSButton *)aButton;

// other methods here

@end
```

In the ButtonTest class, you declare the two methods that will be discussed here. The method doWhenButtonPressed: is called in response to an external event, which will be executed when the user presses the button. The setupButton: method, on the other hand, is used to initialize the target-action mechanism so that the button-press event will be associated with the target object. These methods can be declared as follows:

```
// file ButtonTest.m

@implementation ButtonTest

- (void) doWhenButtonPressed:(id)button
{
        NSLog(@"We received a button press event");
}

- (void) setupButton:(NSButton *)aButton
{
        [aButton setAction:@selector(doWhenButtonPressed:)];
        [aButton setTarget:self];
}

// other methods here

@end
```

The setupButton: method contains the important part of implementation. The parameter to that method is an NSButton object, which is the class used in Cocoa to represent buttons in the user interface. You can assume that this method is called from some other place, probably in the same class, with an NSButton object as argument. The first step is to set the action, that is, the method that will be called when the button pressed event is fired. To do this in a generic way, you pass a selector for the doWhenButtonPressed: method.

The second step in the implementation is to set the target for the action defined in the previous line. In this case, you want the target to be the same object, since you are using a selector for a method implemented in the ButtonTest class. As a result, the button object will use self as a target for the message selector provided in the setAction: method.

Although my example is applicable to an NSButton, the technique used here is completely general. Any UI control can use the target-action pattern to set up the event handling mechanism between the source of events and the consumer. This is a very flexible mechanism that allows different classes and libraries to talk to each other with little knowledge about how they work or even their public interface. A great advantage of such a mechanism is that it reduces the number of classes and protocols that you need to maintain, unlike in other languages where there is no way to provide a dynamic link between objects.

Dynamically Responding to Messages

You have seen how it is possible for classes to send generic messages to a target object without even knowing the name of the message. That is achievable through the use of selectors. Another important aspect of class-based designs is to be able to respond, in a flexible way, to messages that are sent to an object.

In Objective-C, there is the standard option of creating methods and having messages routed to them automatically by the language runtime. However, there are cases where you might want to change the way in which the methods accepted by an object are dispatched. For example, consider a class that needs to relay messages to a helper class. One option is to create a new method for each of the methods in the helper class that want to replicate, as you will see in the next section.

Creating a Proxy Object

For example, consider the original class called MortgageSecurity, which is responsible for mortgage-related calculations. Its interface can be defined as follows:

```
// file MortgageSecurity.h

@interface MortgageSecurity : NSObject

- (void)calculateDebt;

- (void)reapraise;

- (void)calculateTaxes;

@end
```

```
// file MortgageSecurity.m

@implementation MortgageSecurity

- (void)calculateDebt
{
        // code that calculates remaining debt in the mortgage
}

- (void)reappraise
{
        // code used to reapraise the value of a mortgage
}

- (void)calculateTaxes
{
        // method that calculated the amount of taxes in a mortgage
}

@end
```

There are three methods used to calculate quantities associated with a mortgage, such as the amount of taxes and the total debt, as well as the reappraisal value. This is a complex class, so you are not interested in the inner workings of each method. What you want to do, however, is provide a simple proxy object for the original class. This is necessary, for example, when you want to create a façade object so that you can hide the real class in an easier-to-use interface.

The proxy class would include a reference to the MortgageSecurity class and the necessary code to redirect messages.

```
// file SecurityProxy.h

@interface SecurityProxy : NSObject

@property(retain) MortgageSecurity *security;

- (void)calculateDebt;

- (void)reappraise;

- (void)calculateTaxes;

@end
```

The interface in this case is very similar to the interface for MortgageSecurity. You want to provide the major functionality present in the original class, so you need to replicate its interface. The class also contains a property that can be used to store a pointer to a MortgageSecurity object so that it can be later used to route the incoming messages.

The implementation of SecurityProxy contains the code necessary to redirect message calls.

```
// file SecurityProxy.m

@implementation SecurityProxy

- (void)calculateDebt
{
        [_security calculateDebt];
}

- (void)calculateTaxes
{
        [_security calculateTaxes];
}

- (void)reappraise
{
        [_security reappraise];
}

@end
```

As you can see, each method in SecurityProxy acts just as a front end for the corresponding method in the MortgageSecurity class. They use the security property as the target for messages and make a call to exactly the same method. If any parameters had been passed, you would need to supply them to the target object as well.

A client of SecurityProxy would be unaware of the difference between that class and MortgageSecurity, since they both offer the same interface. However, the dependency between these two classes is big. If any detail about the interface of MortgageSecurity changes, then a corresponding change needs to be made in SecurityProxy as well. Without such a manual change, the illusion of the proxy class will be lost and the classes will start to have different interfaces.

Using forwardInvocation

As you can see, maintaining a proxy class using this programming style is very time-consuming. A better solution based on the dynamic features of Objective-C is available, however. What you need is a way of receiving a generic message and routing it to a target object without having to duplicate the message name in your interface.

Such a feature is provided by the forward invocation mechanism. Forward invocation is the process whereby the runtime calls a special method, forwardInvocation:, to decide how messages not present in a class interface should be handled. This dynamic feature is available to any Objective-C class implementing the forwardInvocation: method, which is used automatically by the runtime system whenever a method is not found in the target class.

Therefore, a simpler way to rewrite the class above is to use the forward invocation mechanism to receive and process messages directed to the MortgageSecurity class. This results in the following interface:

```
@interface SecurityProxy : NSObject

- (void)forwardInvocation:(NSInvocation *)anInvocation;

@property (retain) MortgageSecurity *security;

@end
```

The new interface for SecurityProxy still contains a property that stores the MortgageSecurity object. However, the list of methods that are also supported by MortgageSecurity is gone, replaced by the single method forwardInvocation:. The implementation of the new proxy class, therefore, depends only on the inner workings of forwardInvocation.

```
@implementation SecurityProxy

- (void)forwardInvocation:(NSInvocation *)anInvocation
{
        SEL selector = anInvocation.selector;
        if ([_security respondsToSelector:selector])
        {
                [anInvocation invokeWithTarget:_security];
        }
        else
        {
                [super forwardInvocation:anInvocation];
        }
}

@end
```

The implementation of forwardInvocation: needs to follow a similar pattern across all Objective-C classes because of how it interacts with the message dispatching system. The first task is to decide if you want to handle the message. To do so, you can retrieve the message selector from the NSInvocation object.

In this case, the test you want to perform is against the interface of the MortgageSecurity class. Therefore, you send the respondsToSelector: message to the security property to determine if this message should be handled or not. If the message is present on the security object, then you use the invokeWithTarget: to perform the method invocation.

> **Note** The `forwardInvocation:` method uses `invokeWithTarget:` on the `NSInvocation` object,
> instead of `performSelector:`, even though you also have a selector. The reason for this difference is
> that `performSelector:` is not able to handle an arbitrary number of parameters. The `NSInvocation`
> object, on the other hand, contains a parameter list provided by the runtime system, and has the internal
> logic necessary to send the message along with the parameters. Moreover, with `forwardInvocation:` the
> Objective-C runtime is responsible for storing any return value on the `NSInvocation` object, and passing
> them back to the point of the message call as a return value, which is something you cannot do using
> `performSelector:`.

If the message received by `forwardInvocation:` cannot be handled by the security object, then you
call `forwardInvocation:` on the parent class. This is done so that you don't change any of the default
behavior of forwardInvocation, including the standard implementation on `NSObject`.

Simulating Multiple Inheritance

The `forwardInvocation:` method may be used in many cases in which the functionality of a method
is provided by another class. When that happens, the class using `forwardInvocation:` is responsible
for relaying the message to the target object, which will ultimately respond to the message.
As you can see, `forwardInvocation:` has many similarities with the standard method dispatching
mechanism of Objective-C. As such, you can think of this method as a way of implementing your
own customized inheritance mechanism. Using such features you can, for example, design objects
that are able to respond to messages from two or even more classes.

For example, consider the class `SecurityProxy` discussed in the previous section. That class is
able to respond to any message in the `MortgageSecurity` interface. From a client's point of view,
SecurityProxy acts as a type of MortgageSecurity object.

However, you may want to extend this example a little further. Suppose that you also want to
respond to requests for a second interface, `FixedIncomeSecurity`, defined as follows:

```
// file FixedIncomeSecurity.h

@interface FixedIncomeSecurity : NSObject

- (void)calculateAmortization;

- (void)calculateEquivalentBond;

@end
```

This interface provides two additional methods of calculation that you would like to support on the
SecurityProxy class. Unfortunately, Objective-C doesn't provide multiple inheritance (as discussed
in a previous chapter), which means that you cannot use the standard message dispatching
mechanism to achieve this.

The solution, in this case, comes in the form of a modified use of the forwardInvocation: method. You will extend the test for valid selectors in the implementation of forwardInvocation:, and therefore allow for messages that are members of either of the two classes that you want to support. The following code displays the contents of the modified interface for SecurityProxy:

```
// file SecurityProxy.h

@interface SecurityProxy : NSObject

- (void)forwardInvocation:(NSInvocation *)anInvocation;

@property (retain) MortgageSecurity *mortgageSec;

@property (retain) FixedIncomeSecurity *fixIncomeSec;

@end
```

Here you add a new property, named fixIncomeSec, which will hold a pointer to the FixedIncomeSecurity object so that the desired behavior will be available to the class when needed. You also have a new implementation section for the modified class, as follows:

```
// file SecurityProxy.m

@implementation SecurityProxy

- (void)forwardInvocation:(NSInvocation *)anInvocation
{
        SEL selector = anInvocation.selector;
        if ([_mortgageSec respondsToSelector:selector])
        {
                [anInvocation invokeWithTarget:_mortgageSec];
        }
        else if ([_fixIncomeSec respondsToSelector:selector])
        {
                [anInvocation invokeWithTarget:_fixIncomeSec];
        }
        else
        {
                [super forwardInvocation:anInvocation];
        }
}

@end
```

The code on forwardInvocation: has changed to provide support for the methods in FixedIncomeSecurity. This is done in a way similar to what was previously achieved for MortgageSecurity methods. The fixIncomeSec property is tested using the respondsToSelector: message. Finally, unrecognized messages are submitted to the default forwardInvocation: method in NSObject.

Implementing respondsToSelector:

Notice that, although the implementation above provides many of the benefits of multiple inheritance, you should still be careful not to forget the important differences. For example, there is no parent-child relationship between SecurityProxy and any of the two security classes you have seen in this section. Thus, the compiler will not be able to make the standard type checks that are allowed when you are using classes derived from a single super class.

On the other hand, Objective-C's runtime can be used to tweak even more the relationship between classes by using dynamic messages. One of these messages has been encountered before: respondsToSelector:, which is used to determine if an object can respond to a particular message.

You have been using respondsToSelector: to determine if an object can answer to a particular method call using their corresponding selector. However, if another object makes the same method call using SecurityProxy as a target, it will receive a negative response. The result is NO because none of these methods are a real part of the list of messages supported by SecurityProxy.

If you wish to add this additional level of support for SecurityProxy, you may decide to change the implementation of respondsToSelector: in order to fix this problem. A possible implementation would work according to the following lines:

```
// file SecurityProxy.h

@interface SecurityProxy : NSObject

- (void)forwardInvocation:(NSInvocation *)anInvocation;

- (BOOL)respondsToSelector:(SEL) sel;

@property (retain) MortgageSecurity *mortgageSec;

@property (retain) FixedIncomeSecurity *fixIncomeSec;

@end
```

The interface has changed to accommodate the new method, respondsToSelector:, which will be used to determine if a message can be processed by the SecurityProxy class. This method will override the existing, standard implementation, which returns true only for methods that have been defined as part of the class interface.

```
// file SecurityProxy.m

@implementation SecurityProxy

- (BOOL)respondsToSelector:(SEL) sel
{
        if ([super respondsToSelector:sel])
        {
                return YES;
        }
        if ([_fixIncomeSec respondsToSelector:sel]
```

```
               || [_mortgageSec respondsToSelector:sel])
        {
               return YES;
        }
        return NO;
}

- (void)forwardInvocation:(NSInvocation *)anInvocation
{
        SEL selector = anInvocation.selector;
        if ([_mortgageSec respondsToSelector:selector])
        {
               [anInvocation invokeWithTarget:_mortgageSec];
        }
        else if ([_fixIncomeSec respondsToSelector:selector])
        {
               [anInvocation invokeWithTarget:_fixIncomeSec];
        }
        else
        {
               [super forwardInvocation:anInvocation];
        }
}

@end
```

The new implementation of respondsToSelector: is now able to check not only for compile-time defined methods (using the standard implementation supplied by NSObject), but also check with the two other objects mortgageSec and fixIncomeSec to determine if the method is valid for the SecurityProxy class. Here is an example of how this feature can be used by client code:

```
- (void) testSecurityMethods
{
        SecurityProxy *sp = [[[SecurityProxy alloc] init] autorelease];
        sp.mortgageSec = [[[MortgageSecurity alloc] init] autorelease];
        sp.fixIncomeSec = [[[FixedIncomeSecurity alloc] init] autorelease];

        // this method is defined at compilation time
        BOOL res = [sp respondsToSelector:@selector(forwardInvocation:)];
        NSLog(@"the response is %d", res); // response is 1

        // this method is defined dynamically
        res = [sp respondsToSelector:@selector(calculateEquivalentBond)];
        NSLog(@"the response is %d", res); // response is 1
}
```

This code puts together the classes described earlier and shows how they can be used to answer simple questions about their capabilities. The method testSecurityMethods starts by creating an instance of the SecurityProxy class. For this object to work, it needs two others: an instance of MortgageSecurity and an instance of FixedIncomeSecurity. They are both assigned to the corresponding properties mortgageSec and fixIncomeSec, respectively, which are part of

SecurityProxy. Finally, you send the respondsToSelector: message to the SecurityProxy instance, the first time querying about forwardInvocation:, which is a method that is really defined in the public interface. The second request, however, checks for the calculateEquivalentBond method, which is part of the FixedIncomeSecurity class. Both requests return YES, as you expected when designing the new respondsToSelector: method.

Avoiding Method Calls

If you are an experience C programmer, after seeing all of the dynamic features I have described in this chapter, you might have one thought or two about the performance of message sending in Objective-C. After all, you know that the runtime will try to find an implementation for a method by searching the hierarchy of classes in which the target object is member. Moreover, if the search fails, the runtime will try to use the forwardInvocation: method so the object has a "second chance" at responding to that message.

All this runtime behavior certainly has a cost. The good news is that Apple is always optimizing the implementation of this search mechanism. Even then, however, there are times when it is too expensive to use the standard dynamic dispatch. It turns out that Objective-C also has a reasonable solution for this problem, based again on a smart use of selectors to get the implementation of a method.

To understand how you can minimize or even avoid in certain cases the cost of method dispatch, it is necessary to know how methods are implemented. A method implementation is just a regular C function with two special parameters: the first parameter is a pointer to the object, which you already know as self. The second parameter is the selector used in the method call, which is available to any method and can be referenced using the _cmd special variable.

These two parameters are hidden when you create methods in the @implementation section of a class, but they are always present. It turns out that you can retrieve a pointer to the actual C function that is called when a method is dispatched. Such an implementation function is referenced by the runtime using the IMP type. The automatic handling of IMP function pointers is just one of the many details that the language arranges for us during compilation time.

To see how this feature can be used to improve performance, let's consider an example. The class UseIMP has a method called simpleMethod: that just prints an integer value to the logging screen.

```
// file UseIMP.h

@interface UseIMP : NSObject

- (void) simpleMethod:(int)param;

- (void) callSimpleMethod;

@end
```

In the first version of the class, you have a method named callSimpleMethod, which repeatedly calls simpleMethod.

```
// file UseIMP.m

@implementation UseIMP

- (void)simpleMethod:(int)param
{
        // implementation here
        NSLog(@"method called with value %d", param);
}

- (void) callSimpleMethod
{
        int i;
        for (i=0; i<10; ++i)
        {
                [self simpleMethod:i];
        }
}

@end
```

There is nothing wrong with this class, but there is room for performance improvements. The main issue here is that by calling the same method inside a loop you are forcing the runtime system to repeatedly perform the same dispatching sequence. While this is not so bad for a small number of repetitions, the overhead could become very high with a larger number of iterations.

To avoid this problem, you can directly retrieve the implementation function for simpleMethod: and store it in an IMP variable. The new interface will have an added method.

```
// file UseIMP.h

@interface UseIMP : NSObject

- (void) simpleMethod:(int)param;

- (void) callSimpleMethod;

- (void) callWithImplementation;

@end
```

The code for callWithImplementation looks like this:

```
typedef void (*MY_FUNC)(id, SEL, int);

- (void) callWithImplementation
{
        SEL selector = @selector(simpleMethod:);
        IMP imp_func = [self methodForSelector:selector];

        MY_FUNC myFunc = (MY_FUNC)imp_func;
        int i;
```

```
      for (i=0; i<10; ++i)
      {
             myFunc(self, selector, i);
      }
}
```

You start by defining a name for the type that represents a void function receiving an id, a selector, and an integer. In the definition of callWithImplementation, you first retrieve the selector for simpleMethod:. Then, you get the implementation using methodForSelector:, a method that returns an IMP (which in practice is just a function pointer). Thus, you cast that function pointer into a type that you can call directly with the required parameters, which is stored in the myFunc variable. Once the function pointer has been assigned, you can use it to directly call the contents of simpleMethod.

Notice that by calling directly the function pointer returned by methodForSelector:, you are bypassing the whole dynamic dispatch mechanism. Dynamic dispatch was allowed to run only once, when methodForSelector: is called. After that point, all you're doing is a direct pointer access to the function, which is executed at almost the same speed as a normal function call. As a result, this code performs much better than a set of repeated message calls to simpleMethod:. The difference in runtime performance becomes much more pronounced as the number of repetitions increase.

Finally, here is some sample code to test your UseIMP class:

```
- (void) testUseImp
{
      UseIMP *useImp = [[[UseIMP alloc] init] autorelease];
      [useImp callWithImplementation];
}
```

Calling testUseImp will result a sequence of ten lines displayed in the logging window, as expected.

In general, the example above gives you a blueprint for performance improvements based on the suppression of dynamic message dispatch. If you have a segment of code that needs to be optimized, here are some steps you can follow:

- Determine if dynamic dispatch can be eliminated. This is possible when, in a particular context, the same message is being sent to the same object a large number of times. To have a better baseline, use a profiler to determine where most of the time is being spent on your code.

- Once a method has been selected, you can use methodForSelector: to retrieve the IMP pointer for that particular object. Notice that methodForSelector: itself uses the runtime system to find the target method implementation, so the result is guaranteed to be correct.

- Use the IMP function retrieved above to make a direct function call. This can be done by passing directly the two hidden parameters (self and the method selector), along with any additional parameters needed by the method.

After you repeat this process for a few method calls occurring in some inner application loops, it is possible to dramatically improve the performance of the resulting Objective-C code. However, due to the low level manipulations that are necessary when using this technique, you should avoid using it unless there is a real performance bottleneck in your application. Remember that, for most desktop software, it is only in rare situations that the performance of Objective-C code may become an issue that needs to be addressed like this.

Summary

In this chapter, I discussed some of the dynamic dispatch features provided by Objective-C. The availability of such features is one of the advantages of working with a language that has a rich runtime system. Through the use of dynamic dispatch, it is possible not only to work benefits from the standard message dispatch system based on single inheritance, but also bend some of its rules when necessary.

You saw how to work with selectors, with examples of how they can be used to make classes more generic and less dependent on particular interfaces. You discussed a few cases where selectors are used in the Cocoa frameworks to connect clients and services, without adding any explicit compile-time references between them, so they can be connected at runtime.

I also discussed in this chapter the forwardInvocation: method, which gives programmers a clean way to process messages that are not recognized at compile time. Using this mechanism, it is possible to intercept messages that have been received but not matched to any member of your class interface.

With forwardInvocation:, you can decide to send unrecognized messages to some other object that knows how to answer them properly. You saw that, when this happens, a class effectively adopts the interface of another. The result can be interpreted as a simulated form of multiple inheritance in which you can selectively adopt only the desired parts of the interface from two or more classes.

Up to this point you have created objects without much regard for how they will be stored or disposed of after the end of their usage. Although Objective-C doesn't have automatic garbage collection (at least not by default), it has a powerful memory management schema that assists programmers in the important task of conserving memory. This will be the main topic for the next chapter.

Chapter 8

Memory Management

Complex memory management is one of the main problems that developers need to deal with when working with the C programing language. The power provided by direct manipulation of memory addresses, which is the hallmark of effective C programming, may also become a difficult issue when one needs to manually manage the location of those objects in memory. Objective-C, although retaining the power of the C programming language, also introduces a better way of organizing and managing memory. To simplify the use of memory-using objects, the language provides techniques that are fully based on OOP principles.

As you will see, one of the advantages of working with an object-oriented language that emphasizes runtime features is that memory management can be streamlined and mostly delegated to system libraries, which can do much of the complex work. Programmers in Objective-C can concentrate on the practical use of objects to represent their application domain, instead of bothering with low-level memory management schemes.

Although managing memory is much easier in Objective-C than in pure C programming, it is important to remember that it is still based on a manual memory management framework. In other words, there is no automatic garbage collector (GC) controlling memory, as in other languages such as Java and C# (Objective-C has provided GC for desktop applications, but it is being discontinued in favor of Automatic Reference Counting, which is described later in this chapter). Therefore, you need to realize that there are advantages and disadvantages to this kind of memory management scheme.

Garbage collection makes memory use almost trivial. There is no need to worry about how objects are allocated and when they will be released. The system does everything for you. There are some disadvantages, however. Experience has shown that either a GC system is too inefficient (a major problem that can be found in many GC-based languages) or it is so complex that it takes a lot of computer resources to run. This is the case of Java, for example, where GC has been constantly improved for more than a decade, resulting in a complex system that needs a lot of memory to run effectively.

The fact that Objective-C doesn't rely on GC means that it can run anywhere, from large workstations to memory-constrained devices such as cell phones. And all of this is possible while still maintaining the high performance of a C-based language.

The secret of Objective-C memory management is the use of a reference-based model for data, with a small number of simple rules that make it almost straightforward to allocate and release memory in an application. In this chapter, you'll learn the rules that you need to master in order to write correct Objective-C code. After you understand the concepts behind memory management, I will also cover the latest technique provided by Apple compilers through ARC (Automatic Reference Counting), which practically removes the need for manual intervention in the memory management mechanism.

Dealing with Memory Issues

Before you learn how to manage memory properly, it is important to understand the types of memory errors that may be encountered in the course of developing Objective-C applications. Memory bugs, unlike other logical bugs, are among the most difficult to fix because they usually present themselves far away from where the real error occurred. Therefore, it is important to develop techniques to identify memory issues as soon as they happen, as a way to insure against even more complex problems that can take longer to fix.

Types of Memory Problems

In Objective-C, due to its heritage from C, there are a number of memory errors that programmers have to deal with. Among them are the following:

- *Dangling pointers*: A dangling pointer occurs when you are pointing to an object or other area of memory that is not valid anymore. In C, this may happen for several reasons, such as accessing a pointer that was freed. In Objective-C, dangling pointers may occur because an object was released by mistake. When this happens, a new access to the variable will most probably crash the application because all the data that was previously stored there has been reused.

- *Out-of-bound array access*: Since arrays and pointers are equivalent in C, array accessing can result in access to pointers out of the allocated area. This is a common memory error that occurs in most C-based applications. Objective-C programmers, however, can avoid many of these issues by using a collection such as NSArray instead of native arrays. Although NSArray may not be as fast as a native array, it provides automatic protection against this type of unwanted array access. For performance-critical code, it is always possible to convert from the use of collections to native arrays, when that becomes necessary.

- *Memory leaks*: A memory leak is a point of a program where some memory becomes inaccessible, even though it was not released by the system. Memory leaks are possible both in C and Objective-C, only changing the mechanism by which memory is released. In Objective-C this happens because the user of an object didn't call release on a variable by the end of a method (for local variables) or when an object was deallocated (for instance variables). Memory leaks are an insidious type of error because they don't cause an immediate crash. The way you perceive a memory leak is by an increased memory use, which happens every time the offending code is run. After some time this may end up consuming all the memory available for the application, and causing sluggishness and even crashes.

Identifying Memory Bugs

One of the main tools a programmer has against memory issues is the use of debugging applications and libraries. Xcode has a good number of helper tools that can be used to locate and fix error problems.

Let's first consider memory crashes. A great tool for diagnosing memory crashes is the Xcode debugger. The first thing you can do with a debugger is to reproduce the error and see a stack trace showing where the crash happened (see the example in Figure 8-1). Once you have the location of the error, you can add a breakpoint in the lines just before it happens. This way you can have a clear view of the variables and their contents around the area where the error has occurred, and you will be able to determine what caused the incorrect behavior.

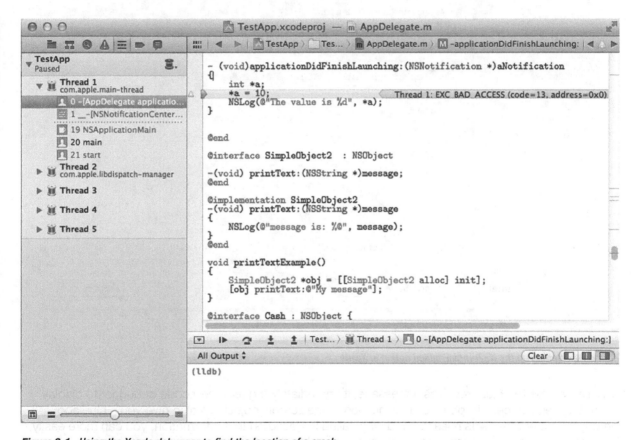

Figure 8-1. Using the Xcode debugger to find the location of a crash

Once you understand what caused a crash by looking at the variables and the code that is being executed, you can design a plan to fix the faulty code.

Xcode also provides a great tool called NSZombieEnabled that checks for access to deallocated objects. This flag, when passed to the application running under Xcode, will tell the application to create NSZombie objects when releasing a pointer. So, instead of just having the memory released, the Objective-C libraries will set up an object of type NSZombie, which is useful to diagnose cases in which a disposed object is receiving messages after it was released. To setup the NSZombieEnabled option, you need to select the menu options Product ➤ Scheme ➤ Edit Scheme, and then click the arguments tab. On the "Arguments Passed on Launch" screen, check the checkbox for NSZombieEnabled (see Figure 8-2).

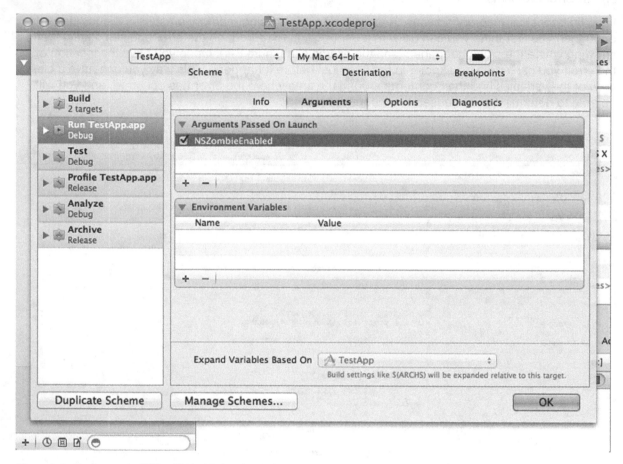

Figure 8-2. *Setting up the NSZombieEnabled option in Xcode*

When an NSZombie object receives a message, it immediately triggers the Xcode debugger to display where the illegal access happened. The location of the zombie object will also give you a clue about the original object that was released and who called it. Based on that information, you can more easily figure out why the object was released by mistake and fix the offending source to get rid of the bug.

Allocating Memory

Memory is the most common kind of resource that needs to be managed by an application. For any software to run properly, it needs to define a way to allocate new memory, as well as a proper scheme to maintain existing references to the allocated memory. Ultimately, the system also needs to determine how to dispose of unused memory blocks.

Objective-C uses a reference-counting mechanism to determine how memory needs to be maintained and disposed. Here is how it works: every object created by the system has an internal counter, which records how many references exist to that object. Each method that creates a new object (such as new or copy) initializes that counter to 1.

If an object is not in use anymore, you need to call the release method, which is part of the NSObject interface. When release is called, it decreases the value of the internal counter. If the counter is positive, nothing happens to the memory; but if the counter ever gets to zero, the object is deleted and removed from memory.

From that you can see that a simple sequence of usage for a new object is to create it using a method such as new, and then call release at the end of its use. If you want to keep an object alive, however, you can always call a method called retain. The role of retain is to increase the internal counter, indicating that a new reference to the object has been added.

Here is a simple example of how reference counting works. Consider the following method, setupProduction, which is used to set up the production system in a Factory class:

```
// file Factory.h

@interface Factory : NSObject

- (void) startProduction;

@end
```

This interface declares a single method, startProduction, that can be used to initiate the production activities for the factory. Before production starts, however, you would like to set up the system with all its components. This is done using the setupProduction method.

```
+ (void) setupProduction
{
        Factory *productFactory = [[Factory alloc] init];
        [productFactory startProduction];

        // do something with productFactory ...

        [productFactory release];
}
```

In this method, you are interested only in the allocation and release of data. Therefore, you start by allocating the Factory object, with a simple alloc/init sequence. The memory management rules say that memory created with a new method has an internal reference count of 1. Then, you use the new object to perform the production initialization steps of startProduction.

Finally, you get to a point where the Factory object is no longer needed. To avoid a memory leak, you need a call to release. In its internal implementation, release will decrement the reference counter and check its value. Since the original value was 1, the counter will drop to zero, and this will tell release to dispose of the object and remove it from memory.

Now, consider what to do if you need to store the Factory object in another location. For example, you may have a factory management class that can be used to manage your own Factory object.

```
// file FactoryManagement.h

/// responsible for managing a Factory object.
@interface FactoryManagement : NSObject
{
        Factory *factory;
}

- (void) setupProductionManagement:(Factory*)factory;

- (void) dealloc;

@end
```

This interface provides a management system for factories. For this purpose, the class needs to store a pointer to the Factory object. The setupProductionManagement: method is responsible for receiving a Factory object and using it to set up the management system. Here is how this can be implemented:

```
// file FactoryManagement.m

#include "FactoryManagement.h"

@implementation FactoryManagement

- (void) setupProductionManagement:(Factory *)aFactory
{
        factory = aFactory;
        [factory retain];
        // perform other setup activities
}

- (void) dealloc
{
        [factory release];
        [super dealloc];
}

@end
```

This example shows how the setupProductionManagement: method uses the Factory object passed as a parameter. First, it saves the pointer to the instance variable factory. However, doing so also requires the use of retain. This is necessary because otherwise the reference to the object passed as a parameter may become invalid after the end of setupProductionManagement:.

After retain is called on the factory object, FactoryManagement is responsible for maintaining the reference counter of the factory object. Therefore, it needs to call release on it when it is no longer needed. The last chance an object has to do this is on the dealloc method, which is called right before it is released by the system.

The implementation of dealloc is responsible for releasing any objects that have been allocated by the class. If a class holds one or more additional resources for its operation, it should also implement a dealloc method to guarantee that such resources will be correctly released at the end of its operation. Failure to implement dealloc properly is a cause of most memory management failures, which can cause not only higher-than-normal memory usage patterns, but also more severe application logical issues and possibly even crashes.

Rules of Reference Counting

As you saw in the previous section, reference counting as implemented by the Objective-C libraries is a simple technique that allows the system to determine when an object should be removed from memory. But for it to work, programmers need to regularly follow a few rules. Although the rules may seem unnatural at the beginning, after some experience these rules will just become second nature. Since the rules for memory management using reference counting are uniformly applied across the system, it doesn't take long for programmers to get used to them and take advantage of their convenience.

Reference counting is a system that can be applied in any non-garbage collected language such as C or C++. However, the basic advantage of this particular memory management system in Objective-C is that, unlike in C, all basic libraries uniformly apply the same strategy. Therefore, there is no need to worry about different memory controlling policies being used by different libraries, as is the case with C code. As soon as you have learned how retain and release work, you will be able to understand the memory usage patterns for all libraries in the system, including third-party frameworks.

Reference counting is a technique of memory organization that uses a simple counter attached to each object. The rules of memory management, therefore, equate with the rules for increasing and decreasing the reference counter (which indicates how many references for the current instance exist in memory) for each object.

Here are the rules that you need to follow for reference counting to work. When an object is created, the internal counter is equal to 1. An object is created only by methods that start with new, alloc, or copy. When a client calls one of these methods for a particular object, the resulting pointer is said to be owned by that client. For example, consider the following code:

```
// file ArrayUse.h

@interface ArrayUse : NSObject

- (void) useArray;

@end

// file ArrayUse.m

#import "ArrayUse.h"

@implementation ArrayUse
```

```objc
- (void) useArray
{
        NSArray *myArray = [[NSArray alloc] init];

        // do something with array ...

        // the array is owned by this object. Release it.
        [myArray release];
}

@end
```

The class `ArrayUse` has a single method called `useArray`, where an array is allocated and used. The array is created using the pair `alloc/init`, and the result is assigned to `myArray`. Remember that, being returned by `alloc`, the memory has now a reference count of 1, and you own the resulting object. This also means that you control the lifetime of the object. Since this is a local array, you cannot use it after the method finishes its execution. Therefore, you need to call `release` on myArray to avoid a memory leak.

Now, consider a situation in which myArray is an instance variable, instead of a local variable.

```objc
// file ArrayUse.h

@interface ArrayUse : NSObject
{
        NSArray *myArray;
}

- (void) useArray;
- (void) dealloc;

@end

// file ArrayUse.m

#import "ArrayUse.h"

@implementation ArrayUse

- (void) useArray
{
        myArray = [[NSArray alloc] init];

        // do something with array ...

}
```

```
// other methods using myArray

- (void) dealloc
{
        // the array is owned by this object. Release it.
        [myArray release];
        [super dealloc];
}

@end
```

In this example, myArray is allocated and stored as an instance variable. As you created myArray using new, you own the variable. The difference between this situation and the previous one is that since you are using myArray at a class scope, the proper method to release it is using dealloc. In both cases the useArray class owns the object, the only change being the lifetime of the object.

A result of the ownership rule explained above is that objects created with methods starting with something other than alloc, new, and copy are not owned by the caller of the code. The NSArray class can provide an example of this.

```
- (void) useArray
{
        NSArray *myArray = [NSArray arrayWithObjects:@1, @2, @3, nil];

        // do something with array ...

        // this array was not created with init/new/copy
        // so there is no need for release
}
```

The object myArray was created this time using the method arrayWithObjects:, which is a class method returning a new array. Although in functionality this is very much the same code as the previous example, the way you need to treat the object is surprisingly different. In this case, NSArray is responsible for providing a way to release the object, since the client code is **not** the owner of myArray.

On the other hand, the same issue changes your responsibility when myArray is an instance variable. And this brings us to the next rule of memory management: if you don't own an object, you need to use the retain method to avoid it being deleted by the system. This rule is exemplified by a modification of the previous example. Look at the difference in how an instance variable is treated when it holds a pointer to memory that is not owned by you:

```
// file ArrayUse.m

#import "ArrayUse.h"

@implementation ArrayUse

- (void) useArray
{
        myArray = [NSArray arrayWithObjects:@1, @2, @3, nil];
```

```
        // do something with array ...

        // this array was not created with init/new/copy
        // so we need to retain it:
        [myArray retain];
}

// other methods using myArray

- (void) dealloc {
        // the array is owned by this object. Release it.
        [myArray release];
        [super dealloc];
}

@end
```

Here you can see the difference in how the NSArray object is stored in the myArray instance variable. Since you are using arrayWithObjects:, the resulting instance is not owned by ArrayUse. The outcome is that you need to use retain in order to get ownership of the object and to be able to use it later. If you hadn't used retain, the object stored in myArray would be released by the system at the next available opportunity.

Notice that the implementation of dealloc, however, didn't change. By the time the object of class ArrayUse is destroyed, it owns a reference to myArray. Therefore, it needs to call release on myArray in the same way as before.

The autorelease Method

In the previous section, you learned how to work with the two main methods used for memory management in Objective-C: retain and release. As you have seen, these two methods increase or decrease the internal reference counter for each object, thus allowing the object itself to know how many references exist for it in memory. These two methods work in tandem to guarantee that the object is alive while there are references to it. On the other hand, they will allow memory to be reclaimed when it is no longer used.

A third method is used to cover situations in which it is not possible to use release directly. This happens when you want an object to persist in memory, but you don't want to (or cannot) take responsibility for its further release. A typical situation when this would occur is a method that returns a new object and has a name that doesn't start with new, alloc, or copy (remember that such methods are always allowed to return objects with reference count equal to 1).

Consider a method that returns the sorted elements in an array of integers. That is, it computes a new, sorted array with the same values contained in the original. To do this, it is necessary to create a new array object and return it as a result, which can potentially cause a memory leak. This is the initial implementation:

```
// file SortArray.h

@interface SortArray : NSObject

- (NSArray *) sortIntegerItems:(NSArray *)data;

@end
```

```
// file SortArray.m

#import SortArray.h"

@implementation SortArray

- (NSArray *) sortIntegerItems:(NSArray *)data
{
        NSArray *output =[[NSArray alloc] initWithArray:data];
        [output sortedArrayUsingComparator:^(id obj1, id obj2)
        {
                if ([obj1 integerValue] > [obj2 integerValue])
                {
                        return (NSComparisonResult)NSOrderedDescending;
                }

                if ([obj1 integerValue] < [obj2 integerValue])
                {
                        return (NSComparisonResult)NSOrderedAscending;
                }
                return (NSComparisonResult)NSOrderedSame;
        }];
        return output;   // memory leak happens here
}

@end
```

This code works in the following way. First, a new array is created with the alloc/initWithArray:
combination of messages. The result is a new NSArray (output) that contains a copy of the
original values stored in the parameter data. The next few lines are used to sort the array, using
the sortedArrayUsingComparator: method. This method receives as a parameter a block, which
determines how the elements will be compared (you saw a similar block in a previous chapter).
Finally, the output data is returned to the caller, already containing the sorted elements.

When the output array is created, it has a reference counter initialized to 1. Notice that this is true
because the array object was created with a function that starts with init (initWithArray: in this
case). The sorting procedure doesn't change that fact. Then, when you return the array object,
a conundrum ensues.

- You cannot release the array, because doing so would invalidate it and return
  garbage to the caller. This means that you still want the array output to have a
  reference counter of at least 1.

- You have no way to perform a release in a future moment because there is no
  guarantee that your code will ever receive the output array. For all practical
  purposes, you don't control the lifetime of this object once it is returned from the
  sortIntegerItems: function. Additionally, the caller of this method doesn't own
  the object (according to the rules you saw in the previous section) because this
  method name doesn't start with new, copy, or alloc. This means that the caller
  also cannot release the object.

To solve these problems within the framework of reference counted memory management, NSObject has another method called autorelease, which works along with the concept of memory pools to ensure that objects will be released even in such a situation. The autorelease method signals to the system that this object should stay alive for now, but it will be released as soon as possible by the memory pool mechanism. Here is how this change can be applied to the sortIntegerItems: method:

```
// file SortArray.m

#import SortArray.h"

@implementation SortArray

- (NSArray *) sortIntegerItems:(NSArray *)data
{
        NSArray *output =[[NSArray alloc] initWithArray:data];
        [output sortedArrayUsingComparator:^(id obj1, id obj2)
        {
                if ([obj1 integerValue] > [obj2 integerValue])
                {
                        return (NSComparisonResult)NSOrderedDescending;
                }

                if ([obj1 integerValue] < [obj2 integerValue])
                {
                        return (NSComparisonResult)NSOrderedAscending;
                }
                return (NSComparisonResult)NSOrderedSame;
        }];
        return [output autorelease];
}

@end
```

Only the last line of the method was altered, so that autorelease can be called on output. As a result, now you don't need to worry about memory leaks due to a failure of releasing the returned array. The caller of this function will have the opportunity to receive a valid object, and when the array is not referenced anymore, the system will take care of calling the release method on it.

In the case of NSArray objects, using autorelease is not the only way to solve the preceding problem, however. Remember that you just need to call release or autorelease in an object that you own. You own the output array because alloc was called to create the new object. However, there is another way to create an NSArray without using alloc: you just need to use one of the class methods that build a new NSArray. For example, this is how you can write the method above without the help of autorelease:

```
@implementation SortArray

- (NSArray *) sortIntegerItems:(NSArray *)data
{
        NSArray *output = [NSArray arrayWithArray:data];
        [output sortedArrayUsingComparator:^(id obj1, id obj2)
```

```
        {
                if ([obj1 integerValue] > [obj2 integerValue])
                {
                        return (NSComparisonResult)NSOrderedDescending;
                }

                if ([obj1 integerValue] < [obj2 integerValue])
                {
                        return (NSComparisonResult)NSOrderedAscending;
                }
                return (NSComparisonResult)NSOrderedSame;
        }];
        return output;  // no memory leak happens here
}

@end
```

The overall algorithm for this method didn't change, but you are now acquiring the NSArray via the arrayWithArray: method, which is provided by the NSArray class itself. Since arrayWithArray: is not one of the methods that trigger ownership of the results, the sortIntegerItems: method is not the owner of the output array. Consequently, there is no need to call release or autorelease in the output object. Notice also that the situation is the same for any caller of sortIntegerItems:. Anyone can call that method without a need to do a release or autorelease.

Using Properties

Using properties (instead instance variables) to hold a new object doesn't change any of the few rules that you learned in the previous section. However, properties have their own attributes, and therefore it is important to clarify how they interact with existing memory management strategies.

When you create a new property, it is possible to determine how it will store any objects assigned to it. Here are the possible memory attributes:

- retain: This attribute indicates that if the property is the target of an assignment, it will receive ownership of the assigned object. This means that a property marked with retain always owns the object that it points to. One advantage of using such properties, however, is that they automatically send a release message to the previously stored object so that you will not forget it. To avoid memory leaks, you need to release any object stored in this kind of property on the dealloc method. A simple way to do so is to assign nil to the property, since this will force a release message to be sent to the currently stored object.

- copy: Unlike the previous case, properties with the copy attribute will not send a retain message to the object, but instead create a copy of it. This means that there is no change in the number of references to the object assigned to the property, and you can change the contents of the property without any changes propagating to the original object. These properties also own the object they copied, so you must release them before the object is released, preferably on the dealloc method.

■ `assign`: This attribute is used for properties that need no special handling of memory. This is the default behavior, in which properties behave very much like a simple instance variable. In this case, there is no change in the behavior of the property with relation to memory management, and you should just use the general memory management rules discussed in the previous section.

The following is an example of how these property attributes interact with memory management and reference counting, by using a class to store book data:

```
// file Book.h
@interface Book : NSObject

- (void) updateBook:(NSString*)name authors:(NSArray*)authors
                      cover:(NSImage*)image;

@property (assign) NSString *bookName;
@property (copy) NSArray *authors;
@property (retain) NSImage *coverImage;

@end
```

Consider a class named Book where you store information about a book, such as the book name, list of authors, and a cover image. This class contains all of these elements as properties, which you will update according to their attributes. The class also has a method, updateBook:authors:cover:, which is responsible for updating the book data with the passed parameters.

The first property, bookName, has been defined as using the assign attribute.

```
// file Book.m

#import Book.h

@implementation Book

- (void) updateBook:(NSString*)name authors:(NSArray*)authors
                      cover:(NSImage*)image
{
        self.bookName = name;
        [name retain]; // retain is needed here
        // other code here
}

- (void) dealloc
{
        [self.bookName release];
        [super dealloc];
}

@end
```

In the first part of the updateBook:authors:cover: method, you are responsible for storing the value name on the bookName property. As bookName is declared using the assign attribute, just assigning the parameter name to bookName doesn't change the ownership of the object or its internal reference counter. Therefore, you need to manually send a retain message to the name object in order to avoid it being released by other owners of this object. As you acquire ownership of the property bookName, however, you need to guarantee that it will be eventually released. This is performed by the dealloc method, where you have to add code to release the property self.bookName.

The second property, authors, has a copy attribute. The following example shows how you can handle that property:

```
@implementation Book

- (void) updateBook:(NSString*)name authors:(NSArray*)authors
                          cover:(NSImage*)image
{
        self.bookName = name;
        [name retain];              // retain is needed here
        self.authors = authors; // no need for retain
}

- (void) dealloc
{
        [self.bookName release];
        self.authors = nil;
        [super dealloc];
}

@end
```

As the property authors has a copy attribute, what you have stored internally is not the original object itself, but a copy. Also according to the rules of memory management, the copied object, which the copy: method returned, is owned by whomever created it. This means that you need to release the copy at the end of its use, or in the dealloc method, as you see in the example above. Notice that I use the frequently employed trick of assigning nil to the object instead of calling release. By assigning nil, you leave the property setter to do the release, while at the same time resetting the value of the property to a known value.

The advantage of using a copy property is that you don't need to worry about any changes to the object by external clients. If the property authors were declared instead as retain or assign, any changes to the NSArray performed outside of your class would be reflected in the value stored in the authors property. Because you are using the copy attribute, however, you can rely on the fact that the value will not change.

Finally, the following code is needed to support a retain property:

```
@implementation Book

- (void) updateBook:(NSString*)name authors:(NSArray*)authors
                          cover:(NSImage*)image
```

```
{
        self.bookName = name;
        [name retain];          // retain is needed here
        self.authors = authors; // no need for retain
        self.coverImage = image;
}

- (void) dealloc
{
        [self.bookName release];
        self.authors = nil;
        self.coverImage = nil;
        [super dealloc];
}

@end
```

It turns out that using properties with the retain attribute is very similar to using properties with the copy attribute. During an assignment, the synthetized methods for the property are responsible for two things: releasing any existing values previously stored, and sending a retain message to the object being assigned. From your point of view, however, the only additional code you have to write is an explicit release when dealloc is called. To perform this, you use the same trick of assigning nil to the coverImage property. The synthesized property handler will be responsible for releasing the previous value and storing nil in its place.

Autorelease Pools

In the previous sections I discussed the use of autorelease. This message is sent to an object that needs to be released by the current owner, even though this action shouldn't happen at least until the control has returned to the caller. The autorelease message is very important to simplify memory management in such situations. The autorelease method can also help you to write more concise code. Look at the following example:

```
- (void) replaceName:(NSString*)newName
{
        NSString *oldName = _bookName;
        _bookName = newName;
        [oldName release];
}
```

The replaceName method operates on the bookName property declared in the Book class. To replace bookName with newName, you need to store the current object in a new variable called oldName before you perform the assignment. This is necessary because you need to release the current object and such a release could change newName object as a side effect. Using autorelease, however, you can simplify this code in the following way:

```
- (void) replaceName:(NSString*)newName
{
        [_bookName autorelease];
        _bookName = newName;
}
```

In this case, you are using autorelease as a delayed release so that newName will be assigned before any real change occurs.

The seemingly magical mechanism behind autorelease is called an autorelease pool. The pool is just a data structure that stores pointers to objects that need to be released in the future. Then, whenever the system libraries call the memory pool, the objects contained in such data structures are released. In general, there is an autorelease pool per application thread, which is called whenever the application has returned from an event handling callback, for example.

Every application has at least one memory pool. The memory pool in the principal thread is installed in the main function. There are two ways to install such memory pool. The first way is using the NSAutoreleasePool object. Here is an example:

```
int main()
{
        NSAutoreleasePool *pool = [[NSAutoreleasePool alloc] init];

        // main application loop is here

        [pool release];
        return 0;
}
```

I display here only the parts of the main function that deal with an autorelease pool. The pool object is first created by sending the alloc message to NSAutoreleasePool. The creation of this object guarantees that the autoreleased objects will be stored in the pool and will stay alive until the pool is drained (or release is called on it).

The second way to create an autorelease pool is using the @autoreleasepool keyword. While this is very similar to create an NSAutoreleasePool object, the keyword allows you to define a block of statements that will be executed under the same autorelease pool. The release of the objects stored in the pool as well as the creation and release of the pool itself is handled by the compiler. Here is an example:

```
int main()
{
        @autoreleasepool
        {
                // additional statements here
        }
        return 0;
}
```

While I have shown only examples of autorelease pools on the main function, there is nothing preventing you from creating other autorelease pools at certain points in the application. In fact, if you are creating code that needs to create and destroy a large number of objects, it may be beneficial to create an intermediate autorelease pool to process all objects that need to be released in that segment of code.

The main advantage of creating additional autorelease pools is that you can reduce the total amount of memory needed by your code. This happens because such an intermediate pool will anticipate the release of some of the objects held in memory. If you see a situation where there is high memory consumption caused by a large number of used objects, creating an autorelease pool might be a good way to recover some of the memory that is being allocated by your code.

Using ARC

Everything that you have seen in this chapter assumes that you are using the `retain/release/autorelease` methods for memory management. While these are the building blocks of memory management in Apple's Objective-C libraries, there are other ways to achieve the same results with less effort on the part of the programmer.

An alternative way to handle memory is to use the Automatic Reference Count (ARC) system, which was recently proposed by Apple and implemented in their latest compiler. ARC is a system that automatically adds the reference count handling code to your program in such a way that you don't need to deal with memory management. Although the usual methods for reference counting are still in use, you cannot directly call `retain`, `release`, or `autorelease`, so that the compiler can automatically maintain the balance or `retain` and `release` calls.

Apple has introduced ARC as an alternative to manual memory management so programmers don't need to worry about calling the right sequence of methods affecting the internal reference counter of objects. At the same time, ARC is a substitute for garbage collection (GC), a technique of automatic memory management that was available for a few platforms, including desktop applications in the Mac OS X. While GC has a number of advantages, Apple has concluded that ARC provides much of the same features of garbage collection, while at the same time being a predictable system that will dispose of memory as it becomes inaccessible.

In GC-based systems, there is frequently a lag time between objects becoming inaccessible and memory recollection, which sometimes translates into unresponsiveness in the application. While this is not a big problem on desktop machines, the fact that Objective-C targets small devices like cell phones and tablet computers makes it much more difficult to support GC across all platforms where Objective-C is deployed. By writing applications that use ARC, programmers can take advantage of the wide use of this technology and have the same code deployed on each supported platform.

Before you use ARC, it is necessary to inform the compiler that you want it to generate ARC-enabled code. There are no runtime changes needed to support ARC code, since the same messages that you have seen before will be generated by the compiler. However, the code generation phase will need to analyze the current objects in use by the application, and add the necessary message calls to either `retain`, `release`, or `autorelease`. The necessary compiler settings are available from the Xcode in the Project Settings panel (see Figure 8-3).

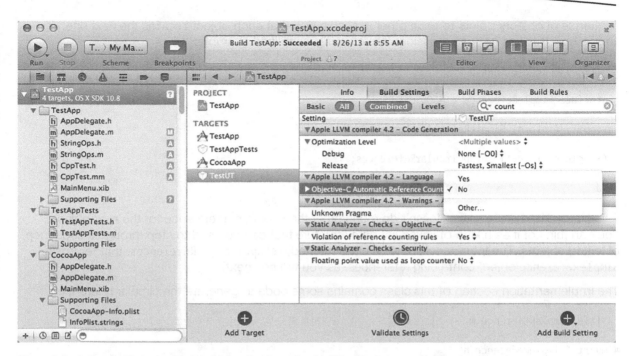

Figure 8-3. Project Settings panel in Xcode showing the option for Objective-C automatic reference counting

To use ARC, you just need to make a few changes to your existing code. The most important change is to remove any calls to methods such as `retain`, `release`, and `autorelease`. These are the functions that directly manipulate the reference counter status for each object in the system. With ARC, you need to relinquish these tasks to the compiler and allow it to choose the best option for each situation. The compiler does this by analyzing the usage patterns for each variable.

For instance, if the variable is holding an object that is returned to the calling function, the ARC-enabled compiler knows that it needs to add an `autorelease` call in order to avoid a dangling pointer. Similarly, if a variable is created inside a method (using a call to `alloc` for example) and never referenced outside it, the compiler deduces that the variable needs to be released to prevent a memory leak.

Another change that needs to be done prior to using ARC in your code is to remove the memory-related attributes attached to properties. For example, ARC doesn't honor attributes such as `retain` or `assign`. The reason is that these decisions should be done at a compilation-analysis level. The goal of ARC is to prevent the kind of manual allocation thinking that is represented by `retain` and `assign` attributes.

The next change when using ARC is to think about the structure of the memory you are allocating, in order to avoid memory leaks caused by circular references. A circular reference happens when a sequence of objects points to each other in such a way that each object retains the next one. To see how this can happen, consider the following, simplified example:

```
// file SimpleReference.h

@interface SimpleReference : NSObject

@property (retain) SimpleReference *nextObject;

+ (SimpleReference*) setupCircularReferences;

@end
```

This class, SimpleReference, doesn't do much other than contain a reference for the next object. You can think of it as a kind of linked list data structure that can be used to step through a sequence of linked objects. The interface also has a class method, setupCircularReferences, that returns a SimpleReference object containing references, as you will see next.

The implementation section of this class contains some code to generate the circular references:

```
// file SimpleReference.m

#import "SimpleReference.h"

@implementation SimpleReference

+ (SimpleReference*) setupCircularReferences
{

        SimpleReference *r1 = [[SimpleReference alloc] init];
        SimpleReference *r2 = [[SimpleReference alloc] init];
        SimpleReference *r3 = [[SimpleReference alloc] init];

        // create circular references

        r1.nextObject = r2;
        r2.nextObject = r3;
        r3.nextObject = r1;

        return [r1 autorelease];
}

@end
```

This code implements a simple method that allocates three SimpleReference objects and sets them up in a way that will generate a circular reference. The reason why this happens is that the nextObject property is declared using the retain attribute. Therefore, each time you add an object to the linked list, you are creating a retained reference.

The problem of such circular references is that they don't work nicely with reference counting. Suppose now that you have the following helper class:

```
// file SimpleReferenceUtil.h

@interface SimpleReferenceUtil : NSObject

@property (retain) SimpleReference *aReference;

- (void) createReference;

@end
```

This class holds and retains a SimpleReference object, using the property aReference. Here is the implementation:

```
// file SimpleReferenceUtil.m

#import "SimpleReferenceUtil.h"

@implementation SimpleReferenceUtil

- (void) createReference
{
        self.aReference = [SimpleReference setupCircularReferences];
}

@end
```

After the creation code is executed, the class SimpleReferenceUtil will have a retained pointer to an instance of the SimpleReference class. As a result of the circular references contained inside SimpleReference, the three objects contained there will still have a positive reference counter even after you try to call release on the aReference property. These objects will constitute an unused and inaccessible area of memory, that is, a memory leak.

Using ARC, you can avoid this situation by declaring at least one of the pointers to have the attribute weak. When a property is marked with a weak attribute, the compiler will generate code in such a way that an object will be released when there are only weak variables pointing to it. Going back to the previous example, by using weak properties (or variables marked with the __weak modifier), you can solve the problem of circular references. Here is how you could modify the interface of the SimpleReference class:

```
// file SimpleReferenceUtil.h

@interface SimpleReferenceUtil : NSObject

@property (weak) SimpleReference *aReference;

- (void) createReference;

@end
```

With this new interface and under ARC compilation settings, the property aReference is not allowed to retain the objects it points to. Of course, you also have to provide a way to retain the reference using a non-weak property or variable. But you can do this in a way that will not introduce circularity, such as using an external array, like this:

```
+ (SimpleReference*) setupReferences:(NSMutableArray*)refs
{
        SimpleReference *r1 = [[SimpleReference alloc] init];
        SimpleReference *r2 = [[SimpleReference alloc] init];
        SimpleReference *r3 = [[SimpleReference alloc] init];

        // create weak circular references

        r1.nextObject = r2;
        r2.nextObject = r3;
        r3.nextObject = r1;

        [refs addObject:r1];
        [refs addObject:r2];
        [refs addObject:r3];
        return r1;
}
```

This time you have a list of objects being added to the refs array, which will be enough to avoid any of the objects being prematurely released. This happens because, as these objects are inserted into the NSArray, they are retained as part of the normal operation of array instances. After these extra (retained) references are created, the objects will not be released at the end of the method, as it would happen if you had only weak references.

Summary

In this chapter I gave an overview of memory management in Objective-C. You saw the importance of memory management as a technique to avoid programming errors resulting from incorrect memory accesses. Using memory correctly is necessary in order to avoid common issues such as memory leaks, which cause unresponsive applications and ultimately crashes for lack of memory resources.

It is difficult to write correct software without knowing how objects are created, held in memory, and ultimately disposed. While Objective-C doesn't use garbage collection of unused memory (mainly for performance reasons), the Foundation framework provides a simple mechanism for memory management that is consistently followed throughout the system.

There are three methods that control how memory is released or retained in memory: retain, release, and autorelease. These methods are present in every object that is derived from NSObject, and they provide a fine control of when memory should be freed by an application. These methods are the building blocks for every memory management scheme in Objective-C.

You learned how to use autorelease pools to facilitate the use of objects that are controlled by autorelease. By carefully employing autorelease pools, it is possible to reduce the amount of memory necessary for a particular algorithm, since memory will be freed more frequently. In a graphical application that uses large objects such as images and sound files, this is the kind of change that can make a difference in performance and ease of use for your product. Autorelease pools can, in some situations, also be helpful for performance reasons: since you are postponing memory release to some later time, you may have to spend less time overall to manage the immediate release of objects.

You saw examples of how the memory management messages interact with properties and their different attributes. Properties can be used to simplify many of the techniques of memory management, since they can automatically retain or release the objects they hold. By carefully choosing the attributes of properties, you can simplify a great deal of your code while making use of the features provided by the Objective-C compiler.

Finally, I discussed Automatic Reference Counting, the new technology in which the compiler is responsible for deducing the correct instructions for retaining or releasing memory. To use ARC, you just need to follow some conventions about how to handle memory references and activate the compile-time settings. The result is a very fast and robust system, with low memory consumption and reduced opportunities for programming errors.

In the next chapter, I will introduce key-value programming, a technique that is used throughout Cocoa and many other third-party libraries. With key-value programming, you will be able to use not only dynamic code through messages, but also dynamic data that can be accessed in a generic way.

Chapter 9

Key-Value Coding

In previous chapters you saw several ways in which Objective-C programmers can use OOP concepts to work with code. For example, developers can enjoy the dynamic nature of the language to implement polymorphic functionality through message passing, and even add new methods to existing classes employing the concept of protocols.

Another aspect of OOP, however, regards the access to data contained in objects. Although it is wise to avoid direct access to data managed by an object, Objective-C provides a well-defined process for getting and setting data using the property mechanism. Properties make data available to other objects, while at the same time retaining the ability to control how this data will be shared.

Properties, however, are not the only way to share data across objects. In this chapter I will discuss key-value coding (KVC), a generic access mechanism for data publishing based on the functionality of the NSObject hierarchy. Key-value coding has been devised to allow data to be exchanged among objects through the use of keys, which are encoded as a string. In KVC, therefore, it is not necessary to call a different method for each data element; instead, a simple interface can be used to get and set a wide range of data.

Another reason why key-value programming is an important topic is that it is used in so many Objective-C libraries. For example, the CoreData framework, used to store and retrieve data from databases as well as other repositories, employs a model based on KVC to save and retrieve data objects. With KVC, data can be accessed through a simple interface, avoiding the need to create multiple subclasses when the only difference between objects is in the set of values they contain.

The Concept of Key-Value Coding

Key-value coding is a specification for a set of interfaces that allow objects to access properties using just a string as the identifier. The string is called the key and is used to access the stored value of the property.

The client side of this specification is very simple, and it uses two methods to read and set a particular property. The valueForKey: method is responsible for accessing the value stored in a particular key. The key object is an NSString, so that you can access different objects types using the same interface. The second method is setValue:forKey:, which is used to set the value object for a particular key.

One of the best things about KVC is that there is very little you need to do to support access to your instance variables—if you are willing to provide complete access to your data. By default, KVC is enabled through its implementation on NSObject, so you just need to call valueForKey: in any NSObject-derived object to have access to the data, like so:

```
// file: KVSample.h

// sample interface containing three variables
@interface KVSample : NSObject
{
        int anInt;
        double aDouble;
        NSString *aString;
}

- (id) init;

+ (void) accessData;

@end
```

This is a simple class interface containing three instance variables: an integer, a double, and a string variable. There is also an init method and a class method called accessData, for testing purposes. Here is how these instance variables can be accessed using KVC:

```
// file: KVSample.m

#import "KVSample.h"

@implementation KVSample

- (id) init
{
        KVSample *obj = [super init];
        if (obj)
        {
                obj->anInt = 10;
                obj->aDouble = 11.0;
                obj->aString = @"test";
        }
        return obj;
}

+ (void) accessData
{
        KVSample *sample = [[KVSample alloc] init];
        NSNumber *a = [sample valueForKey:@"anInt"];
        NSLog(@"int value: %@", a);
        NSNumber *b = [sample valueForKey:@"aDouble"];
```

```
    NSLog(@"double value: %@", b);
    NSNumber *c = [sample valueForKey:@"aString"];
    NSLog(@"double value: %@", c);
    [sample release];
}

@end
```

The init method used here is straightforward and similar to other init methods used in Objective-C. In the initialization section of the class, you assign test values to each of the instance variables present in KVSample. They will contain the values 10, 11.0, and "test".

The method accessData is just an example of how any other client can use KVC to read data stored in an Objective-C object. For this to work, you need to provide the name of the data you want to access as a key to valueForKey:. The runtime system knows the name of each instance variable in your class and will convert the name you passed as a key into a proper address for the variable containing the data.

Avoiding Direct Access

From the previous example, you can see that the default behavior of classes derived from NSObject is to allow access through the KVC mechanism. However, you may not want this kind of access to be granted. For example, if you are defining a scriptable interface, you may want to maintain a few instance variables out of the reach of external code. For another example, if the class contains an instance variable that holds a password, you may want to restrict access to that variable from scripts interacting with your application.

To disable the default behavior, KVC provides a method named accessInstanceVariablesDirectly. This method can be overridden in a derived class to signal that you don't want to grant the default level of access to all instance variables. Here is how this method can be declared:

```
// file: KVSample.h

@interface KVSample : NSObject
{
    int anInt;
    double aDouble;
    NSString *aString;
}

- (id) init;

+ (BOOL) accessInstanceVariablesDirectly;

+ (void) accessData;

@end
```

As in the implementation section, you can add the method, returning NO to indicate that variables should not be accessed directly, like so:

```
// file: KVSample.m

#import "KVSample.h"

@implementation KVSample

// other methods implemented here

+ (BOOL) accessInstanceVariablesDirectly
{
        return NO;
}

@end
```

This modified version of KVSample implements the class method accessInstanceVariablesDirectly. This class method returns a false value to indicate that the runtime system should not access the instance variables contained in it. To check that the new implementation is working, you can run the method accessData in this modified version. As a result, you will get the following error message:

```
this class is not key value coding-compliant for the key anInt.
```

Writing Property Assessors

KVC properties can be defined either implicitly, using instance variables, or explicitly, using getters and setters. The syntax for a generic getter method is - (<data type>) <key>, where key is the string you're expecting to receive as the key. For example, if you want to provide access to the instance methods in KVSample, you can write an interface with getters as follows:

```
// file: KVSample.h

// sample interface containing three variables
@interface KVSample : NSObject
{
        int _anInt;
        double _aDouble;
        NSString *_aString;
}

- (int) anInt;

- (double) aDouble;

- (NSString*)aString;
```

```
+ (void) accessData;

// other methods here
@end
```

Notice that this time you updated the instance variable names to have a leading underscore, a common naming convention used to distinguish them from the property name.

Now you need to provide the getter implementation for the declared KVC data.

```
// file: KVSample.m

#import "KVSample.h"

@implementation KVSample

- (id) init
{
        KVSample *obj = [super init];
        if (obj)
        {
                obj->_anInt = 10;
                obj->_aDouble = 11.0;
                obj->_aString = @"test";
        }
        return obj;
}

- (int) anInt
{
        return _anInt;
}

- (double) aDouble
{
        return _aDouble;
}

- (NSString*)aString
{
        return _aString;
}

// other methods here
@end
```

Now you can call the accessData method on KVSample using the following sample code:

```
- (void) testKVSample
{
        [KVSample accessData];
}
```

This will now work without any issues, since all the keys used by accessData have a proper getter implementation, which returns the content of the instance variables. For example, when this section of the code is executed

```
[sample valueForKey:@"aDouble"]
```

the Objective-C runtime will check for a getter method named aDouble, and return the response received from that message, when sent to the target object sample. The runtime also stores the returned value, of type double, into an NSNumber object, so that you can handle the return value uniformly, through an OOP interface.

Modifying Values

The other side of KVC handles the modification of values passed to the target through the use of a string key. The interface to this functionality in the client side is also very uniform and employs the setValue:forKey: method.

Here is an example of how the class method accessData can be modified to set the initial values for the exported keys aDouble, anInt, and aString:

```
@interface KVSample : NSObject
{
        int _anInt;
        double _aDouble;
        NSString *_aString;
}

- (int) anInt;

- (double) aDouble;

- (NSString*)aString;

- (void) setAnInt:(int) val;

- (void) setADouble: (double) val;

- (void) setAString: (NSString*) str;

- (id) init;

+ (BOOL) accessInstanceVariablesDirectly;

+ (void) accessData;

@end
```

This modified interface adds a group of set<Key>: methods that receive an input value and use it to update its respective instance variable. Here is how these methods can be implemented:

```
- (void) setAnInt:(int) x
{
        _anInt = x;
}

- (void) setADouble: (double) x
{
        _aDouble = x;
}

- (void) setAString: (NSString*) s
{
        _aString = s;
}
```

Finally, using these setters you can change the code of accessData so that the contents of the aString, anInt, and aDouble keys can be updated to new values:

```
+ (void) accessData
{
        KVSample *sample = [[KVSample alloc] init];

        [sample setValue:@20 forKey:@"anInt"];
        [sample setValue:@44.0 forKey:@"aDouble"];
        [sample setValue:@"another value" forKey:@"aString"];

        NSNumber *a = [sample valueForKey:@"anInt"];
        NSLog(@"int value: %@", a);

        NSNumber *b = [sample valueForKey:@"aDouble"];
        NSLog(@"double value: %@", b);

        NSNumber *c = [sample valueForKey:@"aString"];
        NSLog(@"double value: %@", c);
}
```

Here, you take the sample instance of KVSample and send to it three messages, each message with a value for one of the supported keys for this object.

As you can see from this code, KVC supports keys that store values of all common data types, such as int, double, and NSString. There are other support types as well, such as float, char, and long. Essentially, all native data types are supported by the KVC interfaces. The BOOL type is also supported in two ways. A key for a BOOL type called enabled, for example, can be mapped to either to the getter -(BOOL)isEnabled or to the getter -(BOOL)enabled. If any of these two getter methods are found, they will be used to return the required value. On the other hand, the setter method has to be called setEnabled: in this case.

> **Note**   The Foundation framework defines a way for classes to validate the value passed to
> setValue:forKey:. The validate<key>: method can be added to a KVC-compliant class to determine
> if such an argument is valid. However, the user of a KVC class is responsible for calling validate<key>:
> when necessary. You should check if the class you're using provides parameter validation, and use it as
> defined in the class' interface.

KVC and Properties

While reading the preceding description of the relationship between keys and values, and how they map to getters and setters, you might have noticed a similarity between these concepts and the concept of properties. Although KVC and properties are two independent technologies, they have been designed with complementary features so that they can interact nicely with each other.

The most obvious relationship between properties and the values exposed by KVC-compliant objects is that they use getters and setters, which map very closely to underlying instance variables in the current class. What this means is that by defining properties you can simplify even more the process of creating KVC-compliant classes.

Using this equivalence relationship between properties and key-value pairs, you can rewrite class KVSample with the following, simpler interface:

```
// file: KVSample.h

// sample interface containing three variables
@interface KVSample : NSObject

@property int anInt;

@property double aDouble;

@property (retain) NSString *aString;

- (id) init;

+ (BOOL) accessInstanceVariablesDirectly;

+ (void) accessData;

@end
```

Notice that you now have three properties representing the three instance variables stored in the class. You were able to remove the declaration of instance variables from the interface because they are implicitly created when the compiler processes the property definitions.

You were also able to remove the group of methods acting as getters and setters. These methods are now defined implicitly, since they are synthesized during compilation time along with their corresponding properties. Additionally, these changes make memory management easier, since you can use keywords such as retain or copy to perform the desired memory management policy.

Here is the simplified implementation of the KVSample class:

```
// file: KVSample.m

#import "KVSample.h"

@implementation KVSample

- (id) init
{
        self = [super init];
        if (self)
        {
                self.anInt = 10;
                self.aDouble = 11.0;
                self.aString = @"test";
        }
        return self;
}

+ (void) accessData
{
        KVSample *sample = [[KVSample alloc] init];
        NSNumber *a = [sample valueForKey:@"anInt"];
        NSLog(@"int value: %@", a);
        NSNumber *b = [sample valueForKey:@"aDouble"];
        NSLog(@"double value: %@", b);
        NSNumber *c = [sample valueForKey:@"aString"];
        NSLog(@"double value: %@", c);

        [sample setValue:@20 forKey:@"anInt"];
        [sample setValue:@44.0 forKey:@"aDouble"];
        [sample setValue:@"another value" forKey:@"aString"];
        [sample setValue:@YES forKey:@"enabled"];

        a = [sample valueForKey:@"anInt"];
        NSLog(@"int value: %@", a);
        b = [sample valueForKey:@"aDouble"];
        NSLog(@"double value: %@", b);
        c = [sample valueForKey:@"aString"];
        NSLog(@"double value: %@", c);
}

+ (BOOL) accessInstanceVariablesDirectly
{
        return NO;
}

@end
```

After removing all the setters and getters from the implementation, you get a much cleaner and more maintainable code. You may also want to change the way the properties are accessed, using the more concise dot notation to refer to the data instead of the leading underscore instance variables you have been using.

Using Structures

In the previous sections you learned how to use KVC to expose simple properties, defined with scalar data types such as numbers or strings. In the case of numbers, the values are automatically converted into object wrappers such as NSNumber. Working with structures is similar. You don't need to worry about the process of wrapping the data, however, since the runtime libraries already know how to create the necessary objects for any user-defined structure.

The secret of structured data use with the KVC system is the automatic conversion from structs into NSValue objects performed by the runtime libraries. An NSValue, as its name implies, is an object capable of holding any value, such as numbers, strings, or even structs with user-defined data types. Once data has been stored in an NSValue, it is immutable and can later be converted to the desired target type.

Here is an example class that demonstrates how structures can be used with KVC. First, you need to use typedef to name a user-defined type.

```
// file KVStructSample.h

typedef struct
{
        int anInt;
        double aDouble;
}
SampleStruct;
```

Then, a new class is defined with a single data item of type SampleStruct.

```
// file KVStructSample.h

@interface KVStructSample : NSObject
{
        SampleStruct _structValue;
}

@property SampleStruct structValue;

@end
```

A property of type SampleStruct was added to simplify the implementation, but you could do the same using only instance variables, as you have seen previously. Now, the implementation for the class is responsible for initializing the object. You also have a class method that can create a new instance and display its data.

```
// file KVStructSample.m

@implementation KVStructSample

- (id) init
{
        KVStructSample *obj = [super init];
        if (obj)
        {
                SampleStruct val = { 1, 2.0 };
                obj.structValue = val;
        }
        return obj;
}

+ (void) accessData
{
        KVStructSample *sample = [[KVStructSample alloc] init];
        NSValue *val = [sample valueForKey:@"structValue"];
        SampleStruct structVal;
        [val getValue:&structVal];
        NSLog(@"The value is %d and %lf", structVal.anInt, structVal.aDouble);
        [sample release];
}

@end
```

The first method, init, sets the initial value for the property of type SampleStruct. For this purpose, you need to create a new variable of the given structure type, and copy it to the instance variable structValue.

The accessData method shown here is just an example of how to use such a class. It creates an instance of KVStructSample, then retrieves an NSValue object by sending a valueForKey: message. The NSValue object returned by valueForKey: contains a SampleStruct value. To recover the value, you need to use the getValue: method, which receives as a parameter a pointer to the user-defined structure. Then you can proceed to print the values of the components of the structure, anInt and aDouble, which will be displayed in the logging window as values 1 and 2.0.

Accessing Objects Through Key Paths

Once you are able to access scalar data and structures contained in objects through KVC-compliant keys, the next level of functionality is required: that is, being able to do the same for properties defined with an object type. For example, a Factory object may contain one or more Employee objects. These objects could be made accessible through a KVC-style interface.

To make generic objects available through KVC, the runtime system supports not only the concept of simple keys, which are composed of a single word, but also the idea of composed keys, which are determined using a full path notation. In a path definition, Objective-C uses the dot (.) as a separator between segments of the path so that you can specify all the elements in the containment hierarchy between the base object and the desired property.

Using a key path, the runtime system is able to traverse the list of objects specified by the dot-separated elements. Then, it is possible to retrieve or modify elements based on their key path specification.

To have a better understanding of how this process works, consider the class BankEmployee, which stores information about a single bank employee, including a property called salary. Here is the interface definition:

```
// file BankEmployee.h

@interface BankEmployee : NSObject

@property double salary;

- (id) init ;

// other properties and methods here

@end
```

Only the salary property is displayed here, along with the init method. The implementation of init is similar to what you have seen in other examples.

```
// file BankEmployee.m

#import "BankEmployee.h"

@implementation BankEmployee

- (id) init
{
        self = [super init];
        if (self)
        {
                self.salary = 200000.0;
        }
        return self;
}

@end
```

Notice that, for test purposes, you are initializing the salary property to a constant that will be retrieved later. Now consider using an object of this class as part of a Bank class, with the following interface:

```
// file Bank.h

@interface Bank : NSObject

@property (retain) BankEmployee *employee;
```

```
+ (void) accessBank ;

- (id) init;

@end
```

You have a property in this class as well as in the previous examples, but this time the property is not a native data type or a `struct`; the property is now an object of type `BankEmployee`. You use the `init` function to create a new object of that type, with its default value. The method `accessBank` shows how to access the contents of this object-based property using a key path:

```
// file Bank.m

#import "Bank.h"

@implementation Bank

- (id) init
{
        Bank *obj = [super init];
        if (obj)
        {
                obj.employee = [[BankEmployee alloc] init];
        }
        return obj;
}

+ (void) accessBank
{
        Bank *bank = [[Bank alloc] init];

        id res = [bank valueForKeyPath:@"employee.salary"];
        NSLog(@"The salary is %@", res);
}

// you need to release employee
- (void) dealloc
{
        self.employee = nil;
        [super dealloc];
}

@end
```

Notice the use of the `valueForKeyPath:` method inside the `accessBank` method. You need to pass a dot-separated path relative to the target object in order to access the desired property. The value returned by this message call is an object of type `NSValue`, similar to what you have seen in the previous examples. The result of the `accessBank` method will be that the default salary of `200000.0` is printed to the logging window.

Accessing Collections

Another common situation occurring when working with KVC is that one or more keys correspond to a collection of objects. When this happens, you need to use some of the collection-oriented methods that are capable of interacting with arrays or sets of elements that are created as a result of the request.

The KVC specification provides a way to access members of a collection that are used internally. For example, suppose that you have an array called employees. KVC can access the elements of this array either directly (through the instance variable name), through a property, or using a pair of accessing methods. Let's use the method access way, just to illustrate how this can be done in general. In this case, if you want to expose a property called bankEmployees, you need to provide a property getter called objectInEmployeesAtIndex:. The following modifications in the class Bank would be necessary to provide support for a bankEmployees property through KVC:

```
// file Bank.h

@interface Bank : NSObject
{
        NSArray *employees;
}

- (NSUInteger) countOfBankEmployees;

- (id) objectInBankEmployeesAtIndex:(NSUInteger)index;

+ (void) accessBankData;

- (id) init;

@end
```

First, notice that you have the values stored in an internal NSArray object called employees. The interface to KVC is implemented with the two methods countOfBankEmployees and objectInBankEmployeesAtIndex:. These methods are similar in functionality to the methods count and objectAtIndex: present in the NSArray class. Here is an implementation for this class:

```
@implementation Bank

- (id) init
{
        self = [super init];
        if (self)
        {
                self->employees = @[[[[BankEmployee alloc] init] autorelease]];
        }
        return self;
}
```

```
- (NSUInteger) countOfBankEmployees
{
        return self->employees.count;
}

- (id) objectInBankEmployeesAtIndex:(NSUInteger)index
{
        return self->employees[index];
}

- (void) dealloc
{
        [self->employees release];
        [super dealloc];
}
@end
```

The init method is responsible for setting up the initial contents of the array. I am creating an NSArray with a single element just for demonstration purposes. Then you have the implementation for count and objectIn<key>AtIndex:. Since you have an internal array with the contents you want to publish, the implementation of these methods is trivial. But you don't need to limit yourself to using an array as the underlying implementation. Any collection of objects can be used to store the data for this interface.

Next, you need to release the resources in this class using dealloc, which is similar to what you have seen in other cases. Finally, I will show you how to use Bank with a method class called accessBankData:.

```
+ (void) accessBankData
{
        Bank *bank = [[Bank alloc] init];

        NSArray * res = [bank valueForKeyPath:@"bankEmployees"];
        NSLog(@"The first employee is %@", res[0]);
        [bank release];
}
```

First, use alloc to create a new object. Then you can use valueForKeyPath: to retrieve the bankEmployees array. You can see that an array was returned, even though bankEmployees only exists as a set of methods providing access to that named property. Finally, you are able to print the first element of the array using the modern array notation for NSArray manipulation.

Returning a collection is a useful feature, but that's not the only thing that KVC can do with data collections. A client can request that some operations be applied to a data set and the result of the operation returned as the value for the given key. These special operations become part of the key, in what can be seen as a mini-language for collection manipulation. Here is a quick list of some of the operations that can be applied in a key path.

- ■ @avg: Returns the average value for all the elements contained in the indexed collection.

- ■ @max: Returns the maximum value for a property, across a given collection named in the key path.

- ■ @min: Returns the minimum value for a property, across a given collection named in the key path.

- ■ @sum: Returns the sum of all entries specified by the defined key path, over a given collection name.

Using these properties, you can perform quick calculations based on the content of arrays and sets, which can be useful to simplify certain operations on objects. In all of these operations, the runtime is responsible for collecting the data and running the operation in order to return the desired value, without any intervention by the target class.

For a simple example of using operators as part of the key path, consider the following class method:

```
+ (void) accessBankSalaries
{
        Bank *bank = [[Bank alloc] init];

        id res = [bank valueForKeyPath:@"bankEmployees.@sum.salary"];
        NSLog(@"The total salary amount is %@", res);
        [bank release];
}
```

The class method accessBankSalaries is responsible for computing the total salary paid by the bank. This is performed by the KVC system, receiving as input the full key path along with a @sum operator. When this code is run, the KVC system will look first for the collection, which is provided as the first element of the key path. Then, the operator @sum is applied to the property salary of the preceding path. Finally, the computed quantity is returned as the value associated to the key path.

Responding To Undefined Keys

KVC establishes a mechanism by which clients can make a request for properties that are stored on objects, while using only a generic string key as input. Therefore, the runtime system is effectively being used to decouple callers from classes implementing the requested functionality. Since you are not relying on compilation, all operations involving KVC involve property checks that will be performed only during execution time. Therefore, it is possible that some of these property checks will be unsuccessful and will generate undesired errors.

In this case, thorough testing is the best way to completely avoid problems at runtime. However, in order to mitigate some of the issues caused by incorrect KVC key access, Objective-C has provided an additional method named valueForUndefinedKey:. By implementing this method, classes can enable an effective scheme to handle undefined keys given as input.

A particular implementation of the method valueForUndefinedKey: can be used to supply a value even when a key is not recognized as valid by the KVC system runtime. This way, valueForUndefinedKey: functions as a "last chance" way to return a value requested by users. For example, the next method avoids an error for undefined key and simply returns 0 as the default response:

```
- (id)valueForUndefinedKey:(NSString *)key
{
        return [NSNumber numberWithInt:0];
}
```

KVC and KVO

KVC is a technology that is used in several areas of the Cocoa frameworks. One such area where KVC is heavily used is the key-value observing (KVO) system for data observing and notification, which is employed throughout CoreData, among other examples. KVO is a mechanism by which objects can respond to changes in the value of observed properties. In other words, KVO is a general notification mechanism that relies on KVC to determine how to access keys and their corresponding values.

There are two main elements in a KVO solution: observers and observation targets. To become an observer, you need to call the method addObserver:forKeyPath:options:context: on a suitable target. Then the observer also needs to implement the method observeValueForKeyPath:ofObject:change:context:. This method is called every time a change happens to the observed object. Finally, the client can stop observing an object by calling the removeObserver: method.

To become a KVO target, an object needs to be compliant with KVC as a first step. This means that KVC properties need to be exposed to clients, as discussed in the previous sections. This guarantees that NSObject will able to manage the properties exposed in the object, while at the same time making these properties available for observers. Every time a property in the object changes, subscribed observers will be notified automatically.

Let's see an example of how this works in practice. Suppose that you are creating a BankPayroll class, which uses the BankEmployee class previously discussed. You are interested in knowing when the value of the salary property changes, so that the payroll calculations can be kept up to date. Here is how this can be implemented using KVO:

```
@interface BankPayrool : NSObject
{
        BankEmployee *employee;
        double _currentSalary;
}

- (id) initWithEmployee:(BankEmployee *)anEmployee;

- (void) startObserving;

+ (void) useBankPayroll;

@end
```

You store two instance variables: one for the employee object and another with current salary information. Here is the implementation file:

```objc
@implementation BankPayrool

- (id) initWithEmployee:(BankEmployee *)anEmployee
{
        self = [super init];
        if (self)
        {
                employee = anEmployee;
                [employee retain];
        }
        return self;
}

- (void) dealloc
{
        [employee removeObserver:self forKeyPath:@"salary"];
        [employee release];
        [super dealloc];
}

- (void) startObserving
{
        [employee addObserver:self forKeyPath:@"salary"
                                        options:NSKeyValueObservingOptionNew
                                        context:nil];
}

- (void) observeValueForKeyPath:(NSString *)keyPath
                                        ofObject:(id)object
                                           change:(NSDictionary *)change
                                          context:(void *)context
{
        if (object == employee)
        {
                [self setValue:
                 [change objectForKey:NSKeyValueChangeNewKey]
                                forKey:@"currentSalary"];
                NSLog(@"current salary is now %lf", _currentSalary);
        }
}
@end
```

Finally, you may use the code above by implementing a sample class method, useBankPayroll, which changes the salary property. As a result, you will see a log message showing the new salary value, as received by the BankPayroll class.

```
+ (void) useBankPayroll
{
        BankEmployee *employee = [[BankEmployee alloc] init];
        BankPayrool *payroll = [[BankPayrool alloc] initWithEmployee:employee];

        [payroll startObserving];
        [employee setValue:@300000.0 forKey:@"salary"];
        [payroll release];
        [employee release];
}
```

First, you create the employee object, since it will be used as a parameter for the BankPayroll class. Then you send the startObserving message, which registers the payroll object as an observer of employee. Finally, you set a new value for the property salary on employee. This will trigger a notification to payroll, which will print some information to the logs.

Summary

In this chapter, you explored the key-value coding system in Objective C. KVC is a set of conventions and methods that allow generic data access using only a string key or key path. To access data using KVC, you just need to use the valueForKey: message. You can also modify exposed data using the method setValue:forKey:. This simple interface can be used to interact with native or user-defined (struct) data types. KVC also allows you to interact with embedded objects using key paths, where the full property names are separated using a dot notation.

KVC has provisions to work with collections objects, as well as for single values like integers and strings. For collections, you need to expose either a standard Objective-C collection such as NSArray and NSSet, or implement methods equivalent to count and objectAtIndex:, which are part of NSArray. I didn't cover all the options you may have when supporting collections, but the online documentation for KVC is very readable and has all the details you need.

Finally, I showed you how key-value observing (KVO) interacts with KVC. KVO leverages the KVC system to create a notification mechanism on top of it. In this way, objects may not only access properties exposed through keys, but they can also be notified when there is a change in these properties.

In the next chapter, you will see an important application of the OOP concepts discussed up until now. For this purpose, I will show you how Objective-C supports basic and advanced interaction with the file system using the Foundation framework.

Chapter 10

The File System

One of the highlights of working with Objective-C is the availability of high quality libraries that can be used to access most of the resources provided by the operating system. In this chapter, I will show you some of the classes and methods that are used to interact with external storage files in the Foundation framework.

There are different ways to interface with the file system in Objective-C. First, the Foundation framework has a few methods that can be used for simplified file access, both reading and writing. These methods have been added to classes such as NSString and NSData, and offer a convenient way to access files without having to worry about the lower level details of how they are stored. The internal machinery of objects such as NSString will do all the steps necessary to read or write its data to disk.

On the other hand, there are moments when it is important to have a finer control of how files are accessed. For example, large files may take a long time to access. You can avoid these kinds of large I/O delays by using an asynchronous interface. Offering this level of control is the goal of specialized classes such as NSStream, NSInputStream, and NSOutputStream. They allow programmers to determine the details of file access, such as the size of the internal buffers used to transfer data. It is also possible to hold the data and make it available to external files only when deemed necessary by the application. I will give examples of how these classes work and develop a truly asynchronous solution for data transfer to files.

Specifying Locations with NSURL

To access files in the Foundation framework you frequently need to create a NSURL, which is an object that represents a single URL. A URL (uniform resource locator) is an identifier used by the operating system to locate a particular resource. URLs can be used not only to locate files, but also for remote resources such as web pages or FTP files. You are concerned here only with local resources, however.

A URL for a local file starts with the file:// sequence. Therefore, to access a file located at /Users/user1/file.txt, for example, you should use the URL file:///Users/user1/file.txt.

Most file-related methods in Cocoa use NSURL objects instead of (or in addition to) string-based path names. The reason is that NSURL objects have several advantages when compared to standard paths. First, path names are system-specific. For example, some systems have forward slashes as separators, while others use back slashes or colons as separators. URLs were created to abstract these differences.

Another service that NSURL provides is keeping track of a file once it is accessed. If a file is moved in the file system, for example, the NSURL object can keep referencing it, even though the path has changed.

Finally, URLs are not limited to representing local files. You can use an URL to work with remote files using a number of protocols. While you may need to change your code to handle such remote resources, the representation of the location remains unchanged. That is another reason why Cocoa libraries prefer to deal with NSURLs whenever possible: in this way, there is no need to change the representation when using remote versus local resources.

Reading and Writing Text Files

Once you have a correct location for the file you want to access (most of the time in the form of a NSURL object), the next step is to read or write the contents using one of the Cocoa objects that interact with the file system.

The first object that I will cover in this chapter is NSString. When working with text files, NSString may be the simplest way to interact with the file contents—unless there is some additional structure in the file, such as XML, for instance. Let's see an example of how to read from a text file with NSString using a class called FileReader.

```
// file FileReader.h

@interface FileReader : NSObject

+ (void) readTest;

- (void) readFile:(NSString*) fileName;

@end
```

You have two methods in this class: an instance method called readFile: and a class method called readTest.

```
// file FileReader.m

#import "FileReader.h"

@implementation FileReader

- (void) readFile:(NSString*) fileName
{
        NSURL *url = [NSURL URLWithString:fileName];
```

```
        NSError *error;
        NSString *str = [NSString

                            stringWithContentsOfURL:url
                            encoding:kCFStringEncodingUnicode
                            error:&error];

        NSLog(@"String is %@", str);
}

+ (void) readTest
{
        FileReader *reader = [[FileReader alloc] init];
        [reader readFile:@"file:///Users/oliveira/testFile"];
}

@end
```

The readFile: method operates as follows. First, it creates a NSURL object using the URLWithString: method. Once a URL object has been created, it is used to initialize a string with its content. The stringWithContentsOfURL:encoding:error: is responsible for opening the URL and transferring its contents to the NSString internal buffer. This method requires an encoding type, which determines how the text in the file will be represented. This option varies depending on the type of language used for encoding the text. Finally, the method returns an error object in its last parameter whenever an error condition is generated.

> **Note** NSString also allows the contents to be read from a file path, instead of a URL. Although this is convenient, in most situations you should prefer using an NSURL instead. This will help in maintaining portability and making your program able to use different URL types.

Similarly, NSString can also be used to write data to a text file. The following code shows how a FileWriter class can be implemented:

```
// file FileWriter.h

@interface FileWriter : NSObject

+ (void) writeTest;

- (void) writeFile:(NSString*) fileName content:(NSString*)data;

@end
```

The FileWriter class has a method that is used to write the content data, passed as the second argument, into the file defined by the parameter fileName. A testing procedure is also given in the writeTest class method.

```objc
// file FileWriter.m

#import "FileWriter.h"

@implementation FileWriter

- (void) writeFile:(NSString*) fileName content:(NSString*)data;
{
        NSURL *url = [NSURL URLWithString:fileName];

        NSError *error;
        BOOL res = [data writeToURL:url
                        atomically:NO
                          encoding:NSUnicodeStringEncoding
                             error:&error];
        if (!res)
        {
                NSLog(@"error writing to file %@", [error userInfo]);
        }

}

+ (void) writeTest
{
        FileWriter *writer = [[FileWriter alloc] init];
        [writer writeFile:@"file:///Users/oliveira/testFile2"
                content:@"This is the content of the file written by"
                        " the file writer."];

}

@end
```

You can quickly see that the writeFile:content: method is just a wrapper over NSString functionality. The method writeToURL:atomically:encoding:error: is responsible for taking the text stored in the data variable and writing it to the file at the location determined by the given NSURL object. The parameter atomically determines if the process is performed in an atomic way by the file system. To guarantee atomicity, Cocoa uses a buffer to store data until the whole file has been written, and then renames the file to its destination URL. The encoding parameter is similar to the encoding you saw when reading from a file. Finally, the error parameter is used only when an error condition needs to be reported.

Reading and Writing Binary Data

The examples above show you how to operate with a text file. In these cases, it is easy enough just to use NSString to manipulate the contents of the file and read or write it. However, most applications also need to access files that are in binary format. Examples include compressed files, images, and other proprietary formats that cannot be just modified with a text editor.

To accomplish this for small files, you may just use the counterpart of NSString for binary data: NSData. To simplify the process of manipulating such binary files, Cocoa enabled NSData with methods that can read and write data to disk storage, in the same way that NSString does.

When reading a binary file, you need to be able to provide a buffer where the data will be temporary stored and a way to retrieve the data after it had been read. NSData implements this functionality by default, leaving to programmers only the task of processing the resulting data.

For an example of how this works, you will write a class that reads data and prints a few bytes of it in the log, like so:

```
// file ReadBinaryData.h

@interface ReadBinaryData : NSObject

- (NSData*)readData:(NSString*)fileName;

+ (void) testRead;

@end
```

This interface contains only two methods: readData:, which takes as argument the name of the file that you want to read, and testRead, a class method that tests the functionality in readData:.

```
// file ReadBinaryData.m

#import "ReadBinaryData.h"

@implementation ReadBinaryData

#define MAX_DATA_SIZE 1024

- (NSData*)readData:(NSString*)fileName
{
        NSURL *url = [NSURL URLWithString:fileName];

        NSError *error;
        NSData *data = [NSData dataWithContentsOfURL:url options:NSDataReadingUncached error:&error];

        if (data == nil)
        {
                NSLog(@"error reading file: %@", [error userInfo]);
        }
        else
        {
                int data_size = (int)[data length];

                unichar array[MAX_DATA_SIZE];
                int size = data_size;
                if (data_size > MAX_DATA_SIZE) size = MAX_DATA_SIZE;
```

```
            [data getBytes:array length:size];
            NSString *dataStr = [NSString stringWithCharacters:array length:size];
            NSLog(@"first bytes of data are: %@", dataStr);
        }
        return data;
}

+ (void) testRead
{
        ReadBinaryData *reader = [[ReadBinaryData alloc] init];
        [reader readData:@"file:///Users/oliveira/testFile"];
        [reader release];
}

@end
```

In the first part of the implementation file you define the constant MAX_DATA_SIZE, which is used to determine the maximum amount of characters you would like to display from the file.

The readData: method creates a NSURL object containing the file name, and then uses it as a parameter to the dataWithContentsOfURL:options:error: method. The first parameter to this method is the file URL, followed by an option that determines if the file will be cached or memory-mapped, for instance. The last parameter (error) is a pointer to an NSError object, which is used only in the case in which a failure was detected.

If the data returned by dataWithContentsOfURL:options:error: is valid, you retrieve a small portion of its first part and print it to the logging window. This can be accomplished with getBytes:length:, a method in NSData that returns the stored bytes using an auxiliary memory array whose length is determined by the second parameter. You use a simple array of characters, and you copy only the first characters for testing purposes. In practice, you would need to use one or more iterations to retrieve all the data stored in NSData and do something useful with it.

The testRead method is used to exercise the functionality in ReadBinaryData. You create an object of that class, and then send a readData: message to it with the name of a sample file that you have stored in your home directory as parameter. As a result, part of the file should be printed to the application log.

NSData can also write data to a file, similarly to the way NSString works. To avoid repeating a similar example, let me show just the contents of writeData:, a method that uses NSData to output an array of bytes to a binary file:

```
- (void)writeData:(int*)numbers length:(int)size
                     dest:(NSString*)fileName
{
        NSURL *url = [NSURL URLWithString:fileName];

        NSError *error;
        NSData *data = [NSData dataWithBytes:numbers length:sizeof(int)*size];
        BOOL ok = [data writeToURL:url
                                options:NSDataWritingAtomic
                                    error:&error];
```

```
    if (!ok)
    {
            NSLog(@"error writing to file: %@", [error userInfo]);
    }

}
```

This time you create an NSData object to contain the array of integers that was passed as argument to the writeData:length:dest: method. The length of the data to be stored is determined by sizeof(int)*size, which gives the numbers of bytes necessary to store the data in the array.

The next step is to use the writeToURL:options:error: method from NSData to write the array to disk. This method has an options parameter that can be used to determine how the file will be written to disk. In this case, I requested the file to be written atomically, that is, all the bytes will be written to a temporary file and then moved to the right location when finished. If an error occurs while this method is executed, the error variable will be used to store a message describing what happened.

Using NSStream

Using NSString and NSData to manipulate files is convenient, but it is not a scalable solution. A problem with these simple classes is that the programmer doesn't have much control over the I/O process. But the biggest problem with this model of file access is that NSString and NSData perform synchronous operations: that is, the current thread of the application has to wait until the whole file is processed. This may be acceptable for small files and simple applications, but it doesn't scale when files increase in size or when you need quick response times.

Therefore, in many situations it becomes impractical to use NSString or NSData as a solution for file access. Cocoa provides a better way of controlling file operations through the NSStream class and its relatives. NSStream has better ways to control how a file is accessed, and is able to divide the work in smaller chunks that can be handled by the applications without creating long pauses.

NSStream has a generic interface that is implemented by NSInputStream and NSOutputStream. Both of these classes share the same model for file access, which is based on the use of delegates. Essentially, when using an NSStream you need to define a delegate object that will be called when it is time to perform an I/O operation.

The other interesting aspect of NSStream is that it can be used not only to access files. Its internal model can also be applied to any URL, such as web resources or FTP files. It can also be used to connect directly to network sockets, although this application is beyond the scope of the current chapter. Everything that you are going to learn, however, can be used (with minor changes) to access network sockets used on client/server applications, for example.

Reading Files

To read files with NSStream, you need to set up an NSInputStream, and then establish a delegate that will read data as it becomes available. This kind of interface avoids the problem of large I/O delays by using an asynchronous mechanism that triggers an event only when data is available for consumption.

The first step in using an NSInputStream is to define the object responsible for receiving the events triggered by the data-reading interface. Normally, the event handling code is added to your main delegate object, but you may want instead to create a dedicated class for data handling.

Let's create a class called AsyncDataReader that reads a file using an NSInputStream. The interface for this class has a method to set up the stream and another one to handle the events triggered by the NSStream object.

```
// File AsyncDataReader.h

@interface AsyncDataReader : NSObject <NSStreamDelegate>
{
        NSInputStream *_stream;
        NSMutableData *_data;
}

- (void)setupStream:(NSString*)path;

- (void)stream:(NSStream *)stream handleEvent:(NSStreamEvent)event;

+ (void)testRead;

@end
```

This interface implements the NSStreamDelegate protocol, which is required for objects that want to consume data sent by an NSStream. The class contains two instance variables: an NSInputStream that will be used to read the input file, and an NSMutableData object that will store the contents of the file in memory (NSMutableData is a subclass of NSData that allows adding or removing from its contents). There are three methods in the interface. The setupStream: method is responsible for doing the initial setup of the input stream; it receives a file name as its single parameter. The stream:handleEvent: method is required by the NSStreamDelegate protocol; this is the method called when new data is available for consumption, for example. Finally, a class method called testRead shows how this class can be used.

```
// file AsyncDataReader.m

#import "AsyncDataReader.h"

@implementation AsyncDataReader

- (void) setupStream:(NSString*)fileName
{
        NSURL *url = [NSURL URLWithString:fileName];

        if (_stream == nil)
                _stream = [[NSInputStream alloc] initWithURL:url];
        [_stream setDelegate:self];
        [_stream scheduleInRunLoop:[NSRunLoop currentRunLoop]
                        forMode:NSDefaultRunLoopMode];

        [_stream open];
}
```

This is the first part of the class implementation, where you need to set up the stream for the reading operation. First, you check if the _stream variable is valid, and if not, you use alloc followed by initWithURL: to create the object. The next step is to set the delegate for the NSStream, which in this case is the current AsyncDataReader class.

NSInputStream uses a messaging mechanism to communicate with the delegate object. To achieve this, it is necessary to add the stream object to the run loop of the current thread. This is achieved with the scheduleInRunLoop:forMode: message. To find the current run loop, you can use the currentRunLoop method of the NSRunLoop class. The standard model of operation is then selected with NSDefaultRunLoopMode.

Finally, to start processing the input stream, you need to send the open message to the stream object. This will perform all the initialization steps necessary to open a file and start reading the bytes stored in it.

```
- (void)stream:(NSStream *)stream handleEvent:(NSStreamEvent)event
{
        uint8 bytes[256];
        switch (event)
        {
                case NSStreamEventHasBytesAvailable:
                {
                        if (_data == nil)
                                _data = [[NSMutableData alloc] init];
                        NSInteger len = [(NSInputStream*)stream read:bytes maxLength:256];
                        [_data appendBytes:bytes length:len*sizeof(bytes[0])];
                        NSLog(@"Data received: %ld bytes: ", len);
                        // save data stored in bytes

                }
                        break;
                case NSStreamEventEndEncountered:
                {
                        [_stream close];
                        [_stream removeFromRunLoop:[NSRunLoop currentRunLoop]
                                                            forMode:NSDefaultRunLoopMode];
                        [_stream release];
                        _stream = nil;
                }
                        break;
                default:
                        break;

        }
}
```

The method stream:handleEvent: is the workhorse of this class, since it is responsible for interpreting every message that is delegated by the NSInputStream. There are several types of messages that can be received by the NSStreamDelegate, but you are concerned only with two types: NSStreamEventHasBytesAvailable, which indicates that new data is available for consumption, and NSStreamEventEndEncountered, which is used to signal the end of the stream. These two messages are enough for the most common cases where you just want to read the contents of a file.

In response to the NSStreamEventHasBytesAvailable event, you prepare the _data instance variable to store the received bytes. If _data has not been initialized, you will use the alloc/init pair of messages to create a new NSMutableData object. Next, you need to read the data into an internal buffer, and determine the number of bytes received. This is done by calling the read:maxLength: method. This method will transfer the data stored internally to the bytes array. You need to indicate the maximum length of the buffer, so that the stream will copy only a number of bytes that you can store in the declared buffer.

> **Note**   When setting the number of processed items per event (the size of the buffer in the example above), you have an opportunity to influence the performance of the application. A small buffer will force NSStream to send more messages until the file is completely transferred, which can incur a performance penalty. On the other hand, a buffer that is too large can take a long time to process and can result in delays in your user interface. You should determine the best size for your internal buffer based on some experimentation on what works best for your application.

The next step in the stream:handleEvent: method is to add the data received to the _data object, so that it will be available to other methods when needed. The length of the buffer is determined using the result of the read:maxLength: method. This information is printed to the log, too, for debugging purposes.

The second message handled by stream:handleEvent: is NSStreamEventEndEncountered, which is sent to the delegate object when the stream is closed and has no more data. Each application can define how to respond to this event, but in most cases it is necessary to dispose of the stream object. You need first to close the stream by sending the close message to the _stream instance variable. Then, you need to remove the stream from the message loop. This is accomplished using the removeFromRunLoop:forMode: method. Finally, you can call release on the NSStream object to dispose of its contents. You also set the _stream variable to nil, so it can be later reused without the risk of invoking a released object.

```
- (void) dealloc
{
        [_data release];
        [super dealloc];
}
```

In the dealloc method, you release the _data object that was used to store the bytes transferred from the NSInputStream. By this time, the class should have used the data (although you are not presenting here the methods that make use of _data).

```
+ (void) testRead
{
        AsyncDataReader *reader = [[AsyncDataReader alloc] init];
        [reader setupStream:@"file:///Users/oliveira/testFile"];
}
```

@end

The final part of the implementation section is the testRead method. You create a reader with the standard alloc/init sequence. Then, you send it the setupStream: message, passing as parameter the URL path for the test file that you want to read. As a result of this, the NSInputStream will be created and started. The reader object will receive notifications that indicate important events, such as the availability of data and the end of the stream. You should see messages in the log indicating that the data is being received and read.

Writing to a File with NSOutputStream

Writing to a file using NSOutputStream is similar to reading with an NSInputStream. You still use an event-based strategy to interact with the content of the stream, and subscribe to the event through the use of a delegate that implements the NSStreamDelegate protocol. However, NSOutputStream has its own types of messages that need to be handled by the delegate. The tasks that need to be performed include initializing the stream and sending new data to the stream.

The next code snippet shows the interface for a class that writes data to a file asynchronously using NSOutputStream.

```
// File AsyncDataWriter.h

@interface AsyncDataWriter : NSObject <NSStreamDelegate>
{
        NSOutputStream *_outStream;
        int _position;
}

- (void) setupOutputStream:(NSString*)fileName;

- (void)stream:(NSStream *)stream handleEvent:(NSStreamEvent)event;

- (void)dealloc;

+ (AsyncDataWriter*)testWrite;

@property (retain) NSArray *outData;

@end
```

The class contains a pointer to the NSOuputStream and an integer that determines the current position on the array of output data. There are three instance methods: one sets up the output stream, the next receives messages targeted to the NSStreamDelegate protocol, and the third is a standard dealloc. Finally, you have a testWrite class method that shows how the class can be used.

The setupOutputStream method is responsible for initializing the stream and the data used. I use strings as test data, stored in the outData property. However, it is easy to see how you can do this for any set of data you might have stored in memory.

```
- (void) setupOutputStream:(NSString*)fileName
{
        NSURL *url = [NSURL URLWithString:fileName];
```

```
        if (_outStream == nil)
        {
                _outStream = [[NSOutputStream alloc]
                                        initWithURL:url
                                        append:YES];
                self.outData = @[
                                @"A string\n",
                                @"B values\n",
                                @"C test\n",
                                @"D class\n" ];
                _position = 0;
        }
        [_outStream setDelegate:self];
        [_outStream scheduleInRunLoop:[NSRunLoop currentRunLoop]
                                        forMode:NSDefaultRunLoopMode];

        [_outStream open];
}
```

The initialization on setupOutputStream is performed whenever the variable _outStream is nil. The first step is to create an output stream, loading the URL that was created based on the file name passed as a parameter. Next, you create an array with test data that will be used later to supply the contents to the output file.

You create a releaseStream method that is called whenever the data has been completely transferred to the output file.

```
- (void)releaseStream
{
        [_outStream close];
        [_outStream removeFromRunLoop:[NSRunLoop currentRunLoop]
                                        forMode:NSDefaultRunLoopMode];

        [_outStream release];
        _outStream = nil;
}
```

In this code, you first close the output stream so that no additional data will be accepted for output. Then, you remove the stream from the currentRunLoop; as a result, the delegate object won't receive further event requests for this particular output stream. In sequence, you release the stream and set it to nil, so that it can be later used to write into another file.

Similar to the NSInputStream case, the stream:handleEvent: method is the central piece of the work performed by this class. In this method, you will provide data whenever it has been made available to the application. As a result, the output stream will use the provided data to write to the file named when the stream was created.

```
- (void)stream:(NSStream *)stream handleEvent:(NSStreamEvent)event
{
        char bytes[NUM_ITEMS_IN_ARRAY];
```

```
        switch (event)
        {
                case NSStreamEventHasSpaceAvailable:
                        if (_position < [_outData count])
                        {

                                NSString *element = _outData[_position];
                                [element getCString:bytes
                                                maxLength:NUM_ITEMS_IN_ARRAY
                                                 encoding:NSASCIIStringEncoding];
                                NSLog(@"ss %s %d", bytes, (int)[element length]);
                                [_outStream write:(const uint8_t *)bytes
                                                maxLength:[element length]];
                        }
                        else
                        {
                                [self releaseStream];
                        }
                        position++;
                        break;
                case NSStreamEventEndEncountered:
                        [self releaseStream];
                        break;
                default:
                        break;
        }
}
```

First, you declare a buffer that is used for temporary data transfer. Then, if the event is an NSStreamEventHasSpaceAvailable this means that you need to provide additional data, if any is available. In the code above, you do this by checking if there is a valid position in the outData array, by testing if _position is less than or equal to the number of elements in outData. If there is a valid position, you start getting the corresponding NSString. Then you get a C string (array of characters) out of the NSString using the method getCString:maxLength:encoding:. Once the data has been copied into the bytes array, you send the message write:maxLength: to the _outStream object so that it can transfer the raw data to the output file.

Note   When using the example above, please notice that I employed the constant NUM_ITEMS_IN_ARRAY to simplify the presentation. In practice, you need to be prepared and allocate enough memory to handle data of any size.

If there is no more available data, then you call the releaseStream method, which was described above. When the message received is NSStreamEventEndEncountered, you also release the stream since this indicates that it is not possible to add more data to the output file.

Finally, here is how to use the methods of the class described above:

```
+ (AsyncDataWriter*)testWrite
{
        AsyncDataWriter *writer = [[AsyncDataWriter alloc] init];
        [writer setupOutputStream:@"file:///Users/oliveira/testFile4"];
        return [writer autorelease];
}
```

The `testWrite` method is a class method, which can be called directly to test the behavior of the class. The first step is to create a new instance of `AsyncDataWriter`. Then, you send the `setupOutputStream:` message to the writer. This will set up the stream and try to open it. After that, the stream object will start sending events to the `AsyncDataWriter` object, and as a result it will eventually transfer all the data to the output file.

Although reading or writing data using `NSStream` and its subclasses is not straightforward, it gives the programmer a lot of flexibility. First of all, `NSStream` is adaptable in its purpose: it can be used to read or write to files, network sockets, or in memory buffers. Therefore, the code that you wrote above can be applied in many situations with little change. The other advantage of `NSStream` is its asynchronous behavior. An application that uses `NSStream` will not have any delay caused by data input/output issues, even when working with large files. This is possible because `NSStream` will divide the work into small tasks, and these tasks will be performed as part of the run loop of the application, where all messages (including UI messages) are processed. Therefore, the application will not stop while waiting for completion of these I/O tasks; it will instead continue processing other events in the meantime.

Summary

In this chapter I showed you how to read and write data to files in Objective-C. First, you saw how file paths are represented in the Foundation framework. `NSURL`, being a standard and generic class, is currently the preferred way to encode file paths.

You learned how to read simple files using basic classes available in the Foundation framework. The framework is designed so that common tasks, such as reading a small file, can be performed without much overhead. In fact, it is necessary to call only a single method to read or write a file using the `NSString` interface. Similarly, it is possible to read or write binary files using the `NSData` class, which allows any data format to be stored in memory.

You also learned about the class `NSStream`, along with its concrete implementations `NSInputStream` and `NSOutputStream`. These classes can be used to create an asynchronous interface to the file system. They are also used to communicate with network sockets or other network resources. In this chapter, you have seen the necessary code to read and write data into external files using `NSStream` objects.

With the conclusion of this chapter, you have learned some of the most fundamental techniques used in Objective-C. You now have a good understanding of how object-oriented programming works, and how this style of programming is enabled by the libraries provided with the language. The next chapter summarizes the information you have about the Foundation framework with a reference, covering most of the important classes you will use in a Cocoa-based application.

Reference

The Foundation Framework

In the last few chapters, you learned the basics of the Objective-C language and how to write simple programs using it. In this chapter, I will provide a quick reference on the most common classes used in Objective-C. These classes are contained in the Foundation framework and provide a lot of the groundwork needed to write a complete application.

The first part of the chapter deals with some of the fundamental classes provided by the Foundation framework. These classes, such as NSString and NSValue, are use throughout the system and are the basis upon which everything else is built.

In the second part of the chapter, I give a quick reference on the most common collection classes. These classes are used to store sets of objects, and are manipulated in more complex ways by other classes and algorithms.

Fundamental Classes

The following fundamental classes are used throughout the system and are the basis upon which everything else is built.

NSObject

The NSObject class is the superclass for most other classes in Cocoa. NSObject provides very important services that are used throughout the system, such as allocation, value observation, and method dispatch. In this section, you will find a list of the important methods in this class, and how to interact with them.

- + (void)load: is executed when the class is loaded for the first time. The method is useful for tasks that need to be performed only once in the lifetime of the application.

- + (void)initialize: is called prior to any use of the class. That is, this method runs before the first non-initialize/non-load method is executed, typically at the first object creation. This is unlike the load method, which is called when the class is first loaded into memory.

- ▪ - (id)init: is the default initializer, used generally in an alloc/init sequence.

- ▪ + (id)new: can be used in place of the alloc/init combination.

- ▪ + (id)allocWithZone:(NSZone *)zone; is used to allocate NSObject in a memory area defined by the parameter NSZone, which determines the policy for memory allocation.

- ▪ + (id)alloc; returns a new NSObject using the default NSZone. The object returned is not initialized. Therefore, alloc is frequently used in combination with an init method for the target class. The object returned by alloc is owned by the caller, which should release the object when it is not used.

- ▪ - (void)dealloc; disposes the memory and other resources used by the object. When overridden, this method should always call the version of the superclass to avoid resource leaks in the base classes.

- ▪ - (void)finalize; should be used only when garbage collection is enabled. Its goal is to free any resource used by the object before it is reclaimed by the system. This method is deprecated when using ARC.

- ▪ - (id)copy; returns a new object of the same class as the original object. Similarly to alloc and new, the object returned is owned by the caller, which is now responsible for releasing the object when not in use, to avoid a memory leak.

- ▪ - (id)mutableCopy; returns a mutable copy of the target object. This method is implemented by objects that need to create mutable copies of immutable objects.

- ▪ + (id)copyWithZone:(NSZone *)zone: returns a new object that contains a copy of the target object. Uses the zone parameter as the parameter to allocWithZone:.

- ▪ + (id)mutableCopyWithZone:(NSZone *)zone: returns a copy of the target object that can be later modified. Uses the zone parameter to determine how the object should be allocated, similar to allocWithZone:.

- ▪ + (Class)superclass; returns a class object that identifies that superclass, if the target object is derived from a base case.

- ▪ + (Class)class; returns a class object that identifies the class of the target. The returned object can be later used as the target for class messages. For example, if obj is an object, you can use [[obj class] alloc] to create an uninitialized object of the same class.

- ▪ + (BOOL)instancesRespondToSelector:(SEL)aSelector; returns YES if the target class or one of its superclasses has an implementation for the given selector.

- ▪ + (BOOL)conformsToProtocol:(Protocol *)protocol; returns YES if the target class or one of its superclasses implement the protocol passed as parameter.

- ▪ - (IMP)methodForSelector:(SEL)aSelector; returns the implementation for the given method selector. The IMP value is normally a pointer to a function that is called in response to the given selector.

- + (IMP)instanceMethodForSelector:(SEL)aSelector; returns the implementation for the instance method that corresponds to the given selector (if such an implementation exists). The IMP value can later on be called to execute the selector for a particular object.

- - (void)doesNotRecognizeSelector:(SEL)aSelector; This is a method that can be overridden in subclasses. It is used to determine if the current class does not recognize a selector. A class can return a different value depending on how it wishes to respond to that selector.

- - (id)forwardingTargetForSelector:(SEL)aSelector; overriding this method, you can define a target object for any selector that is not directly handled by the current class.

- - (void)forwardInvocation:(NSInvocation *)anInvocation; forwards the method call represented by the NSInvocation parameter to its appropriate target. This method is normally overridden in classes that need to forward one or more messages to other objects.

- - (NSMethodSignature *)methodSignatureForSelector:(SEL)aSelector; returns the method signature for the given selector. This method is used when it is necessary to determine the parameters or return types for a method at runtime.

- + (NSMethodSignature *)instanceMethodSignatureForSelector:(SEL) aSelector; returns the address of the implementation of the instance method identified by a given selector.

- + (NSString *)description; returns a string used to describe the object. This is usually overridden in classes that need this type of service. You shouldn't rely on the value returned by this method for identification purposes; it is most frequently used for debugging.

- + (BOOL)isSubclassOfClass:(Class)aClass; returns true if the target class is derived from or is the same as the class passed as a parameter. When you feel the need to use this method, first try defining a polymorphic method in your class hierarchy.

NSString

NSString stores an immutable sequence of characters. Most textual data in an Objective-C application is stored as NSString objects. The NSString class provides a rich interface; in fact, many frameworks choose to enrich the NSString interface with additional methods through the use of protocols. Here is a list of the most common methods present in the NSString class:

- - (id)init; is a simple initializer that returns an empty NSString object.

- - (id)initWithCharactersNoCopy:(unichar *)characters length:(NSUInteger) length freeWhenDone:(BOOL)freeBuffer; initializes the string using a pointer to an array of characters, with length defined by the parameter length. The parameter freeBuffer determines if the buffer should be freed after the copy is performed.

- ■ - (id)initWithCharacters:(const unichar *)characters length:(NSUInteger) length; initializes the target NSString object with the characters passed as parameter.

- ■ - (id)initWithUTF8String:(const char *)nullTerminatedCString; initializes the string using the null-terminated C string passed as argument.

- ■ - (id)initWithString:(NSString *)aString; initializes the NSString using another object of the same type.

- ■ - (id)initWithFormat:(NSString *)format, ...; initializes the string using a formatted string. The formatted string follows the same conventions used by the parameters of NSLog, and is an extension of the format used by the printf function in the C standard library. Please refer to the documentation of NSLog for the exact format.

- ■ - (id)initWithFormat:(NSString *)format arguments:(va_list)argList; is similar to the initializer above, but the arguments are passed as a va_list.

- ■ - (id)initWithFormat:(NSString *)format locale:(id)locale, ...; initializes the NSString using a format string. The arguments to the format, however, are interpreted according to the locale object passed as argument.

- ■ - (id)initWithFormat:(NSString *)format locale:(id)locale arguments: (va_list)argList; is similar to the above, but the format arguments are passed as a va_list, instead of directly as a set of values.

- ■ - (id)initWithData:(NSData *)data encoding:(NSStringEncoding)encoding; initializes the NSString object using an NSData object that contains an encoded string. The encoding is determined by the second parameter.

- ■ - (id)initWithBytes:(const void *)bytes length:(NSUInteger)len encoding:(NSStringEncoding)encoding; initializes the NSString using an array of bytes, passed as a pointer. The second parameter determines the length of the array bytes.

- ■ - (id)initWithBytesNoCopy:(void *)bytes length:(NSUInteger)len encoding:(NSStringEncoding)encoding freeWhenDone:(BOOL)freeBuffer; initializes the NSString using an array of bytes, with length determined by the second parameter. The encoding parameter is used to specify the encoding of the data. The last parameter can be used to determine if the buffer will be released at the end of the initialization.

- ■ + (id)string; is a class method that return an NSString object initialized using the init method. It can be used to quickly return a new string. Following the allocation rules of Objective-C, the caller does not own the string returned by this method.

- ■ + (id)stringWithString:(NSString *)string; returns an NSString object, initialized with an existing string.

- ▪ + (id)stringWithCharacters:(const unichar *)characters length:(NSUInteger)length; returns a new NSString object, initialized with the contents of the array pointed by characters. The length of the array is determined by the second parameter.

- ▪ + (id)stringWithUTF8String:(const char *)nullTerminatedCString; returns a new NSString object, initialized with a null-terminated C string.

- ▪ + (id)stringWithFormat:(NSString *)format, ...; returns a new string using a format similar to the one used by NSLog. Check the NSLog documentation for the details of how the format syntax is defined.

- ▪ + (id)localizedStringWithFormat:(NSString *)format, ...; returns a new string object using the format string, similar to the previous method. The format parameters are localized using the current default locale for the user.

- ▪ - (id) initWithCString:(const char *)nullTerminatedCString encoding:(NSStringEncoding)encoding; initializes a string using a null-terminated C character array, which is interpreted according to the encoding passed as the second parameter.

- ▪ + (id)stringWithCString:(const char *)cString encoding:(NSStringEncoding)enc; returns a new string and initializes it with an existing null-terminated array of characters, interpreted according to the encoding passed as a second parameter.

- ▪ - (id)initWithContentsOfURL:(NSURL *)url encoding:(NSStringEncoding)enc error:(NSError **)error; initializes the string using the content of the given URL. For example, this can be used to load the contents of a file or web page. It uses the encoding provided as the second argument. This function may return an error object if a failure occurs.

- ▪ - (id)initWithContentsOfFile:(NSString *)path encoding:(NSStringEncoding)enc error:(NSError **)error; initializes the string with the contents of a file, whose path is determined by the first argument, using the given encoding. This function may also return an error object in case of error.

- ▪ + (id)stringWithContentsOfURL:(NSURL *)url encoding:(NSStringEncoding)enc error:(NSError **)error; returns a new string using the contents of the URL passed in the first parameter, using the given encoding. An error object may be returned in case of failure.

- ▪ + (id)stringWithContentsOfFile:(NSString *)path encoding:(NSStringEncoding)enc error:(NSError **)error; returns a new string initialized with the contents of the file, whose path is given in the first parameter. The file is interpreted using the given encoding. An error object may be returned if a failure occurs.

- ▪ - (id)initWithContentsOfURL:(NSURL *)url usedEncoding:(NSStringEncoding *)enc error:(NSError **)error; initializes the new string using the contents of the given URL object. The contents of the URL are encoded using the second parameter. An error object may be returned on failure.

- ▪ `- (id)initWithContentsOfFile:(NSString *)path usedEncoding:(NSStringEncoding *)enc error:(NSError **)error;` initializes the string object using the contents of the file determined by the `path` parameter. The encoding used is given in the second argument. Finally, an error object may be returned in case of failure.

- ▪ `+ (id)stringWithContentsOfURL:(NSURL *)url usedEncoding:(NSStringEncoding *)enc error:(NSError **)error;` returns a new string, initialized with the contents of the given URL, which may be a local file or a remote resource. The contents are encoded using the second parameter, and an error object may be returned in case of failure.

- ▪ `+ (id)stringWithContentsOfFile:(NSString *)path usedEncoding:(NSStringEncoding *)enc error:(NSError **)error;` returns a new object. The string is initialized with the contents of the file stored in the give path, using the encoding passed as the second argument. An error object may be returned in case of failure.

- ▪ `- (NSString *)stringByAppendingString:(NSString *)aString;` returns a new string object. The target string is concatenated with the argument `aString` and returned as a new object.

- ▪ `- (NSString *)stringByAppendingFormat:(NSString *)format, ...;` returns a new string. The contents of the current target string are concatenated with the formatted string passed as the first argument. The format string may have additional arguments that will be passed to the method.

- ▪ `- (__strong const char *)cStringUsingEncoding:(NSStringEncoding) encoding;` returns a null-terminated array of characters (traditionally known as a C string), using encoding provided as the first parameter. The string is not owned by the caller, and you should copy the string if you intend to use it later.

- ▪ `- (BOOL)getCString:(char *)buffer maxLength:(NSUInteger)maxBufferCount encoding:(NSStringEncoding)encoding;` copies to an array of characters the current contents of the string. The size of the array is passed in the `maxBufferCount` parameter. The encoding used is passed as the third parameter.

- ▪ `- (BOOL)getBytes:(void *)buffer maxLength:(NSUInteger)maxBufferCount usedLength:(NSUInteger *)usedBufferCount encoding:(NSStringEncoding) encoding options:(NSStringEncodingConversionOptions)options range:(NSRange)range remainingRange:(NSRangePointer)leftover;` also copies the contents of the current string into the given array of characters, but it provides more options. Other than the maximum length and the encoding, you can also pass an integer that will be updated with the number of used characters, an options parameter that gives possible ways to interpret the encodings, a given range of characters to be copied, and finally a pointer to a range that will be updated with the remaining range of characters.

- ▪ `- (NSString *)stringByFoldingWithOptions:(NSStringCompareOptions)options locale:(NSLocale *)locale;` returns a new string object with folding options applied. Search options are also applied, as well as the locale in the third parameter.

- - (NSString *)stringByReplacingOccurrencesOfString:(NSString *)target withString:(NSString *)replacement options:(NSStringCompareOptions) options range:(NSRange)searchRange; returns a new string object based on the current string. The new string has occurrences of the given target replaced by the replacement string. You can pass additional options for the replacement, which are of type NSStringCompareOptions. Finally, you can determine the range of replacement using the last parameter.

- - (NSString *)stringByReplacingOccurrencesOfString:(NSString *)target withString:(NSString *)replacement; is a simplified version of the previous method. Returns a new string by replacing any occurrence of target with the replacement string.

- - (NSString *)stringByReplacingCharactersInRange:(NSRange)range withString:(NSString *)replacement; returns a new string based on the current string value, where the range determined in the first parameter is replaced by the replacement string in the second argument.

- - (__strong const char *)UTF8String; return a null-terminated array of characters (a traditional C string) representing the contents of the current string. This method assumes that you're using the UTF8 encoding. The character array returned is not owned by the caller, so you should make a copy of it if you want to use the string later.

- + (NSStringEncoding)defaultCStringEncoding; returns the default encoding for NSString objects. This method can be used as a convenient way to retrieve the current encoding.

- + (const NSStringEncoding *)availableStringEncodings; returns a list of NSString encodings in current use. The sequence of encoding is null-terminated.

- + (NSString *)localizedNameOfStringEncoding:(NSStringEncoding)encoding; returns the localized name of the encoding passed as a parameter.

- - (NSUInteger)length; returns the number of characters in the string.

- - (unichar)characterAtIndex:(NSUInteger)index; returns a single character stored at the location given by index. If the index is invalid, an NSRangeException is generated.

- - (void)getCharacters:(unichar *)buffer range:(NSRange)aRange; copies the sequence of characters determined by range into the given buffer. The method assumes that buffer has enough space to hold all characters in the specified range.

- - (NSString *)substringFromIndex:(NSUInteger)from; returns a new string, initialized with the contents of the current string, starting from the position determined by the first parameter.

- - (NSString *)substringToIndex:(NSUInteger)to; returns a new string, initialized with the contents of the current string, starting from the first character and ending at the index given in the second argument.

■ - (NSString *)substringWithRange:(NSRange)range; returns a new string initialized with the contents of the current string. The substring used is determined by the range parameter.

■ - (NSComparisonResult)compare:(NSString *)string; returns the value of comparing the current string and the string passed as argument.

■ - (NSComparisonResult)compare:(NSString *)string options:(NSStringCompareOptions)mask; returns the value of comparing the current string and the string passed as argument. You can also provide options to determine how the strings should be compared.

■ - (NSComparisonResult)compare:(NSString *)string options:(NSStringCompareOptions)mask range:(NSRange)compareRange; returns the result of comparing a range of the current string and the string passed as argument, using the given comparison options.

■ - (NSComparisonResult)compare:(NSString *)string options:(NSStringCompareOptions)mask range:(NSRange)compareRange locale:(id)locale; compares a given range of the target string with the string passed as the first parameter. This function uses a set of comparison options, and uses the given locale for the comparison.

■ - (NSComparisonResult)caseInsensitiveCompare:(NSString *)string; compares the current string and the string passed as argument using case-insensitive comparison.

■ - (NSComparisonResult)localizedCompare:(NSString *)string; compares the target string and the string passed as argument using the current locale.

■ - (NSComparisonResult)localizedCaseInsensitiveCompare:(NSString *) string; compares the target string and the string passed as the first argument. The comparison is performed using the current locale options.

■ - (NSComparisonResult)localizedStandardCompare:(NSString *)string; compares the target string and the string passed as the first argument. The comparison method used the current locale definitions.

■ - (BOOL)isEqualToString:(NSString *)aString; returns YES when the target string and the argument string have the same content.

■ - (BOOL)hasPrefix:(NSString *)aString; returns YES if the target string starts with the string passed as a parameter.

■ - (BOOL)hasSuffix:(NSString *)aString; returns YES if the target string ends with the string passed as parameter.

■ - (NSRange)rangeOfString:(NSString *)aString; if aString is a substring of the target NSString, then this method returns its location as an NSRange.

■ - (NSRange)rangeOfString:(NSString *)aString options:(NSStringCompareOptions)mask; returns its location as an NSRange if aString is a substring of the target NSString. The comparison is performed according to the options passed as the parameter mask.

- ■ - (NSRange)rangeOfString:(NSString *)aString
options:(NSStringCompareOptions)mask range:(NSRange)searchRange; returns
its location as an NSRange if aString is a substring of the target NSString and
contained in the range searchRange. The comparison is performed according to
the options passed as the parameter mask.

- ■ - (NSRange)rangeOfString:(NSString *)aString
options:(NSStringCompareOptions)mask range:(NSRange)searchRange
locale:(NSLocale *)locale; returns its location as an NSRange if aString is a
substring of the target NSString and contained in the range searchRange. The
comparison is localized using the argument locale.

- ■ - (double)doubleValue; tries to convert the content of the target string into a
double, while skipping initial blank characters.

- ■ - (float)floatValue; tries to convert the content of the target string into a
float, while skipping initial blank characters.

- ■ - (int)intValue; tries to convert the content of the target string into an int,
while skipping initial blank characters.

- ■ - (NSInteger)integerValue; tries to convert the content of the target string into
an NSInteger, while skipping initial blank characters.

- ■ - (long long)longLongValue; tries to convert the content of the target string
into a long long, while skipping initial blank characters

- ■ - (BOOL)boolValue; tries to convert the content of the target string into a BOOL,
while skipping initial blank characters.

- ■ - (NSArray *)componentsSeparatedByString:(NSString *)separator; returns
an array where each element is one of the components of the target string. The
components are determined by the separator passed as a parameter.

- ■ - (NSArray *)componentsSeparatedByCharactersInSet:(NSCharacterSet *)
separator; returns an array where each element is one of the components of
the target string. The components are determined by looking at each of the
members of the set of separators passed as a parameter.

- ■ - (NSString *)commonPrefixWithString:(NSString *)aString
options:(NSStringCompareOptions)mask; returns a new string that
corresponding to the maximum common prefix shared by the target string and
the parameter aString.

- ■ - (NSString *)uppercaseString; returns a new string with the contents of the
current string in uppercase.

- ■ - (NSString *)lowercaseString; returns a new string with the contents of the
target string in lowercase.

- ■ - (NSString *)capitalizedString; returns a new string with the contents of the
target string in capitalized style.

- ▪ - (NSString *)uppercaseStringWithLocale:(NSLocale *)locale; returns a new string with the contents of the target string in uppercase, using the current locale.

- ▪ - (NSString *)lowercaseStringWithLocale:(NSLocale *)locale; returns a new string with the contents of the target string in lowercase, using the current locale.

- ▪ - (NSString *)capitalizedStringWithLocale:(NSLocale *)locale; returns a new string with the contents of the target string in capitalized style, using the current locale.

- ▪ - (NSString *)stringByTrimmingCharactersInSet:(NSCharacterSet *)set; returns a new string based on the contents of the target string. The characters contained in the set passed as a parameter are removed from the resulting NSString.

- ▪ - (NSString *)stringByPaddingToLength:(NSUInteger)newLength withString:(NSString *)padString startingAtIndex:(NSUInteger)padIndex; returns a new string, created by padding the content of the target string with a padding string, passed as the second parameter. The final length of the padded string is given as the argument newLength. You can also determine the index from which the padding will occur.

- ▪ - (void)getLineStart:(NSUInteger *)startPtr end:(NSUInteger *)lineEndPtr contentsEnd:(NSUInteger *)contentsEndPtr forRange:(NSRange)range; returns information about the start and end of the line contained in the range given as the last parameter.

- ▪ - (NSRange)lineRangeForRange:(NSRange)range; returns a range that determines the beginning and ending of the line contained in the original range that was passed as argument to this method.

- ▪ - (void)getParagraphStart:(NSUInteger *)startPtr end:(NSUInteger *)parEndPtr contentsEnd:(NSUInteger *)contentsEndPtr forRange:(NSRange)range; this method is used to calculate the start of a paragraph based on the range that is specified by the range parameter. The information about paragraph beginning and ending positions are saved using the pointers passed as the first three arguments.

- ▪ - (NSRange)paragraphRangeForRange:(NSRange)range; calculates the range of characters containing one or more paragraphs within the input range.

- ▪ - (void)enumerateSubstringsInRange:(NSRange)range options:(NSStringEnumerationOptions)opts usingBlock:(void (^)(NSString *substring, NSRange substringRange, NSRange enclosingRange, BOOL *stop))block; enumerates all substrings of the target string using the block passed as parameter. The block is applied to the range, using the enumeration options determined by the parameter options.

- ▪ - (void)enumerateLinesUsingBlock:(void (^)(NSString *line, BOOL *stop))block; uses the block passed as argument to enumerate each line in the current string, where lines are separated by line break characters.

- - (NSString *)description; returns a short description for the string. This is usually employed only for debugging purposes.

- - (NSUInteger)hash; returns an integer value that can be used as a hash, for example, when inserting the string in a hash table.

- - (BOOL)writeToURL:(NSURL *)url atomically:(BOOL)useAuxiliaryFile encoding:(NSStringEncoding)enc error:(NSError **)error; writes the content of the URL passed as the first parameter. An auxiliary file may be used store the data before it is finally copied to the destination. The given encoding is used and an error object is returned in case of failure.

- - (BOOL)writeToFile:(NSString *)path atomically:(BOOL)useAuxiliaryFile encoding:(NSStringEncoding)enc error:(NSError **)error; writes the content of the current string to a file, whose location is determined by the path parameter. The second parameter determines if an auxiliary file should be used during the writing process. The encoding used is determined by the third parameter. An error object is returned in case of failure.

NSMutableString

The NSMutableString class is a subclass of NSString that allows the modification of its contents. Therefore, all methods available for NSString are valid for NSMutableString, but you can also directly modify the contents of the string without having to create new strings for the intermediate results. This class is used in situations where you want to manipulate the value stored in a given string or create a string that is computed from data collected from two or more sources. Here is a list of its methods worthy of mention:

- - (void)replaceCharactersInRange:(NSRange)range withString:(NSString *)aString; replaces all characters in the specified range with the string passed as the second parameter.

- - (void)insertString:(NSString *)aString atIndex:(NSUInteger)loc; inserts the contents of the string passed as the first argument into the target string, starting from the location specified by parameter loc.

- - (void)deleteCharactersInRange:(NSRange)range; is used to remove a subsequence of characters, as defined by the locations in the range parameter.

- - (void)appendString:(NSString *)aString; augments the current string using the characters contained in the aString argument.

- - (void)appendFormat:(NSString *)format, ...; appends a string to the end of the current string, using the format specifier provided. The format is similar to the one used by NSLog.

- - (void)setString:(NSString *)aString; resets the characters stored in the string using the aString argument.

- - (id)initWithCapacity:(NSUInteger)capacity; initializes the target NSMutableString object using the capacity indicated in the first parameter.

- ■ + (id)stringWithCapacity:(NSUInteger)capacity; is a class method that creates and returns a new string, initialized using the given capacity.

- ■ - (NSUInteger)replaceOccurrencesOfString:(NSString *)target withString:(NSString *)replacement options:(NSStringCompareOptions) options range:(NSRange)searchRange; changes the mutable string by replacing occurrences of the target parameter with the replacement defined by the second parameter.

NSValue

An NSValue provides an abstract interface for objects that function as a wrapper for other data types. NSValue is used as the base for other important classes such as NSNumber and NSData. Here is a list of its main methods:

- ■ - (void)getValue:(void *)value; copies the internal value stored in the NSValue to the given storage area.

- ■ - (const char *)objCType; returns a null-terminated array of characters (a C string) that encodes the type of the data stored in the NSValue. This type description is used by other methods in NSValue.

- ■ - (id)initWithBytes:(const void *)value objCType:(const char *)type; initializes an NSValue with the data passed in the value parameter. This method also sets the type of the data to the argument type. Notice that type should not be generated manually; instead use the @encode keyword to find the string corresponding to an existing type.

- ■ + (NSValue *)valueWithBytes:(const void *)value objCType:(const char *)type; returns a new NSValue object with the data passed by address in the value parameter. This method also sets the type of the data to the argument typ. Notice that type should not be generated manually; instead use the @encode keyword to find the string corresponding to an existing type.

- ■ + (NSValue *)value:(const void *)value withObjCType:(const char *)type; is similar to the method above.

- ■ + (NSValue *)valueWithNonretainedObject:(id)anObject; creates a new NSValue, using anObject as its initial value. The advantage of using this method is that it will not retain the passed object, so this might be useful when used with other containers.

- ■ - (id)nonretainedObjectValue; returns the contained data as an id (which is internally treated as a pointer).

- ■ + (NSValue *)valueWithPointer:(const void *)pointer; creates a new NSValue object using the pointer passed as parameter as the contents. This method is useful if you want to store a pointer in a container.

- ■ - (void *)pointerValue; returns the contained data in the target NSValue object as a pointer.

- ■ - (BOOL)isEqualToValue:(NSValue *)value; returns YES if the target objet is equal to the value passed as an argument. The comparison is performed using the appropriate types for the stored value.

NSNumber

NSNumber is a basic class used to manipulate native numbers. The biggest use case for NSNumber is to store native numeric data types on Objective-C collections. This class acts as a shell for numeric subclasses, and therefore presents a common interface to them all, so that you just need to use a single numeric class.

- ■ - (id)initWithChar:(char)value; initializes the NSNumber using a character.

- ■ - (id)initWithUnsignedChar:(unsigned char)value; initializes the NSNumber using an unsigned char.

- ■ - (id)initWithShort:(short)value; initializes the NSNumber using a short value.

- ■ - (id)initWithUnsignedShort:(unsigned short)value; initializes the NSNumber using an unsigned short value.

- ■ - (id)initWithInt:(int)value; initializes the NSNumber using an int value.

- ■ - (id)initWithUnsignedInt:(unsigned int)value; initializes the NSNumber using an unsigned int value.

- ■ - (id)initWithLong:(long)value; initializes the NSNumber using a long value.

- ■ - (id)initWithUnsignedLong:(unsigned long)value; initializes the NSNumber using an unsigned long value.

- ■ - (id)initWithLongLong:(long long)value; initializes the NSNumber using a long long value.

- ■ - (id)initWithUnsignedLongLong:(unsigned long long)value; initializes the NSNumber using an unsigned long long value.

- ■ - (id)initWithFloat:(float)value; initializes the target NSNumber using a float value.

- ■ - (id)initWithDouble:(double)value; initializes the target NSNumber using a double value.

- ■ - (id)initWithBool:(BOOL)value; initializes the target NSNumber using a BOOL value.

- ■ - (id)initWithInteger:(NSInteger)value ; initializes the target NSNumber using an NSInteger value.

- ■ - (id)initWithUnsignedInteger:(NSUInteger)value ; initializes the target NSNumber using an NSUInteger value.

- ■ + (NSNumber *)numberWithChar:(char)value; returns a new NSNumber object and initializes it using a value of type char.

- ■ + (NSNumber *)numberWithUnsignedChar:(unsigned char)value; returns a new NSNumber object and initializes it using a value of type unsigned char.

- ■ + (NSNumber *)numberWithShort:(short)value; returns a new NSNumber object and initializes it using a value of type short.

- ■ + (NSNumber *)numberWithUnsignedShort:(unsigned short)value; returns a new NSNumber object and initializes it using a value of type unsigned short.

- ■ + (NSNumber *)numberWithInt:(int)value; returns a new NSNumber object and initializes it using a value of type int.

- ■ + (NSNumber *)numberWithUnsignedInt:(unsigned int)value; returns a new NSNumber object and initializes it using a value of type unsigned int.

- ■ + (NSNumber *)numberWithLong:(long)value; returns a new NSNumber object and initializes it using a value of type long.

- ■ + (NSNumber *)numberWithUnsignedLong:(unsigned long)value; returns a new NSNumber object and initializes it using a value of type unsigned long.

- ■ + (NSNumber *)numberWithLongLong:(long long)value; returns a new NSNumber object and initializes it using a value of type long long.

- ■ + (NSNumber *)numberWithUnsignedLongLong:(unsigned long long)value; returns a new NSNumber object and initializes it using a value of type unsigned long long.

- ■ + (NSNumber *)numberWithFloat:(float)value; returns a new NSNumber object and initializes it using a value of type float.

- ■ + (NSNumber *)numberWithDouble:(double)value; returns a new NSNumber object and initializes it using a value of type double.

- ■ + (NSNumber *)numberWithBool:(BOOL)value; returns a new NSNumber object and initializes it using a value of type BOOL.

- ■ + (NSNumber *)numberWithInteger:(NSInteger)value; returns a new NSNumber object and initializes it using a value of type NSInteger.

- ■ + (NSNumber *)numberWithUnsignedInteger:(NSUInteger)value; returns a new NSNumber object and initializes it using a value of type NSUInteger.

- ■ - (char)charValue; returns the char value stored in the target object.

- ■ - (unsigned char)unsignedCharValue; returns the unsigned char value stored in the target object.

- ■ - (short)shortValue; returns the short value stored in the target object.

- ■ - (unsigned short)unsignedShortValue; returns the unsigned short value stored in the target object.

- ■ - (int)intValue; returns the int value stored in the target object.

- - (unsigned int)unsignedIntValue; returns the unsigned int value stored in the target object.

- - (long)longValue; returns the long value stored in the target object.

- - (unsigned long)unsignedLongValue; returns the unsigned long value stored in the target object.

- - (long long)longLongValue; returns the long long value stored in the target object.

- - (unsigned long long)unsignedLongLongValue; returns the unsigned long long value stored in the target object.

- - (float)floatValue; returns the float value stored in the target object.

- - (double)doubleValue; returns the double value stored in the target object.

- - (BOOL)boolValue; returns the bool value stored in the target object.

- - (NSInteger)integerValue; returns the integer value stored in the target object.

- - (NSUInteger)unsignedIntegerValue; returns the unsigned int value stored in the target object.

- - (NSString *)stringValue; returns the NSString value stored in the target object.

- - (NSComparisonResult)compare:(NSNumber *)otherNumber; thie method returns a NSComparisonResult that determines how the target object compares to the given parameter.

- - (BOOL)isEqualToNumber:(NSNumber *)number; returns true if the target object is a number and has the same value as the passed argument.

- - (NSString *)descriptionWithLocale:(id)locale; returns a string describing the object. The string is encoded with the given locale.

NSData

NSData is a generic class that provides an envelope for data of any type. The data may be stored, for example, using a C-style array of bytes. NSData is responsible for maintaining the storage of the data contained in it. It's most important function is to define an OO-based interface that can be used, for example, to pass data to other objects, or to store data in a standard container. Here is a list of the methods implemented by NSData:

- - (NSUInteger)length; returns the length of the NSData object.

- - (const void *)bytes; returns the content stored in the NSData object as a C-style array of bytes.

- - (NSString *)description; returns a short description for the NSData object, usually employed for debugging purposes.

■ - (void)getBytes:(void *)buffer length:(NSUInteger)length; copies the bytes stored internally in the NSData object to the buffer passed as the first argument. The maximum number of bytes to be copied is given by the length argument.

■ - (void)getBytes:(void *)buffer range:(NSRange)range; copies the bytes stored internally in the NSData for the given range in the buffer passed as the first argument.

■ - (BOOL)isEqualToData:(NSData *)other; returns YES if the target NSData object is equal to the given NSData object.

■ - (NSData *)subdataWithRange:(NSRange)range; returns a new NSData object with part of the data stored in the target NSData, determined by the range given as the first parameter.

■ - (BOOL)writeToFile:(NSString *)path atomically:(BOOL)useAuxiliaryFile; writes the contents of the NSData object to a file determined by the path argument. If useAuxiliaryFile is true, a temporary file is used to store the intermediate stages of data transfer.

■ - (BOOL)writeToURL:(NSURL *)url atomically:(BOOL)atomically; writes the contents of the NSData object to a file or network resource determined by the given URL. If useAuxiliaryFile is true, a temporary file is used to store the intermediate stages of data transfer.

■ - (BOOL)writeToFile:(NSString *)path options:(NSDataWritingOptions) writeOptionsMask error:(NSError **)errorPtr; writes the contents of the NSData object to a file determined by the given path. If useAuxiliaryFile is true, a temporary file is used to store the intermediate stages of data transfer. The data writing options are used and an error object is returned in case of failure.

■ - (BOOL)writeToURL:(NSURL *)url options:(NSDataWritingOptions) writeOptionsMask error:(NSError **)errorPtr; writes the contents of the NSData object to a file or network resource determined by the given URL. If useAuxiliaryFile is true, a temporary file is used to store the intermediate stages of data transfer. The data writing options are used and an error object is returned in case of failure.

■ - (NSRange)rangeOfData:(NSData *)dataToFind options:(NSDataSearchOptions)mask range:(NSRange)searchRange; finds the data associated with the given dataToFind in the target NSData using the search options in the mask parameter and in the range determined by searchRange. Returns the range of the data if it is found.

■ + (id)data; creates a new, empty NSData object.

■ + (id)dataWithBytes:(const void *)bytes length:(NSUInteger)length; creates a new NSData object and initializes it with the C-style array of bytes, with size given by length.

- ▪ + (id)dataWithBytesNoCopy:(void *)bytes length:(NSUInteger)length;
  creates a new NSData object and initializes it with the C-style array of bytes, with
  size given by length. The array is not copied by this method.

- ▪ + (id)dataWithBytesNoCopy:(void *)bytes length:(NSUInteger)length
  freeWhenDone:(BOOL)b; creates a new NSData object and initializes it with the
  C-style array of bytes, with size given by length. The last parameter determines
  if the array is released when the object is deallocated.

- ▪ + (id)dataWithContentsOfFile:(NSString *)path
  options:(NSDataReadingOptions)readOptionsMask error:(NSError **)
  errorPtr; creates a new NSData object with the contents of the file in the given
  path. Uses the reading options and returns an error object in case of failure.

- ▪ + (id)dataWithContentsOfURL:(NSURL *)url options:(NSDataReadingOptions)
  readOptionsMask error:(NSError **)errorPtr; creates a new NSData object
  with the contents of the file or network resource in the given URL. Uses the
  reading options and returns an error object in case of failure.

- ▪ + (id)dataWithContentsOfFile:(NSString *)path; creates a new NSData object
  initialized with the contents of the file determined by path.

- ▪ + (id)dataWithContentsOfURL:(NSURL *)url; creates a new NSData object
  initialized with the contents of the file or network resource determined by url.

- ▪ - (id)initWithBytes:(const void *)bytes length:(NSUInteger)length;
  initializes the target NSData object with the C-style array of bytes, with length
  given by the second argument.

- ▪ - (id)initWithBytesNoCopy:(void *)bytes length:(NSUInteger)length;
  initializes the target NSData object with the C-style array of bytes, with length
  given by the second argument.

- ▪ - (id)initWithBytesNoCopy:(void *)bytes length:(NSUInteger)length
  freeWhenDone:(BOOL)b; initializes the target NSData object using a C-style array
  of data, with length determined by the second argument. If the last argument is
  YES, then the array is freed when the data is not used anymore.

- ▪ - (id)initWithContentsOfFile:(NSString *)path
  options:(NSDataReadingOptions)readOptionsMask error:(NSError **)
  errorPtr; initializes the target NSData object using the data stored in the file
  determined by path. Uses the read options, and returns an error object in case
  of failure.

- ▪ - (id)initWithContentsOfURL:(NSURL *)url options:(NSDataReadingOptions)
  readOptionsMask error:(NSError **)errorPtr; initializes the target NSData
  object using the data stored in the file or network resource determined by url.
  Uses the read options, and returns an error object in case of failure.

- ▪ - (id)initWithContentsOfFile:(NSString *)path; initializes the target NSData
  object using the data stored in the file determined by path.

- ■ - (id)initWithContentsOfURL:(NSURL *)url; initializes the target NSData object using the data stored in the file or network resource determined by url.

- ■ - (id)initWithData:(NSData *)data; initializes the target NSData object using the NSData that was passed as argument.

- ■ + (id)dataWithData:(NSData *)data; returns a new NSData object and initialize it using the NSData object that was passed as argument.

NSMutableData

NSMutableData is a subclass of NSData that can be used to modify the data in place. As such, NSMutableData can be used whenever an NSData is needed. Here are the available methods:

- ■ - (void *)mutableBytes; returns a pointer to the data stored in the target object. You can use that pointer to modify the data, as long as you use only the previously allocated size.

- ■ - (void)setLength:(NSUInteger)length; determines the length of the memory buffer used to store data internally.

- ■ - (void)appendBytes:(const void *)bytes length:(NSUInteger)length; appends the data passed as the first parameter to the internal buffer. The data is assumed to have size given by the length parameter.

- ■ - (void)appendData:(NSData *)other; appends the data stored in the NSData object passed as a parameter.

- ■ - (void)increaseLengthBy:(NSUInteger)extraLength; changes the internal data representation so that it will have its size increased by the quantity extraLength.

- ■ - (void)replaceBytesInRange:(NSRange)range withBytes:(const void *) bytes; changes the data stored internally so that the bytes determined by range parameter are substituted by the second argument.

- ■ - (void)resetBytesInRange:(NSRange)range; resets the part of the internal data buffer, as determined by the parameter range. The data in the given range is reset to a zero value.

- ■ - (void)setData:(NSData *)data; resets the internal data buffer so that it will contain the same data as the NSData object passed as argument.

- ■ - (void)replaceBytesInRange:(NSRange)range withBytes:(const void *) replacementBytes length:(NSUInteger)replacementLength; replaces part of the internal buffer stored in the target object with the sequence of bytes pointed by the pointer replacementBytes. The exact part of the internal data is determined by the range parameter. The size of the replacement array is given by the replacementLength parameter.

- ■ + (id)dataWithCapacity:(NSUInteger)aNumItems; creates and returns a new object of type NSMutableData with capacity given by aNumItems.

- + (id)dataWithLength:(NSUInteger)length; creates and returns a new object of type NSMutableData with length given by the length parameter.

- - (id)initWithCapacity:(NSUInteger)capacity; initialize the target object using the given capacity.

- - (id)initWithLength:(NSUInteger)length; initializes the target object using the length parameter.

Collection Classes

The collection classes are responsible for storing objects that can be later retrieved by the application. There are several classes of collections in the Foundation Framework. These classes are classified according to how the data is stored or retrieved. The classes also determine if the collection is mutable or immutable. In the next section you will find the classes most commonly used to maintain collections in Objective-C.

NSArray

NSArray is a very basic class in the Foundation framework. It provides an OO implementation of the concept of a sequential storage collection. Elements are stored in adjacent locations, and can be retrieved using an index-based approach. Here is a list of the instance and class methods provided by NSArray:

- - (NSUInteger)count; returns the number of elements contained in the NSArray object.

- - (id)objectAtIndex:(NSUInteger)index; returns the object stored at the given index.

- - (NSArray *)arrayByAddingObject:(id)anObject; creates a new array by taking the current elements of the target object and adding the object passed as an argument.

- - (NSArray *)arrayByAddingObjectsFromArray:(NSArray *)otherArray; creates a new NSArray using the contents of the target object and adding all the objects in the array in the second parameter.

- - (NSString *)componentsJoinedByString:(NSString *)separator; returns a string created by concatenating all the elements of the target array, with a separator determined by the first parameter.

- - (BOOL)containsObject:(id)anObject; returns true if anObject is contained in the target NSArray.

- - (NSString *)description; returns a brief description of the target object. Normally used for debugging purposes.

- - (NSString *)descriptionWithLocale:(id)locale; returns a short description, using the locale passed as argument.

■ - (NSString *)descriptionWithLocale:(id)locale indent:(NSUInteger)level; returns a short description using the locale from the first parameter, and indents the description by the number of levels as determined by the second argument.

■ - (id)firstObjectCommonWithArray:(NSArray *)otherArray; returns the first object contained in the target array that also occurs in the otherArray.

■ - (void)getObjects:(id __unsafe_unretained [])objects range:(NSRange) range; copies the objects stored in the target array to the C array of ids. You need to pass a range of objects that will be copied.

■ - (NSUInteger)indexOfObject:(id)anObject; returns the index of anObject in the target array, if anObject is found. Otherwise, this method returns NSNotFound.

■ - (NSUInteger)indexOfObject:(id)anObject inRange:(NSRange)range; returns the index of anObject in the target array if anObject is found in the range passed as the second argument. Otherwise, this method returns NSNotFound.

■ - (NSUInteger)indexOfObjectIdenticalTo:(id)anObject; returns the index of anObject in the target array, if anObject is found using a memory address comparison. Otherwise, this method returns NSNotFound.

■ - (NSUInteger)indexOfObjectIdenticalTo:(id)anObject inRange:(NSRange) range; returns the index of the passed object, with an address comparison similar to the one performed by the previous method. The object is searched only on the passed range.

■ - (BOOL)isEqualToArray:(NSArray *)otherArray; returns YES only if the target array has the same elements as otherArray, in the same order.

■ - (id)lastObject; returns the last object stored in the target array.

■ - (NSEnumerator *)objectEnumerator; returns an NSEnumerator object, which can be used for enumerating the target object. With an NSEnumerator object, you can use the nextObject method to successively visit each element of the target array.

■ - (NSEnumerator *)reverseObjectEnumerator; returns an NSEnumerator object for the target array. However, the enumeration runs from the back to the front of the array.

■ - (NSData *)sortedArrayHint; returns a sorting hint that can be used with other sorting methods.

■ - (NSArray *)sortedArrayUsingFunction:(NSInteger (*)(id, id, void *)) comparator context:(void *)context; returns a new sorted NSArray, where the comparison between elements is done by the passed comparison function. The context data is passed to the comparator.

■ - (NSArray *)sortedArrayUsingFunction:(NSInteger (*)(id, id, void *)) comparator context:(void *)context hint:(NSData *)hint; is similar to the previous method, but it also uses a hint that speeds up sorting, as returned by the sortedArrayHint method.

- `- (NSArray *)sortedArrayUsingSelector:(SEL)comparator;` sorts the target NSArray using the selector passed as argument.

- `- (NSArray *)subarrayWithRange:(NSRange)range;` returns a new NSArray object that contains only the range of objects as determined by the parameter range.

- `- (BOOL)writeToFile:(NSString *)path atomically:(BOOL)useAuxiliaryFile;` writes the data stored in the target NSArray to a file determined by path. If the second parameter is YES, then a temporary file is used to store the intermediate stages of the file transfer.

- `- (BOOL)writeToURL:(NSURL *)url atomically:(BOOL)atomically;` writes the data stored in the target NSArray to a file or network resource determined by url. If the second parameter is YES, then a temporary file is used to store the intermediate stages of the file transfer.

- `- (void)makeObjectsPerformSelector:(SEL)aSelector;` calls the selector passed as the first parameter for each object contained in the target NSArray.

- `- (void)makeObjectsPerformSelector:(SEL)aSelector withObject:(id)argument;` calls the selector passed as the first parameter for each object contained in the target NSArray. Each call passes the argument object as parameter to the selector.

- `- (NSArray *)objectsAtIndexes:(NSIndexSet *)indexes;` returns a new NSArray that contains all objects stored in the target NSArray at the given indices.

- `- (id)objectAtIndexedSubscript:(NSUInteger)idx ;` returns a single object stored in the target NSArray at the given index.

- `- (void)enumerateObjectsUsingBlock:(void (^)(id obj, NSUInteger idx, BOOL *stop))block;` calls the block passed as argument for each object of the target NSArray.

- `- (void)enumerateObjectsWithOptions:(NSEnumerationOptions)opts usingBlock:(void (^)(id obj, NSUInteger idx, BOOL *stop))block;` calls the block passed as argument for each object of the target NSArray, using the options determined by opts.

- `- (void)enumerateObjectsAtIndexes:(NSIndexSet *)s options:(NSEnumerationOptions)opts usingBlock:(void (^)(id obj, NSUInteger idx, BOOL *stop))block ;` calls the block passed as argument for each object in the index set contained in the target object, using the options determined by opts.

- `- (NSUInteger)indexOfObjectPassingTest:(BOOL (^)(id obj, NSUInteger idx, BOOL *stop))predicate ;` returns the first object satisfying the predicate block passed as argument.

- `- (NSUInteger)indexOfObjectWithOptions:(NSEnumerationOptions)opts passingTest:(BOOL(^)(id obj, NSUInteger idx, BOOL *stop))predicate;` returns the object satisfying the predicate block passed as argument. The order in which the elements are tested is determined by the opts parameter.

- ▪ - (NSUInteger)indexOfObjectAtIndexes:(NSIndexSet *)s options:(NSEnumerationOptions)opts passingTest:(BOOL (^)(id obj, NSUInteger idx, BOOL *stop))predicate ; returns index of the object satisfying the predicate block passed as argument. The order in which the elements are tested is determined by the opts parameter

- ▪ - (NSIndexSet *)indexesOfObjectsPassingTest:(BOOL (^)(id obj, NSUInteger idx, BOOL *stop))predicate; returns an index set for the objects satisfying the predicate block passed as argument.

- ▪ - (NSIndexSet *)indexesOfObjectsWithOptions:(NSEnumerationOptions)opts passingTest:(BOOL (^)(id obj, NSUInteger idx, BOOL *stop))predicate; returns an index set for the objects satisfying the predicate block passed as argument. The order in which the elements are tested is determined by the opts parameter.

- ▪ - (NSIndexSet *)indexesOfObjectsAtIndexes:(NSIndexSet *)s options:(NSEnumerationOptions)opts passingTest:(BOOL (^)(id obj, NSUInteger idx, BOOL *stop))predicate; returns an index set for the objects satisfying the predicate block passed as argument. Only the objects indicated by the first parameter are used. The order in which the elements are tested is determined by the opts parameter

- ▪ - (NSArray *)sortedArrayUsingComparator:(NSComparator)cmptr; returns a new sorted array using the comparator given as argument.

- ▪ - (NSArray *)sortedArrayWithOptions:(NSSortOptions)opts usingComparator:(NSComparator)cmptr; returns a new sorted array using the comparator given as argument, and using the provided sort options.

- ▪ - (NSUInteger)indexOfObject:(id)obj inSortedRange:(NSRange)r options:(NS BinarySearchingOptions)opts usingComparator:(NSComparator)cmp; returns the index of the given object in the range r of the target NSArray object. The search is performed using the given options and uses the comparator provided as the last argument.

- ▪ + (id)array; returns a new, empty array.

- ▪ + (id)arrayWithObject:(id)anObject; returns a new array with a single object.

- ▪ + (id)arrayWithObjects:(const id [])objects count:(NSUInteger)cnt; returns a new array with a set of objects determined by the C-style array. The number of elements in the array is given by cnt.

- ▪ + (id)arrayWithObjects:(id)firstObj, ...; returns a new NSArray with a set of objects determined by the sequence of arguments to the method. The list of arguments must be terminated with nil.

- ▪ + (id)arrayWithArray:(NSArray *)array; returns a new array initialized using the objects in the given array.

- ▪ - (id)initWithObjects:(const id [])objects count:(NSUInteger)cnt; initializes an NSArray object with the objects in the C-style array passed as the first argument. The number of such objects is determined by cnt.

- - (id)initWithObjects:(id)firstObj, ... ; initializes an NSArray with a set of objects determined by the sequence of arguments to the method. The list of arguments must be terminated with nil.

- - (id)initWithArray:(NSArray *)array; initializes the target NSArray object using an existing NSArray.

- - (id)initWithArray:(NSArray *)array copyItems:(BOOL)flag; initializes the target NSArray using an existing NSArray object. The items are copied only if the flag is YES.

- + (id)arrayWithContentsOfFile:(NSString *)path; creates a new NSArray object using the contents of the file determined by the path parameter.

- + (id)arrayWithContentsOfURL:(NSURL *)url; creates a new NSArray object using the contents of the file or network resource determined by the url parameter.

- - (id)initWithContentsOfFile:(NSString *)path; initializes a NSArray object using the contents of the file determined by the path parameter.

- - (id)initWithContentsOfURL:(NSURL *)url; initializes an NSArray object using the contents of the file or network resource determined by the url parameter.

NSDictionary

An NSDictionary is an associative collection. That is, it provides an association between objects and their corresponding keys. The NSDictionary class gives support to some of the most common operations on such associative collections. Here follows a list of its methods:

- + (id)dictionary; returns a new empty NSDictionary object.

- + (id)dictionaryWithObject:(id)object forKey:(id <NSCopying>)key; returns a new NSDictionary object with a single object set to the given key.

- + (id)dictionaryWithObjects:(const id [])objects forKeys:(const id []) keys count:(NSUInteger)cnt; returns a new NSDictionary object with the given set of objects assigned to the keys in the second parameter. The number of such objects and keys is determined by the parameter cnt.

- + (id)dictionaryWithObjects:(const id [])objects forKeys:(const id <NSCopying> [])keys count:(NSUInteger)cnt; returns a new NSDictionary with the objects and keys given as C-style arrays, with the number of such objects and keys given by the parameter cnt. The key are copied into the container.

- + (id)dictionaryWithObjectsAndKeys:(id)firstObject, ...; returns a new NSDictionary object with the objects and keys determined by the arguments to the method. The list of objects and keys must be ended by nil.

- + (id)dictionaryWithDictionary:(NSDictionary *)dict; returns a new NSDictionary object with the same objects and keys as the parameter dict.

- ■ + (id)dictionaryWithObjects:(NSArray *)objects forKeys:(NSArray *)keys; returns a new NSDictionary object with objects and keys determined by two NSArray objects. The two arrays must have the same number of elements.

- ■ - (id)initWithObjects:(const id [])objects forKeys:(const id [])keys count:(NSUInteger)cnt; initializes a NSDictionary object with the given set of objects assigned to the keys in the second parameter. The number of such objects and keys is determined by the parameter cnt.

- ■ - (id)initWithObjects:(const id [])objects forKeys:(const id <NSCopying> [])keys count:(NSUInteger)cnt; initializes an NSDictionary object with the given set of objects assigned to the keys in the second parameter. The number of such objects and keys is determined by the parameter cnt. The keys are copied, and no changes are made to their initial values.

- ■ - (id)initWithObjectsAndKeys:(id)firstObject, ... ; initializes the target NSDictionary object with a list of objects and their respective keys as supplied in the list of parameters. The list must be terminated by nil.

- ■ - (id)initWithDictionary:(NSDictionary *)otherDictionary; initializes the target NSDictionary object with the contents of another instance of NSDictionary.

- ■ - (id)initWithDictionary:(NSDictionary *)otherDictionary copyItems:(BOOL)flag; initializes the target NSDictionary object with the contents of another instance of NSDictionary. The values contained in otherDictionary are copied and are not retained internally.

- ■ - (id)initWithObjects:(NSArray *)objects forKeys:(NSArray *)keys; initializes the target NSDictionary object with objects and their respective keys. Objects and keys are supplied are two NSArray objects.

- ■ + (id)dictionaryWithContentsOfFile:(NSString *)path; creates a new instance of NSDictionary and initializes it with the contents of the file determined by path.

- ■ + (id)dictionaryWithContentsOfURL:(NSURL *)url; creates a new instance of NSDictionary and initializes it with the contents of the file or network resource identified by the url parameter.

- ■ - (id)initWithContentsOfFile:(NSString *)path; initializes the target NSDictionary using the contents of the file identified by the path parameter.

- ■ - (id)initWithContentsOfURL:(NSURL *)url; initializes the target NSDictionary using the contents of the file or network resource identified by the url parameter.

- ■ - (NSUInteger)count; returns the number of objects stored in the target NSDictionary object.

- ■ - (id)objectForKey:(id)aKey; returns the object that corresponds to the key provided as the first parameter.

- ■ `- (NSEnumerator *)keyEnumerator;` returns an `NSEnumerator` object that can be used to step through the elements of the `NSDictionary`.

- ■ `- (NSArray *)allKeys;` returns a new `NSArray` containing all keys stored in the target `NSDictionary` instance.

- ■ `- (NSArray *)allKeysForObject:(id)anObject;` returns a new `NSArray` containing all keys associated with anObject in the target `NSDictionary`.

- ■ `- (NSArray *)allValues;` returns a new `NSArray` containing all values stored in the target `NSDictionary`.

- ■ `- (NSString *)description;` returns a short description of the `NSDictionary` instance. Usually employed for debugging purposes.

- ■ `- (NSString *)descriptionWithLocale:(id)locale;` returns a short description of `NSDictionary` instance, using the supplied locale.

- ■ `- (NSString *)descriptionWithLocale:(id)locale indent:(NSUInteger)level;` returns a short description of the `NSDictionary` instance, using the supplied locale, and indented by the level indicated in the last argument.

- ■ `- (BOOL)isEqualToDictionary:(NSDictionary *)otherDictionary;` returns YES if the targeted `NSDictionary` has the same objects and keys as the supplied dictionary.

- ■ `- (NSEnumerator *)objectEnumerator;` returns an `NSEnumerator` object, which can be used to step through the elements of the `NSDictionary`.

- ■ `- (NSArray *)objectsForKeys:(NSArray *)keys notFoundMarker:(id)marker;` returns a new `NSArray` that contains all objects that are associated with one of the keys stored in the first argument. A marker is used to indicate that a particular key has no association in the target `NSDictionary`.

- ■ `- (BOOL)writeToFile:(NSString *)path atomically:(BOOL)useAuxiliaryFile;` writes the content of the `NSDictionary` to a file indicated by the path parameter. If the second argument is YES, then a temporary file is used to hold the transferred content until the whole data is stored.

- ■ `- (BOOL)writeToURL:(NSURL *)url atomically:(BOOL)atomically;` writes the content of the `NSDictionary` to a file or network resource indicated by the url parameter. If the second argument is YES, then a temporary file is used to hold the transferred content until the whole data is stored.

- ■ `- (NSArray *)keysSortedByValueUsingSelector:(SEL)comparator;` returns a new `NSArray` containing the set of keys stored in the `NSDictionary`, sorted by value according to the selector passed as argument.

- ■ `- (void)getObjects:(id __unsafe_unretained [])objects andKeys:(id __unsafe_unretained [])keys;` copies the set of objects and keys contained in the `NSDictionary` into the C-style arrays provided as parameters.

- ■ `- (id)objectForKeyedSubscript:(id)key;` returns the object corresponding to the given key in the target `NSDictionary`.

- ■ - (void)enumerateKeysAndObjectsUsingBlock:(void (^)(id key, id obj, BOOL *stop))block; calls the block argument for each key stored in the target NSDictionary.

- ■ - (void)enumerateKeysAndObjectsWithOptions:(NSEnumerationOptions)opts usingBlock:(void (^)(id key, id obj, BOOL *stop))block; calls the block passed as argument for each key stored in the target NSDictionary, using the given enumeration options.

- ■ - (NSArray *)keysSortedByValueUsingComparator:(NSComparator)cmptr; returns a new NSArray containing all the keys stored in the NSDictionary instance, sorted according to the comparator object passed as an argument.

- ■ - (NSArray *)keysSortedByValueWithOptions:(NSSortOptions)opts usingComparator:(NSComparator)cmptr; returns a new array containing all keys stored in the target NSDictionary, sorted according to the given options, and using the comparator object cmptr.

- ■ - (NSSet *)keysOfEntriesPassingTest:(BOOL (^)(id key, id obj, BOOL *stop))predicate; returns a NSSet object containing all the keys stored in the target NSDictionary that pass the test determined by the predicate parameter.

- ■ - (NSSet *)keysOfEntriesWithOptions:(NSEnumerationOptions)opts passingTest:(BOOL (^)(id key, id obj, BOOL *stop))predicate; returns a NSSet object containing all the keys stored in the target NSDictionary that pass the test determined by the predicate parameter. The enumeration is performed according to the enumeration option opts.

NSHashTable

An NSHashTable is a simple collection class where the elements are stored in an array. Each element in the hash table is associated to a hash key. The key is then used to find the exact position where the element will be stored. The following is a list of the methods:

- ■ -(id)initWithOptions:(NSPointerFunctionsOptions)options capacity:(NSUInteger)initialCapacity; initializes the NSHashTable object using the provided options and an initial capacity defined by the second argument.

- ■ - (id)initWithPointerFunctions:(NSPointerFunctions *)functions capacity:(NSUInteger)initialCapacity; initializes the NSHashTable object with a set of pointer functions and defines the initial capacity of the hash table.

- ■ + (id)hashTableWithOptions:(NSPointerFunctionsOptions)options; creates and initializes the NSHashTable object with the options passed as the first argument.

- ■ + (id)hashTableWithWeakObjects; returns a new hash table with weak references to the objects contained in the target object. This method is deprecated and should be substituted by the following method.

- ■ + (id)weakObjectsHashTable; is similar to the previous method, and is the preferred one.

- - (NSPointerFunctions *)pointerFunctions; returns the pointer functions stored in the target NSHashTable object.

- - (NSUInteger)count; returns the number of elements contained in the target NSHashTable object.

- - (id)member:(id)object; determines if the object passed as the first argument is contained in the target NSHashTable. If the answer is YES, then the object is return. Otherwise, the return value is nil.

- - (NSEnumerator *)objectEnumerator; returns an NSEnumerator object, which can be used to step through the elements of the target NSHashTable object.

- - (void)addObject:(id)object; adds a new object to the NSHashTable.

- - (void)removeObject:(id)object; removes the parameter object to the target NSHashTable.

- - (void)removeAllObjects; cleans up the target NSHashTable object by removing all elements stored internally.

- - (NSArray *)allObjects; returns an NSArray that contains all object stored in the NSHashTable.

- - (id)anyObject; returns one of the objects contained in the target NSHashTable. There is no guarantee that the object returned is chosen randomly.

- - (BOOL)containsObject:(id)anObject; returns YES if the object passed as the first argument is contained in the target NSHashTable.

- - (BOOL)intersectsHashTable:(NSHashTable *)other; returns YES if there are elements that are contained both in the target NSHashTable object and in the parameter other.

- - (BOOL)isEqualToHashTable:(NSHashTable *)other; returns YES if other is equal to the target NSHashTable object. That is, the two hash tables must contain the same elements.

- - (BOOL)isSubsetOfHashTable:(NSHashTable *)other; returns YES if the hash table passed as a parameter is a subset of the target NSHashTable. That is, every element contained in other must also be in the target object.

- - (void)intersectHashTable:(NSHashTable *)other; removes any element from the target NSHashTable that is not part of the hash table passed as an argument.

- - (void)unionHashTable:(NSHashTable *)other; includes in the target NSHashTable object any element contained in the hash table passed as an argument that is not already included.

- - (void)minusHashTable:(NSHashTable *)other; removes from the target NSHashTable any element that is included in the other hash table.

- - (NSSet *)setRepresentation; creates a new NSSet object that contains all elements from the target NSHashTable object.

NSSet

An NSSet object represents a simple collection of objects. You should use an NSSet when the main goal is to query for containment in the set. This class also provides other set operations, such as intersection, union, and subset extraction, for example. Here are the methods:

- + (id)set; creates a new, empty NSSet object.

- + (id)setWithObject:(id)object; creates a new NSSet object and initializes it by adding the object passed as parameter.

- + (id)setWithObjects:(const id [])objects count:(NSUInteger)cnt; creates a new NSSet object and initializes it by adding the objects passed as a C-style array. The number of such object is determined by the parameter cnt.

- + (id)setWithObjects:(id)firstObj, ... ; creates a new NSSet object and initializes it by adding the objects as a list of arguments. The list must be terminated by nil.

- + (id)setWithSet:(NSSet *)set; creates a new NSSet object and initializes it by adding all the elements of the set passed as a parameter.

- + (id)setWithArray:(NSArray *)array; creates a new NSSet and initializes it by adding all the elements contained in the NSArray passed as parameter.

- - (id)initWithObjects:(const id [])objects count:(NSUInteger)cnt; initializes a NSSet object by using the elements contained in the C-style array objects. The number of such objects is given by cnt.

- - (id)initWithObjects:(id)firstObj, ... ; initializes a NSSet object by adding the objects given as argument. The list of objects must have nil as the last element.

- - (id)initWithSet:(NSSet *)set; initializes a NSSet object by adding all elements contained in an existing NSSet object.

- - (id)initWithSet:(NSSet *)set copyItems:(BOOL)flag; initializes a NSSet object by adding all the elements contained in an existing NSSet. If the second argument is YES, then the elements are copied, and the original values are not used.

- - (id)initWithArray:(NSArray *)array; initializes a NSSet object by adding all the elements contained in the NSArray passed a parameter.

- - (NSUInteger)count; returns the number of elements stored in the target NSSet object.

- - (id)member:(id)object; returns the parameter object if it is contained in the target NSSet object. Otherwise, this method returns nil.

- - (NSEnumerator *)objectEnumerator; returns an NSEnumerator object, which can be used to step through the objects contained in the target NSSet object.

- - (NSArray *)allObjects; returns a new NSArray containing all the objects stored in the target NSSet object.

- - (id)anyObject; returns any of the objects currently stored in the NSSet. There is no guarantee which element will be returned.

- - (BOOL)containsObject:(id)anObject; returns YES if the target NSSet contains the object passed as a parameter.

- - (NSString *)description; returns a short description for the target NSSet object.

- - (NSString *)descriptionWithLocale:(id)locale; returns a short description for the NSSet object, using the locale specified.

- - (BOOL)intersectsSet:(NSSet *)otherSet; returns YES if the target NSSet has at least one element in common with the given parameter otherSet.

- - (BOOL)isEqualToSet:(NSSet *)otherSet; returns YES if each element of the target NSSet is also contained in otherSet and both sets have the same number of elements.

- - (BOOL)isSubsetOfSet:(NSSet *)otherSet; returns YES if each element of the target NSSet is also an element of the otherSet.

- - (void)makeObjectsPerformSelector:(SEL)aSelector; executes the selector aSelector for all elements of the target NSSet object.

- - (void)makeObjectsPerformSelector:(SEL)aSelector withObject:(id) argument; executes the selector aSelector for all elements of the target NSSet object. The second parameter is passed as an argument to the selector.

- - (NSSet *)setByAddingObject:(id)anObject; creates a new NSSet and initializes it by adding a single object as the anObject parameter.

- - (NSSet *)setByAddingObjectsFromSet:(NSSet *)other; creates a new NSSet and initializes it by adding all objects from the set passed as the first argument.

- - (NSSet *)setByAddingObjectsFromArray:(NSArray *)other; returns a new NSSet and initializes it by adding all members of the NSArray other.

- - (void)enumerateObjectsUsingBlock:(void (^)(id obj, BOOL *stop))block; executes the block passed as argument for all elements of the target NSSet.

- - (void)enumerateObjectsWithOptions:(NSEnumerationOptions)opts usingBlock:(void (^)(id obj, BOOL *stop))block; executes the block for all elements of the target NSSet, using the options passed in the first argument.

- - (NSSet *)objectsPassingTest:(BOOL (^)(id obj, BOOL *stop))predicate; returns a new NSSet object containing all the elements of the target set that pass the test determined by the predicate argument.

- - (NSSet *)objectsWithOptions:(NSEnumerationOptions)opts passingTest:(BOOL (^)(id obj, BOOL *stop))predicate; returns a new NSSet object that contains all the objects in the target NSSet that passed the test determined by the predicate argument. The enumeration of the object is performed according to the options in opts.

Summary

In this chapter, I provided a quick reference for the most important classes contained in the Foundation framework. I limited the exposition to the most commonly used interfaces, so that you can quickly refer to the methods that are contained in these classes.

In the first part of the chapter, I presented a reference for some of the basic classes, such as NSObject, NSString, and NSValue. These classes are the foundation of the services provided by Cocoa. The second part of the chapter is a reference for a few of the most common collection classes, such as NSArray, NSDictionary, and NSSet.

In the next few chapters, I will start covering the tools and the environment available to Objective-C developers. The first thing you will learn about is the Objective-C compiler, along with its most important configurations. I will show you some of the common ways to use the compiler, and how to tweak its options to achieve different levels of performance, logging, or memory use.

Part 3

The Tools

Chapter 12

The Compiler

To use Objective-C effectively, it is important to understand the basic infrastructure of the language. The compiler plays a special role in the software development cycle, since it determines how source code is translated into executable programs. In the Apple environment, two main compilers are employed: gcc, the traditional compiler used by Mac OS X, and the new clang compiler based on LLVM (Lower Level Virtual Machine), which has been developed as an open source project by Apple and others during the last few years.

The compiler is responsible for translating your program into binary instructions that will be directly executed by the CPU. Every source file has to be processed first, but when it comes time to generate code you have some latitude on deciding how the resulting code will be produced. You can influence the code generation process using some of the building settings available either through Xcode or through the command line interface for the compilers.

In this chapter, you will take a look at several options provided by the Objective-C compilers and how to use them to write better code for your target platforms. You'll first consider the compilers available for the Apple platform: GCC, the original open source compiler used by Mac OS X, and LLVM clang, the more modern option that is currently the officially supported compiler on Xcode.

You will then learn about the main building options that can be accessed directly from the Building Settings window in Xcode, including a quick list of the most used compiler and linker-related options. Then I will show you the ways in which you can access the compiler from the command line.

Finally, I will discuss some of the ways in which the Objective-C compiler has evolved over the last few years. First, I will discuss the integration of ARC (Automatic Reference Counting) with existing projects. You will also learn how to use another practical feature of the Objective-C compiler: its integration with existing C++ code.

Using GCC and LLVM Compilers

The Objective-C compilers used in the platforms supported by Apple have evolved continuously over the last few years. Understanding this evolution will help you make an informed decision between the two compilers, and know when one should be used instead of another.

The compiler used by Mac OS X since its inception has been GCC. GCC is an open source compiler for C, C++, and other languages. The fact that it is an open source project with an active community of developers and supporters made a big difference in the choice of the platform. It means that everyone can benefit from improvements introduced by open source enthusiasts all over the world. Moreover, users are not restricted to wait for fixes and updates provided by Apple. Instead, they can find solutions for common problems and perform their own updates if necessary. GCC is the most commonly used open source compiler in the world, which means that it is supported in many different operating systems and processors.

Although the GCC compiler has been used for several years, some of its shortcomings have become a difficult obstacle for the evolution of the Objective-C language. One of the problems is the lack of support for plug-ins, which can be used to perform important tasks other than compilation, such as documentation, diagnostics, and performance measurement. This problem was felt exactly at a moment when Apple was introducing new features to Objective-C such as ARC, an improved literal syntax, and better integration with the Xcode IDE.

To continue the evolution of the language in a cleaner base, Apple decided to support a more modern, but still open source, compiler for Objective-C. The choice was the product of the LLMV clang project, a modern open source compiler that has been developed from the ground up to address many of the shortcomings of GCC.

The LLMV compiler was initially used as an additional option for compilation, but as of this writing, it has become the officially supported compiler for Objective-C in all Apple-supported platforms. Other than the internal advantages of the new code in clang, which is important mostly for developers of the compiler itself, LLVM clang provides much better error messages in general than the older versions of GCC. That alone is a great advantage of using LLVM, since it may become at times difficult to grasp the meaning of a particularly cryptic error message. LLVM usually also provides options that make it easier to fix common errors.

For example, consider the following fragment of code that contains an error and a call to `printf`:

```
// file hello.c

#include <stdio.h>

int main()
{
    printf("Hello %s");
    return 0;
}
```

Here is the message produced by GCC:

```
> gcc hello.c

hello.c: In function 'main':

hello.c:5: warning: too few arguments for format

hello.c:5: warning: too few arguments for format
```

While this messages points out where the problem has been detected, it gives little clue about the exact location where the underlying code is incorrect, other than the line where the error occurs. Here is the same error message returned by clang:

```
> cc hello.c

hello.c:5:19: warning: more '%' conversions than data arguments [-Wformat]

    printf("Hello %s");
                 ~^
1 warning generated.
```

In this case, you see that not only is the error identified, as with GCC, but its location is directly pointed out in a very easy format.

Another advantage of LLVM is its tighter integration with Xcode, made possible by its new internal architecture. For example, by using LLVM, Xcode can more easily extract error information and diagnostics in a format that is simpler to parse and display.

For these reasons, I will consider LLVM as the default compiler in the discussion of compiler features in the next few sections. Notice, however, that most of the current features of Objective-C are accessible for either compiler. However, new technologies such as ARC are made available first on LLVM clang. This is another reason why you should make sure that your code compiles correctly on clang as way to guarantee that it will be supported in the future.

Changing Compiler Options in Xcode

Xcode is an integrated environment that has helpful tools for every phase of the development cycle. In particular, Xcode enables programmers with tools to define the compiler options that are most adequate for the final product they need to deliver. For example, in the Xcode Settings window, it is possible to help the compiler define the necessary parameters for how it is going to produce executable code.

To access the Settings window, click the top-level node in the Project Navigator. This will bring up the Settings Editor. Then, click the project you want to edit, and you will see the list of settings. Click Building Settings at the top of the window to access the building options. Figure 12-1 shows what the Building Settings window looks like for an example project.

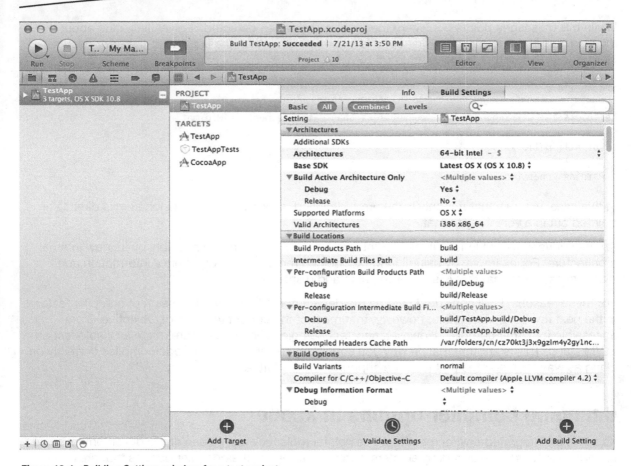

Figure 12-1. Building Settings window for a test project

Here is a list of the most common settings that you can access from the Building Settings window:

- *Architectures*: The Objective-C compiler can generate code for a number of architectures, including 32-bit Intel, 64-bit Intel, and ARM (used on mobile devices). This setting is normally defined automatically when you create a new project, but you may want to change this when creating desktop application, for example, that may work either on 32-bit or 64-bit architectures.

- *Base SDK*: The SDK is the set of Objective-C libraries that together comprise the complete programming environment and API for Mac OS X or iOS applications. Major SDK releases occur one or more times per year. You can decide which SDK to use based on the devices that you want to support. Older devices don't support the latest SDKs, so you need to decide if you want to compromise on features or on wider availability of the code.

- *Supported Platforms*: The two main platforms are Mac OS X and iOS.

- *The Build Locations Settings*: This set of options determines the location for several outputs generated during the building process. For example, you can decide where to put final products, intermediate object files, debugging files, among others.

- *Default Compiler*: You can define here the compiler used, either GCC or LLVM clang. The default nowadays is LLVM, but your code may depend on a feature that exists only in GCC. In this case, you should try to update your code for the medium term so that it will become compatible with the other compiler as well.

- *Precompiled Header Files*: If you set this option to yes, you can define the name of a header file that will be pre-compiled. This option is commonly used to increase the speed of compilation for large projects. When this setting is turned on, the compiler creates a pre-processed representation of the included files, which is then reused throughout the project.

- *Run Static Analyzer*: One of the features of the LLVM clang compiler is the ability to perform syntactic analysis. For example, such analysis can detect memory leaks or areas in which the arithmetic overflow operations may happen. You can run the static analyzer manually by calling it from the Product ➤ Analyze menu (or Shift + Command + B). This option lets you call the static analyzer automatically for each run of the compiler.

- *Validate Built Product*: This is another optional step that can be triggered from the menu, but it can also be called automatically for each compilation run. The product validation checks the outputs of the compiler and the build system, and verifies that they comply with the rules of software distribution for that particular platform.

- *Code Signing Identity*: For builds that require code signing, such as when you're distributing code through the App Store, this step will create the necessary information for code signing. You need to supply a signing identity, which is determined through encryption keys that can be retrieved from the Apple Developer's web site.

- *Deployment Target*: You can change the deployment target for the resulting binaries in such a way that you can choose which operating systems will be able to run the code you generated. Usually this is used to maintain compatibility with particular libraries that you're using in the application as well as with some older devices and CPU models.

Running the Compiler from the Command Line

Depending on your workflow, it may be desirable to run the compiler directly from a command line window instead of using Xcode for development. For example, you may be using an external text editor or programming environment. This is the case if you decide to use vim as the text editor for everything related to Objective-C files, instead of using the Xcode IDE. In these occasions, it is easier to use a command line tool to build the whole project, rather than switching to Xcode just to perform compilations.

Other times, you may want to create a quick app for testing purposes, and that may be easier to do from the command line, if you know the exact steps to follow. Whatever your reasons for accessing the command line, it is just as easy as running Xcode, once you get the right compiler options and build system in place.

There are two ways to use the command line compiler on Mac OS X. The first option is to rely on Xcode for project management and use the command line to trigger the Xcode-controlled build. This method relies on the xcodebuild tool, which is made available when Xcode is installed. The second option is to use your preferred project management tool, such as make, cmake, or scons, and create build scripts that will work independently from Xcode. I will briefly explain these two options.

To use the first method, the Xcode-managed project called from the command line, you just need to call xcodebuild as a command line program and pass to it a few arguments to determine where the project located, as well as other build-time options that can control certain settings on the executable output.

For example, suppose that you have a project called TestProj. The file where such a project would be stored would be called TestProj.xcodeproj. You can call the Xcode building system from the command line using the builder command xcodebuild. This command is responsible for loading the project file where the build information is stored, running the selected target, and calling the compiler and other tools as necessary to build the resulting project. With the TestProj.xcodeproj file, this would work as follows:

```
xcodebuild -project TestProj.xcodeproj
```

Then xcodebuild will build the whole project, emitting messages such as the following, until the project is completely built:

```
CpResource TestProj.sqlite build/Release-macos/TestProj.app/TestProj.sqlite
    cd /Users/coliveira/MacApps/TestProj
    setenv PATH "/Applications/Xcode4.app/Contents/Developer/Platforms/iPhoneOS.platform/Developer/
usr/bin:/Applications/Xcode4.app/Contents/Developer/usr/bin:/Users/coliveira/src/cappuccino/bin:/
Applications/Xcode.app//Contents/Developer/Platforms/iPhoneOS.platform/Developer/usr/bin/:/usr/
texbin:/opt/local/bin/:/sw/bin:/sw/sbin:/usr/bin:/bin:/usr/sbin:/sbin:/usr/local/bin:/usr/X11/bin:/
usr/X11R6/bin:/Users/oliveira/Downloads/plan9/port/bin"

    builtin-copy -exclude .DS_Store -exclude CVS -exclude .svn -exclude .git -exclude .hg -strip-
debug-symbols -strip-tool /Applications/Xcode4.app/Contents/Developer/Toolchains/XcodeDefault.
xctoolchain/usr/bin/strip -resolve-src-symlinks /Users/oliveira/MacApps/TestProj/TestProj.sqlite /
Users/oliveira/MacApps/TestProj/build/Release-macos/TestProj.app
...
```

The xcodebuild command has a number of common options that can be used to tweak the command line build process. For example, you can use the -list option to identify all the schemes, targets, and building configurations.

```
$ xcodebuild -list -project TestProj.xcodeproj

Information about project "TestProj":
    Targets:
        TestProj
```

```
        OptTkUI
        OptTkUITests
        TestProjOrganizer
        TestProjOrganizerTests

    Build Configurations:
        Debug
        Release

    If no build configuration is specified and -scheme is not passed then "Release" is used.

    Schemes:
        TestProj
        TestProjLite
        OptTkUI
        TestProjOrganizer
```

Another option that provides useful information about the system is showsdks, which lists all target sdks installed in your machine.

```
$ xcodebuild -showsdks

OS X SDKs:
        Mac OS X 10.7                    -sdk macosx10.7
        OS X 10.8                       -sdk macosx10.8

iOS SDKs:
        iOS 6.1                         -sdk iphoneos6.1

iOS Simulator SDKs:
        Simulator - iOS 6.1             -sdk iphonesimulator6.1
```

The interesting thing about xcodebuild is that it can perform the same tasks as the internal builder of Xcode. Therefore, it is very easy to transition from an IDE-based workflow to a command line-based one. However, the downside is that it requires that the project was initially created using Xcode. Some developers prefer to avoid it, therefore the next method, an external tool for managing project dependencies, would be more suitable for them.

Dependency management tools such as make are used to keep track of the dependencies between artifacts in an application. When a source artifact changes, the outputs that depend on that source file will be rebuild as needed.

Since the project dependencies in a typical Mac OS X UI application are complex, make is more frequently used for console-based applications. A simple example would be a console application called hello, composed of three Objective-C files: main.m, Hello.h, and Hello.m. Here is a simple make file that could be used to build this project:

```
# file Makefile
#
TARGET = hello

OBJ = Hello.o main.o
```

```
all: build

main.o: main.m Hello.h
        cc -o main.o main.m

Hello.o: Hello.m Hello.h
        cc -o Hello.o Hello.m

build: $(OBJ)
        cc $(OBJ) -o $(TARGET)

clean:
        rm -f *.o $(TARGET)
```

This project has only one main file (main.m) and a class (Hello). The makefile describes how each file depends on the others. Thus, the build depends on the object files stored in the $(OBJ) variable. The object files are built from the source files main.m and Hello.m. Each dependency line is composed of the name of the target file followed by a colon and the list of dependencies. Therefore, for example, the main.o object file depends on Hello.h. Similarly, Hello.o depends on Hello.h. This means that when Hello.h is changed, make will rebuild the targets that depend on it, such as Hello.o and main.o.

The command to rebuild a target is listed after the dependency list, started by a tab character. For example, to rebuild Hello.o, the command used is

```
cc -o Hello.o Hello.m
```

Using makefiles may be easier when you are creating simple projects, but it can quickly become hard to track all the dependencies in a project. Therefore, makefiles are used with Objective-C only when the code is designed to work in multiple platforms and is mixing other languages that are not supported directly by Xcode. You should refer to the documentation of make in the Apple developer's library if that is the case.

Code Optimization

One of the main reasons to use compilation options to change the behavior of the Objective-C compiler is when you are trying to achieve some optimization goal. For example, you may want to optimize the compiled code to achieve maximum speed. Or you may be more interested in creating compact executables that occupy less space in a mobile platform, for example. The options in this section can be used to drive these two different ways of performing code optimization.

Speed Optimization

The primary method to optimize Objective-C is using one of the -O settings. The -O settings (the O means "optimize") are used to define the level of optimization you need. The setting is generally followed by a number, which determines how much optimization is performed at that particular level.

The lowest level of optimization is -O0, which means no optimization at all. This is used primarily when you want to disable optimizations in your code, mainly for debugging purposes, or to determine a baseline for performance measurement.

The first level of meaningful optimization is -O1. You can apply this level if you desire some speed optimization but you don't want to bother to run the full set of optimization levels available for that particular platform. The next level of optimization, -O2, adds some additional improvements that can make your code even faster. On the other hand, adding more optimizations can make your build run a little slower than normal.

The -O3 level is the most aggressive, and it also requires the most time to run. Use this level if you need high performance code and you don't care much about the time it takes to get a full build. This is usually used when creating a release version of your project. You can also have an -O4 level, which adds not only compilation optimization, but also linking-time optimizations that consider all object files as they are linked.

Space Optimization

Another useful optimization target on Objective-C is to minimize the space used by the whole application. This option has become popular in the last few years as applications have become larger and as, at the same time, they are required to run on very small devices such as the iPhone and the iPod touch.

With space optimization, you tell the compiler to generate code that occupies minimum space, instead of reducing execution speed. This is necessary because sometimes space optimization may come at the expense of speed optimization. For example, the compiler may at times generate faster code by adding some repeated sections of code. A well-known case of this is loop-unrolling optimizations, which increase the size of code to speed up loops at runtime. On the other hand, as a result of reducing the amount of code generated in the executable, it may be necessary to spend more time during execution.

The main way to optimize space on Objective-C compilers is to use the -Os option. This option performs optimization steps that try to reduce the resulting size of the target code. This option will also take precedence whenever there are conflicts, such as other options to improve performance in ways that can increase the size of the executable binaries.

ARC Support

ARC is a technology that allows Objective-C programmers to write code without the use of explicit reference counting mechanisms such as `retain` and `release`. The main goal of ARC is to free programmers from an activity that may result in common mistakes that are difficult to debug and fix. This happens because, while it is not hard to learn the rules of memory management under Objective-C, it is possible to make allocation mistakes that can cause memory leaks, heap corruption, or even crashes.

Trying to solve some of these memory management issues, Apple has introduced ARC as a feature of the LLVM compiler. With ARC, the compiler can analyze how objects are used in an Objective-C application and determine where they should be retained or released. It works automatically in the great majority of cases, and requires only a few hints on memory usage in cases such as circular references.

In this section, I cover only the compiler options used to support ARC in Objective-C. For an introduction to ARC and how it can be used to simplify memory management in Objective-C applications, please refer to Chapter 8 for further information.

This first thing necessary to use ARC is to make sure that you're using the LLVM compiler instead of GCC. It is possible that ARC may become available in GCC in the future, but currently this is a technology implemented on LLVM clang only. To determine which compiler is used, select the Building Options window. To find it, click the target in the left panel (this is the top-level element of the Project Navigator) and click the project name. The Project Settings will be displayed, and you can select from one of the two options at the top of the window: Info and Building Settings. Click the Building Settings option. The Settings window will appear, as shown in Figure 12-2.

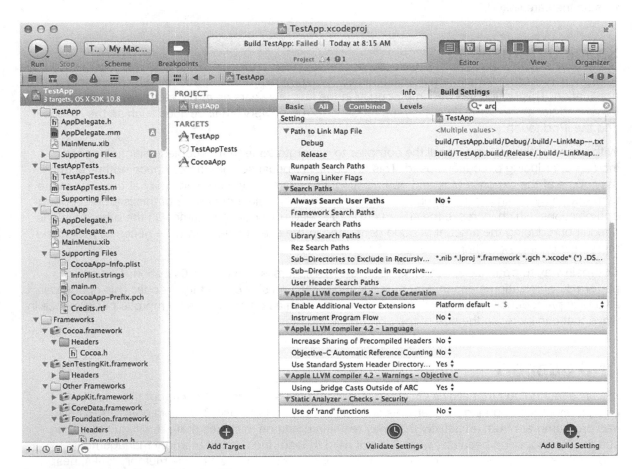

Figure 12-2. Project Settings window for ARC properties

The first thing is to select, in the Build Options section, the option "compiler for C/C++/Objective-C." Then, in the drop-down, select "default compiler (Apple LLVM compiler 4.2)."

The Project Settings window contains ARC options in the section "Apple LLVM compiler 4.2 – Language." The option desired is the "Objective-C Automatic Reference Counting." By setting that value to Yes, you will have ARC enabled on your project. To use ARC, you also need to make sure that `retain` and `release` are not used, along with other issues discussed in Chapter 8.

Compiling Objective-C++

As you have seen in the previous chapters, Objective-C is a proper superset of the C programming language, and both languages can be mixed without any problem. In particular, every function and expression created in C can also be interpreted as valid Objective-C code.

Due to the fact that Objective-C was designed to avoid conflicts with the C programming language, a useful property of it is that you can also easily mix Objective-C with C++ code without major problems. The result of the combination of Objective-C code with C++ is sometimes described as Objective-C++, but there is effective no difference from the point of view of Objective-C programmers. Anything that is specific to Objective-C remains the same when Objective-C and C++ are mixed. The only difference is that now you can use C++ constructs in addition to C.

Objective-C++ programming can be easily enabled using Xcode. The compiled language in Xcode is largely defined by the extension of the source file. For example, files with the .m extension are processed as Objective-C files, while .c files are processed as plain C files. To be able to mix C++ and Objective-C, you just need to create files with the extension .mm instead of .m. Xcode will use this extension as an indication that the file contains C++ code and will provide the correct options to the compiler so that C++ and Objective-C may be fully recognized as part of the build.

The following code is a simple example of mixed C++ and Objective-C code. While explaining how C++ works is completely outside the scope of this book, you can easily see the combination of non-C features such as class definitions with the creation and use of Objective-C objects.

```
class Logger
{
public:
        void addLog(NSString *s);
};

void Logger::addLog(NSString *s)
{
        NSLog(@"here is my message: %@", s);
}
```

This code defines a C++ class called `Logger`, and is responsible for sending string messages to the console. You may notice that the `addLog`, despite being a C++ member function, accepts a parameter of type `NSString`, which is an Objective-C object.

Next, you can use this class from inside of a normal Objective-C method as follows:

```
- (void) createCppObj
{
        Logger logger;
        logger.addLog(@"my message");
}
```

The logger object is declared as having type Logger, which is a C++ class. You can call methods in logger just as you would do in a normal C++ source file.

Finally, the next example shows how to create a C++ class that contains Objective-C objects as member variables. This code describes a type of collection class where you can add elements and check the size of the collection.

```
class MyCollection
{
public:
        MyCollection();
        ~MyCollection();
        void add(id obj);
        int size();
private:
        NSMutableArray *array;
};
```

The first part is the definition of the C++ class. There are four public member functions and one private member variable of type NSMutableArray. They are defined as follows:

```
MyCollection::MyCollection()
{
        array = [[NSMutableArray alloc] init];
}

MyCollection::~MyCollection()
{
        [array release];
}

void MyCollection::add(id obj)
{
        [array addObject:obj];
}

int MyCollection::size()
{
        return (int)[array count];
}
```

The first method is called the constructor and it is called automatically when the object is created. This method will allocate and initialize a new Objective-C object of type NSMutableArray. The object is stored in the array member variable (similar to an instance variable).

The second method is a destructor, and it runs when the object is destroyed. When this happens, you want to release the array object to avoid a memory leak.

The next two objects implement the add and size operations. They are just thin wrappers around the corresponding functionality provided in the NSMutableArray class.

This class can be used as shown:

```
- (void) useMyCollection
{
        MyCollection * c = new MyCollection;
        c->add(@"test 1");
        c->add(@"test 2");
        NSLog(@"the size is %d", c->size());
        // This will print "the size is 2"
}
```

> **Note**   Objective-C with C++ constructs frequently provide the same features using a different syntax. For this reason, I don't recommend that you mix the two languages, unless you know very well what you want to achieve with them. Most frequently, programmers mix Objective-C and C++ to be able to access libraries in both languages. Even in that case, try to evaluate your project and see if there are other alternatives to using both languages in the same code base.

Summary

In this chapter, you learned about the Objective-C compiler, the most important tool for software development for Mac OS X and iOS. The compiler is responsible for reading your source code and translating it into executable code, normally stored in a format that can be directly run by the processor.

The current compiler for the Objective-C language, LLVM clang, has a number of options that affect the qualities of the resulting output. Attributes such as the speed of the binary code, its size, or the inclusion of debugging information are defined by options passed to the compiler during the compilation process. It is important that, as an Objective-C developer, you become familiar with the options that affect the result of programs in the C and Objective-C languages.

A feature of the Objective-C compiler is that it is able to recognize not only plain-C and Objective-C syntax, but also C++ as well. This means that you can mix code using both languages to take advantage of the best features of both. Xcode can be used to generate correct results when you create files with the .mm extension.

While the compiler is a very important tool for programming development, in the Objective-C world it doesn't generates its output without the help of other tools. An important tool that is closely associated with the Objective-C compiler is the preprocessor. The preprocessor runs in an initial phase that prepares the source to be seen and processed by the compiler. While these days the preprocessor is rarely used as a separate program, it is still useful to understand the rules of how it works and performs the initial code preparation. This is the main topic of the next chapter, where you will learn about the features of the Objective-C preprocessor.

The Preprocessor

Objective-C comes with a powerful preprocessor that can simplify the input of repetitive code into a program. For example, the preprocessor can be used to import header files, which are used to make class definitions available to other parts of the application. The preprocessor is also used to define macros, which can work both as constants or to perform simple substitution based on arguments.

Despite all its functionality, however, the preprocessor may be the source of numerous programming pitfalls if you are not careful with its usage. Due to the fact that the substitutions performed in the preprocessing stag are not immediately checked by the compiler, there is the possibility of introducing faulty code by means of subtle interactions between the elements introduced by the preprocessor.

In this chapter, I present the main features of the preprocessor and show you how to avoid some of its rough edges. You will first learn in detail how the preprocessor works and the additional tools it makes available to Objective-C programmers. In the first section, I will explain how macros work and how they can be used to define new symbols and parameter-based substitutions. You will also learn about some common pitfalls of macros and how to avoid them. Next, you will see the facilities available in Objective-C for including header files. Handling file inclusion is one of the most important tasks performed by the preprocessor, and you will see how it is performed, as well as the options you have to control the process.

Defining Macros

One of the important tasks of the preprocessor is to define symbolic names for values commonly used in a program. For example, suppose that you have an algorithm that processes file paths, and in a particular platform the file path has a limit of 255 characters. This can be represented with the help of a new macro, like so:

```
#define MAX_PATH_LENGTH 255
```

The syntax is composed of just the #define and a macro name, followed by whatever symbol or expression you want to use (you will see later what to do when the expression is longer than a single line). The macro definition mechanism in the Objective-C preprocessor is based on literal substitution. This means that whenever the preprocessor sees the defined symbol, it performs the substitution with the value that was supplied during definition, like so:

```
- (BOOL)checkPathSize:(NSString *)path
{
        if ([path length] > MAX_PATH_LENGTH )
        {
                NSLog(@"Error: the path length is invalid");
                return NO;

        }
        return YES;
}
```

As used in the example above, macro names behave like variables, but there are some important differences. First, the substitution happens even before the code is compiled. That is, the compiler itself never sees the symbol MAX_PATH_LENGTH, only the resulting substitution. Thus, there is no memory associated with a macro symbol, unlike variables, which are usually stored in memory, and you can manipulate their memory content using operators such as &.

Another consequence of the way macros are processed is that they can do more than substitute for constant values. For example, while not recommended, the following kind of code is valid (and has even been used by some programmers in the old days):

```
#define BEGIN {
#define END }

void myFunction(int val)
BEGIN
        if (val > 0)
        BEGIN
                NSLog(@"value is positive");
        END

END
```

This is possible because the processor blindly performs macro substitutions, and the compiler will only deal with the result of these substitutions after they are completed.

To avoid surprises when dealing with macro substitutions, C and Objective-C have a convention saying that macros should be named in uppercase, so as to distinguish them from normal symbols. This may not solve all the problems that can be generated by macros, but at least it can alert the programmer that you're dealing with a preprocessed symbol instead of a normal variable.

Macros with Parameters

Another feature of macros is that they can also take parameters, with a syntax that is similar to function calls. To declare a macro that receives two parameters and returns the largest one, for example, you can use the following code:

```
#define MAXIMUM(a, b)    (a) > (b) ? (a) : (b)
```

This says that the macro MAXIMUM has two parameters, and its substitution value comes after the declaration. Using the ternary operator, the macro checks the two values passed as parameters. When the first value is greater than the second, it is returned; otherwise the macro returns the second value.

The general syntax for macros with parameters is a macro name right after the #define directive, followed by the parameters between parentheses. Unlike functions, the parameters are not typed, so you can enter anything you want as arguments, including variables, keywords, or operators, for instance.

The body of the macro follows right after the list of parameters. You can use any expression in the body. Unlike a function, a macro is not compiled the first time it is seen. The macro's body is only used when it is needed for a substitution. When that happens, the preprocessor will make the parameter replacements and paste the result at the location of the occurrence. Only after this process occurs will the compiler have a chance of checking the contents of the macro.

Macros cannot be split into multiple lines as functions can. However, the preprocessor recognizes the backslash character (\) as a line continuation mark. Therefore, you can enter multiline macros, as long as each line that needs to be joined to the next is terminated by a backslash. For example, using the rule for joining adjacent lines, the previous macro can also be written as

```
#define MAXIMUM(a, b)  \
   (a) > (b) ? \
        (a) : \
        (b)
```

Notice how each line is terminated by a backslash, except for the last line, which indicates the end of the macro.

Macro Operators

Another peculiarity of macros is that they provide their own operators, which can perform useful transformations when used on parameterized macros. These operators are supplied as a way of simplifying common tasks that are often needed when putting macro substitutions together.

The first operator is the string conversion transformation, also known as stringify because it converts any value or expression passed as a parameter into a C-style null terminated string.

The string conversion operator uses a leading # character to indicate that the following macro parameter will be converted into a string. Here is an example:

```
#define EXP_TRUE(expr) \
  if (expr) \
    NSLog(@"the following expression is true: %s", #expr)
```

This macro can be used to determine if an expression evaluates to a true value. It does this by simply using an if statement where the test argument is used as the expression itself. If such an expression evaluates to true, then the logging statement is called and the stringify operator will convert whatever expression was passed as a parameter into a string, which will then be sent to the logging terminal.

You can pass to this macro any expression that evaluates to YES or NO. For example, consider the following function:

```
- (void) useMacro
{
        EXP_TRUE(2 + 3 > 4);
}
```

Here, the expression used by the preprocessor is composed of the whole contents between parentheses. The preprocessor will find the macro name EXP_TRUE, substitute the required parameter with the expression passed as argument, and paste the result into the same location in the output source file. Then, when the expression #expr is seen by the preprocessor, it triggers a transformation into a null-terminated string. The result of the macro processing is therefore the following:

```
- (void) useMacro
{
        if (2 + 3 > 4)
                NSLog(@"the following expression is true: %s", "2 + 3 > 4");
}
```

As you can see, the ability of the preprocessor to convert generic expressions into strings can be very useful for debugging purposes. For example, a commonly used standard macro is assert; contained in the header file assert.h, it determines if a given expression is true. If not, then the program stops and a message is printed saying that the assertion failed. The assert macro is very useful to diagnose exceptional conditions as soon as they happen.

```
- (double)squareRoot:(double) x
{
        assert(x > 0);
        // perform calculations here
}
```

This code checks that x is a positive number before doing anything else. If the parameter is incorrect, the program will stop immediately.

Another operator that is less frequently used is the concatenation operator (##). This operator is used when you provide two symbols, and its goal is to create a new symbol that is the concatenation of them. The main use of the concatenation operator is to create unique names, which are sometimes necessary when working with complex macros. Here is a simple example of its usage:

```
#define VARIABLE_NAME(partA, partB) \
  partA ## _ ## partB
```

This macro just pastes together the two parameters, separated by an underscore, into a new symbol. The macro can then be used as follows:

```
- (void)useMacroConcatenation
{

        int VARIABLE_NAME(my, variable) = 10;
        NSLog(@"the value is %d", my_variable);
}
```

Notice that, in the first line, the VARIABLE_NAME macro creates a new variable name that is composed of two parts. These parts are named as partA and partB in the macro definition. In this sample application, the result is the variable name defined as the first part, followed by an underscore, and concatenated to a second part. You can clearly see that this happened as desired when the composite name is used in the next line as argument to NSLog, which will print the value 10, as currently stored in the variable.

Similar to the #define directive, the preprocessor also provides #undef, which is capable of removing the definition of a macro from memory. This is useful when you want to guarantee that a macro is not in use in a particular segment of the code. Another use case would be to redefine the value of an existing macro, such as after executing the following line through the preprocessor:

```
#undef VARIABLE_NAME
```

You can now be sure that the symbol VARIABLE_NAME is free, and it can be defined in a different way if needed.

Common Pitfalls

Using macros with parameters may be a fast and useful mechanism in some situations, but you should be warned against using it frequently. Here are a few reasons.

First, it is difficult to diagnose compilation problems with macros. Since the whole body of the macro is substituted before proper compilation starts, there is no way for the compiler to accurately tell what is going on. When a compilation error occurs inside a macro substitution, you will usually see only a reference to the line, with an actual error that has little to do with the contents of that line. Modern compiler may improve on this issue, but diagnostics are still more difficult to perform on macros than in normal code.

Debugging macros is also a difficult task, in part because of the compilation issues described above. This gives you limited options when working with a debugger, for example, since it is not possible to find the exact line in a macro where something is going wrong. A possible way to at least partially solve this issue is to generate a preprocessed file and verify its output. You can do this in Xcode by going to the menu Product ➤ Generate Output ➤ Generate Preprocessed file. The resulting file is usually very large because it includes all header files imported via the #include or #import directives. But it may be useful to locate the exact transformations introduced by the preprocessor.

A related issue is that a macro can manipulate its parameters in a way that doesn't result in valid C or Objective-C code. For example, consider the MAXIMUM macro presented above and the code that is substituted when you use it in the following way:

```
- (void)useMacro
{
        int i = 10;
        NSLog(@"the maximum is %d", MAXIMUM(11, i++));
}
```

The problem with this code is that the macro MAXIMUM is using the argument i++ in two places of its definition. While the natural response for the value of MAXIMUM with the arguments displayed above should be 11, the reality is that the operation i++ is evaluated twice. This means that, in this case, the printed result will be different from the expected. In other situations, not only can this happen but also the results may even become undefined, causing bugs that are difficult to fix.

> **Note**   As you can see in the previous example, macros increase the risk that their arguments will be evaluated incorrectly. While it is possible to avoid some of these problems by creating temporary variables, for example, the best strategy is to avoid using macros whenever possible. If necessary, avoid passing expression as macro arguments, unless they have been designed for this purpose.

Conditional Compilation

Another important use of macros is to define conditional compilation statements, which will be processed by the compiler only when some compile-time condition is true. These conditional operations are different from normal conditionals such as the if statement because they operate even before the compiler starts its work.

The #if Directive

For instance, the #if directive can be used to define sections of code that will be processed only when a particular compile-time condition is true. Usually, the condition involves a simple arithmetic comparison, and the following lines of code are passed to the compiler only if the condition evaluates to true. All such lines are included until the next #endif directive is found. Here is an example:

```
- (int) getSupportLevel
{
#if VERSION > 5
        return 2;
#endif
```

```
#if VERSION >= 2 && VERSION <= 5
        return 1;
#endif

#if VERSION < 2
        return 0;
#endif
}
```

In this method, the level of support in the application is defined based on the value of the VERSION macro. The tests occur during compilation time, and only one of the options will ever be true. As a result, one of the support levels (0, 1, or 2) will be returned by the method getSupportLevel.

The #if directive can also be followed by an #elif directive. By analogy with #if, the #elif directive is similar to an else if statement, but evaluated at compile time. Finally, the #if or #elif directives can also be followed by an #else directive, which includes the lines that should be compiled only when the previous tests are false. Considering these additional directives, you can more clearly write the previous example using #elif and #else:

```
- (int) getSupportLevel
{
#if VERSION > 5
        return 2;
#elif VERSION >= 2 && VERSION <= 5
        return 1;
#else
        return 0;
#endif
}
```

The #ifdef Directive

In other cases, the condition that you want to test for compilation may involve the definition of other existing macros. This is commonly the case when a macro is used to signify the presence of a particular feature. For example, the GCC compiler predefines the macro __GNUC__ so that you can detect when a program is being compiled by GCC. Other compilers and compiler features have similarly defined macros that can be used for conditional compilation.

You can write code that will be compiled only when a particular macro is defined by using the #ifdef and #ifndef directives. The first one is similar to an #if, but it checks only if the symbol entered directly after has been defined in the current file. Similarly, the #ifndef looks at the macro symbol following it and will execute the next lines if the symbol has not been defined. Here is an example:

```
- (void) detectGCCCompiler
{
#ifdef __GCC__
        NSLog(@"This is the GCC compiler");
#endif

#ifndef __GCC__
        NSLog(@"This is not the GCC compiler");
#endif
}
```

Another way to test if a symbol has been defined is by using the defined macro operator. This operator is useful when you want to create more complicated tests.

```
- (BOOL) systemIsSupported
{
#if defined(__GCC__) && VERSION > 3
        return YES;
#else
        return NO;
#endif
}
```

> **Note**   To define a preprocessor symbol you have at least two options: use a #define directive to introduce the macro, or use the –D option in the GCC (or LLVM) compiler. For example, using –DIS_DEBUG_VERSION will define the macro symbol IS_DEBUG_VERSION. Xcode also allows a preprocessor symbol to be defined in its project settings screen, but this is later translated into a –D option to the compiler.

The Import Mechanism

One of the main uses of the preprocessor is to insert the necessary definitions for elements employed by a particular source file. For example, you have learned that when creating a class you should have a header file with the class interface definition (with extension .h) and an implementation file with method implementations for that class. The header for a class needs to be imported into an implementation file whenever the class is used.

There are two ways to import header files into an implementation file. The first way is to use the #include mechanism. The #include directive is present in both C and Objective-C. It provides the basic functionality of inserting the contents of the referred files into the current source file. Thus, you can benefit from the several libraries available in the Objective-C standard library, as well as from external libraries.

The #include mechanism is used primarily in C libraries because it is the only available with the C (and C++) language, and it requires additional work for defining new header files. To use #include, you just need to say which header file you need to access, like so:

```
#include <stdio.h>
```

This will import the contents of the standard I/O C library into you program. Using this library, you can call functions such as printf (printing facility) or fopen (open a file).

Defining files that can be #included into a file requires a little more preparation. Here is the standard organization of a header file that is imported using #include:

```
#ifndef INCLUDED_MYFILE
#define INCLUDED_MYFILE

// file contents here

#endif
```

Here, INCLUDED_MYFILE is a unique identifier that is used only in this header file. At first this structure may seem unnatural, but its main goal is to avoid processing the same header multiple times for the same source file. For this purpose, each header file has its own unique symbol that is defined at the top. Usually the name of the macro symbol is derived from the file name. Thus, if the file is called Employee.h, the inclusion macro might be named INCLUDED_EMPLOYEE_H.

The result of this schema is simple to interpret: first, check if the unique symbol has been defined. If not, first define the symbol, and then compile the contents of the header file. If the symbol is already defined, however, this means that it is the not the first time the preprocessor has visited the current file. Therefore, the contents of the header file will be skipped, avoiding multiple inclusions.

The second way to include files is unique to Objective-C, and it is implemented with the #import directive. The main difference between #import and #include is the fact that the first one will automatically take care of multiple inclusions, and therefore won't need the conditional macro inclusion scheme explained above.

With #import, the preprocessor has an internal database, so that it already knows which files have been previously processed. This technique guarantees that a file will be processed only once. As a result, you don't need to use conditional compilation tricks, such as the one explained above.

The #import and #include directives can have files specified in two ways: the file name can be enclosed in angle brackets or in double quotes. The difference between these two methods of defining the imported file is the way the file name will be searched. When you use angle brackets, the implicit assumption is that the preprocessor will search on all system include directories. These directories can be determined by a combination of system settings. For example, you can get them listed in the Xcode include path configuration tool. Or you can have such directories added to the GCC/LLVM command line interface with the -I option.

On the other hand, you can use double quotes to delimiter the header file name. In that case, the implicit indication is that the preprocessor will search on the current directory for any file with the specified name. Therefore, the double quoted version can be used to input you own header files, which will compose the list of classes on your own project.

In general, double quoted header names imply that the header is user-created. Similarly, header names delimited by angle brackets indicate that the file is part of the system or some other external library. It is important to maintain consistency in the use of these two options, so that you can avoid mistakes by always importing the correct header file.

Best Practices for Header Files

Given the necessary and widespread use of header files in Objective-C, one needs to follow a few conventions to maintain a basic system organization and avoid performance problems. These best practices are sometimes not necessary for simple projects, but become increasingly important when the size of the project grows, and especially when there are many developers working in the same application.

The first rule that should be followed is to include only class and function definitions in header files. Including the implementation of methods or functions in a header file is not a valid practice, because most header files are designed to be included in more than one place in the system. Having the same function definition occur twice in different files may cause a linking error, since the linker doesn't know which version of your function or method should be maintained.

Another rule of thumb is to avoid nested inclusion of header files whenever possible. The reason is that, because the preprocessor will perform file inclusions recursively, having too many header files included inside the main header file will force an increase in compilation time for every client of that class. In other words, in an include file, only add the bare minimum that will allow the class interface to be defined.

It is clear that it is sometimes necessary to transitively include a header file; for example, when declaring a subclass of an existing class, you need to include the header file for the parent class so that its definition can be seen by the compiler. However, in other situations, it is possible to avoid the direct inclusion of header files and, as result, reduce the complexity of the application.

There are a few ways to avoid including additional header files. For example, you can use the @class keyword in Objective-C to introduce a class name whenever that class is to be used as part of a class interface. In a class interface definition, this is generally all you need, unless you require access to the data or methods in a class. Here is a common example:

```
// file MyInternalClass.h

@class MyExternalClass;

@interface MyInternalClass : NSObject
{
        MyExternalClass *externalObject;
}

-(MyExternalClass*) getExtObject;

@end
```

Notice that MyExternalClass is used here only as part of the interface for MyInternalClass. In this case, you don't really need to use an #import directive; just the @class declaration is enough to tell the compiler what kind of symbol is MyExternalClass. From that point on, MyExternalClass is recorded by the compiler as the name of a class, which can be used, for example, to define a instance variable or as a parameter for other methods. Later on, you will need to import the header file for MyExternalClass, but only when you're ready to write the method implementations.

```
// file MyInternalClass.m

#import "MyExtenalClass.h"

@implementation MyInternalClass

- (MyExternalClass*) getExtObject
{
        // implementation here ...
}

@end
```

Another option that you have to minimize the transitive inclusion of other files is the creation of minimal headers, where exactly one class is defined and not much else. In particular, external dependencies are avoided in the interface and moved to the implementation section. The goal of this technique is to avoid external dependencies as much as possible by adding only the interfaces and functions that you really need in the class interface.

For example, suppose that you are creating a new class that uses three other library header files. Instead of creating a header that includes references to the three other libraries, you can just define a small interface that doesn't have external dependencies. To help with avoiding dependencies, you can create an anonymous protocol that contains all the properties you need in terms of dependencies to external libraries. Then, in the implementation file, you are free to import the head files for each library you're using. Such a judicious separation of interface and implementation will facilitate the importing and utilization of your class by other clients. A side effect of this kind of judicious use is a project that is easier to maintain and faster to build.

Summary

Preprocessing is the first task that is performed on a source file as it is prepared to become an input to the compiler. As such, this is an important operation that needs to be mastered in order to get the most from the Objective-C programming environment.

The preprocessor does a number of transformations based the symbols that have been defined using the #define facility, for example. These macros can be used for simple substitutions, both with and without parameters. Parameterless macros act just like a compile-time constant. On the other hand, macros with parameters are able of much more sophisticated substitutions. You have seen some of the common pitfalls of employing macros, and why you should avoid their extensive use when there are other available options.

The preprocessor is also able to perform conditional compilation based on compile-time expressions that can be evaluated to determine if a block of code will be compiled or not. This kind of conditional compilation is normally used for compatibility reasons, and can be used, for example, to create applications that are able to run in multiple platforms.

Finally, you have seen another important task performed by the preprocessor: including header files for externally defined classes and functions. Such header files contain interface or function definitions that can be made readily available to other clients. The include mechanism can be implemented using either the #include or #import directives, and you have seen the advantages and disadvantages of each of these options.

Using the knowledge you acquired about the compiler and the preprocessor, you will start looking at some common programming tasks that can be performed by employing the features of Objective-C. In the next chapter, you will learn how to use these language facilities to create unit tests. You will see that Objective-C and the Cocoa framework provide outstanding support to test-driven development through their libraries as well as through the Xcode IDE.

Chapter 14

Unit Testing

Unit tests are the basis of a programming strategy that promotes the creation of individual checks for each feature implemented in an application. Unit tests can also be created to verify that a piece of code complies with some particular requirement. For example, if you are creating a method that adds two numbers, a unit test can be written to verify that the response is correct for some particular cases. Although you cannot prove that a piece of code works by just testing for specific values, running unit tests can improve your confidence that the code is indeed returning results that comply with your requirements.

Another use for unit tests and associated tools is in what is called test-driven development (TDD). TDD is a software methodology that requires that every feature of a program be thoroughly specified using unit tests even before it is written. That is, with TDD, programmers use new tests to drive the development of code, which will ultimately satisfy the requirements of the written tests.

Unit test-based development is a great way to explore the modularity of object-oriented languages such as Objective-C. In fact, unit test frameworks became popular in part due to the ability of OOP to create well-defined interfaces, with objects that have few dependencies on external code.

Testing frameworks such as OCUnit leverage these OOP features in order to make unit testing available to programmers using Objective-C. In this chapter, I provide an overview of the support for unit testing in Objective-C using OCUnit and Xcode. You will learn how to quickly create unit tests in new or existing projects. You will also learn how to manage and run sets of unit tests using the Xcode IDE. Finally, you will see an example of how to employ TDD programming strategies to write code in Objective-C.

Unit Test Frameworks

Conscientious programmers have always strived to create tests that could be used to exercise the functionality they are implementing. Therefore, testing methodologies have predated the development of OOP languages, and have always played an important role in the creation of high quality code. However, OOP languages such as Objective-C provide an indispensable tool to make effective unit testing easier to accomplish. At the same time, the features of OOP have contributed to the creation of a common interface for unit testing, which can be leveraged by programmers working across teams or companies.

The most influential OOP-based testing framework is SUnit, a unit-testing library created in Smalltalk. While Smalltalk popularity as a programming language has declined during the last decade, many of its original ideas, such as a solid runtime support for message-based polymorphism, have remained strong. These ideas have even been included in other mainstream languages such as Objective-C, JavaScript, and Ruby. The influence of Smalltalk also extends to unit testing technology such as SUnit, which is still nowadays used almost verbatim by these newer languages. Thus, Java has JUnit, while Objective-C has OCUnit, a library that follows a very similar design approach and interface as the one introduced by Smalltalk with SUnit.

In this chapter, I discuss the features of OCUnit that are used to support the creation and execution of unit tests. I will concentrate the discussion on OCUnit mainly because it is a de-facto standard in the Objective-C world. One of the main reasons for this status is the support from Apple, as the official testing library deployed along with Xcode. The IDE allows programmers to add testing targets based on OCUnit, as well as run tests and display the results as part of the Log Navigation panel. For all these reasons, OCUnit is currently the natural choice for the implementation of unit tests in Objective-C.

Note   Remember that OCUnit is not the only testing framework that can be used with Objective-C. In fact, there are other testing frameworks written in Objective-C that have been made available as open source. It is also appropriate to employ frameworks written directly in the C, such as CUnit. The fitness of a particular testing framework depends much more on the needs of the project itself rather than on the requirements of the language. For example, in some large projects, the amount of code written in Objective-C is small compared to other C and/or C++ legacy code. This is a situation where it could be more convenient to use a C or C++-based testing tool.

Adding Unit Test Targets

I assume in this chapter that you are using Xcode to create and build your project. Adding unit testing through command line tools is possible, but it is highly dependent on the building tool you're using and is usually not supported by Apple. That's why in this chapter I only describe the procedure for creating unit tests using Xcode.

Xcode projects can be divided into a number of targets, which are used to organize the various outputs that can result from a single project. A target within a project is generally an executable, depending on the platform and environment that you want to support. A unit test target allows you to create a separate executable whose purpose is to run test cases against production code. In this way, you can neatly separate code that is specific to the application from code that is used only to test the application.

Moreover, Xcode supports two kinds of test targets, each one linked to a particular kind of tests. A *logical test* is one in which you are interested in testing only the correctness of a particular method or class in isolation. For this kind of test, Xcode only needs to be able to find the code for the tested methods and include it in the executable of the unit test target.

A second kind of unit test is an *application test*. These tests are run not in complete isolation, but in the context of an application. For example, they can be used to determine if the buttons in a particular window have the correct labels. Or you can use them to verify that a certain value will be updated when a menu option is clicked. Because of their own nature, application tests depend on the platform in which they are set up and on the toolkit used for that particular environment.

> **Note** Due to the environment-specific features that are inherent to application tests, in this chapter I will consider only logical tests, as they are valid in any platform that is supported by Objective-C (and they may work even in non-Apple environments). If you intend to use application-specific unit tests, just check the programming manual for your target environment. Apple provides that information along with Xcode for both Mac OS X and iOS targets.

There are two ways to add unit tests to your code. The first, and simplest one, is adding a testing target when creating the project. The New ➤ Project menu option will let you create a new application from one of several project types. If you select OS X Application, and then Cocoa Application, you will be presented with the window displayed in Figure 14-1. Make sure you click the "Include Unit Tests" options, and Xcode will generate the new project with an associated unit test target.

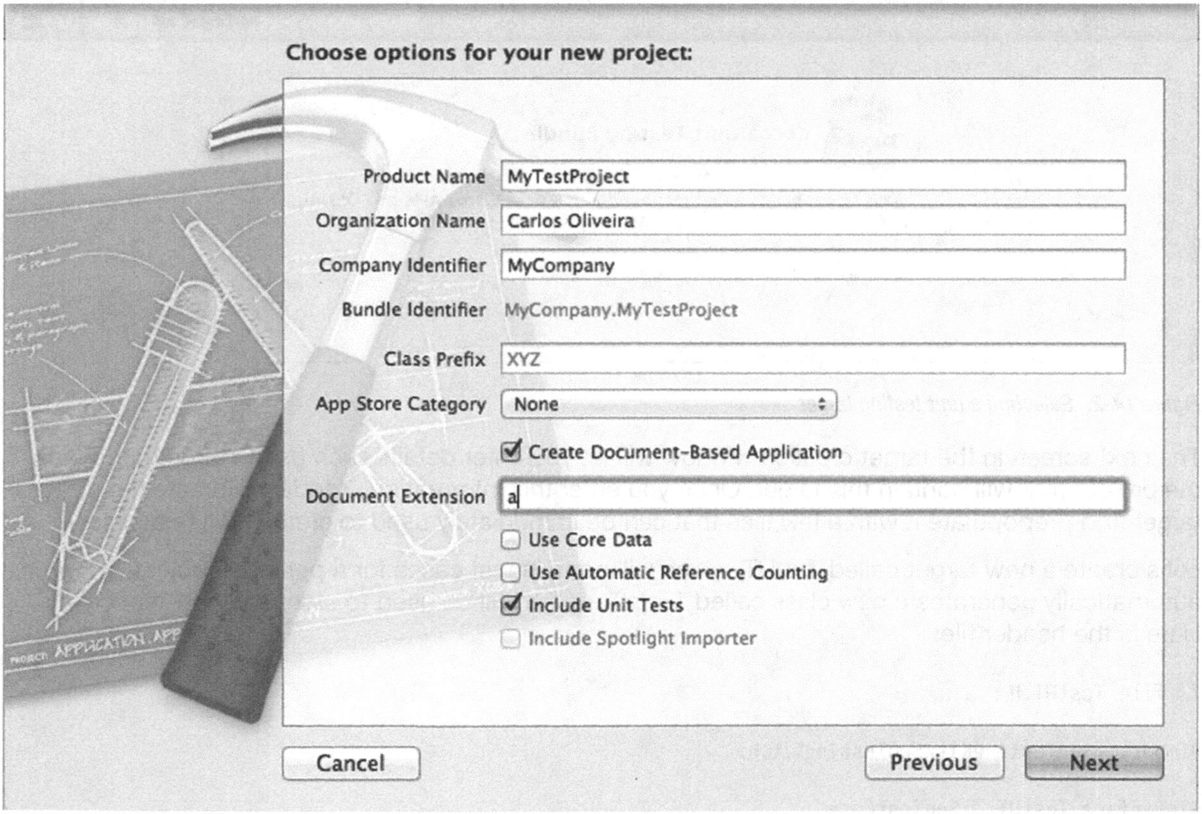

Figure 14-1. Including unit tests in a new project

The second way to include unit tests is by adding a new target to an existing project. Xcode allows you to create a new target, which is a generic name for the IDE support to generate a new executable. Suppose that you have an existing project to which you want to add a set of unit tests. You can add new targets by using the New ➤ Target menu while the project is open. On the left side, select the "Other" option. You will see a few items, from which you can select "Cocoa Unit Testing Bundling." The target selection window is displayed in Figure 14-2.

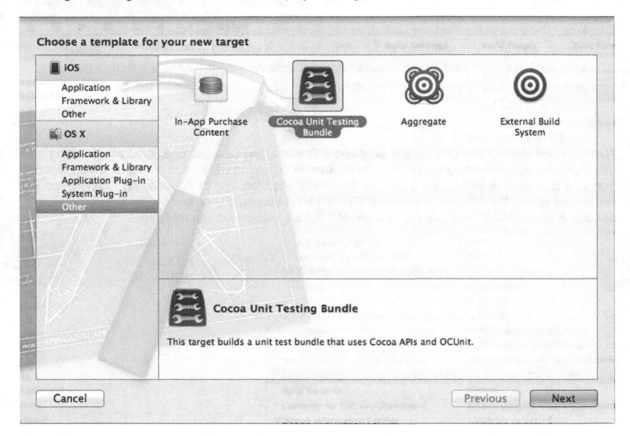

Figure 14-2. Selecting a unit testing target

The next screen in the target creation window will let you enter details such as the target name and the project that will contain this target. Once you enter this information, Xcode will create the new target and prepopulate it with a few files that can be immediately used to create new test cases.

Let's create a new target called TestUT, which will contain test cases for a personal project. Xcode automatically generates a new class called TestUT, which will be used to store any new test cases. Here is the header file:

```
// file TestUT.h

#import <SenTestingKit/SenTestingKit.h>

@interface TestUT : SenTestCase

@end
```

The symbol SenTestingKit used above is the name of the framework that contains OCUnit. The default class inherits from SenTestCase, so that it can use all the methods made available by OCUnit. Here is the corresponding implementation file:

```
// file TestUT.m

#import "TestUT.h"

@implementation TestUT

- (void)setUp
{
    [super setUp];

    // Set-up code here.
}

- (void)tearDown
{
    // Tear-down code here.

    [super tearDown];
}

- (void)testExample
{
    STFail(@"Unit tests are not implemented yet in TestUT");
}

@end
```

Notice how the implementation file already gives you a few of the methods that are frequently needed in a unit testing class. You need first to understand how each of these methods cooperated during the execution of test cases.

The setUp method is responsible for initializing the testing environment for your test case. You can add here any code that is common to each of the tests you want to run in the test class. For example, if you need a database connection available for each of your tests, you can write the code that creates the connection as part of the setUp method.

Similarly, the tearDown method is used to finalize the environment used by each test case in this class. In the case of the database connection, you may want to close the connection here, so you don't need to repeat that code in each test case.

Creating New Tests

Creating test cases in OCTest is a simple process. You just need to add methods to the test class, which in this case is called TestUT. The methods don't even need to be added to the public interface, since the OCTest framework will take care of running any test case included in the implementation section. The only requirement is that the method representing a test case starts with the word test, returning void and with no expected parameters. Therefore, you can add a new test case as follows:

```
- (void)testExample
{
        // This code will be run by OCUnit
        STAssertTrue(TRUE, @"sample test");
}
```

While the mechanics of adding tests is simple, much more important is to determine logically when a new test should be added to your list of test cases.

In theory, the number of test cases that can be written for most non-trivial methods is unlimited. However, in practice you should write tests only to make sure that certain aspects of your implementation return correct results. For example, here is a method that adds one unit to an integer argument:

```
- (int) addOne:(int)value
{
        // implementation here
}
```

It is not possible to test for every integer value. However, it makes sense to write tests that check the accuracy of the method for positive integers, negative integers, and for zero, for example.

```
- (void)testExample
{
        // create obj here...
        STAssertEquals([obj addOne:2], 3, @"test 2");
        STAssertEquals([obj addOne:-3], -2, @"test -3");
        STAssertEquals([obj addOne:0], 1, @"test 0");
}
```

In general, it is useful to create tests that apply not only to the general cases, but also to corner cases. For example, if the method is supposed to work only for positive numbers, you should check what happens when zero is passed as the argument, since it is common to have errors at such boundary cases.

Another rule of thumb is to add new test cases whenever a new unforeseen case has been found. For example, if you find a bug in your code, it can be very useful to add a test case to check that the bug has been correctly fixed. This is important not only to guarantee that the current code is accurate, but also that future revisions of your code will not have the same error. These types of tests are also called regression tests, because they avoid the regression of previously fixed bugs into working code.

Running Tests in Xcode

Building a testing target in Xcode and creating new tests is just half of the process of using a unit testing methodology for software development. Once the tests have been created, you need to actually run them in your development environment and verify that they all pass. Xcode allows you to run tests from inside the IDE, so that you can easily fix any issues raised during the testing procedure.

If you have a previously set up testing target in your project, you can use menu option Product ➤ Tests (or the keyboard shortcut ⌘+U), and the tests defined for your project will be executed. You have two ways to access the results. The first is a list of all tests that were executed in the test target. To see them, you can use the Log Navigator from the menu bar, choose View ➤ Navigators ➤ Show Log Navigator (or the keyboard shortcut ⌘+7). This will display the log navigator on the left side of the Xcode screen. Click the logs that correspond to the testing action, and you will see the complete logs for the execution of the testing target. If everything has been successful, you should see a list of tests marked in green.

The second way you can access the results of unit tests is through the Issue Navigator, whenever there is a failure in one or more unit tests. When that happens, Xcode generates an issue that is listed along with other issue categories in its own navigator. You can access this view using the main menu by choosing View ➤ Navigators ➤ Issue Navigator. Then, look at the problems (listed in red), which will indicate if one or more unit tests have failed in the last execution. You can click the issue, which will lead the code editor directly to the position of the failed unit test. You can also double-click the issue, in which case a new editor window will appear, with the cursor at the exact location of the error. You can now edit the test or the code being tested in order to fix the issue.

OCUnit Assertion Macros

As you have seen in the previous example, you need to use assertion expressions to determine if a test is returning the expected results. Using assertions to determine test correctness is so common that OCTest has defined several macros for this purpose. These assertion macros can determine if two values are equal, different, or conform to some other relation.

Most of the assertion macros in OCTest have a common interface. The general pattern is that the name of the assertion starts with STAssert, followed by the type of test this macro is supposed to perform. For example, STAssertEquals is where the test for equality is performed.

The arguments for each of these assertion macros also follow a similar pattern. The first parameters are the objects or values to which the test applies. For example, in STAssertEquals, the first two parameters are the objects tested for equality. Then, the next parameter is a string that describes the meaning of the test. This parameter is displayed in the Xcode test log when an assertion fails. Therefore, it is important to give an appropriate description that can make it easier to spot a problem when it happens.

Another common feature of the assert macros is that the description can accept formatting parameters in a way similar to NSLog. This is expressed in the macros by specifying the last parameter with the ". . ." syntax.

Here is a list of the commonly used assertion macros in OCUnit.

- STAssertEquals(value1, value2, description, ...): This macro succeeds whenever the two values are the same. Otherwise, the test fails with the given description. This macro works with non-object values, such as numbers, structs, or generic pointers.

- STAssertEqualObjects(obj1, obj2, description, ...): This macro succeeds whenever the two objects are the same. Otherwise, the test fails with the given description. This macro works for objects, and tests for equality using the isEqual: method. A failure occurs when isEqual: for the objects return false or either of the objects is nil.

- STFail: This is a macro that always fails. It is convenient to use STFail in situations when a particular code path should never be taken, such as

```
- (void)testExample
{
        int value = [myObj fileOperation];
        switch (value)
        {
        case ERROR_NO_SPACE:
        case ERROR_INCORRECT_FILE_NAME:
                STFail(@"Failing test for unsupported value");
                break;

        // other cases go here...
        default:
                break;
        }
}
```

In this example, you have a switch statement whose value depends on a method that you are testing. The return value needs to be validated by the test case in order to determine its correctness. Among the values returned by the method, you want to make sure that the values ERROR_NO_SPACE and ERROR_INCORRECT_FILE_NAME are not allowed. One way to check for this condition is to use a switch case and call STFail when these two values are returned. While not shown here, you might have many other cases to validate.

- STAssertEqualsWithAccuracy(value1, value2, accuracy, description, ...): This macro compares the first and second values using the given accuracy. If the comparison fails, then the description is used to give a hint of what went wrong. This comparison macro is useful when dealing with floating point values where accuracy indicates a small acceptable difference between these two values.

- STAssertNil(expression, description, ...): This macro tests if the given expression has nil value. Otherwise, a failure is reported using the provided description.

- STAssertNotNil(expression, description, ...): This macro tests if the given expression has non-nil value. Otherwise, a failure is reported using the provided description.

- **STAssertTrue(expression, description, ...)**: This macro tests if the given expression has a YES value. Otherwise, a failure is reported using the provided description.

- **STAssertFalse(expression, description, ...)**: This macro tests if the given expression has a NO value. Otherwise, a failure is reported using the provided description.

- **STAssertThrows(expression, description, ...)**: This macro tests is the given expression throws an exception when executed. If an exception is not thrown, a failure is reported using the provided description.

An exception is an Objective-C mechanism that signals the occurrence of an unexpected error. Libraries can generate exceptions when they can't recover from a particular error. You can also generate an exception using the @throw keyword. The following is an example of throwing an exception, and detecting it with an assert macro. This method is used to return the first character of a string. If the string is empty, the method raises an exception using the @throw keyword.

```
- (char)getFirstChar:(NSString *)string
{

        if ([string length] < 1)
        {
                @throw [[NSException alloc] initWithName:@"firstChar"
                        reason:@"StringIsEmpty" userInfo:nil];
        }
        return [string characterAtIndex:0];
}
```

This method will check if there is at least one character and return it. If the string is empty, it creates an NSException object, which describes the exception, and uses the @throw keyword to generate the exception signal. The following test can be used to guarantee that the exception is generated:

```
-   (void)testGetFirstChar
{
        StringOps *so = [[StringOps alloc] init];
        STAssertThrows([so getFirstChar:@""], @"checks for exception on empty string");
}
```

This test will call the getFirstChar: method using an empty string. This will check that the exception is thrown as required and succeeds when that happens.

- **STAssertThrowsSpecific(expression, exception_class, description, ...)**: This macro tests that the given expression throws a specific exception, named in the second parameter, when executed. If the exception is not thrown, a failure is reported using the provided description.

- **STAssertNoThrow(expression, description, ...)**: This macro tests that the given expression doesn't throw an exception when executed. If an exception is thrown, a failure is reported using the provided description.

■ STAssertNoThrowSpecific(expression, exception_class, description, ...): This macro tests that the give expression, when executed, doesn't throw an exception of the type listed on the send parameter. If the exception is thrown, a failure is reported using the provided description.

Test-Driven Development

Test-driven development (TDD) is a strategy for software development that goes much further than simply adding tests to a project. The central idea of TDD is that writing tests should precede the development or real code. The reasoning behind TDD is that good code should always have tests that guarantee that it works. On the other hand, having tests helps us focus on the development of particular features, with the goal of achieving the desired functionality.

These characteristics of TDD lead to a specific workflow that is somewhat different from the standard coding techniques used by most developers. The idea is to use the set of unit tests as the driver for new functionality in the project. This means that the first thing you need to do when adding a new class or method to the project is to create tests that will guarantee that the new code behaves as desired.

For example, suppose that you want to add a new method to the class StringOps that calculates the reverse of a string. According to TDD, the first thing you need to do, even before you write anything in the interface of the class, is to create a new method called testReverse.

```
- (void)testReverse
{
        STFail(@"not implemented");
}
```

This test will fail as expected. But this is an important feature, because in TDD you want tests to fail until the desired functionality has been correctly implemented. Thus, the next thing to do is to create a class called StringOps. Then, the test can be updated with the following code:

```
- (void)testReverse
{

        StringOps *so = [[StringOps alloc] init];
        STAssertTrue(so != nil, @"check object created");
}
```

This test should compile and run correctly after you import the header file for StringOps. The test just checks that you can create an object of type StringOps, a trivial test that should work.

Now that you are passing the test for creation of a StringOps object, the next step is to add a method implementing the operation of string reversal. The first thing is to create a test for this.

```
- (void)testReverse
{

        StringOps *so = [[StringOps alloc] init];
        STAssertTrue(so != nil, @"check object created");

        STAssertEqualObjects([so reverse:@"ABC"], @"CBA", @"check string reversal");
}
```

At the same time, you need to add a corresponding method in the `StringOps` class so that the test will compile.

```
#import <Foundation/Foundation.h>

@interface StringOps : NSObject

- (NSString*)reverse:(NSString *)string;

@end
```

As for the implementation of the `reverse:` method, you will start with a simple implementation that just returns the original string.

```
#import "StringOps.h"

@implementation StringOps

- (NSString*)reverse:(NSString *)string
{
        return string;
}

@end
```

This algorithm is clearly incorrect but, again, that is the strategy of TDD: start with a failing test and only then create a valid implementation that will validate the test. By clicking ⌘+U (run tests), you will see a failing test that needs to be fixed. The error reads "`'ABC' should be equal to 'CBA' check string reversal`." Click the error, and the editor will be positioned at the location of the failing test.

Now, you will write an implementation that makes that test succeed. You will use a simple algorithm that iterates through the string and interchange the characters, returning a new `NSString`.

```
- (NSString*)reverse:(NSString *)string
{
        char* cstr = (char*)[string UTF8String];
        int size = (int)[string length];
        int i, j;
        for (i=0, j=size-1; i<size/2; ++i, j--)
```

```
        {
            char c = cstr[i];
            cstr[i] = cstr[j];
            cstr[j] = c;
        }

        return [NSString stringWithCString:cstr encoding:NSUTF8StringEncoding];
}
```

The input value is used to create a null-terminated C-style string employing the UTF8String method. Then, you use a simple loop to iterate through the characters of the C array, interchanging their positions so as to reverse them. After the array has been reversed, you create and return a new string using the class method stringWithCString:encoding:, which takes as parameters a null-terminated array of characters and the desired encoding (in this case you use the standard UTF8 encoding).

After running the tests once again, you should see that testReverse is now passing. This indicates that the implementation of reverse has produced the indicated results. As in any testing procedure, you should add other tests for the same method to increase your confidence in its correctness. For example, you can add a new assertion to make sure that empty strings are correctly handled.

```
- (void)testReverse
{

    StringOps *so = [[StringOps alloc] init];
    STAssertTrue(so != nil, @"check object created");

    STAssertEqualObjects([so reverse:@"ABC"], @"CBA", @"check string reversal");

    STAssertEqualObjects([so reverse:@""], @"", @"check empty strings");

}
```

To proceed with this using TDD, you should first start with an example that fails, by replacing the second parameter with @"A", for instance. When you see the failure, replace it with the correct result, @"", and run the tests again. This should succeed, giving you confidence that the tests and the tested code are behaving as desired.

> **Note** The simple example given above shows all the steps you need to follow to use a test-driven development approach with Objective-C. The advantage of using TDD is that you can concentrate at each step on a small feature. Then, when you're done with the implementation of that step, the execution of the associated tests will give you confidence in its correctness. The TDD procedure is very different from standard development techniques where you write code and subsequently use ad hoc procedures for testing, which happens only when the feature is ready.

Summary

In this chapter, you explored unit testing, a programming practice that has been frequently used to improve code quality and reduce the number of defects in software products. Unit testing methodologies have the added benefit of providing fast development cycles where programmers are able to produce code and test its correctness in quick succession.

Objective-C is the ideal environment for the development of programs using a unit testing methodology. Its support for object-oriented technologies means that it is easier to decompose code into smaller chunks that can be tested independently. Objective-C also offers a complete test framework, called SenTestingKit, which implements the OCUnit library. OCUnit is based on SUnit, the first widely used solution for unit testing, created for the Smalltalk language.

You have learned how to integrate unit testing targets into an existing Objective-C project and how to add such targets to new projects. Then, I discussed examples of the types of tests that you can add to unit testing cases. The OCUnit framework offers a rich set of testing macros that facilitate the detection of most programming conditions. Examples are macros that test if their arguments are nil, equal to, or different from other objects, or throw a particular kind of application-defined exception.

Finally, you have seen how these features can be used to support Test-driven development, a programming methodology that uses unit tests as the driving force to implement new features, while providing some assurance that the implementation is correct for the provided tests. Since TDD supports an incremental development method, it has been successfully used to develop software with higher quality and fewer bugs. The fact that code developed in this way is frequently tested also reduces the risk that changes will generate undesired side effects and hidden bugs, which are much more difficult to track down after a complete feature has been implemented.

Testing code is just one facet of programming, although an important one. In addition, it is very important to understand how to deal with programming errors that may eventually get into later phases of the development cycle. Programming faults are a common occurrence, even on projects that have an extensive policy for code verification through unit testing. In the next chapter, you will learn the features provided by Xcode to facilitate the identification and removal of software errors. You will also see some of the debugging techniques that can be used by Objective-C programmers, leveraging the features supported by Objective-C.

15

Debugging

Any programmer knows how difficult it is to write defect-free software. That is why every platform has a number of integrated debugging aids, which give support in the task of identifying, reproducing, and fixing programming bugs. Xcode provides a complete solution for writing and debugging programs, which makes it much easier to find bugs in new or existing applications. In this chapter, I explain how to use these debugging features.

You will initially learn how general debugging methods can be applied to Objective-C programs. For this purpose, I explain some general debugging strategies that are valuable for finding and fixing errors in any programming language. Then, you will see how the Objective-C environment, which includes Xcode and related command line tools, can be used to support these general debugging strategies.

Using examples when necessary, I will describe how to employ Xcode features such as breakpoints, watch windows, conditional expressions, and the logging terminal. I also talk about how to use command line tools such as gdb and LLVM debuggers.

General Debugging Strategies

Debugging software is a task that requires significant intellectual effort and a different mindset from other programming activities. While programming, you are in a "creator" mode, constantly trying to produce good software designs and adding new features to existing code; while debugging, you will be mostly in a "researcher" mode, trying to figure out where a particular issue might be hiding. This difference in perspective is a reason why so many people find it difficult to find and fix bugs efficiently.

Finding problems in a piece of software is, in many ways, similar to detective work. You need to have a well-established process to evaluate possible causes and find the root cause of the bug. Just like a detective, you start with data collection, which will be later used to detect exactly where the problem is occurring. Only then can you proceed to creating and validating a hypothesis about how to solve that particular issue.

Here is a summary of the steps necessary for a well-structured debugging strategy.

1. *Data Collection*: Gathering data is the first step in solving a debugging problem. You need to collect all the information that is relevant to the issue you're trying to fix. To this end, there is a very important tool that you need to consider using: a case that can reproduce the problem. A bug that cannot be reproduced is very difficult to solve, because you cannot track down the situations that generated the problem in the first place. The first goal of your information gathering process should be to determine how to reliably reproduce the bug. Only then can you start to determine a fix for the issue.

2. *Defining a Hypothesis*: The next step, after you have a way to reproduce the issue, is to create a hypothesis of why this is not working. For example, you might be initializing a variable incorrectly. Or a step in your algorithm is missing. Whatever your educated guess about the origin of the problem, you should follow up with a plan to test that hypothesis. This usually involves more information gathering, such as looking at the application logs, or running the application on the debugger. By doing this, you will have a better idea about the root cause of the bug you're trying to fix. The process of making an educated guess and trying to prove that guess with data should be repeated until you find one or more possible cause for the observed problem. Once you find something that points to incorrect behavior, you will also have an initial idea about how to fix it. This knowledge comes as a side effect of the process you followed in order to find the issue and is a result of the data collection you performed.

3. *Applying a Fix*: After you test your hypothesis and determine that it corresponds to the root cause of the problem, it is time to apply a fix to the code. This may be just a small change that corrects a minor logic mistake. But it can also, in some cases, result in a large change or even a redesign of your application. It all depends on how severe the problem is and your strategy for dealing with the perceived issue.

4. *Creating One or More Unit Tests*: If you are creating unit tests, as explained in the previous chapter, this is a good time for another test case. There are two reasons why you may want to add unit tests. First, during coding, unit tests are very useful because they allow you to focus on a single issue as you proceed. Instead of worrying about everything else that might be wrong in your program, a unit test allows you to concentrate on a particular bug, and work towards making the code work as desired. Once you have the unit test set up, make sure it passes and then go back to test the complete application. A second way in which unit tests happen is in checking for regressions: when regularly executed, a unit test will automatically tell you if the problem ever occurs in the future. This gives you a good guarantee that the program will continue to work as desired, even in the presence of changes that may be introduced in the future.

The general steps outlined above can be performed in any programming language. However, as you will see, Objective-C provides a unique set of tools that facilitate the work of developers that need to fix one or more issues in their code. This is made possible not only by the characteristics of the language itself, but also by the programming environment, which includes the debugger (gdb or LLVM debugger) and the Xcode integrated debugger (which works with the support of the command line debugger).

In the next sections, you will get an overview of the debugging tools that can be used to implement the steps discussed above. In particular, you will want to employ tools that simplify the process of gathering data concerning the programming bug. Using this information, you can then use the debugging environment to test the hypothesis and verify if the proposed solution can fix the reported bug.

Debugging with Xcode

One of the best features of Xcode is the tight integration of development tools, where debugging plays an important role. The integrated debugger in Xcode is a front end to gdb (or LLVM debugger, depending on the debugging settings used in your project). The great advantage of debugging with Xcode is the visual feedback you receive when using the IDE. For example, you can create breakpoints by simply clicking the line where you want to stop the execution. Or you can verify the value of a local variable by hovering over the variable name in the editor. This is a real time saver when compared with the operation of a standard debugger.

Controlling Program Execution

The first set of instructions you will want to learn for effective debugging control are the ones used for program execution. With these instructions, a programmer is able to run, stop, or step into functions and methods written in C or Objective-C code. Such commands provide the essential parts of a debugging session, since you need to have some way of controlling the execution of the application if you want to have a chance of observing what the code is doing.

To start the execution of an application, you need to use the run command. This instruction will load the program executable and read all the debugging information contained in it. The debugger will also request that the program be immediately executed by the operating system. After that point, the program is loaded into memory and you can start defining breakpoint stops and other useful properties for the debugging session.

The run command in Xcode will execute the program as desired. You can use the menu Product ➤ Run to access this functionality. You can also use the ⌘ +R keyboard shortcut.

The step operation is used to move a single step in the source code. This means that all the instructions in the current line are executed, and the application stops when the next line is reached. To execute a single step of the program, you have two options: *step into* will jump either to the next line or to the first line of any user function or method that is executed by the current line. You use step into when you want to jump into a method that is being called by the current line of code.

The other step option, *step over*, will go directly to the next line of code, without stopping on any other user code that might be called in the current line. Both step execution options are available from the Product ➤ Debug menu. You can also use the F6 keyboard shortcut to perform a step-over and F7 to do a step-into.

Adding Breakpoints

To add a breakpoint with Xcode, just click the left border of the editor panel. A small annotation in the form of a red circle will be added to the line to indicate that a breakpoint exists for that location. You can also add or remove a breakpoint to a line using the ⌘+K keyboard shortcut.

Creating conditional breakpoints is easy with Xcode. The first thing you need to do is to create a normal breakpoint as described above. Then, Ctrl+click the breakpoint indicator and select "edit breakpoint." A new panel will show up with the available options. The first option you will see is Condition. There you can add any expression involving local variables that are active at the time the breakpoint is activated.

To remove an existing breakpoint, Ctrl+click the breakpoint indicator. You will see the option to delete the breakpoint. Alternatively, you may want to temporarily disable the breakpoint instead of removing it completely. By disabling a breakpoint, you retain any properties it might have (for example, if you added conditional expressions to it). Then, if you need any of these properties, you can reactivate the breakpoint. If you delete the breakpoint, however, you need to reenter any property it had in the first place.

When defining a new breakpoint, you can decide to make it conditional on an expression, so that the breakpoint will be activated only when it passes a particular predefined test. You can add such conditional breakpoints by Ctrl+clicking the breakpoint indicator and selecting the "Edit Breakpoint" option. The resulting screen is displayed in Figure 15-1. You can add a new expression to the condition field, as desired. In the example displayed in Figure 15-1, I am adding a breakpoint that will be activated only when the variable index is negative.

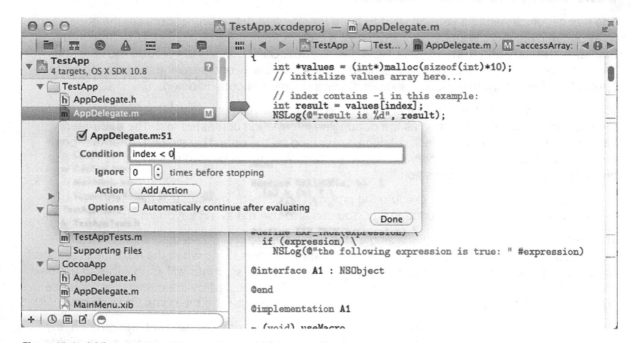

Figure 15-1. Adding a conditional breakpoint in Xcode

Another option you have when creating breakpoints is to define the number of times that the breakpoint can be ignored. For instance, this is useful when you know that the breakpoint will be executed as part of a loop, which repeats for a set number of times. Just define the number of times it should ignore the breakpoint.

Still another option is available for breakpoints in Xcode: you have the ability to run one or more actions whenever the breakpoint is reached. The kind of action may be executing a script, playing a sound, or just sending a message to the log window. I am particularly fond of the message logging option. By using it, you have functionality similar to the use of NSLog or other print statements, but without the need to recompile the application. Thus you can decide, right in the middle of a debugging section, which messages are most useful to understand the execution of the program. You can also add new messages as necessary to get more details.

These options for breakpoint execution give a lot of flexibility to programmers that need to find a bug quickly. By learning how to control breakpoints, you can minimize the number of instructions sent to the debugger while also getting better data that you can use to make decisions about the proper fix for a software bug.

Watching Expressions

Another feature of the debugging system in Xcode is the availability of an expression watcher. That is, you can define expressions that will be evaluated and displayed automatically by the IDE. Using the watching expressions, you can, for example, analyze the values of particular variables during the execution of the program. If the contents of such variables differ from the expected, you may get a better understanding of how the application works and use that information to fix the bug.

To add an expression watcher, you need to access the debug area and display the Variables view (if you can't see this view, click the split window icon at the top right of the debug area). Once the Variables view is visible, Ctrl+click the view and select the option "Add Expression." This allows you to add either a single variable, or an expression containing variables or other elements such as method calls and operators.

After you enter the expression you want to watch, the value will be evaluated regularly. The debugger will reevaluate the expression whenever there is a change in the state of the program, such as when the debugger advances the program from one step to the next, or when a function is executed. By using such expressions, it becomes easy to understand the changes performed by your algorithm in a nutshell. Moreover, you can change the variable or expression you want to watch without having to recompile the application or even restart it.

Investigating Local Objects

Another feature of the Variables view is the ability to have quick access to the contents of every local variable in the current method. This is made available as a standard feature in the Variables view. By displaying the value of local variables, you reduce considerably the need to add new expressions: frequently, the local variables comprise the most important memory locations for the current algorithm.

Once you have access to the local variables in a particular context, you can drill down on their contents, so as to reveal instance variables for each object stored locally. Similarly, you can observe the contents of structures by clicking their internal elements.

Probably the most important element of the list of local variables is the self variable. This shows you information about the current object (the object where the current method was called). Therefore, from self you can retrieve information such as the exact type of the current object, the list of instance variables, and the state of each of these variables.

Using the Variables view, you can not only observe values, but also make direct changes. For example, suppose you found that a particular variable has an incorrect value. You suspect that the method would work well if that variable had been correct, but you would like to test this hypothesis without building and restarting the application.

The easy way to perform such a test is to Ctrl+click the variable you want to change, and then select the "Edit Value" option. This will allow you to update the value of the selected variable without having to restart the debugging session. Figure 15-2 shows an example of how to perform a value update. From that point on, the current method will use the updated value as if the program had created the value as part of its normal operation. Depending on the result of this test, you can then make the necessary changes in the code to fix the bug, or at least to reduce the scope of the problem.

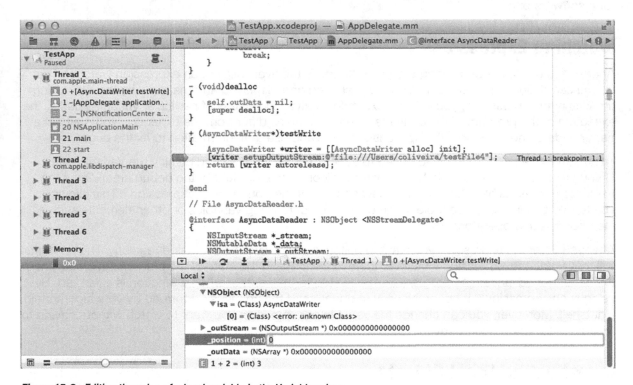

Figure 15-2. Editing the value of a local variable in the Variables view

Using the Logging Console

The logging console is another simple, but highly effective, tool for finding issues with programs written with Objective-C or other programming languages supported by the Mac OS X and iOS platforms. The logging terminal is a simple way to send text messages that can be later accessed by programmers.

When using Xcode, the console is readily available as one of the windows in the debug panel. To print something to the console, just use NSLog, as you have been seeing in the examples throughout this book. After an application is shipped and run by Mac OS X, the logs can be viewed and searched using the Console application (displayed in Figure 15-3), which is available in any installation of the system. Similarly, the console data is available for iOS devices using the iTunes application, for example.

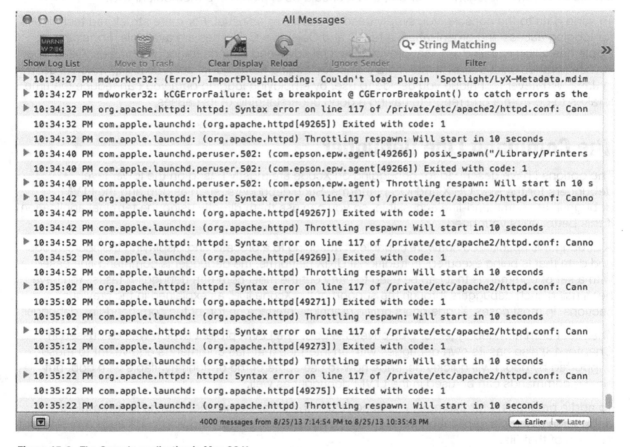

Figure 15-3. The Console application in Mac OS X

The main way in which the console is used is to print relevant information in such a way that it becomes easier to identify the causes of a programming problem. There are two main situations in which the console can be used: for immediate debugging purposes or for permanent logging.

The first use case of immediate logging is easy to understand: during a debugging session you can use the console to print values that you want to observe. In this sense, using the logging facilities is similar to using the debugger with expression watches, with the only disadvantage that you need to recompile the application to get the results. On the other hand, logs are easier to visualize and allow for the observation of several repetitions of the debugged code, until a problem is detected. Debugging by printing useful information is such a common debugging technique that most programmers have used it at one point or another.

The second use case for logs is for long-term data collection. To really work, this use has to precede the occurrence of a real bug, so that you can have access to previous information. The main strategy for long-term logging is that you should print logging data whenever you make a programming decision that can possibly result in an error. At these logical places, you should also be adding the considered data to the logs. By recording such decisions, you can make it easier to later determine the sequence of facts that lead to a bug. Logging information is a very powerful ally when considering some categories of errors, and it should be explored in a methodical way.

To send data to the console, you simply need to use NSLog as usual. For more structured techniques for logging access and organization, a few C and Objective-C libraries are available. For example, Apple has a library called asl that provides several advanced options for logging to files. Other open source libraries exist that simulate more complete logging frameworks such as log4j, which is used in Java. Whatever technique you decide to use, by employing logging data you can reduce the time it takes to go from a bug report to having a good understanding of its causes.

The Command Line Debugger

The options I have described for debugging on Xcode are mostly based on the lower level debuggers for the Mac OS X and iOS platforms. Such debuggers, such as gdb and the LLVM debugger, are command-line accessible, so you can use them directly using the terminal application if this better suits your needs.

A debugger is specialized software capable of attaching to a process and displaying the source code and data that is being executed. In traditional UNIX platforms, the debugger is command-line based, with a set of commands that can be used to carry out the most common debugging tasks. You have been using such debuggers through the support of the Xcode IDE, as explained in the previous sections. In most cases, Xcode offers only a graphical interface on top of the command-line debugger.

The most common debugger for Objective-C is gdb. The LLVM project (which was discussed in Chapter 13) also has its own debugger, with an interface that has commands equivalent to those supported by gdb. I will quickly describe how to use some of the options available with gdb, but similar commands can be used in the LLVM debugger as well.

To add a breakpoint, for example, you need to use the break command. Here is an example of debugging a sample application that contains a file called a.c. The following code adds a breakpoint at line 5 of that file:

```
oliveira:~ $ gdb a
GNU gdb 6.3.50-20050815 (Apple version gdb-1752) (Sat Jan 28 03:02:46 UTC 2012)
Copyright 2004 Free Software Foundation, Inc.
GDB is free software, covered by the GNU General Public License, and you are
welcome to change it and/or distribute copies of it under certain conditions.
Type "show copying" to see the conditions.
There is absolutely no warranty for GDB.  Type "show warranty" for details.
This GDB was configured as "x86_64-apple-darwin"...
Reading symbols for shared libraries .. done

(gdb) break a.c:5
Breakpoint 1 at 0x100000f04: file a.c, line 5.
(gdb)
```

Just as with Xcode, a breakpoint defines a location in your code where you want to stop execution. Once your application is stopped at a breakpoint you can investigate the content of variables and other memory addresses, or the sequence of calls in the call stack, for example. You can enter that information in a number of ways. The first way to set up a breakpoint is to enter the file name followed by a line number. It is also possible to create a breakpoint using only the name of a C function. Here's how to set up a breakpoint in the main() function:

```
(gdb) break main
Note: breakpoint 1 also set at pc 0x100000f04.
Breakpoint 2 at 0x100000f04: file a.c, line 5.
(gdb)
```

You can now run the program using the run command.

```
(gdb) run
Starting program: /Users/coliveira/a
Reading symbols for shared libraries +........................ done

Breakpoint 1, main () at a.c:5
5           printf("Hello world");
(gdb)
```

This will load the executable and run the program until a breakpoint is found. As you can see in the example above, the first breakpoint was reached, and as result the program stopped for debugging.

Once a program is stopped at a breakpoint location, there are several operations that can be performed to control its execution. For example, you can step to the next line of code with the next command.

```
(gdb) next
11          say_hello();
(gdb)
```

You can also step into the code that is executed in the current line. For example, this code would result in the execution of the following instruction:

```
(gdb) step
say_hello () at a.c:5
5           printf("Hello again");
(gdb)
```

You may also continue the execution of the program until the next breakpoint is reached.

These few examples show how you can simulate practically all of the debugging instructions available in Xcode through the command-line debugger. The debugger, however, provides a rich instruction set that is much more comprehensive than what the visual debugger can offer. In fact, the Xcode debugging sessions also expose the command-line debugger through the debug panel.

To see the debugger prompt, click View ➤ Debug Area ➤ Activate Console. This will display the debugging console, which shows some of the commands that have been executed by the debugger. It also has a prompt, which you can use to enter new debugging instructions, using syntax similar to the examples you have seen so far. For more information about how the debugger works in your environment, check the manual that ships with Xcode.

Debugging Memory Issues

Memory problems are some of the most difficult to track down using a debugger. The main reason for this difficulty is that in many cases a memory-related issue manifests itself far away from the point where the real problem occurs. For an example, consider a problem caused by a premature object release, like in the following method:

```
- (void) getArrayValue
{
        NSArray *values = @[ @0, @1, @2, @3];
        NSArray *numbers = values;

        // do something with the values array here.

        [values release];

        // do something else here...

        id two = numbers[2];
        NSLog(@"number is %@", two);
}
```

This code fails because at some point the array values are also stored in the variable numbers. However, after using values, the code releases it, without also invalidating the reference stored in number.

In a more general case, an object may be released in one part of your application, when in fact it is still needed somewhere else. The future access to the object, however, may take several seconds or minutes to occur, as happens in many typical desktop applications. In the case of a client-server application, on the other hand, it may even take days between the incorrect release and the future access to a released object.

Similar memory corruption issues, such as illegal array access, invalid pointers, etc., may be hard to track due to the distance between the error and the access failure. This is the reason why we need additional help when tracking such memory errors. Just stepping over the code may not be enough to catch defects that result from memory management issues.

Thankfully, Xcode has a number of features that can be used to help track such annoying memory errors. The first one you will learn about is the ZombieObject option.

Using NSZombie

NSZombie is a debugging aid that is able to detect incorrect access to objects that have been previously released. In such a scenario, a message is incorrectly sent to an object that is no longer available, causing an immediate crash. The resulting problem is difficult to diagnose because the access is not necessarily related to the release operation, which may have happened in a distinct section of code.

The NSZombie option in Xcode involves compiler support and converts all release operations into the creation of an object of the class NSZombie. These are very simple objects whose only function is to print an error when one of its methods is called. After all, since the original object it represents was supposedly released, any access to the object must be the sign of a memory access error.

The advantage of this strategy is that, instead of receiving an unhelpful crash, you will see an immediate and clear error message detailing that a message was sent to a released object. The message will also contain the location where the zombie object was created, which is the same place where the incorrect release occurred. In addition, the zombie object records information such as the type of the released object and the original pointer address. Using this information, it becomes much easier to track down the faulty logic that allowed the bad release to occur in the first place.

To use NSZombie in your application, the following steps are necessary. First, select the scheme for the current project using the menu Product ➤ Scheme ➤ Edit Scheme (or using the Command+< keyboard shortcut). Then, you should select the Arguments tab at the top of the panel. On arguments passed on launch, check "NSZombieEnabled." On the Diagnostics tab, you should also click the option "Enable Zombie Objects" in the Memory Management group.

When setting the NSZombie options, make sure that you're modifying the debug profile, since there is a performance penalty for using these options. They should be necessary only during debugging sessions and not on the release versions of your application.

Using the guardmalloc Library

While NSZombie is a great tool to detect memory issues when accessing objects, it doesn't help you when you're using traditional C types such as structures and arrays. For this purpose, you should turn to guardmalloc, the debugging library for general memory allocation.

To add support for guardmalloc in your debugging environment, you first need to access the debug scheme. Just select the menu option Product ➤ Scheme ➤ Edit Scheme. Then, click the Diagnostics tab on the top of the panel. Click the Enable Guard Malloc option box, which is listed in the Memory Management group.

The guardmalloc library is a replacement for the standard allocation library used by methods such as alloc. The difference between guardmalloc and other allocation libraries is that it organizes memory is such a way that an incorrect access will immediately generate an exception (or crash). The way guardmalloc works is by exploiting the virtual memory system present in most modern processors.

By allocating a page of virtual memory for each request, guardmalloc makes sure that the virtual memory system will detect any misuse of that memory. For example, suppose that you, by mistake, try to access an array with a negative number.

```
- (void) accessArray:(int) index
{
        int *values = (int*)malloc(sizeof(int)*10);
        // initialize values array here...

        // index contains -1 in this example:
        int result = values[index];
        NSLog(@"result is %d", result);
        free(values);
}
```

The method above uses the parameter index to access a value in the values array. The method is not checking the value of index, however, which results in a reference to a negative position in the C array. If you're not using `guardmalloc`, this kind of reference can succeed but will return incorrect results, which makes it much more difficult to debug. The reason is that you would need to audit all of the code to find the exact place where the incorrect access happened. This is very difficult to do, especially in a multithreaded application where the memory can be modified by several concurrent execution threads.

With `guardmalloc`, however, this and other places where memory is allocated directly are guarded using the virtual memory instructions employed by the processor. Therefore, an incorrect access, as show above, will generate an immediate crash in the application. If you are running in debug mode, this is helpful because the debugger will show the exact place where the crash occurred. Using the debugger, you will be able to determine the conditions that triggered the crash and fix it before it can result in further problems. The `guardmalloc` is one of the most useful tools available to fix basic memory access problems in C and Objective-C. Use it whenever you see suspicious memory corruption problems, and you will most probably identify a place where incorrect memory access is occurring.

Additional Tools

While the debugger is the most visible and hands-on tool used during the process of detecting and fixing programming errors, it is not the only device that you should be using for this purpose. A number of other applications can give you additional help in the process of correcting software defects. They complement the standard set of tools that have been used by most programmers, and give you an advantage in the difficult task of keeping the system current and bug-free.

In the next sections, I discuss two tools that have become indispensable aids in software development. Version control systems are used to maintain several versions of the code of applications of all sizes. They facilitate the communication between members in a team and can even simplify the task of finding bugs. Second, I discuss bug track systems, which are essential to maintain up-to-date information about bugs and other issues observed by testers and other users of application software.

Version Control Systems

The most common additional tool used for debugging issues is a version control system (VCS). A number of open source VCS tools have emerged in the last few years; they currently offer the same level of sophistication as the best commercial VCS applications. The leading open source tools for version control are subversion and git. These two systems have different implementation philosophies, but they are both high quality tools that can be effectively used for fine-grained control of software updates.

With subversion, you have a client-server system that can store multiple revisions of a set of source files. You can quickly make changes to files and have these changes stored in a server and available for a group of programmers. Git is another open source VCS; it uses a distributed methodology for source control, where each developer has a complete copy of the revisions, which can work independently of a server. In such a system, developers can collaborate by sharing the modifications they implemented locally. This contrasts with the methodology used by subversion, where all modifications are stored in a centralized location.

The main advantage of using such a system as a helper for tracking programming errors is that you can use it to see how the system evolved, and how this evolution interacted with the problem you're trying to solve. For example, the blame functionality that is implemented both by subversion and git allows the developer to determine exactly when a change was added to a particular file. This information can help you determine if a particular change was made by mistake or if it was a valid part of a new feature. The logs available along with blame can also be used to determine who made the changes in question.

Another thing you can do with a VCS is to move your copy to an earlier version and see if the bug was still there. This kind of exploration is extremely helpful during the initial phases of bug fixing, when you're still gathering as much information as you can about the problem and how it interacts with the other parts of the system. This kind of investigation is so useful that git has even introduced a software mode for investigation of older releases. The bisect option is used to navigate through the history of the project with a binary search strategy. You can do the same with subversion, however, which allows you to determine exactly when a bug was introduced in the source code.

Bug Tracking Systems

The bug tracking or ticket system is another indispensable tool when working with software defects. A ticket system can help make your process easier to follow, so that you can prioritize the efforts in software development and error removal. A good bug tracking system will allow you to keep detailed information about how, when, and where a particular error is occurring. The bug tracking system also provides a common collaboration tool, so that developers, testers, and users can have access to the same information about failures detected in the system. With this information, it is possible to tackle more complex problems and share all the information generated by everyone involved with the system.

You should use the bug tracking system to store instructions to reproduce the bug; describe the error with as much detail as you can; store data about the environment where the software is running; and plan the process of fixing the bug, with the amount of effort necessary, target date, and other related information. All this information can be used to drive the debugging process, so that you can have a broader perspective of how fixing the bug fits with other activity in the system. You can also use the VCS to coordinate with other software engineers and guarantee that no efforts are duplicated in the process.

While these are not the only tools used in the discovery and eradication of software defects, such applications are the ones that you will find more frequently on the lists of most used. They have helped in improving the quality of software for many groups of users, and they might just be a good choice for your development efforts.

Summary

Software bugs are a common problem that afflicts any programming team, independent of how careful they might be. It is therefore important to use tools to facilitate the process of finding and fixing software bugs as they are discovered.

The Objective-C language has a great ecosystem, with debugging tools that are tightly integrated to the environment. The Xcode IDE has a large number of features that can be used to automate the debugging process. Features such as a visual debugger, visual breakpoints, and data watchers make it a valuable instrument for the several activities necessary to fix software defects.

The programming environment also has other valuable tools for detection and correction of memory issues. The NSZombie mechanism is used to generate code that intercepts messages sent to incorrectly released objects. The guardmalloc debugging library is used to detect invalid accesses to memory, such as array references to locations that lie beyond the end of the allocated memory. The guardmalloc library uses the hardware for effective handling of memory barriers, and it is therefore able to accurately determine the location where such erroneous accesses are executed.

Finally, you have seen a few tools that can be used to support the debugging process. Applications such as git and subversion are not specific to Objective-C, but they offer new possibilities, such as examining older versions of the source code. It is also possible to determine exactly who worked on a particular version of a source file, which is helpful when working in a large team. Bug tracking systems, on the other hand, are used to maintain a detailed description of software faults. They are helpful in storing instructions for reproducing a bug, or the necessary steps to fix an existing issue.

I finished this chapter with the overview of the most important aspects of Objective-C and its programming environment. In the next chapter, you will get a complete example of a typical Objective-C application written for Mac OS X. You will see how the concepts we have explored so far can be put together into a working program that is able to benefit from the integration with the Cocoa framework.

Part 4

Writing Apps for OS X and iOS

Part

Writing Apps for OS X and iOS

Chapter 16

Building OS X GUI Applications

Objective-C is most commonly used in the implementation of applications that employ the Cocoa frameworks. As an Objective-C programmer, your will most certainly be involved in the creation of iOS apps or full OS X applications. In this chapter, I will discuss application development for OS X. For this purpose, you will learn about Cocoa UI, the framework used to develop graphical applications that conform to the UI standards of OS X.

Xcode offers an object-oriented approach to creating graphical interfaces, and this approach needs to be well understood before you will be able to take full advantage of its possibilities. Unlike other environments, GUI applications created with Xcode are not created using code (although that could be done if necessary). Instead, objects are designed with a graphical editor and saved to a file, which is then loaded directly by the Cocoa application.

Such graphical applications depend on the dynamic behavior of windows, views, and control objects provided by Cocoa. Using standard Objective-C technologies, these objects can be manipulated in Xcode and later loaded into your application using the nib file format. When loading the nib from a file, Objective-C guarantees that the saved properties and connections will be present at runtime.

Initially, I will explain how to create a sample UI application in Xcode. Then, you will see how the Cocoa framework is used to save and load the state of the graphical interface, including properties and connections between objects, so that you can spend less time coding and more time designing the UI of an application in an intuitive way. I will discuss the hierarchy of UI objects that is based on the NSResponder class.

In the last part of this chapter, I will provide a complete example of a UI application written in Cocoa. The application is able to receive events from the system menus. You will also learn how to draw on the screen using Cocoa libraries and how to respond to user events such as mouse movements and key presses.

An Overview of UI Creation with Cocoa

The first step in creating graphical applications in OS X is to plan the look of the UI. For this initial design you can employ any of the existing UI design applications. A few groups work with professional graphics applications such as Photoshop, but there are many other options on the market. If you are working in a small group or are a single developer, you may just use a hand-drawn design to guide you through this initial phase.

This resulting UI design work then needs to become an implementation, where developers try to achieve the requirements specified in the UI design document using their programming tools. This phase of the work will result in a working interface, which can be used for functional testing. This version will later have programming functionality added, towards a complete implementation of the application.

Setting Up a Cocoa Project

Creating a new project in Objective-C is a simple task, which can be accomplished completely from inside the IDE. You can tell Xcode to invoke the new project wizard by going to File ➤ New ➤ Project (or using the keyboard shortcut ⇧+⌘+N). The project wizard that appears as a result will show all the project types available in your local Xcode configuration. The wizard allows you to select a new project based on a desired project type. The list of project types is divided based on a target operating system. For Mac OS X, there are the following available project types in Xcode (see Figure 16-1):

- **Application**: This is the main type of project used by end-user developers that need to create user-facing applications. There are options for both graphical and console-based applications, as you will see next.

- **Framework and Library**: These project types are used to create software components that can be later used by other applications. A framework is a library created in Objective-C that can be more easily integrated into object-oriented applications or other libraries. You also have the option of creating C or C++ based libraries that can be imported by other languages.

- **Application Plug-in**: A plug-in is a special type of library that can be imported by applications during runtime. This allows such applications to add or remove plug-ins as needed, or even installing new plug-ins from a web site. Since the APIs used by a plug-in depend on the internal design of the target application, the resulting plug-ins are application-specific. Among the standard options available on Xcode, you can create plug-ins for the Address Book, the Installer application, and for Automator. Other plug-in types may be available in your machine if they were installed with software from third-party vendors.

- **System Plug-in**: These plug-ins are used to extend the operating system or some of the fundamental applications of Mac OS X, such as Finder. Among other options, you can create Mac OS X plug-ins that can serve as a preference panel in the Preferences application, a quick look plug-in for Finder, a screen saver, and a Spotlight importer.

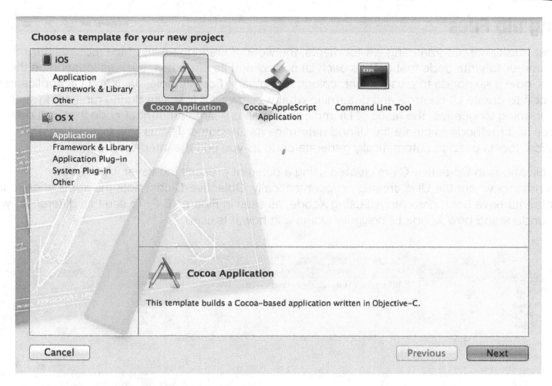

Figure 16-1. Selecting a new Xcode project for the Mac OS X

In this chapter, we are interested in creating applications that are located in the Applications tab. The following options are available:

- **Cocoa Application**: This project type can be used to create traditional window-based applications in Mac OS X. I will use this type of project as an example because it is the most commonly used to create end-user applications.

- **Cocoa-AppleScript Application**: This project type is used when creating applications programmed in AppleScript, a scripting language developed by Apple for Mac OS X. AppleScript is not very popular nowadays, but it is still available to support some of the technologies in Mac OS X.

- **Command Line Tool**: Use this project type to create applications that run only in the command line. These applications don't need to be Objective-C based, and may be written in other languages such as C or C++ instead. However, it is still possible to use Objective-C's foundation framework to streamline the development of command line applications, especially if they interact with other Mac OS X technologies that are only available through Objective-C frameworks.

After selecting a new application and clicking the Next button, you will be presented with a screen that requests some basic information necessary to create the project, including the directory where the file will be located

Using nib Files

In most traditional programming environments, the work of creating an interface requires the programmer to write code that defines each UI control and its attributes, such as location on the screen, how it responds to a user event, colors, and others. For example, Java and C# applications use code to create UI controls and determine what windows will look like during runtime. In such programming languages, the result of UI implementation is a large amount of code that includes classes and methods to create the UI and determine its attributes. That is true even when a graphical tool is used to automatically generate code as you edit the interface.

UI applications in Objective-C are created using a different process, however. Unlike other environments where the UI is created programmatically, Objective-C connects the application to live objects that have been prearranged using Xcode, as seen in Figure 16-2. To see this difference, you must understand how Xcode UI designer works and how it is used.

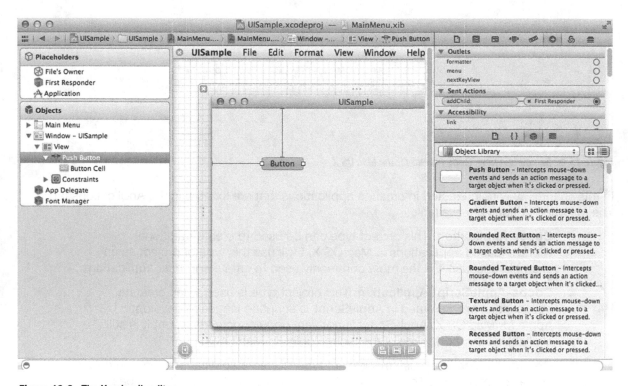

Figure 16-2. The Xcode nib editor

At the heart of Xcode UI design abilities is the functionality of Cocoa UI objects. A Cocoa UI has the behavior necessary for runtime manipulation, which is performed by the Xcode editor. Additionally, UI objects can be saved directly to a file and restored to the same state they were in during design time. This file, called a nib file (the meaning is NexTSTEP Interface Builder), is a saved representation of a set of objects. The nib file is commonly saved with a xib extension, since it uses XML for data encoding. Your application can later restore the representation of these objects by just requesting Cocoa to read the file into memory.

Therefore, in a sense you are not telling how a set of objects should be created, as in other languages. Instead, you are manipulating in Xcode the same objects that will be later loaded in the application. This means that you can configure the object, and no code will be necessary to set it up later, other than the generic Cocoa code that reads it from the xib file. Additionally, all the complexity of initially creating objects through Xcode is hidden from the application. No code needs to be generated or compiled for this purpose, even if you added hundreds of objects to the UI, or made thousands of changes to these objects. This is very difficult to achieve with traditional tools that just generate code.

Another advantage of xib files is that they can be loaded on demand. If you have a xib file that holds the UI for a part of your application that is seldom used, it will not impact the loading time for the whole application. Again, this is not possible with traditional code-generation technologies, because the code needs to be generated, compiled, and loaded, even if it is rarely used in practice.

These features of UI controls using xib files show the great flexibility you have when designing graphical applications in Xcode. And this is one of the reasons why the Mac OS X allows the creation of much more complex interfaces, compared to other operating systems. The next sections will provide an overview of the facilities provided by Xcode for the design of such applications.

The Cocoa UI Classes

At the heart of Xcode UI design abilities is the support provided by a set of classes in the Cocoa framework. These UI classes define the runtime abilities of graphical objects. A Cocoa UI object encapsulates all the behavior necessary for runtime manipulation, which is achieved by editing a nib file in Xcode. Additionally, UI objects can be easily saved to a xib file and restored to the same state they were in at the moment of its creation.

When manipulating objects in Xcode, you are in fact determining how these objects will appear and interact at runtime. The runtime behavior is defined not only by static properties such as colors and locations, but also by the relationship between objects appearing in the window. For this to work, you are allowed not only to change the visible properties of the UI objects, but also to wire objects using connections, which are defined by a set of *outlets* and *actions*.

Each object edited in Xcode can have one or more outlets. An outlet is a slot that can be filled with connections to other objects. So, for example, an NSWindow object has an outlet called menu. This outlet is used to send updates to the application menu, or to read any menu properties when necessary. You are responsible for defining the connection between a menu object and the NSWindow menu outlet during UI design with Xcode. After you do all the wiring of the objects, that configuration is frozen in the xib file, which can be later restored when it is time to display the window.

UI Objects in Cocoa also have actions. An action is a method in an object that is made available for connection at design time. Xcode will display all actions made available by a particular UI object in the property panel, in the "Received Action" list. To use these actions, you need to connect the object that generates an event to an object that has a target, which will be in the receiver end. See Figure 16-3 for an example.

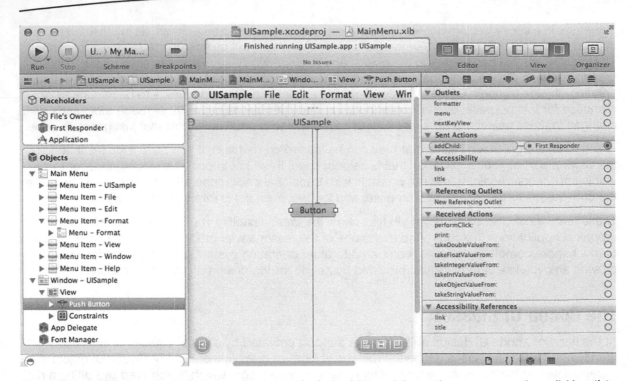

Figure 16-3. An NSButton control with its associated properties in the right panel. Among them, you can see the available outlets, sent actions, referencing outlets, and received actions

When a Cocoa application starts, one of the first things it does is to load one or more nib files. This xml file is then used to restore the saved objects, so they can be loaded to memory with the exact same properties and connections they had when designed in Xcode. This provides the initial states for the objects.

The connections established in Xcode are also visible by the Objective-C code once the application starts. Each outlet is translated into an instance variable in the corresponding object, so that Objective-C can use those variables to send a message to the desired control. These connections, then, close the gap between the design-time properties of object and their runtime behavior, which is defined by the code you write in Objective-C classes.

Outlets and Actions in Objective-C

You have seen how outlets and actions are fundamental to establish the connections between objects that are created in a xib file. However, these connections need to be accessible from Objective-C if this interface has to be used at runtime by your code. Xcode uses some simple conventions to connect Objective-C code with outlets and actions used in the UI.

To provide an outlet in your Objective-C class, you can simply add the IBOutlet modifier, like so:

```
#import <Cocoa/Cocoa.h>

@interface AppDelegate : NSObject <NSApplicationDelegate>
{
        id IBOutlet menuBar;
}

@property (assign) IBOutlet NSWindow *window;

@end
```

This class declares an application delegate, which will respond to events sent to the application. The class contains two outlets that can be accessed by the Xcode UI designer. These outlets are marked by the IBOutlet keyword. In fact, IBOutlet has no effect during compilation time, but is viewed by Xcode when your class is loaded in the editor.

When a nib file is loaded by Cocoa, it will have information about which objects are assigned to which outlets. Thus, after a nib file is loaded, the connections are restored and the outlets point to the right object. Thus, if you connect the menu bar object to the menuBar outlet in Xcode, the connection will be valid when the application is loaded in Objective-C.

The Cocoa UI Hierarchy

The hierarchy of graphical objects in Cocoa is rooted in NSResponder. This is the common object because it offers the behavior for answering to application events that is common to all graphical elements. NSWindow and NSView, which are used to implement windows and generic views, are all decedent from NSResponder.

The functionality provided by NSResponder includes the following:

- **Responding to mouse events**: mouseDown:, mouseDragged:, mouseUp:, mouseMoved:, mouseEntered:, rightMouseDown:, among others.

- **Responding to key events**: keyDown:, keyUp:, performMnemonic:, interpretKeyEquivalent:, among others.

- **Responding to other miscellaneous events**: cursorUpdate:, scrollWheel:, helpRequested:, etc.

- **Responding to miscellaneous action messages**: cancelOperation:, capitalizeWord:, insertNewLine:, insertTab:, indent:, moveBackward:, moveToBeginningOfDocumentAndModifySelection:, moveToLeftEndOfLine:, moveLeft:, moveRight:, pageUp:, pageDown:, scrollLineUp:, selectWord:, selectLine:, showContextHelp:, among many others.

- **Managing window restoration**: restoreStateWithCoder:, among others.

- **Responding to menu events**: setMenu:

This is just a small selection of the interface made available by NSResponder, which makes it a fundamental class in Cocoa UI programming. Subclasses such as NSWindow, NSApplication, and NSView further refine the standard behavior provided by this class.

The NSWindow Class

The NSWindow class provides the behavior necessary for all windows in Cocoa, including top-level windows, utility windows, and dialogs. They all share some common code to display, move, resize, and manage the content of the window.

Here are some common features available to any window deriving from NSWindow:

- **Defining the size of the window**: setFrameOrigin:, setFrameTopLeftPoint:, setMinSize:, performZoom:, showsResizeIndicator, among others.

- **Configuring window properties**: setBackgroundColor:, setStyleMask:, setOpaque:, setHasShadow:, among others.

- **Getting information from a window**: windowNumber, deviceDescription, canBecomeVisibleWithoutLogin, among others.

- **Managing the main window status**: isMainWindow, canBecomeMainWindow, makeMainWindow, among others.

- **Managing child and attached windows**: addChildWindow:ordered:, removeChildWindow:, parentWindow, among others.

- **Managing title bars**: standardWindowButton:, showsToolbarButton, among others.

The API provided by NSWindow encompasses the main functionality available in standard Mac OS X windows. Cocoa encapsulates this behavior in NSWindow, and you can set up how much of this functionality is used during design time using Xcode, or at runtime by calling the methods of NSWindow as needed.

The Window Controller Object

The window controller is an important part of the design of graphical applications. Unlike other GUI toolkits, most of the customization code in Cocoa is not written as a subclass of NSWindow. Instead, Cocoa uses window controller objects to handle most of the programmatic behavior of real NSWindow instances in the system.

This is possible again because you can redirect messages to certain objects at design time using Xcode and nib files. When you need to handle a particular type of action, it is not necessary to crate a subclass of a given UI object. Instead, you can just use Xcode to connect the object to a certain action in the window controller object. This guarantees that you will have a modified behavior, without the need to create a subclass of any particular UI object.

In general, events directed to an NSWindow are directed to the window controller for immediate response. Thus, the window controller can be seen as the headquarters for the functionality provided in a window. You can further divide this responsibility to other controllers as necessary, but many simple applications have a single window controller that responds the requests for the whole window.

In a large application, each window can have its own window controller, which responds to messages sent to that window. Other controls can also have their own associated controller, if their behavior is complex enough that requires this level of customization.

The Delegate Object

Among the outlets provided by Cocoa UI objects, one of the most important is the delegate outlet. A delegate is an object that automatically receives messages and notifications that are sent to a particular UI control or window. By setting an object as the delegate for a UI control, you will be able to process messages destined to that control. That is the main mechanism by which UI events are processed in a Cocoa-based application.

For an example of setting delegates on the Xcode UI, consider the Window object, which is an instance of the NSWindow class. If you select that object and click the Connections Inspector (in the panel on the right side), you will see the list of outlets. One of these outlets is the delegate object, which is a present in every object of the class NSWindow, as shown in Figure 16-4.

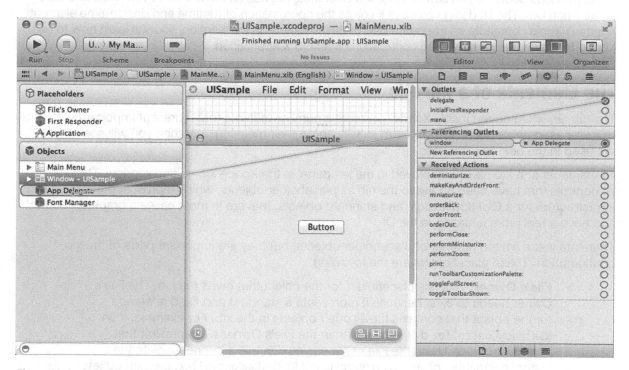

Figure 16-4. *Connecting the delegate for an NSWindow object*

To set the delegate object, you can connect it to the desired received receiver in the same way you can connect any other outlet. The object you want to use is the File's Owner (i.e., the object that owns this xib file). Click the outlet connection icon and drag it to the File's Owner placeholder, and you will see the outlet changing to indicate the new connection.

Once a delegate connection has been established, you can start adding methods to the delegate class to process the events sent by the window object. Such a delegate class should conform to the NSWindowDelegate protocol, which defines methods that are sent to the delegate for processing. Here is a list of methods that can be implemented in the delegate class:

- **Window movement messages**: windowWillMove:, windowDidMove:, windowDidChangeScreen:, among others.

- **Window minimization messages**: windowWillMiniaturize:, windowDidMiniaturize:, windowDidEndLiveResize:, among others.

- **Window update messages**: windowDidUpdate:, windowDidExpose:, windowDidBecomeMain:, windowWillClose:, among others.

Using Xcode for UI Design

In the previous sections you saw how Cocoa UI objects provide all the elements you need to create feature-rich UIs. The UI design process involves the coordination of runtime and design-time elements. Xcode UI tools constitute an important part of this workflow. In this section, you will learn how to use Xcode to define the windows and controls of a Mac OS X application.

The Elements of a nib File

The nib fie, when edited inside Xcode, presents a number of items that represent important elements of a UI-based application. You will learn initially about their meaning, and then you will see how they are used in the next few sections.

All elements of a nib file are displayed in the left panel in the Xcode xib editing window. They include UI controls that have been added to the nib as placeholder objects, which represent parts the design infrastructure for a GUI application, and standard objects, that are in most cases a graphical control and have a real representation in the UI.

There are just a limited number of placeholder objects, but they are important parts of the xib configuration. These placeholders are the following:

- **File's Owner**: This is a placeholder for the object that owns the nib. The File's Owner needs to exist because it represents a standard and fixed reference for the object that contains the all other objects in the xib. For example, if an NSWindowController owns the xib, then the File's Owner will represent that controller object. Using the File's Owner, you can make connections to the instance variables of your own subclass of NSWindowController, through outlets that will be automatically recognized from your source file instance variables. You can use these outlets as the main connection between your code in Objective-C and the objects instantiated in the xib.

- **First Responder**: In a window, the first responder is the object that has the focus at the moment. The first responder then receives several default events, such as keyboard events. You can think about the first responder as the default target for events that happen in a window.

- **Application**: This object is a reference to the NSApplication class. This placeholder object can be used as the target of standard messages that impact the whole application, such as Quit, for example. You can also use this object to receive messages directed to your own subclass of NSApplication, if you have decided to create such a subclass.

Other than the placeholder objects, there are normal UI objects that are have been placed in the xib file. These objects appear in a hierarchical way, depending on how they contain each other. For example, it is common to add a window object the xib, which will contain one or more controls to display information, and a menu object. Figure 16-5 shows an example that displays the placeholder objects and the normal objects for a sample application.

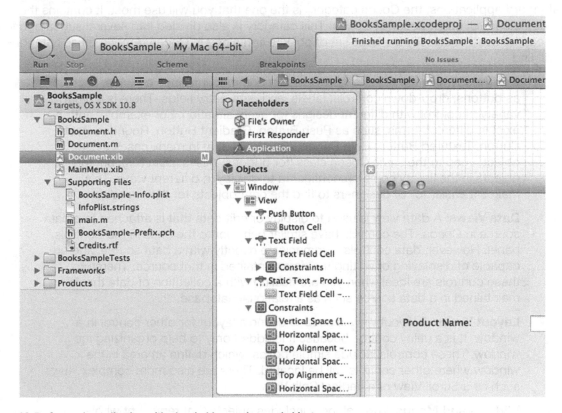

Figure 16-5. A sample application with placeholders and normal objects

You can interact with objects in this panel by clicking them. When you click an object, it becomes the selection used in other panels, such as the properties panel. Then you can make changes to the properties of that object as needed.

The Object Library

The object library is a panel in Xcode that displays a list of all objects that can be used to create UIs. If an object is listed in the library, you can quickly add it to the xib, and have it as part of the interface you're designing. These objects can also be customized using the properties panel and moved to the location you desire.

The library is organized according to categories, which can be accessed from the pull-down control at the top of the object library panel. The main categories include Cocoa, Address Book, Automator, and WebKit. Separate categories can be added to object library by third parties. For example, you can add additional object libraries or use open source libraries from the Web.

For standard applications, the Cocoa category is the one that you will use most. It contains the basic objects for UI construction in Cocoa. This category is also divided into several subcategories, which can be used to classify the large set of objects contained in Cocoa. Among these categories you will find

- **Controls**: These are objects that represent common interface controls, such as buttons, drop-down controls, labels, and data-entry fields. There is a great variety of control with different designs for every situation. For example, buttons exist in different forms, such as Push Button, Gradient Button, Rounded Rect Button, Textured Button, Help Button, etc. Notice that in many cases these objects map to the same Cocoa class (for buttons, this is NSButton), but the objects in the library come preconfigured to display in different ways. This makes it easier for UI designers to find the right objects for their needs.

- **Data Views**: A data view is used to display or edit data that is attached to a data source in Cocoa. The controls have similar behavior to the ones in the Controls panel. However, data controls communicate directly with a data source, and are capable of displaying or editing the data contained in that source. Therefore, these controls are ideal when you are dealing with a collection of data that is maintained in a data source such as a relational database.

- **Layout Views**: A layout view is used to define a layout for other control in a window. It is a utility control, because it is added only to help organizing the window. These controls include simple boxes, which define an area in the window where other controls will be located. There are also more complex views such as a Scroll View or a Vertical Split View.

- **Widows and Menus**: This category includes objects that represent whole windows, toolbars, and menus that can be displayed in the top of the menu bar. There are also different windows to choose from, including a standard Window, a Panel (which is small secondary window), a Textured Window, and a Window with Drawer.

Creating a Main Window

The first step in the UI creation is to add at least one window to the nib. This is done by selecting one of the window objects from the object library panel. There are several types of windows that you can use in your UI.

- **Window**: The standard option is a Cocoa window with buttons for closing, minimizing, and maximizing. This style of window should be good enough for most uses, including editing windows and informational windows.

- **Panel**: A panel is normally used for transitory purposes. For example, you may want to use it to display drawing tools, for the properties of a selected element, or for the selection of styles in a document. Panel windows are not supposed to be used for a long time, so they have smaller controls that are less frequently used.

- **Textured Window**: A textured window has many of the same properties of a standard window. However, it has distinctive background and borders, which make it more appropriate for applications that can be used as tools. For example, iTunes is uses this style of main window: its main purpose is not to edit data, but to work as a tool for music playing.

- **HUD Window**: This style of window is more indicated for transient data or informational purposes. For example, you can use it for help information, or to display properties of a selected element in the application.

To add a main window to the nib file, just drag the window object into the edit area. You will see that the window will appear as part of the xib design. The window will also be added to the panel of objects, displayed on the left side. By clicking in one of these items, you will be able to change the properties of the window or configure its outlets and actions.

Adding Menus

Working with menu bars is easy with Xcode. First, a menu bar is present in the initial xib created by Xcode. It is displayed along the top of the editor window and you can click its representation to edit the necessary items. You can change the configuration of the menus by double-clicking an item and editing its label.

To change the connections for these menu items, you can click and drag the items to the object that is supposed to respond to it. There are a few targets that are commonly used to respond to menu events. The first is the Application placeholder object. For example, for menu commands such as Quit, or Minimize, the application has default methods that can be used to respond to such common requests.

The second object that is a common target for menu events is the application delegate. This object is used to handle events that happen at the application level and need to be handled with some customized response. Let's see, for example, how the application can handle a menu item called Save Document.

The first step is to add an action method to the delegate object. Here is an example of the delegate interface:

```
#import <Cocoa/Cocoa.h>

@interface AppDelegate : NSObject <NSApplicationDelegate>
{
        // store an outlet to the menu bar
        id IBOutlet menuBar;
}
```

```
@property (assign) IBOutlet NSWindow *window;

// an action called by a menu event
- (IBAction)onSaveDocument:(id)sender;

@end
```

This interface declares a method named onSaveDocument:, which is marked as an IBAction. Remember that IBAction is just another name for void, but when used in an interface file it tells Xcode that this method can be connected to other controls at design time.

In Xcode, when selecting the AppDelegate object in the xib file, you will now see onSaveDocument: as another action available in the Received Actions section. To connect this new action to its source, click and drag from the circle on right side of the action to the desired menu item (in this case the Save item). After you release the mouse, the connection will be established and displayed, as in Figure 16-6.

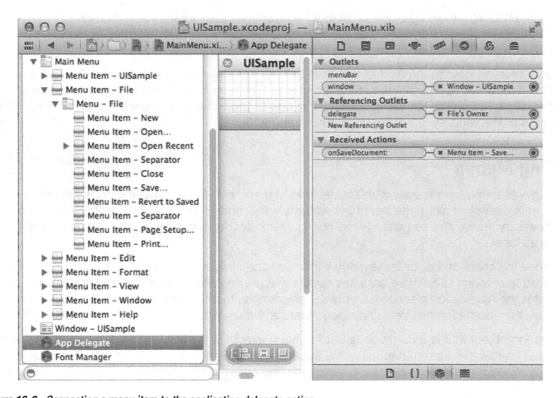

Figure 16-6. Connecting a menu item to the application delegate action

Making Changes After a nib Is Loaded

Any nontrivial application needs some customization to the plain style of a control. While several customizations can be done using Xcode UI design features, some changes are more easily done in code. For example, if the same update needs to be done to several controls, it may be easier to make the change via a for loop rather than manually performing the change during design. At the same time, it would be nice to be able to perform such changes before the interface is displayed to users.

Therefore, it is useful to have a way to execute code after the nib file has been loaded, but right before it is presented to the user. This is exactly what is possible with the windowControllerDidLoadNib method, which is part of the NSDocument interface. Here is an example:

```objectivec
- (void)windowControllerDidLoadNib:(NSWindowController *)aController
{
  [super windowControllerDidLoadNib:aController];

  // make updates here ...
}
```

If, instead of an NSDocument interface, you use a view controller class to manage your code, there is a similar method that is run right after the nib file has been loaded. It is called viewDidLoad (this method is also called even if the UI is created programmatically, but if you know that the UI is created from a nib file, then you can guarantee that the nib was loaded):

```objectivec
- (void)viewDidLoad{
    [super viewDidLoad];

    // make your changes here
}
```

Last, if you are subclassing a control (that is, a subclass of NSView), you should be able to implement the awakeFromNib method. This method is called right after the view has been read from the nib file, so you can use this opportunity to add your own customizations.

Coding a UI Application with Objective-C

In the previous sections, you saw how the design aspects of UI creation interact in Xcode, resulting in the creation of a nib file that represents these objects on disk. The next step is to use Xcode to control these objects at runtime. Here you can use all the features of Objective-C, in combination with the rich set of runtime features made available by Cocoa UI objects.

While I don't have the space needed to introduce all the features of UI libraries in Cocoa, I will present a simple drawing application as an example of coding an UI in Objective-C. At the same time, I will explain the meaning of these classes and methods as they are introduced so you can have an idea of how such applications work. For the complete source code and support files, please access this book's web page on my web site at http://coliveira.net.

The application I introduce here is an interactive app that can be used to create and display a graph. A graph is a specialized chart that can be used to show the connection between items known as graph nodes. Graphs are used in several applications to analyze the structure of connected elements. Examples of such structures include computer networks and transportation networks.

The main Function

In Objective-C as in C, the application starts execution in the main function. If you have a simple application that doesn't need a lot of customization, you can just delegate the responsibility of main to NSApplicationMain, a function exported by NSApplication that performs the needed initialization.

```
//
//  file: main.m
//  Graph Application

#import <Cocoa/Cocoa.h>

int main(int argc, char *argv[])
{
    return NSApplicationMain(argc,  (const char **) argv);
}
```

The AppDelegate

Let's start with the application delegate. As you saw above, this delegate receives events that have been routed in the nib using the Xcode nib editor.

```
/* AppDelegate */

#import <Cocoa/Cocoa.h>

@interface AppDelegate : NSObject
{
    IBOutlet id selectNumberOfNodesWindow;
        IBOutlet id numberOfNodesControl;
        IBOutlet id minDistField;
        IBOutlet id applyDistControl;
        int numberOfNodesControlCanceled;
}
- (id)getSelectNumberOfNodesWindow;
- (id)getNumberOfNodesControl;
- (id)getNumberOfNodesApplyDistControl;
- (id)getNumberOfNodesDistField;
- (int)getNumberOfNodesControlCanceled;
- (IBAction)closeSelectNumberOfNodesWindow:(id)sender;
- (IBAction)cancelSelectNumberOfNodesWindow:(id)sender;
- (IBAction)setApplyMinDistOnNumberOfNodesWindow:(id)sender;
@end
```

The application has a number of outlets that represent fields in the UI. For example, there is a field that stores the number of nodes in the window. Notice that all these fields are marked as IBOutlet, which is used to tell Xcode that these variables are mapped to outlets. Then, notice that the last three methods have a return value of IBAction. This is used to tell Xcode these methods should be mapped to actions in the nib editor.

Next, you have implementation of the AppDelegate.

```objc
#import "AppDelegate.h"

@implementation AppDelegate

- (id)getSelectNumberOfNodesWindow
{
        return selectNumberOfNodesWindow;
}

- (id)getNumberOfNodesControl
{
        return numberOfNodesControl;
}

- (int)getNumberOfNodesControlCanceled
{
        return numberOfNodesControlCanceled;
}
```

These first three methods simply return the ids for a few UI controls. These ids define the window that displays the number of nodes, a control with the number of nodes, and a control used to cancel the operation.

```objc
- (IBAction)cancelSelectNumberOfNodesWindow:(id)sender
{
        printf("The window was canceled\n");
        numberOfNodesControlCanceled = 1;
        [NSApp stopModal];
}

- (IBAction)closeSelectNumberOfNodesWindow:(id)sender
{
        numberOfNodesControlCanceled = 0;
        [NSApp stopModal];
}

- (IBAction)setApplyMinDistOnNumberOfNodesWindow:(id)sender;
{
        if ([sender state] ==  NSOffState) {
                [minDistField setEnabled:NO];
        } else {
                [minDistField setEnabled:YES];
                [selectNumberOfNodesWindow makeFirstResponder:minDistField];
        }
}
```

These three methods are use to respond to messages sent by a modal window defined in the application. The model window is used to define the number of nodes in the editor. Notice that, in the first two methods, you have a call to the method stopModal in the NSApp object. stopModel is used to close a modal window (in this case the modal window is a small dialog).

```
- (id)getNumberOfNodesApplyDistControl
{
        return applyDistControl;
}

- (id)getNumberOfNodesDistField
{
        return minDistField;
}

@end
```

The last two methods are necessary just to return stored information, such as the number of nodes in the distribution.

The GraphView Interface

The GraphView.h file is used to define the interface for graph drawing routines. Most of the code is related to defining the instance variables necessary during the drawing operations.

```
/* GraphView: viewer for graph drawing. */

#import <Cocoa/Cocoa.h>

#include <graph.h>

// This class implements the viewer, which displays the graph and
// takes care of editing operations.
@interface GraphView : NSView
{
        NSBezierPath *path;              // path used by the main graph
        NSBezierPath *sg_path;           // path used by the sobreposed graph
        NSAffineTransform *transform;    // transformation used to draw on scale
        Graph *G;                        // Main graph
        Graph *sG;                       // Sobreposed graph
        IBOutlet id Document;            // Pointer to the document
        IBOutlet id _posField;           // Field in the status bar showing position
        IBOutlet id scroller;
        IBOutlet NSSlider *_slider;
        int *_associatedPoints;          // pointer to a vector of associated points
        int _nPoints;                    // number of points in this graph
        double _sliderValue;             // the value of the slider widget
        int _clickedNode;                // node that was last clicked
        int _deleteEdgeMode;             // 1 if the current mode is "delete edge"
}
```

```
-(void) refreshView;
-(void)setBezierPaths;
-(NSBezierPath *) getPath;
-(void)startDeleteEdgeMode;
-(Graph *) getGraph;
-(IBAction)sliderChanged:(id)sender;
-(void) refreshView;
-(void)drawNodeNumbers;
-(int)findClickedNode:(NSPoint)loc;
-(void)moveNode:(int)clickedNode to:(NSPoint)loc;
-(void)addSobreposedGraphToPath;
-(void)addGraphToPath;
-(void)mouseMoved:(NSEvent *)theEvent;
@end
```

Notice that this file, like most files in a Cocoa application, starts with the command #import
<Cocoa/Cocoa.h>. Then you will see a list of necessary variables, with a few outlets used by Xcode.
Among the methods declared, you can also see an action that is used during the UI design phase.

The GraphView Implementation

This file is at the heart of the drawing application you are exploring. The class defined here,
GraphView, is a subclass of NSView. As you have seen before, NSView is responsible for managing an
area of the screen. In this case, GraphView manages all the area of the editor, being responsible for
editing operations from users. This class manages events such as keyboard, mouse movements,
and window resize operations, for example.

The file starts with a few useful definitions, such as min and max that will be used in some
calculations later in this class implementation. A few functions are defined in pure C for additional
speed, but most of the file implements the GraphView class using Objective-C methods.

```
#import "GraphView.h"
#import "MyDocument.h"
#include <common.h>

#define NODE_RADIUS 4

#define min(x,y)  (x<y ? x : y)
#define max(x,y)  (x>y ? x : y)

static int change_points_associated_to_edges(graph_node *graph_node, int a, int b, void *data);
static int find_edge_at_point(graph_node *graph_node, int a, int b, void *data);

struct for_each_edge_data {
        Graph *G;
        int movedNode;
        int secondMovedNode;
        int edgeFound;
        NSPoint *loc;
        NSBezierPath *path;
```

```
        NSBezierPath *sg_path;
        GraphView *v;
        double sliderValue;
};
```

The for_each_edge_data struct is used to store useful information about edges of the graph. An edge is just a line connecting two nodes in the graph. This struct is used to store data that needs to be quickly accessed by the methods of GraphView.

```
@implementation GraphView

/**************************************
 * Generic options for the window.
 **************************************/


// This is necessary to say that we want to use a coordinate
// system with origin in the upper left corner.
- (BOOL)isFlipped
{
        return NO; // should be YES to change
}

// This is necessary to say that we want to process
// keyboard events
- (BOOL)acceptsFirstResponder
{
    return YES;
}
```

These two methods override the existing options from NSView. The first one determines that the coordinate system used by the view is not inverted with relation to the default coordinate system. The default coordinate system starts in the upper left corner. You can try to flip it to get a more conventional coordinate system that starts in the lower left corner.

The second method determines that this view accepts first responder. This means that you are able to send keyboard commands directly to the view, among other events that depend on the first responder.

```
/**************************************
 * Initialization of window and structures.
 **************************************/


// initialize the window.
// Note: This is called after initWithFrame:
-(void)awakeFromNib
{
        [[self window] setAcceptsMouseMovedEvents:YES];
        // create the path  (retain avoids the path being GC'ed after return of method)
        path = [[NSBezierPath bezierPath] retain];
        sg_path = [[NSBezierPath bezierPath] retain];
        transform = [[NSAffineTransform transform] retain];
        _associatedPoints = 0;
```

```
        _sliderValue = 1.0;
        _clickedNode = 0;
        _deleteEdgeMode = 0;
        [self setBezierPaths];
}
```

The method awakeFromNib overrides the same name on the parent class. In awakeFromNib, you should do any initialization necessary before the view is displayed. This method is called right after the nib file has been used to create the UI. This means that at this point all properties and connections in the nib have been restored and are accessible to the NSView.

This code is calling methods to establish the initial status of the GraphView. For example, you can see two of the variables storing a new object of NSBezierPath. This object will be later on used to create Bezier curves. The method also allocates an NSffineTransfor object, which will be used to transform the location and size of nodes and edges on the GraphView.

Notice how this method calls setAcceptsMouseMovedEvents:. This is necessary because standard NSView objects don't receive mouse messages. To be able to process then, you need to make a request using the method named above.

```
// deletes memory previously allocated
-(void)dealloc
{
        if (_associatedPoints)
                Delete(_associatedPoints);
        [path release];
        [sg_path release];
        [transform release];
        [super dealloc];
}
```

The dealloc method ,is responsible for releasing all the data associated with this view. It will delete the screen locations stored in _associatedPoints. It will also release the path, sg_path, and transform objects. It also calls dealloc in the base class.

```
// draw the shapes
- (void)drawRect:(NSRect)aRect
{
        //
        // first draw the shapes
        [transform concat];                 // call the current transformation
        [[NSColor redColor] set];           // set color to red
        [path stroke];                      // draw the shapes
        [[NSColor blueColor] set];          // set color to blue
        [sg_path setLineWidth:2];           // define line width
        [sg_path stroke];                   // draw the sobreposed graph
        //
        // then draw nodes numbers
        if (G) {                            // if the graph is loaded
                [self drawNodeNumbers];     // draw the nodes
        }
}
```

This method is responsible for drawing the contents of the view. In fact, when this method is called, most of the decisions have already been made. The only thing it does is to ask the paths used by GraphView to be redrawn. If the graph has been initialized, it also draws node numbers near the nodes.

```
// delete an edge that is located at location "loc"
-(int)deleteEdge:(NSPoint)loc
{
        //
        // adjust the necessary data
        struct for_each_edge_data data;
        data.G = G;
        data.loc = &loc;
        data.edgeFound = 0;
        data.sliderValue = _sliderValue;
        //
        // pass data to find_edge_at_point
        gr_for_each_edge_dir(G, find_edge_at_point, &data);
        //
        // change drawing
        if (data.edgeFound) {
                [self setBezierPaths];          // creates again the shapes
                [self setNeedsDisplay:YES];     // redraw the screen
        }
        return 1;
}
```

The deleteEdge method ,uses the gr_for_each_edge_dir function to do the hard work of finding an edge (it uses a C function for performance reasons). Once an edge has been found, the work is relegated to the setBezierPaths method and the view is redrawn.

```
// process mouse down event
- (void)mouseDown:(NSEvent *)theEvent
{
        NSPoint loc = [self convertPoint:[theEvent locationInWindow] fromView:nil];
        if ( _deleteEdgeMode) {
                [self deleteEdge:loc];
                [[NSCursor arrowCursor] set];
                _deleteEdgeMode = 0;
                return;
        }
        _clickedNode = [self findClickedNode:loc];
        if (_clickedNode) printf("node clicked is %d\n", _clickedNode);
}
```

This method is called when a mouseDown: action is sent to the GraphView. The first thing this method does is to determine the exact location where the event happened. This is done with the help of the locationInWindow method, which is part of the NSEvent object. ,If the view is in delete edge mode, then you request the edge to be deleted, and the cursor is set to the normal arrow mode. Otherwise, the only thing you do is to print the number of the node that was clicked.

```objc
- (void)mouseUp:(NSEvent *)theEvent
{
        NSPoint loc = [self convertPoint:[theEvent locationInWindow] fromView:nil];
        if (_clickedNode) {
                //
                // correct the location using the zoom factor
                loc.x /= _sliderValue;
                loc.y /= _sliderValue;
                //
                // update the location of the node
                gr_set_pos(G, _clickedNode, loc.x, loc.y);
                //
                // change the position of each individual edge
                struct for_each_edge_data data;
                data.movedNode = _clickedNode;
                data.loc = &loc;
                data.G = G;
                data.path = path;
                gr_for_each_adjacent_edge(G, _clickedNode,
change_points_associated_to_edges, &data);
                //
                // do the same to the superposed graph, if it exists
                if (sG) {
                        data.G = sG;
                        data.path = sg_path;
                        gr_for_each_adjacent_edge(sG, _clickedNode,
change_points_associated_to_edges, &data);
                }
                //
                // restore original location, and move position of node
                loc.x *= _sliderValue;
                loc.y *= _sliderValue;
                [self moveNode:_clickedNode to:loc];
                [self setNeedsDisplay:YES];
        }
        _clickedNode = 0;
}
```

The mouseUp: method ,responds to mouse events sent to the GraphView. This method will first get the location where the mouse was clicked, using the locationInWindow method of NSEvent. Then, the code proceeds to update the nodes and edges if there was a clicked node. First, the zoom factor from the slide control is applied and the position of the node is updated. Then, the position of each connected edge is also updated. The superposed graph is also updated, when available. Finally, the method calls the internal moveNode:to: method and redraws the view.

```
- (void)mouseDragged:(NSEvent *)theEvent
{
        NSPoint loc = [self convertPoint:[theEvent locationInWindow] fromView:nil];
        if (_clickedNode) {
                [self moveNode:_clickedNode to:loc];
                [self setNeedsDisplay:YES];
        }
}
```

The mouseDragged: method ,is called when the mouse has moved while the user is pressing the mouse button. In this view, you use the moveNode:to: method to give an instant feedback when a node was clicked. Then the method calls the setNeedsDisplay method to redraw the view.

```
-(void)setBezierPaths
{
        [path removeAllPoints];
        G = [Document getGraph];
        if (G) {
                int n = gr_nverts(G);
                if (_associatedPoints && n > _nPoints) {
                        Delete(_associatedPoints);
                        _associatedPoints = 0;
                }
                if (!_associatedPoints) {
                        _associatedPoints = NewVec(int, n);
                        if (!_associatedPoints) {
                                printf("error creating vector of associated points\n");
                                return;
                        }
                        _nPoints = n;
                }
                [self addGraphToPath];
        }
        [sg_path removeAllPoints];
        sG = [Document getSobreposedGraph];
        if (sG) {
                [self addSobreposedGraphToPath];
        }
}
```

The setBezierPaths ,is used to initialize all the paths in the view. A Bezier path is an object that determines how a path will be drawn by Cocoa. You can use Bezier paths to draw complex paths, including lines, rectangles, circles, and arcs. You just need to set up the Bezier path and ask the path to be drawn on the view after it has been constructed. This method is setting up the internal Bezier path to draw each of the lines it needs to display the graph on the screen.

```
// this function is called for each edge, and data has the required information
static int draw_the_edge(graph_node *graph_node, int a, int b, void *data)
{
        // reads data and unpack it
        struct for_each_edge_data *myData = (struct for_each_edge_data*) data;
        Graph *G = myData->G;
```

```
        NSBezierPath *path = myData->path;
        //
        // adds the position (in the path) of point to the data associated to this
        // edge of the graph so that we remember it later.
        int *point = (int*)malloc(int,sizeof(int));
        *point = [path elementCount];
        gr_set_data(G, a, b, point, 1);
        //
        // add edge to the path
        NSPoint p1, p2;
        nodePos *pa, *pb;
        pa = gr_get_pos(G, a);
        pb = gr_get_pos(G, b);
        p1.x = pa->x;
        p1.y = pa->y;
        p2.x = pb->x;
        p2.y = pb->y;
        [path moveToPoint:p1];
        [path lineToPoint:p2];
        return 1;
}
```

The draw_the_edge function is a helper function that will draw an edge using the data that was passed. The important part of this method is how it manipulates the Bezier path, using the moveToPoint: and lineToPoint: methods. These methods create the path that will later be drawn on the screen when the Bezier path is complete.

```
// draw the shape of a node in position given by p, into the bezier path
void draw_node(nodePos *p, NSBezierPath *path)
{
        NSPoint pos;
        pos.x = p->x-NODE_RADIUS;
        pos.y = p->y-NODE_RADIUS;
        [path moveToPoint:pos];
        pos.x += 2*NODE_RADIUS;
        [path lineToPoint:pos];
        pos.y += 2*NODE_RADIUS;
        [path lineToPoint:pos];
        pos.x -= 2*NODE_RADIUS;
        [path lineToPoint:pos];
        pos.y -= 2*NODE_RADIUS;
        [path lineToPoint:pos];
}
```

This function does a similar work for the nodes in the graph. It manipulates the Bezier path, so that the nodes in the graph are draw. The node representation is just a small square with size defined by NODE_RADIUS.

```
// starts adding the edges to the path. Calls function draw_the_edge to do the job.
-(void)drawEdges:(Graph*)_G withPath:(NSBezierPath*)_path
{
        struct for_each_edge_data data;
        data.path = _path;
        data.G = _G;
        gr_for_each_edge_dir(_G, draw_the_edge, &data);
}
```

The drawEdges:withPath: is responsible for retrieving the right parameters, calling the draw edge function for each edge in the graph.

```
// adds the shapes of the graph to path. Uses drawEdges and drawNodes
- (void)addGraphToPath
{
        int i, n;
        n = gr_nverts(G);
        [self drawEdges:G withPath:path];
        for (i=1; i<=n; i++) {
                nodePos *p = gr_get_pos(G, i);
                _associatedPoints[i-1] = [path elementCount];
                draw_node(p, path);
        }
}
```

The method addGraphToPath has the responsibility of drawing the complete graph to the Bezier path. It will first draw the edges using the drawEdges:withPath:, then draw each of the nodes of the graph.

```
// Convenience function to add superposed graph.
-(void)addSobreposedGraphToPath
{
        [self drawEdges:sG withPath:sg_path];
}
```

The user can choose to use a superposed graph in the application. This is performed using the above method.

```
-(void)drawNodeNumbers
{
   int i;
   int n = gr_nverts(G);
   for (i=0; i<n; i++) {
           NSPoint loc;
                loc.x = gr_get_x_pos(G, i+1);
                loc.y = gr_get_y_pos(G, i+1);
                char num[32];
                sprintf(num, "%d", i+1);
                [[NSString stringWithCString:num] drawAtPoint:loc withAttributes:0];
   }
}
```

This method draws numbers that correspond to each node. To draw a string in the screen, you use the `drawAtPoint:withAttributes:` method of `NSString`. This extension of `NSString` will directly draw the string to the view using the given location.

```
- (int)findClickedNode:(NSPoint) loc
{
        int i;
        int n;
        if (!G) return 0;
        n = gr_nverts(G);
        for (i=1; i<=n; i++) {
                double x = gr_get_x_pos(G, i);
                double y = gr_get_y_pos(G, i);
                double radius = _sliderValue > 1 ? NODE_RADIUS * _sliderValue : NODE_RADIUS;
                x *= _sliderValue;
                y *= _sliderValue;
                if (i==1) printf("%lf %lf: loc i\n%lf %lf: nodePos i\n",
                 loc.x, loc.y, x, y);
                if (x-radius <= loc.x && x+radius >= loc.x
                 && y-radius <= loc.y && y+radius >= loc.y)
                        return i;
        }
        return 0;
}
```

This method provides a simple way to determine if a node was clicked at the specified location. It just goes through the list of nodes and returns the index of the node that is intersected by the given location.

```
static int change_points_associated_to_edges(
        graph_node *graph_node, int a, int b, void *data)
{
        struct for_each_edge_data *dt = (struct for_each_edge_data*)data;
        int u = a < b ? a : b;
        int v = a < b ? b : a;
        int point = *((int*)gr_get_data(dt->G, u, v));
        if (a < b)  point++;
        [dt->path setAssociatedPoints:dt->loc atIndex:point];
        return 1;
}
```

This is a helper function that associates data to a particular node in the graph using the `setAssociatedPoints:atIndex:` method of `NSBezierPath`.

```
-(void)moveNode:(int)clickedNode to:(NSPoint)loc
{
        int point = _associatedPoints[clickedNode-1];
        loc.x /= _sliderValue;
        loc.y /= _sliderValue;
        loc.x -= NODE_RADIUS;
        loc.y -= NODE_RADIUS;
        [path setAssociatedPoints: &loc atIndex:point];
```

```
        loc.x += 2*NODE_RADIUS;
        [path setAssociatedPoints: &loc atIndex:point+1];
        loc.y += 2*NODE_RADIUS;
        [path setAssociatedPoints: &loc atIndex:point+2];
        loc.x -= 2*NODE_RADIUS;
        [path setAssociatedPoints: &loc atIndex:point+3];
        loc.y -= 2*NODE_RADIUS;
        [path setAssociatedPoints: &loc atIndex:point+4];
}
```

The moveNode:to: method is responsible for relocating a node to a new location and performing all the associated modifications. The first step is to retrieve the point that was clicked. Then, you update the Bezier path so that the node will be redrawn at the location determined by the second argument.

```
-(NSBezierPath *) getPath
{
        return path;
}

-(Graph *) getGraph
{
        return G;
}
```

The last two methods just provide an easy way to retrieve data. The first method returns the main path used by the view. The second method returns the graph that stores the information for all nodes and edges that are displayed.

```
-(void) refreshView
{
        [self setBezierPaths];
        [self setNeedsDisplay:YES];
}
```

The refreshView method is just a convenient way to redraw the screen. It resets the Bezier path objects and then asks the view to redisplay its contents.

```
-(IBAction)sliderChanged:(id)sender
{
        [transform scaleBy:1/_sliderValue];
        _sliderValue = [_slider floatValue];
        [transform scaleBy:_sliderValue];
        [self setNeedsDisplay:YES];
}
```

This action is called whenever the slider control sends a new event. Remember that an action is normally wired using the Xcode editor (although you can also do that using code). The current method responds to this event by getting the value stored in the slider object (which is wired to the _slider ivar) and using it to define the new scale of the transform for the objects draw in the window. Then, the method asks for the view to be redrawn.

```
- (void)keyDown:(NSEvent *)theEvent
{
        NSString *keyChar = [theEvent characters];
        if ( [keyChar isEqualToString:@"c"] ) {
                [self setNeedsDisplay:YES];
                printf("you typed c\n");
        }
}
```

The OS calls the keyDown: method whenever a new key press has occurred in the window where GraphView is the primary responder. To get the characters that have been pressed, you can use the characters method on the event object. In this method, you are testing if the user pressed the "c" character, and calling the display function when that happens.

```
-(void)startDeleteEdgeMode
{
        _deleteEdgeMode = 1;
        [[NSCursor disappearingItemCursor] set];
}
```

This method is called when the delete edge mode is starting, which just means setting a flag on the _deleteEdgeMode instance variable. The interesting part here is how to set a new cursor on the NSView; you just need to retrieve the cursor you want (in this case it is disappearingItemCursor) and then call the set method.

```
// this function is called for each edge, and says if and edge is in the position
// pointed by data.
static int find_edge_at_point(graph_node *graph_node, int a, int b, void *data)
{
        //
        // read and unpack data data
        struct for_each_edge_data *myData = (struct for_each_edge_data*) data;
        if (myData->edgeFound) {
                return 1;
        }
        Graph *G = myData->G;
        //
        // make a local copy of myData->loc, because we don't want to change
        // its value (and this caused a bug in the past)
        NSPoint aloc = *(myData->loc);
        NSPoint *loc = &aloc;
        //
        // correct the coordinates according to the zoom value
        loc->x /= myData->sliderValue;
        loc->y /= myData->sliderValue;
        //
        // find coordinates of the edge in the screen
        double x1 = gr_get_x_pos(G, a);
        double y1 = gr_get_y_pos(G, a);
        double x2 = gr_get_x_pos(G, b);
        double y2 = gr_get_y_pos(G, b);
```

```
        //
        // if |x1-x2| < |y1-y2| then it is better to invert the roles of x and y,
        // because otherwise the test of the slope is not very efficient (and doesn't work
        // for vertical lines)
        if (abs(x1-x2) < abs(y1-y2)) {
                swap(double, x1, y1);
                swap(double, x2, y2);
                swap(double, loc->x, loc->y);
        }
        //
        // define equation of the line determined by the two points
        double m = (x2-x1 == 0) ? 0 :(y2-y1)/(x2-x1);
        double x = loc->x;
        double y = m * (x - x1)  + y1;
        //
        // correcting values: radius is the distance around the edge
        double radius = 4.0;
        //
        // checks if point intersects with line
        if (x >= min(x1, x2) && x <= max(x1, x2)
                && y-radius <= loc->y && y+radius >= loc->y) {
                myData->edgeFound = 1;
                myData->movedNode = a;                  // store the nodes adjacent to the edge
                myData->secondMovedNode = b;            // ditto
                gr_remove_edge(G, a, b);                // remove the edge
        }
        return 1;
}
```

This function is coded in C for performance reasons. Its goal is to detect edges, when the user clicks in a particular area of the screen. The code may seem to be complex, but the idea behind it is just to follow the straight line connecting two points in the graph, and return which edge (if any) was clicked by the user.

```
// use this for mouse movement:
- (void)mouseMoved:(NSEvent *)theEvent
{
        NSPoint loc = [self convertPoint:[theEvent locationInWindow] fromView:nil];
        //
        // update the location in field in the toolbar
        char str_pos[1024];
        sprintf(str_pos, "(%.0lf, %.0lf)", loc.x, loc.y);
        [_posField setStringValue: [NSString stringWithCString:str_pos]];
}

@end
```

This method is called when the user moves the mouse. What it does is to first define the location where the click was performed. Then, it stores the location in a string, for debugging purposes. The string is then stored in the position field in the interface.

Summary

In this chapter, you learned about the UI-based features of Cocoa. As you have seen, the strengths of Objective-C are used by Cocoa to support a style for UI construction that offers a lot of freedom and reduces the amount of code necessary to create a rich UI experience.

One of the central concepts of the GUI development in Mac OS X is the support for nib files. A nib is a file-based representation of objects that can be manipulated using a graphical tool such as Xcode. Objects are created and modified through the editor, but they can be saved and loaded later by your application.

In this chapter, I initially provided an overview of the hierarchy of UI classes in Cocoa. They all derive from the NSResponder class, which is responsible for handling UI-based events. Other important classes, such as NSWindow and NSView, implement additional features that are shared by all windows and views in the system.

Finally, I gave a complete example of an application that handles user input from menus and from direct interaction, such as keyboard key presses and mouse movements. The application is used to draw graphics on the screen that represent a set of points and connected lines. You have seen how to use Bezier paths to draw items in the screen, and how to perform other common tasks such as drawing strings.

In the next chapter, I will discuss the support for mobile programming available in Cocoa. Through Cocoa Touch, the mobile extension available for the iOS platform, Objective-C provides everything you need to run your code on mobile devices such as the iPhone and the iPad. For this purpose, you will use most of the concepts introduced in this chapter, along with a set of specialized classes from the Cocoa Touch framework.

Building iOS Apps

Cocoa Touch is the Objective-C framework used to create rich mobile applications for iOS, the operating system that powers the iPhone, iPad, and iPod touch. While using technologies that are similar to the desktop-based Cocoa, Cocoa Touch provides a simplified architecture in comparison to the full-featured Mac OS X frameworks. Cocoa Touch also provides access not only to Touch-based UI controls, but also to mobile resources such as the camera and the accelerometer. With Cocoa Touch, developers have access to the hardware managed by iOS, including many features that are not available to Mac OS X applications.

In this chapter, you will get an overview of the programming environment for developing mobile applications with Xcode. I start the discussion with some information about the difference between mobile apps and full-featured applications written for Mac OS X. You will learn about the new UI controls that have been developed specifically for Touch-based interfaces. You will also learn how to create new apps and deploy these apps to iOS targets.

Finally, I will conclude the chapter with a complete example, which shows how to use Objective-C to interact with several important classes included in Cocoa Touch. This example will also show you some fundamental concepts of graphical iOS programming such as animations. Additionally, it will show you how to interact with Touch-based controls and respond to events in a mobile device.

iOS Programming

Creating applications for iOS has many similarities with desktop application development. First, you will be using the same programming language, Objective-C, with some of the same base libraries, including all features available in the Foundation framework. Common classes such as NSArray, NSDictionary, and many others in the Foundation framework remain unchanged, and will work as described in the first part of this book.

On the other hand, there are several important differences that a programmer needs to consider when creating iOS applications. Understanding these differences is necessary to develop effective apps for iOS.

Memory Limitations

First, there is the issue of memory usage. In a modern desktop operating system such as Mac OS X, the memory available is plentiful and there are few situations where you need to worry about it. For example, unless you are writing software to manipulate video or other large data files, you never need to worry about memory usage. In particular, you almost never have to consider the memory consumed by normal elements of the graphical interface such as UI controls, images, or small sound files.

This is not the case on mobile devices. They have limited memory, and some popular models of iPhones and iPod touch don't have enough resources to run every kind of application you may conceive. Therefore, you need to work with and around the limitations of the platform, and make sure that your app is using resources wisely.

Another reason mobile apps use memory differently is that the system doesn't employ virtual memory. Virtual memory is a concept created for desktop machines where, if you don't have enough space, the system will swap part of what it has stored in memory to disk in order to create an additional memory area. This results in a large memory space, which is available to all applications (as long as they don't use all memory at the same time). But this is not the case with mobile devices: their limitations don't allow for a complex virtual memory system, so they need to work only with the memory that is directly available to them.

Limited Multiprocessing

Another difference manifests itself in the processing capabilities of these devices. While it is possible to have multiple applications working at the same time in a desktop machine, mobile devices with iOS limit the amount of multitasking it can perform at any time. This is done in order to conserve power in the device, and to allow users to run longer periods without recharging the battery. This is a point, however, that has changed in the last few years: initially, Apple didn't allow any multitasking on iOS. While new generations of the system have introduced background tasks, for example, it still doesn't have the same ability for concurrency as in Mac OS X. As a consequence, it is still important to conserve processing resources in your mobile apps.

Another issue that you should consider is app responsiveness. Remember that app users are trying to access information quickly, so they don't have the attention span needed to wait for long loading times, as has become common for desktop applications. For example, a desktop user is willing to wait 30 seconds for Photoshop to start because he or she will use that program for several hours. But an app user is not going to interact with your app for more than a few minutes or even seconds. It doesn't make sense to wait for the load time if you just want to tweet something or check the weather.

These considerations relating to limited memory, limited amount of multiprocessing, and the required short loading times make the design of mobile apps very different from desktop applications. This means that you can rarely take a desktop application and convert it directly to iOS (even though a lot of the code may compile). You can still use a lot of your code, but it needs to be employed in a context where the design of the app makes sense as part of a mobile environment.

UI Classes in iOS

Another aspect that marks a difference between mobile and desktop applications is the way user input is processed. Desktop applications GUIs are primarily driven by mouse and keyboard. These two input devices, however, don't exist on iOS. Although it is possible to attach a keyboard to an iOS device, it is awkward to type on most iOS apps. And the use of a mouse pointer has been replaced by direct manipulation by users.

This difference is reflected in the style of the UI used in mobile applications. To support these differences between iOS and Mac OS X programming, iOS introduced a set of UI controls that are tailored to be used with gestures instead of the mouse and keyboard. These controls have been encapsulated as a set of unique UI classes defined by Cocoa Touch. The classes are collected and shipped in an Objective-C framework called UIKit.

Container Classes

Containers are the first type of UI-related classes I will discuss. They define how objects are organized in the screen and how they relate to each other. Here are the most important classes in this category:

- UIWindow: A UIWindow represents a managing window for the app. In iOS, windows occupy the full screen, since there is no multiprocessing between two windows of different applications. Windows can contain other controls, such as toolbars and views. The UIWindow class is typically not subclassed, since it is possible to achieve most customizations through delegates or window controllers.

- UIView: A UIView is a rectangular area inside an app window. A view can respond to user input and manage other views. UIView objects are frequently associated to a view controller, used to respond to common notification messages. UIView is a parent class to most UI controls in Cocoa Touch, such as labels, buttons, and date pickers, for example.

- UIToolbar: A toolbar object of type UIToolbar is used to manage buttons and related controls. Toolbars in the iPhone are generally displayed in the lower part of the screen. You can add or remove buttons from a UIToolbar in order to provide a limited number of options to your users.

- UINavigationBar: This is also a bar that can contain other controls. In iOS, however, a navigation bar sits at the top of the window. The navigation bar contains a default item that points to the previous location. This control manages each new screen that is displayed in the context of the app, so you can go back in the list of views by using such navigation buttons.

UI Controls

Cocoa Touch also comes with a large number of single-purpose controls that can help users to make selections, visualize, and input data. Here follows a list of additional control classes made available in the UIKit that are used to support Touch-based input (see Figure 17-1):

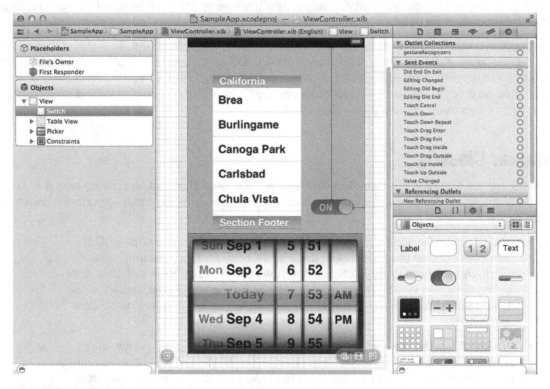

Figure 17-1. An Xcode nib design view, showing some of the UI controls in UIKit

- UILabel: This class is used to create label objects. A label can display text or images in any part of an NSView. The text can be formatted using RTF, which may be generated by most text editors.

- UITextField: A class representing an input field, where users can enter data such as e-mail addresses, contact names, or passwords using the screen-based keyboard. The UITextField class knows how to control the display of the screen-based keyboard, showing and hiding it when the control is selected or deselected.

- UIButton: This class is able to display a simple button, which can be customized with text or images. The main functionality of the button is sending a message to a declared action in the view controller, which will in turn execute the necessary code for the requested function.

- UISegmentedControl: This control displays a segmented surface that you can touch to access different parts of a view. It is frequently used in mobile apps for iPhone, due to the lack of space in the smaller screen.

- **UISwitch**: The switch allows the user to select one of two states. It is consistently used in the Settings application for options with a YES/NO answer.

- **UIProgressView**: This view can be used to display progress in long running operations, so the user knows that the app is active, although in a wait state, while the operation is being performed.

- **UIActivityIndicatorView**: This is similar to the **UIProgressView** in purpose, but it is used when you don't know how long an activity will take. On the other hand, you shouldn't show this control if the operation takes too long, because it gives little clue to the user about how long it will take to move from this busy state.

- **UIPickerView**: This versatile UI control can be used to select one among several items. When clicked, this control displays a large selection wheel that makes it easier for the user to click the desired option.

Setting Up a Cocoa Touch Project

You can create an iOS app in a way that is very similar to other projects in Xcode: by using the project wizard to determine the kind of project that needs to be created. To generate a new project using the project wizard, you can use the menu by going to File ➤ New ➤ Project (or using the keyboard shortcut Shift+Command+N). The project wizard will be displayed and list all the project types available in your local Xcode installation. Select "Application" in the iOS category, and you will see the list of available applications types, as show in Figure 17-2.

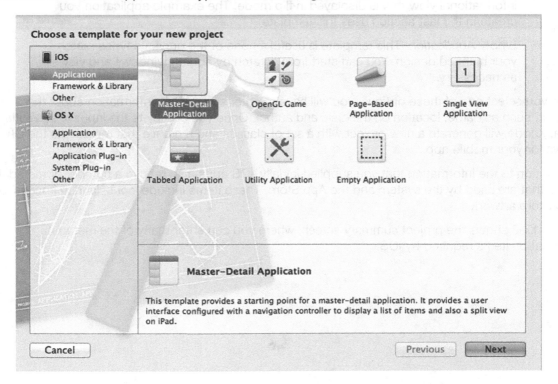

Figure 17-2. The project template selection screen in the new project wizard

Among iOS application types, the following are of interest for mobile apps developers:

- *Master-Detail Application*: These are applications that present a master view, where you can summarize the contents of the app, and a detail view, which can be used for editing and visualization of selected parts of the content. This kind of app is used on the iPad only, since the iPhone generally doesn't have enough screen space to handle the master and detail views at the same time.

- *OpenGL Game*: This template category is used to generate game apps. The application is set up so that you can access an OpenGL view, which allows developers to create 2D and 3D images for their games.

- *Page-Based Application*: Creates a new application where data is displayed using a book metaphor. The application uses a `UIPageViewController`, which automates the process of managing the views that correspond to each page.

- *Single View Application*: This template generates a simple app that contains a single `UIView`.

- *Tabbed Application*: Generates an app that uses a tabbed interface to display content. This format is useful to drill down into data that can be represented in a tabular format, such as databases, phone books, and shopping lists, among others. The tabbed app automatically supplies the navigational tools to move between tabs, such going to the previous or next screen.

- *Utility Application*: This is an application that has only one view, with possibly an informational view that is displayed in flip mode. The example application you create in the last section uses this template.

- *Empty Application*: This template is useful if none of the previous types match your planned design. You can start from scratch by adding windows and views as necessary.

After you select one of these options, you will have to enter some basic information about the project, such as name, location on the disk, and author. Once you complete the input of this initial data, Xcode will generate a new project with a set of classes and a nib file that represents the UI views for your mobile app.

In addition to the information that you supplied initially, iOS apps also require a number of metadata items that are used by the system and the App Store. These items include icons, launch images, and App Store artwork.

Figure 17-3 shows the project summary screen, where you can enter many of the metadata information items required by iOS.

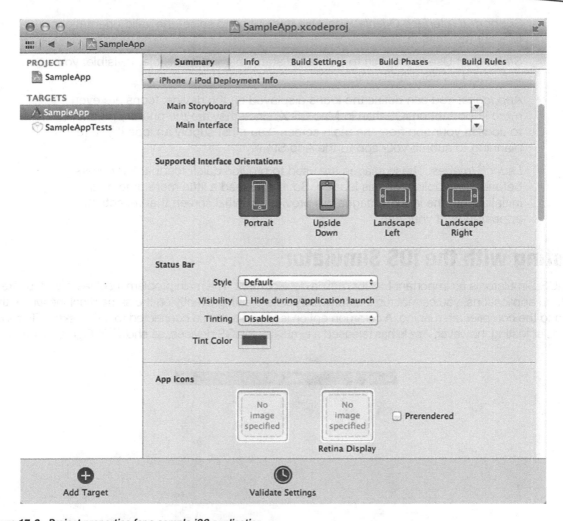

Figure 17-3. Project properties for a sample iOS application

Here are some of the main properties you should use to create a customized application:

- *Bundle Identifier*: Indicates the identifier for your application and is used as a unique id that can be employed to track your app in the App Store.

- *Version*: The version number of an app is visible in the App Store and should be updated when a new version is created. I don't have space to describe the process of adding apps to the App Store, but you can use the online resources available at developer.apple.com to familiarize yourself with the requirements.

- *Devices*: Use this option to determine if the app will target the iPhone, iPad, or both devices. You can also start with one device and later add support to a different type, if you prefer.

- *Deployment Target*: Use this option to determine the target version of iOS. Devices with an older version of iOS may not be able to run software that targets the latest versions. On the other hand, you will be able to use more advanced features by selecting a newer target.

- *Supported Interface Orientations*: Use this option to select the valid orientations for your application.

- *Status Bar*: Use this option to define if a status bar will be visible. If visible, you can select its color and style.

- *App Icons*: You can define the icons displayed on the device. Icons are even more important on iOS than in Mac OS X, since they are the primary means to access your app from the main screen. You must supply an icon if you're planning to submit your app to the App Store.

- *Launch Images*: These images are used to provide quick feedback for users, before your application has loaded. So, if you need a little more time during initialization, the launch images will provide an initial screen that reflects the appearance of your app.

Testing with the iOS Simulator

The iOS Simulator is an important tool for mobile development. The main problem it solves is that, unlike desktop applications, you cannot run the software you're creating directly on the same machine where the IDE and the compiler are running. A common option is to use a device connected to the desktop. To allow for easier testing, however, Apple has released a simulator for iOS devices, as shown in Figure 17-4.

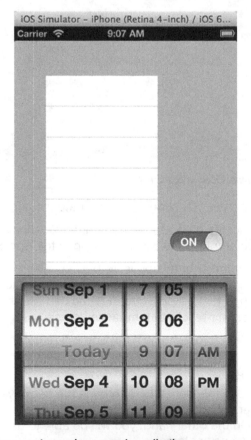

Figure 17-4. The iOS Simulator in iPhone mode, running a sample application

The iOS Simulator can be used to test most of the aspects of an application, such as memory management issues and simple UI interaction, without having to load the app into a real iOS device. Also, the simulator allows you to run the app in several simulated devices and find possible issues that would be harder to track if you had to manually install your app on several different iPhones and iPads.

To start the simulator, you can use the scheme selection tool located on the main toolbar. Make sure that you select the simulator scheme you want, either iPhone or iPad, in the scheme selection tool. Depending on the type of app you created when choosing a new iOS project, you default choice may be the iPhone or the iPad, unless you already have a real device connected to your Mac.

After the proper scheme is selected, you can select Product ➤ Run from the main menu (or press the Command+R keyboard shortcut) to run the project. This will start the iOS Simulator if it is not already active. Xcode will transfer your app to the directory location used by the simulator, and you application will be started.

The simulator has several options that control how the simulated hardware behaves. At the most basic level, you can define what kind of device is being simulated. You can choose between the iPhone and the iPad when selecting the schema used on Xcode. Once the simulator has started, you have additional options to select the specific hardware configuration you want to test. For example, suppose that you started with the simulator for the iPhone. Then, you can select the menu Hardware ➤ Device and select one of the configurations from the list. For example, my version of the iOS Simulator has the following options:

- iPad
- iPad (Retina)
- iPhone
- iPhone (Retina 3.5-inch)
- iPhone (Retina 4-inch)

Your options may be different, depending on the particular release of the simulator. You can also select the iOS version used, such as 5.1 or 6.0, under the menu option Hardware ➤ Version.

Another thing you can vary in your tests using the simulator is the orientation of the device. This allows you to determine if rotation is being correctly handled by your code. You can simulate rotation by clicking on the menu Hardware ➤ Rotate Right (or using the key combination Command+➔), or Hardware ➤ Rotate Left (key combination Command+⬅). You can also simulate pressing some of the buttons that are unique to the iPhone and iPad, such as the Home button (Shift+Command+H) and the Lock button (Command+L).

Finally, you can also simulate some special conditions that occur only on such mobile devices. First, you can use the app to pretend that a low memory condition was reached. This allows you to detect possible problems in the handling of memory problems that might go undetected until such a low memory situation occurs. You can also use the simulator to fake an in-call, so you can see if your app would have a problem with switching from a call to the normal flow of the program and vice versa.

An Example iOS Application

I conclude this chapter with a complete example of an iOS application. This sample app simulates a list of index cards that can be helpful for students learning topics for an exam or acquiring new words in a foreign language.

The main UI for the app is simple, with buttons for the next and previous index card, and an option to reveal the hidden information for the card. The app also supports playing a sound file for each index card; this can be a useful method for memorization.

In the next sections, I will introduce each of the main files in the application. After each method, I explain what it does, when it is called, and which objects are used in the implementation. After you go through this application, you will have a good idea of how such apps are organized and how they interact with the Cocoa Touch libraries. For the complete files for the sample app, check the web page from this book on my web site at http://coliveira.net.

The Main File

The main file for the app is responsible for initializing the Cocoa Touch libraries and running the main loop. This is not difficult to do, however, since you can use the UIApplicationMain. The only other work is to make sure that the autorelease pool for the application has been initialized. This is done by called alloc/init on class NSAutoreleasePool.

```
//
//   main.m

#import <UIKit/UIKit.h>

int main(int argc, char *argv[])
{
    NSAutoreleasePool *pool = [[NSAutoreleasePool alloc] init];
    int retVal = UIApplicationMain(argc, argv, nil, nil);
    [pool release];
    return retVal;
}
```

The MainViewController Interface

It is the responsibility of a view controller to determine how its corresponding view will respond to events that are directed to it. The interface of the MainViewController declares a number of slots (with the keyword IBOutlet) and actions (with the keyword IBAction), so that the UI can send messages to this object when new events occur.

```
#import "FlipsideViewController.h"

@interface MainViewController : UIViewController <FlipsideViewControllerDelegate>
{
        IBOutlet UIView *wordView;
        IBOutlet UILabel *lbWord;
        IBOutlet UILabel *lbTranslation;
```

```
        IBOutlet UIButton *btBuy;
        IBOutlet UIButton *btPlay;
        IBOutlet UIView* ad;
}

- (IBAction)showInfo:(id)sender;

- (IBAction)playSound:(id)sender;

- (IBAction)showPrevious:(id)sender;

- (IBAction)showNext:(id)sender;

- (IBAction)shuffle:(id)sender;

- (IBAction)review:(id)sender;

- (IBAction)buyClicked:(id)sender;

+ (void)syncIsFreeVersion:(BOOL)setValue;

+ (void)refreshTopLevelViewController;

@end
```

The MainViewController Implementation

The MainViewController implementation defines how the controller for the main view interacts with the system. This file implements all the actions that are called from the UI, such as moving to the next and previous card, revealing the contents of the card, and playing a sound.

```
//
// file: MainViewController.m

#import "MainViewController.h"
#import "InfoView.h"
#import "PurchaseController.h"
#import <AVFoundation/AVFoundation.h>

@implementation MainViewController

int currentPos = 0;
struct words
{
    NSString *word, *translation, *file;
} words[] = {
    { @"Ajuda", @"Help", nil },
    { @"Almoço", @"Lunch" , @"Almoco"},
    { @"Restaurante", @"Restaurant", nil},
    { @"Rua", @"Street", nil},
```

```
    { @"Semana", @"Week", nil},
    { @"Supermercado", @"Supermarket", nil},
    { @"Viagem", @"Travel", nil},
};
```

This simple application presents an index card interface, with words on one side of the card and definitions on the other side. This structure is used to maintain the list of words and definitions. A more complex application could store these definitions on a database, but this works enough as a data source for your purposes. The third element of the structure is a file name, where you will store the name of a sound file if it is not the same as the original word.

```
#define maxWords  sizeof(words)/sizeof(*words)
int perm[maxWords];

static MainViewController *ui_controller = nil;

- (void) refreshWord
{
    CGFloat d = 0.9;
    [UIView animateWithDuration:d animations:^{ wordView.alpha = 0.0; }
                     completion:^(BOOL finished){
                         int pos = perm[currentPos];
                         lbWord.text = words[pos].word;
                         lbTranslation.text = words[pos].translation;
                         lbTranslation.hidden = YES;
                     }];

    [UIView animateWithDuration:d animations:^{ wordView.alpha = 1.0; }
                     completion:nil];
}
```

The method refreshWord is responsible for redrawing the current view with a transition. To do this, you use a simple animation performed with the help of a block. The method animateWithDuration: animations:completion: takes as parameter the total duration in seconds and two blocks: the first, which performs the transitional animation, and the second, which determines the final state of the transition.

The animation, in this case, changes the alpha value of the view, which indicates the transparency. When these animations are run, they give the visual impression of fading, with the definition of the current word revealed at the end.

```
- (IBAction)showNext:(id)sender
{
    currentPos =  (currentPos + 1 == maxWords) ? 0 : currentPos + 1;
    [self refreshWord];
}

- (IBAction) showPrevious:(id)sender
{
    currentPos = (currentPos == 0) ? maxWords - 1 : currentPos - 1;
    [self refreshWord];
}
```

These two methods control the current position in the list of index cards. The showNext: method moves to the next available index card in the list. The showPrevious: method returns to the previous position available. Both methods redraw the screen using the fading effect you saw previously with the refreshWord method.

```
- (UILabel*) makeLabel:(NSString*)title width:(CGFloat)w
              height:(CGFloat)h top:(CGFloat)t
{
    CGFloat vw = wordView.frame.size.width;
    CGRect r = CGRectMake(vw/2 - w/2, t, w, h);
    UILabel *l = [[[UILabel alloc] initWithFrame:r] autorelease];
    l.text = title;
    l.textAlignment = UITextAlignmentCenter;
    l.backgroundColor = [UIColor colorWithRed:1 green:1 blue:1 alpha:0.0];
    return l;
}
```

The makeLabel:width:height:top: method creates and returns a new label object, of type UILabel. First, the information passed as parameters is used to initialize the CGRect structure that determines the location and dimensions of the control. Then, a new UILabel is created. The label is initialized with the given title, which is center-aligned. The background color is set to white using the colorWithRed:green:blue:alpha: method of the UIColor class.

```
- (void)resetAdPosition:(UIView *)adView
{
    CGRect adrect = [adView frame];

    AppDelegate *deleg = [[UIApplication sharedApplication] delegate];
    UIWindow *viewCont = deleg.window;

    // get the content frame
    CGRect brect = viewCont.frame;

    // move to location above the toolbar
    adrect.origin.y = brect.size.height - adrect.size.height - 20;

    adView.frame = adrect;
    NSLog(@" height is %lf, y for bar is %lf", adrect.origin.y, brect.origin.y);

}
```

Another common task in a mobile app is to display ads for monetization. You can see an example of how to do this in the method above. The resetAdPosition: shows how easy it is to display ads using the Cocoa Touch UI classes. First, you get the frame that defines the location and position of the existing ad object, which was added during design on Xcode. Then, you get the frame rectangle for the content window, so that you can use the dimensions to adjust the ad control. You need to set these dimensions and save them on the frame property of the ad object. Then, the ad unit will be displayed automatically, with the content served directly by Apple.

```
- (void)viewDidLoad
{
    [super viewDidLoad];
    ui_controller = self;
    [self resetAdPosition:ad];
    [self refreshUi];

    srand(time(NULL));
    // create the initial word permutation
    for (int i=0; i<maxWords; ++i)
    {
        perm[i] = i;
    }
    [self refreshWord];
}
```

The viewDidLoad method is called right after the controller has loaded its resources, including the nib file, but right before the UI is displayed on the screen. Therefore, at this point it is safe to refer to the UI objects in the nib file and well as their corresponding slots.

The first step for viewDidlLoad should always be to call the same method on the parent class, as I do here. In this implementation, the ui_controller variable is initialized, and then a few methods are called to set up the UI as desired. The srand function is from the standard C library, and is used to initialize the random number generator, which will provide the sequence of index cards.

The time function is used here only to provide a reasonable random value with which to initialize the random sequence. Then, you initialize the permutation array with the identity permutation, so that the index cards will be initially presented in the standard sequence.

The last step of the viewDidLoad method is to call the refreshWord, which is responsible for drawing the desired index card on the screen.

```
- (IBAction)shuffle:(id)sender
{
    for (int i=0; i<maxWords; ++i)
    {
        int pos = (int)((rand() % ((maxWords-i) * 10))/ 10.0);
        int t = perm[i];
        perm[i] = perm[i+pos];
        perm[i+pos] = t;
    }
    [self refreshWord];
}
```

The shuffle: method is marked as an IBAction, and is used to receive a notification from the shuffle button on the app's UI. As a result of this message, the app should shuffle the order of the index cards displayed. This is done by first creating a random permutation of the cards. The loop goes through all positions in the perm array, and first generates a random value which is stored in the variable pos. Then, the value stored in the current position is interchanged with the value stored in the random position that was previously calculated.

```objc
- (IBAction)playSound:(id)sender
{
        NSLog(@"Playing a sound...");

        AVAudioPlayer *player;
        NSError *playerError = nil;
        NSString *file_name = words[perm[currentPos]].file;

        if (file_name == nil)
        {
                file_name = words[perm[currentPos]].word;
        }
        file_name = [file_name lowercaseString];

        NSString *path = [[NSBundle mainBundle] pathForResource:file_name ofType:@"mp3"];
        if (!path)
        {
                NSLog(@"Error Loading File");
                return;
        }

        NSURL *fileURL = [[NSURL alloc] initFileURLWithPath: path];
        player = [[AVAudioPlayer alloc] initWithContentsOfURL:fileURL error:&playerError];

        if (!player || playerError)
        {
                NSLog(@"Error creating player %@: %@", file_name,
                        [playerError localizedDescription]);
                return;
        }

        player.volume = 1.0;
        player.numberOfLoops = 0;
        player.delegate = (id<AVAudioPlayerDelegate>)self;

        NSLog(@"calling play method...");
        [player play];
        [fileURL release];
}
```

One of the features of this app is that it is able to play a sound for each index card, when requested by the user. You can use this feature to sound a reminder for the concept in the index card, or to play a recording of the value in the index card. It really helps memorization to have a sound associated to each value.

To achieve this effect, the first thing to do is to retrieve the name of the sound file that will be played. This information is stored in the words data structure, in the file field. The current position is determined using currentPos in association with the perm array, which records the current permutation. If no file name is stored in that position, you generate a file name based on the information stored in the index card.

The first step in loading the sound file is to get the path where it is stored. For this purpose, you can use the method `pathForResource:ofType:`, which is sent to the object that represents the `mainBundle`.

> **Note** A bundle is a collection of files that are distributed along with an application. A bundle is viewed by Cocoa as a unit, and you will see it as a single file in Mac OS X Finder. Cocoa provides several methods to retrieve information from bundles, but for most simple applications you interact only with the main bundle, which is returned by `[NSBundle mainBundle]`.

After you get the path of the required sound resource, you create an `NSURL` object that represents the file. The next step is to create an `AVAudioPlayer` object, initialized with the sound resource URL. Next, you need to set up player options such as volume and number of loops. I also pass to the player object a delegate, which will be responsible for receiving and answering to any notifications generated during the playing process. Finally, the play message is sent to the object, starting the process of playing the sound file.

```
- (void)audioPlayerDidFinishPlaying:(AVAudioPlayer *)player successfully:(BOOL)flag
{
        NSLog(@"Releasing player...");
        [player release];
}
```

The `audioPlayerDidFinishPlaying:successfully:` method is part of the `AVAudioPlayerDelegate` interface and is called when the player object notifies its delegate (remember that the `delegate` property of player was initialized to point to the `MainViewController` object. The only important thing you need to do in this implementation is to release the player object. Otherwise, for each time you played a sound, a new undesirable memory leak would result.

```
- (IBAction)reveal:(id)sender
{
    lbTranslation.hidden = NO;
}
```

The `reveal:` method is another action available during nib design time on Xcode. Its purpose is to display the hidden value for the current index card. By changing the hidden property on this `UILabel` object, the Cocoa Touch libraries are responsible for automatically updating the UI as needed.

```
- (void)flipsideViewControllerDidFinish:(FlipsideViewController *)c
{
    [self dismissModalViewControllerAnimated:YES];
}
```

This method is responsible for closing a modal view when the app has indicated that this is necessary. This is performed by calling the inherited method `dismissModalViewControllerAnimated:`. The value passed to this method indicates if you want an animation effect when the view is removed from the screen.

```
- (IBAction)showInfo:(id)sender
{

    InfoView *c = [[[InfoView alloc] initWithNibName:@"InfoView" bundle:nil] autorelease];

    c. modalTransitionStyle = UIModalTransitionStyleFlipHorizontal;
    [self presentModalViewController:c animated:YES];
}
```

The showInfo: method is an action that can be wired in Xcode during the nib design phase. Its purpose is to display an info box that shows some information about the app, such as its name and current options used. First, you create the new UI view object, which is of type InfoView. The initiWthNibName:bundle: method is the main way to create UI objects that are stored in a nib file. The first parameter defines the name of the nib. The second parameter gives the name of a bundle where the nib file is located. If this parameter is nil, then the nib must be located in the same bundle as the current executable.

The modalTransitionStyle property indicates the transition method used to display the new view. This property is initialized to UIMOdalTransitionStyleFlipHorizontal, so that the view will appear with a horizontal flip effect.

Next, the method displays the modal view in the current screen. The second parameter to presen tModalViewController:animated: is YES when you want to use an animation when the view is first displayed.

```
+ (void) refreshTopLevelViewController
{
        [ui_controller refreshUi];
}
```

The refreshTopLevelViewController method is provided as a helper that is used to refresh the UI controller from other parts of the application. Notice that ui_controller is a static variable that is initialized to point to the current UI controller. The method uses the fact that is valid to send a message to nil objects, so you don't need to check if ui_controller has been initialized before using it.

```
- (BOOL)shouldAutorotateToInterfaceOrientation:(UIInterfaceOrientation)io
{
    // Return YES for supported orientations.
    return (io == UIInterfaceOrientationPortrait);
}
```

The shouldAutorotateToInterfaceOrientation: method is called when the iOS device tries to change orientation. Some applications need to be responsive to orientation changes. For example, a reader application will change how its text is drawn on screen depending on orientation. The parameter passed to this method, UIInterfaceOrientation, indicates the new orientation of the screen. The return value of this method should be YES if you want to change to this new orientation, and NO if you don't wish to change the screen. This sample application will return YES only if the screen orientation if UIInterfaceOrientationPortrait. Therefore, it supports only one screen orientation.

```
- (void)didReceiveMemoryWarning
{
    // Releases the view if it doesn't have a superview.
    [super didReceiveMemoryWarning];
}
```

This method is sent to a view whenever there is shortage of memory in the system. By responding to this method, you make your application promptly recoverable in the case of resource usage problems. This sample application will just call the same method in the superclass, but for more complex apps it is important to consider how to reduce resource usage during low-memory scenarios.

```
- (void)viewDidUnload
{
        [btBuy release];
        btBuy = nil;
        [btPlay release];
        btPlay = nil;
        [super viewDidUnload];
}
```

The viewDidUnload method will release any unused memory when the current view is unloaded from the screen. This is another method that satisfies an important need in a mobile system, since there is a limited amount of memory to work with. By releasing memory that is not in current use, it can be used by other app (or even others views in the same app), while reducing the total resources needed by the system.

```
- (void)dealloc
{
        [btBuy release];
        [btPlay release];
        [super dealloc];
}
```

@end

The dealloc method is responsible for returning the sources used by the class to the operating system. This class uses a few controls, therefore you should release then at this time, in order to avoid undesirable memory leaks. Always remember to call dealloc on the parent class as well, since otherwise you will have a memory leak on the resources managed by the parent.

The FlipsideViewController Interface

The FlipsideViewController is a subclass of UIViewController that is used to respond to messages sent by the flipside control, which displays auxiliary information about the app. The main difference in this controller is that it uses a delegate object, declared ot the type FlipsideViewControllerDelegate. This protocol is used to communicate with the MainWindowViewController, and has only one method called flipsideViewControllerDidFinish:.

```
// file FlipsideViewController.m

#import <UIKit/UIKit.h>

@protocol FlipsideViewControllerDelegate;

@interface FlipsideViewController : UIViewController
{

}

@property (nonatomic, assign) id <FlipsideViewControllerDelegate> delegate;

- (IBAction)done:(id)sender;

@end

// this protocol must be implemented by classes passed as a delegate

@protocol FlipsideViewControllerDelegate

- (void)flipsideViewControllerDidFinish:(FlipsideViewController *)controller;

@end
```

The FlipsideViewController Implementation

The implementation file for FlipsideViewController provides methods that can respond to some of the messages directed to the flipside view.

```
// file FlipsideViewController.m

#import "FlipsideViewController.h"

@implementation FlipsideViewController

@synthesize delegate=_delegate;

- (void)viewDidLoad
{
    // the view is now loaded, call the super class first
    [super viewDidLoad];
    self.view.backgroundColor = [UIColor viewFlipsideBackgroundColor];
}
```

The `viewDidLoad` method is executed when the view is about to be displayed. The only change you make here is on the background color used, which is defined by the method `viewFlipsideBackgroundColor` of the `UIColor` object. `UIColor` is a class that offers common methods to manage colors in iOS devices.

```
- (void)viewDidUnload
{
    // make sure that the parent class is unloaded
    [super viewDidUnload];
    // e.g. self.myOutlet = nil;
}


- (BOOL)shouldAutorotateToInterfaceOrientation:(UIInterfaceOrientation)interfaceOrientation
{
    // Return YES for supported orientations
    return (interfaceOrientation == UIInterfaceOrientationPortrait);
}
```

This method determines if the UI should change orientation when the user rotates the device. This application supports only portrait orientation.

```
#pragma mark - Actions

- (IBAction)done:(id)sender
{
    // notifies the delegate about the action of closing the current view
    [self.delegate flipsideViewControllerDidFinish:self];
}

@end
```

The `done:` action has been set up in Xcode to receive an event when the close button is selected. In this case, the only thing you need to do is to notify the delegate object (which in fact is the `MainWindowController`) that this view needs to close. This is done by calling the method declared in the delegate protocol, as shown in the header file.

Summary

In this chapter, you learned how to create mobile applications that run on iPhone and iPad devices using Objective-C. The Cocoa frameworks are used as the official development environment for iOS applications, thus if you intend to develop mobile applications for the Apple platform, Objective-C is the shortest way to get a working product.

You learned about the differences between iOS apps and applications written for desktop operating systems. These differences show the need for a customized set for Objective-C frameworks, which can be used to control the particular hardware and software requirements of mobile apps. I discussed some of the support provided by Cocoa Touch, including views, windows, and Touch-based UI controls.

In the last part of the chapter, you saw the code of a complete mobile app. I explained how the app uses the Cocoa Touch API to perform actions such as creating new views, playing sound files, and performing simple animations. You saw how these classes work together and with the UIKit framework to control all aspects of the iOS experience.

With this chapter, we reach the end of our overview of the Objective-C language and its environment. The material provided in these chapters contains the essential information you need to start your journey as an Objective-C developer. As you have seen, Objective-C is a modern language with features that make software development feel easy and natural. By taking the OO paradigm further than their competitors such as C++ or Java, Objective-C has enabled the best features of procedural and OO programing to coexist. Now it is time to use it to create your own applications.

Index

Get the eBook for only $10!

Now you can take the weightless companion with you anywhere, anytime. Your purchase of this book entitles you to 3 electronic versions for only $10.

This Apress title will prove so indispensible that you'll want to carry it with you everywhere, which is why we are offering the eBook in 3 formats for only $10 if you have already purchased the print book.

Convenient and fully searchable, the PDF version enables you to easily find and copy code—or perform examples by quickly toggling between instructions and applications. The MOBI format is ideal for your Kindle, while the ePUB can be utilized on a variety of mobile devices.

Go to www.apress.com/promo/tendollars to purchase your companion eBook.

All Apress eBooks are subject to copyright. All rights are reserved by the Publisher, whether the whole or part of the material is concerned, specifically the rights of translation, reprinting, reuse of illustrations, recitation, broadcasting, reproduction on microfilms or in any other physical way, and transmission or information storage and retrieval, electronic adaptation, computer software, or by similar or dissimilar methodology now known or hereafter developed. Exempted from this legal reservation are brief excerpts in connection with reviews or scholarly analysis or material supplied specifically for the purpose of being entered and executed on a computer system, for exclusive use by the purchaser of the work. Duplication of this publication or parts thereof is permitted only under the provisions of the Copyright Law of the Publisher's location, in its current version, and permission for use must always be obtained from Springer. Permissions for use may be obtained through RightsLink at the Copyright Clearance Center. Violations are liable to prosecution under the respective Copyright Law.